MONTAGUE GRAMMAR

CONTRIBUTORS

Michael Bennett
Robin Cooper
M. J. Cresswell
Enrique Delacruz
David R. Dowty
C. L. Hamblin
David Lewis
Terence Parsons
Barbara H. Partee
Robert Rodman
Muffy Siegel
Richmond H. Thomason

MONTAGUE GRAMMAR

EDITED BY

BARBARA H. PARTEE

Departments of Linguistics and Philosophy
University of Massachusetts
Amherst, Massachusetts

ACADEMIC PRESS

New York   San Francisco   London

A Subsidiary of Harcourt Brace Jovanovich, Publishers

ACADEMIC PRESS, INC.
111 Fifth Avenue, New York, New York 10003

United Kingdom Edition published by
ACADEMIC PRESS, INC. (LONDON) LTD.
24/28 Oval Road, London NW1

Library of Congress Cataloging in Publication Data
Main entry under title:

Montague grammar.

    Includes bibliographies and index.
        1.   Generative grammar—Addresses, essays, lectures.
2.   Grammar, Comparative and general—Syntax—
Addresses, essays, lectures.   3.   Semantics—
Addresses, essays, lectures.   4.   English language—
Grammar, Generative—Addresses, essays, lectures.
I.   Partee, Barbara Hall.
P158.M6   415   75-13078
ISBN 0–12–545850–9

To the memory of Richard Montague

CONTENTS

LIST OF CONTRIBUTORS

Numbers in parentheses indicate the pages on which the authors' contributions begin.

Michael Bennett *(119)*, Department of Philosophy, University of Pittsburgh, Pittsburgh, Pennsylvania

Robin Cooper *(311)*, Department of Linguistics, University of Massachusetts, Amherst, Massachusetts

M. J. Cresswell *(261)*, Department of Philosophy, Victoria University of Wellington, Wellington, New Zealand

Enrique Delacruz *(177)*, Department of Philosophy, University of California, Los Angeles, California

David R. Dowty *(201)*, Department of Linguistics, Ohio State University, Columbus Ohio, and the Institute for Advanced Study, Princeton, New Jersey

C. L. Hamblin *(247)*, Department of Philosophy, University of New South Wales, Kensington, New South Wales, Australia

David Lewis *(1)*, Department of Philosophy, Princeton University, Princeton, New Jersey

Terence Parsons *(311)*, Department of Philosophy, University of Massachusetts, Amherst, Massachusetts

Barbara H. Partee *(51)*, Departments of Linguistics and Philosophy, University of Massachusetts, Amherst, Massachusetts

Robert Rodman *(165)*, Department of Linguistics and Non-Western Languages, University of North Carolina, Chapel Hill, North Carolina

Muffy Siegel *(293)*, Department of Linguistics, University of Massachusetts, Amherst, Massachusetts

Richmond H. Thomason *(77)*, Department of Philosophy, University of Pittsburgh, Pittsburgh, Pennsylvania

PREFACE

This volume represents some initial attempts to extend Richard Montague's work on the syntax and semantics of natural languages. Taken together with Montague's collected works on the theory of language,[1] it makes available to linguists and philosophers a view of the range of applications of Montague's theory to problems of syntax and semantics, and some comparisons of Montague's approach to other theories of language. Seven of the authors are primarily philosophers, and five are primarily linguists; their approaches are by no means homogeneous, but all share with Montague a concern for treating semantics as rigorously as syntax and a desire to uncover systematic connections between the two.

The book is intended for two sorts of readers. On the one hand, those who already have some familiarity with Montague's work will be in a position to appreciate the diversity of applications, extensions, competing analyses, and theoretical comparisons that are offered in this collection. On the other hand, those linguists, philosophers, and other students of language who have heard of Montague grammar but have not become acquainted with it may well find some of the papers in this book a gentler introduction to the subject than Montague's work or the few explications of it in print.

For the reader with little or no acquaintance with Montague grammar, I would suggest the following order of reading the articles: *(1)* Lewis; *(2)* Partee; *(3)* Hamblin; *(4)* any of Rodman, Delacruz, Siegel, or Dowty. At some point, it would of course be profitable for the reader to tackle some of Montague's own writings, perhaps with the aid of Partee (1975)[2] or Thomason's introduction[3] to

[1] R. Thomason (Ed.), *Formal philosophy: Selected papers of Richard Montague*. New Haven: Yale Univ. Press, 1974.

[2] Partee, B. Montague grammar and transformational grammar. *Linguistic Inquiry,* 1975, **6,** 203–300.

[3] In Thomason (Ed.), *Formal philosophy*.

Montague (1974). By that time the reader will no longer be a novice and can read the remaining articles in any order.

The volume as a whole can be broken into four parts. The first part consists of the paper by Lewis, which serves as background for and perspective on all that follows. The second part contains the three studies by Partee, Thomason, and Bennett. These three studies all offer extensions of Montague's fragment in "The Proper Treatment of Quantification in Ordinary English"[4] (henceforth PTQ), and overlap considerably in the problems they treat, but with considerable divergence in treatment. The third part contains all of the next six papers: Rodman, Delacruz, Dowty, Hamblin, Cresswell, and Siegel. Each of these focuses on some particular syntactic or semantic problem, one on Russian and the rest concerning English. The fourth part consists of the final paper, by Cooper and Parsons, which deals with theory comparison. I will say more below about each of the contributions.

1. David Lewis's already classic article, "General Semantics," first published in 1971 in *Synthese,* is included here because of the excellent introduction it provides to the philosophical conception of semantics, particularly possible-worlds semantics, the notions of categorial grammar, the critically important extension/intension distinction, certain key notions of pragmatics, and a host of other central concepts and issues in the study of syntax and semantics of natural language. The paper is not merely introductory; it also contains a wealth of original ideas, presented in a very comprehensible style. The paper is not written within the framework of Montague grammar proper, but it provides a clear view of the goals and methods of argumentation of the enterprise in which Montague was engaged.

2. Barbara Partee, "Some Transformational Extensions of Montague Grammar" contains a brief introduction to Montague's general framework and a description of the grammar (syntax and semantics) of a fragment of English given in PTQ. It draws comparisons between Montague's theory and the theory of transformational grammar, and gives some proposals for incorporating some close analogues of familiar transformations (Reflexive, Passive, Tough-movement, Raising) into Montague's system, plus a new rule for forming derived verb phrases from sentences.

3. Richmond Thomason, "Some Extensions of Montague Grammar" offers modifications and extensions of PTQ to deal with many of the same constructions treated by Partee, but in quite different ways. Thomason makes use of a more fully categorial syntax than Montague did in PTQ, and shows the power of the device of "abstracts" in accomplishing this. He also shows how meaning postulates can to a large extent replace transformations in capturing relatedness between sentences.

4. Michael Bennett, "A Variation and Extension of a Montague Fragment of

---

[4]In Thomason (Ed.), *Formal philosophy,* pp. 247–270.

English'' extends a modified version of PTQ to treat adjectives, three-place verbs, Raising, Passive, and other constructions. Bennett's approach is less transformational than Partee's but more so than Thomason's; he offers, for instance, a nontransformational treatment of passive constructions but argues for a transformational account of Raising.

The three papers together provide a good view of the extent to which alternative analyses are possible within the general Montague framework; a comparison of the analyses given could serve as a useful starting point for debate on the extent to which transformations are necessary or desirable in a Montague system.

5. Robert Rodman, "Scope Phenomena, 'Movement Transformations,' and Relative Clauses'' gives rules for forming relative clauses in English in their natural form (as opposed to Montague's **such that** constructions) and discusses how the appropriate "Ross constraints" can be added to the system. He shows that a single kind of syntactic device can simultaneously capture the syntactic restrictions on movement rules and the semantic restrictions on scope interpretation.

6. Enrique Delacruz, "Factives and Proposition Level Constructions in a Montague Grammar'' treats the phenomenon of factivity first raised by the Kiparskys in their paper "Fact.''[5] One important innovation made in this paper is the addition of a distinction in category between "entity-level'' expressions like **the man** and **hit** and "proposition-level'' expressions like **the fact** and **entail.** This distinction makes possible an account of certain kinds of noun complements **(the fact that . . .)** and an explication of some of the phenomena of factivity without resort to the notion of presupposition.

7. David Dowty, "Montague Grammar and the Lexical Decomposition of Causative Verbs'' is concerned with a comparison of the theory of generative semantics and Montague's theory, focusing on arguments for the lexical decomposition hypothesis. Dowty shows how analogues of decomposition analyses can be formulated within the framework of PTQ, making use of translation rules or meaning postulates in place of complex syntactic analyses. Alternative treatments of adverb scope ambiguity are proposed and discussed, extensions of PTQ are given to treat complex causatives like **hammar flat,** and the relation between syntax and derivational morphology is explored.

8. C.L. Hamblin, "Questions in Montague English'' is a short, self-contained article which gives a capsule description of Montague's paper "English as a Formal Language''[6] (EFL) and extends it to account for the semantics of **yes–no** questions and **who/which/what** questions. This paper is the only one in the collection based on EFL, and the only one besides Lewis's to treat nondeclarative sentences. It is easier to read than most of the other papers, and the treatment

---

[5]Kiparsky, P., and Kiparsky, C. Fact. In D.D. Steinberg and L.A. Jakobovits (Eds.), *Semantics: An interdisciplinary reader in philosophy, linguistics, and psychology.* Cambridge: Cambridge Univ. Press, 1971. Pp. 345–369.

[6]In Thomason (Ed.), *Formal Philosophy,* pp. 188–221.

proposed for *wh*-question words is an elegant extension of Montague's treatment of quantifiers.

9. M.J. Cresswell, "The Semantics of Degree" is not strictly within the Montague framework, but draws on Cresswell's own theory elaborated in Cresswell's *Logics and Languages*.[7] Cresswell's theory is similar in spirit to Montague's, the main differences being in the syntax. The paper contains sufficient exposition of Cresswell's theory to make the differences clear; within his framework, Cresswell offers an account of the syntax and semantics of comparative constructions and related degree expressions, and relates his analysis to Bresnan's transformational account of comparatives.[8] The paper also contains an analysis of mass nouns.

10. Muffy Siegel, "Capturing the Russian Adjective" shows that the existence and behavior of the two distinct morphological classes of adjectives in Russian ("long forms" and "short forms") can be elegantly explained by treating the long form adjectives as common noun modifiers (CN/CN) and the short form adjectives as categorially identical to verbs. A wide range of syntactic distributional differences between the two forms are shown to be natural corollaries of this underlying distinction in categories; the same distinction accounts for semantic differences which can be found in positions where long and short forms can both occur. The net result of this study is to turn what looked at first like a problem for the Montague framework (the prediction that adjectives could fit into two distinct categories) into a striking advantage, at least for Russian.

11. Robin Cooper and Terence Parsons, "Montague Grammar, Generative Semantics, and Interpretive Semantics" makes a significant advance in opening up the field of theory comparison. Cooper and Parsons show how a Montague semantics can be incorporated into either a generative semantics or interpretive semantics sort of framework, at least for a fragment that matches that of Montague's PTQ. The equivalence of the generative and interpretive systems is proved for the given fragment; the study naturally opens up questions of whether the equivalence would continue to hold for various extensions of the fragment. The study offers hope of making comparisons between frameworks more straightforward and less polemical, thereby making it easier both to achieve cooperative progress on substantive problems and to look for areas in which alternative frameworks may eventually be shown to differ.

Research in the area of Montague's theory of language and its relation to other theories of syntax and semantics is currently being carried out by many more researchers than could be represented in a single volume. Other scholars working in this area include Renate Bartsch, Joyce Friedman, Dov Gabbay, Roland Hausser, Lauri Karttunen, Asa Kasher, Kiyong Lee, Julius Moravcsik, Stanley Peters, and Helmut Schnelle, a list I am sure is still incomplete.

[7] Methuen and Company, Ltd. London, 1973.
[8] Bresnan, J. Syntax of the comparative clause construction in English, *Linguistic Inquiry*, 1973, **4**, 275–343.

For permission to reprint papers that had earlier appeared elsewhere, I am grateful to the following:

D. Reidel Publishing Company, for permission to reprint David Lewis, "General Semantics" from *Semantics of Natural Language,* edited by D. Davidson and G. Harman (1972), pp. 169-218, and for permission to reprint Barbara Partee, "Some Transformational Extensions of Montague Grammar" from *Journal of Philosophical Logic,* Vol. 2 (1973), pp. 509-534.

John W.M. Verhaar, S.J., editor, *Foundations of Language,* for permission to reprint C.L. Hamblin, "Questions in Montague English," from that journal, Vol. 10 (1973), pp. 41-53.

The Department of Linguistics, University of California at Los Angeles, for permission to print slightly revised versions of papers by Enrique Delacruz and Robert Rodman which originally appeared in Robert Rodman, editor, *Papers in Montague Grammar,* Occasional Papers in Linguistics, No. 2, UCLA (1972).

I also wish to acknowledge the support of NSF Grant GS 39752 in preparing this volume, and to express my gratitude to the contributors and other colleagues whose encouragement and responsiveness made this volume a reality. Many of the contributors join me in acknowledging as well the support of a grant from the Mathematical Social Science Board for a Research Workshop on the Syntax and Semantics of Non-Extensional Constructions, held in Amherst in the summer of 1974, which included among its participants Lewis, Partee, Thomason, Bennett, Delacruz, Dowty, and Parsons, and which provided an opportunity for much fruitful interchange on many of the topics treated in the studies included here.

DAVID LEWIS

GENERAL SEMANTICS*

I. INTRODUCTION

On the hypothesis that all natural or artificial languages of interest to us can be given transformational grammars of a certain not-very-special sort, it becomes possible to give very simple general answers to the questions:

(1)   What sort of thing is a meaning?
(2)   What is the form of the semantic rules whereby meanings of compounds are built up from the meanings of their constituent parts?

It is not my plan to make any strong empirical claim about language. To the contrary: I want to propose a convenient format for semantics general enough to work for a great variety of logically possible languages. This paper therefore belongs not to empirical linguistic theory but to the philosophy thereof.

My proposals regarding the nature of meanings will not conform to the expectations of those linguists who conceive of semantic interpretation as the assignment to sentences and their constituents of compounds of 'semantic markers' or the like. (Katz and Postal, 1964, for instance.) Semantic markers are *symbols*: items in the vocabulary of an artificial language we may call *Semantic Markerese*. Semantic interpretation by means of them amounts merely to a translation algorithm from the object language to the auxiliary language Markerese. But we can know the Markerese translation of an English sentence without knowing the first thing about the meaning of the English sentence: namely, the conditions under which it would be true. Semantics with no treatment of truth conditions is not semantics. Translation into Markerese is at best a substitute for real semantics, relying either on our tacit competence (at some future date) as speakers of Markerese or on our ability to do real semantics at least for the one language Markerese. Translation into Latin might

Davidson and Harman (eds.), Semantics of Natural Language, 169–218. *All rights reserved*
Copyright © 1972 *by D. Reidel Publishing Company, Dordrecht - Holland*

serve as well, except insofar as the designers of Markerese may choose
to build into it useful features – freedom from ambiguity, grammar based
on symbolic logic – that might make it easier to do real semantics for
Markerese than for Latin. (See Vermazen, 1967, for similar criticisms).

The Markerese method is attractive in part just because it deals with
nothing but symbols: finite combinations of entities of a familiar sort out
of a finite set of elements by finitely many applications of finitely many
rules. There is no risk of alarming the ontologically parsimonious. But
it is just this pleasing finitude that prevents Markerese semantics from
dealing with the relations between symbols and the world of non-symbols
– that is, with genuinely semantic relations. Accordingly, we should be
prepared to find that in a more adequate method, meanings may turn out
to be complicated, infinite entities built up out of elements belonging to
various ontological categories.

My proposals will also not conform to the expectations of those who,
in analyzing meaning, turn immediately to the psychology and sociology
of language users: to intentions, sense-experience, and mental ideas, or
to social rules, conventions, and regularities. I distinguish two topics:
first, the description of possible languages or grammars as abstract
semantic systems whereby symbols are associated with aspects of the
world; and second, the description of the psychological and sociological
facts whereby a particular one of these abstract semantic systems is the
one used by a person or population. Only confusion comes of mixing
these two topics. This paper deals almost entirely with the first. (I discuss
the second elsewhere: Lewis, 1968b and 1969, Chapter V.)

My proposals are in the tradition of *referential*, or *model-theoretic*,
semantics descended from Frege, Tarski, Carnap (in his later works), and
recent work of Kripke and others on semantic foundations of intensional
logic. (See Frege, 1892; Tarski, 1936; Carnap, 1947 and 1963, § 9;
Kripke, 1963; Kaplan, 1964; Montague, 1960, 1968, and 1970c; Scott, 1970.)
The project of transplanting referential semantics from artificial to natural
languages has recently been undertaken, in various ways, by several philosophers and linguists (Davidson, 1967; Parsons, 1968; Montague,
1969, 1970a, and 1970b; Keenan, 1969.) I have no quarrel with these
efforts; indeed, I have here adapted features from several of them. I hope,
however, that the system set forth in this paper offers a simpler way to
do essentially the same thing. But simplicity is a matter of taste, and

simplicity at one place trades off against simplicity elsewhere. It is in these trade-offs that my approach differs most from the others.

II. CATEGORIALLY BASED GRAMMARS

A *categorial grammar* in the sense of Ajdukiewicz (Ajdukiewicz, 1935; Bar-Hillel, 1964, Part II) is a context-free phrase structure grammar of the following sort.

First, we have a small number of *basic categories*. One of these is the category *sentence* (S). Others might be, for instance, the categories *name* (N) and *common noun* (C). Perhaps we can get by with these three and no more; indeed, Ajdukiewicz went so far as to do without the category *common noun*. Or perhaps we might do better to use different basic categories; we will consider dispensing with the category *name* in favor of an alternative basic category *verb phrase* (VP), or perhaps *noun phrase* (NP).

Second, we have infinitely many *derived categories*. Whenever $c, c_1, ..., c_n$ ($n \geqslant 1$) are any categories, either basic or derived, we have a derived category which we will write $(c/c_1 ... c_n)$. (However, we will usually omit the outermost parentheses.)

Third, we have context-free phrase-structure rules of the form

$$c \to (c/c_1...c_n) + c_1 + \cdots + c_n$$

corresponding to each derived category. That is to say: for any categories $c, c_1, ..., c_n$, the result of concatenating any expression of category $(c/c_1...c_n)$, then any expression of category c_1, then..., and finally any expression of category c_n is an expression of category c. Accordingly, we will say that a $(c/c_1...c_n)$ *takes* a c_1 and ... and a c_n and *makes* a c. The phrase-structure rules are implicit in the system of derived categories.

Finally, we have a lexicon wherein finitely many expressions – words or word-like morphemes – are assigned to categories. The categories of these lexical expressions may be either basic or derived; unless some lexical expressions belong to derived categories, no non-lexical compound expressions can be generated. Notice that although there are infinitely many derived categories and infinitely many phrase-structure rules, nevertheless with any given lexicon all but finitely many categories and rules will be unemployed. This is true even though many lexica will generate infinitely many compound expressions.

To specify a categorial grammar, we need only specify its lexicon. The rest is common to all categorial grammars. Consider this lexicon:

$$
\left\{
\begin{array}{llll}
\langle a & (S/(S/N))/C\rangle & \langle pig & C\rangle \\
\langle believes & (S/N)/S\rangle & \langle piggishly & (S/N)/(S/N)\rangle \\
\langle every & (S/(S/N))/C\rangle & \langle Porky & N\rangle \\
\langle grunts & S/N\rangle & \langle something & S/(S/N)\rangle \\
\langle is & (S/N)/N\rangle & \langle the & (S/(S/N))/C\rangle \\
\langle loves & (S/N)/N\rangle & \langle which & (C/C)/(S/N)\rangle \\
\langle Petunia & N\rangle & \langle yellow & C/C\rangle
\end{array}
\right\}
$$

It gives us a categorial grammar which is simply a notational variant of this rather commonplace context-free grammar:

$$
S \rightarrow \begin{cases} NP + VP \\ VP + Npr \end{cases} \qquad Npr \rightarrow \begin{cases} Porky \\ Petunia \end{cases}
$$

$$
VP \rightarrow \begin{cases} Adv + VP \\ Vt + Npr \\ Vs + S \end{cases} \qquad \begin{array}{l} NP \rightarrow something \\ Nco \rightarrow pig \\ VP \rightarrow grunts \end{array}
$$

$$
\begin{array}{l} NP \rightarrow Art + Nco \\ Nco \rightarrow Adj + Nco \\ Adj \rightarrow Rel + VP \end{array} \qquad Vt \rightarrow \begin{cases} loves \\ is \end{cases}
$$

$$
Vs \rightarrow believes
$$

$$
Art \rightarrow \begin{cases} a \\ every \\ the \end{cases}
$$

$$
\begin{array}{l} Adj \rightarrow yellow \\ Adv \rightarrow piggishly \\ Rel \rightarrow which \end{array}
$$

There are three peculiarities about the grammar. First, proper nouns are distinguished from noun phrases. Proper nouns or noun phrases may be subjects (though with different word order) but only proper nouns may be objects. Second, there is nothing to prevent inappropriate iteration of modifiers. Third, the word order is sometimes odd. We will see later how these peculiarities may be overcome.

The employed rules in this example are the eight phrase-structure rules corresponding to the eight employed derived categories.

In this example, I have used only derived categories of the form (c/c_1) that take a single argument. I shall adopt this restriction for the most part in practice, but not in principle.

It is apparent that categorial grammars of this sort are not reasonable grammars for natural language. For that matter, they are not reasonable grammars for most artificial languages either – the exception being symbolic logic in Polish notation. Hence, despite their elegance, categorial grammars have largely been ignored since the early 1950's. Since then, however, we have become interested in the plan of using a simple phrase-structure grammar as a base for a transformational grammar. The time therefore seems ripe to explore *categorially based transformational grammars*, obtained by taking an Ajdukiewicz categorial grammar as base and adding a transformational component. So far as I know, this proposal has been made only once before (Lyons, 1966), but it seems an obvious one.

It is obvious that by adding a transformational component to the categorial grammar of our example, we could rectify the word order and filter out inappropriate iterations of modifiers. Less obviously, we could provide for noun phrase objects by means of a transformational component together with a few additional lexical items – items that need never appear in the final generated sentences.

If reasonable categorially based transformational grammars can be given for all languages of interest to us, and if this can be done under the constraint that meanings are to be determined entirely by base structure, so that the transformational component is irrelevant to semantics, then it becomes extremely easy to give general answer to the questions: What is a meaning? What is the form of a semantic projection rule? Let us see how this can be done.

III. INTENSIONS FOR BASIC CATEGORIES

In order to say what a meaning *is*, we may first ask what a meaning *does*, and then find something that does that.

A meaning for a sentence is something that determines the conditions under which the sentence is true or false. It determines the truth-value of the sentence in various possible states of affairs, at various times, at various places, for various speakers, and so on. (I mean this to apply even to non-declarative sentences, but postpone consideration of them.) Similarly, a meaning for a name is something that determines what thing, if any, the name names in various possible states of affairs, at various times, and so on. Among 'things' we include things that do not actually exist, but *might* exist in states of affairs different from the actual state of affairs. Similarly, a meaning for a common noun is something that determines which (possible or actual) things, if any, that common noun applies to in various possible states of affairs, at various times, and so on.

We call the truth-value of a sentence the *extension* of that sentence; we call the thing named by a name the *extension* of that name; we call the set of things to which a common noun applies the *extension* of that common noun. The extension of something in one of these three categories depends on its meaning and, in general, on other things as well: on facts about the world, on the time of utterance, on the place of utterance, on the speaker, on the surrounding discourse, etc. It is the meaning which determines how the extension depends upon the combination of other relevant factors. What sort of things determine how something depends on something else? *Functions*, of course; functions in the most general set-theoretic sense, in which the domain of arguments and the range of values may consist of entities of any sort whatever, and in which it is not required that the function be specifiable by any simple rule. We have now found something to do at least part of what a meaning for a sentence, name, or common noun does: a function which yields as output an appropriate extension when given as input a package of the various factors on which the extension may depend. We will call such an input package of relevant factors an *index*; and we will call any function from indices to appropriate extensions for a sentence, name, or common noun an *intension*.

Thus an *appropriate intension for* a sentence is any function from indices to truth-values; an *appropriate intension for* a name is any function from indices to things; an *appropriate intension for* a common noun is any function from indices to sets. The plan to construe intensions as extension-determining functions originated with Carnap. (Carnap, 1947, § 40, and 1963.) Accordingly, let us call such functions *Carnapian intensions*. But whereas Carnap's extension-determining functions take as their arguments models or state-descriptions representing possible worlds, I will adopt the suggestion (Montague, 1968; Scott, 1970) of letting the arguments be packages of miscellaneous factors relevant to determining extensions.

We may take indices as n-tuples (finite sequences) of the various items other than meaning that may enter into determining extensions. We call these various items *coordinates* of the index, and we shall assume that the coordinates are given some arbitrary fixed order.

First, we must have a *possible-world coordinate*. Contingent sentences depend for their truth value on facts about the world, and so are true at some possible worlds and false at others. A possible world corresponds to a possible totality of facts, determinate in all respects. Common nouns also have different extensions at different possible worlds; and so do some names, at least if we adopt the position (defended in Lewis, 1968a) that things are related to their counterparts in other worlds by ties of strong similarity rather than identity.

Second, we must have several *contextual coordinates* corresponding to familiar sorts of dependence on features of context. (The world coordinate itself might be regarded as a feature of context, since different possible utterances of a sentence are located in different possible worlds.) We must have a *time coordinate*, in view of tensed sentences and such sentences as 'Today is Tuesday'; a *place coordinate*, in view of such sentences as 'Here there are tigers'; a *speaker coordinate* in view of such sentences as 'I am Porky'; an *audience coordinate* in view of such sentences as 'You are Porky'; an *indicated-objects coordinate* in view of such sentences as 'That pig is Porky' or 'Those men are Communists'; and a *previous discourse coordinate* in view of such sentences as 'The aforementioned pig is Porky'.

Third, it is convenient to have an *assignment coordinate*: an infinite sequence of things, regarded as giving the values of any variables that may occur free in such expressions as 'x is tall' or 'son of y'. Each variable employed in the language will accordingly be a name having as its intension, for some number n, the *nth variable intension*: that function whose value, at any index i, is that thing which is the nth term of the assignment coordinate of i. That thing is the extension, or value, of the variable at i. (Note that because there is more than one possible thing, the variable intensions are distinct: nothing is both the n_1th and the n_2th variable intension for two different numbers n_1 and n_2.) The extensions of 'x is tall' of 'son of y' depend on the assignment and world coordinates of indices just as the extensions of 'I am tall' and 'son of mine' depend on the speaker and world coordinates. Yet the assignment coordinate cannot naturally be included among features of context. One might claim that variables do not appear in sentences of natural languages; but even if this is so, it may be useful to employ variables in a categorial base. In any case, I seek sufficient generality to accommodate languages that do employ variables.

Perhaps other coordinates would be useful. (See the Appendix.) But let us stop here, even though the penalty for introducing a superfluous coordinate is mere clutter, while the penalty for omitting a needed one is inadequacy. Thus an *index* is tentatively any octuple of which the first coordinate is a possible world, the second coordinate is a moment of time, the third coordinate is a place, the fourth coordinate is a person (or other creature capable of being a speaker), the fifth coordinate is a set of persons (or other creatures capable of being an audience), the sixth coordinate is a set (possibly empty) of concrete things capable of being pointed at, the seventh coordinate is a segment of discourse, and the eighth coordinate is an infinite sequence of things.

Intensions, our functions from indices to extensions, are designed to do part of what meanings do. Yet they are not meanings; for there are differences in meaning unaccompanied by differences in intension. It would be absurd to say that all tautologies have the same meaning, but they have the same intension: the constant function having at every index the value *truth*. Intensions are part of the way to meanings, however, and they are of interest in their own right. We shall consider later what must be added to an intension to obtain something that can do *all* of what a meaning does.

We may permit Carnapian intensions to be partial functions from indices, undefined at some indices. A name may not denote anything at a given possible world. 'Pegasus', for instance, denotes nothing at our world, so its intension may be taken as undefined at any index having our world as its world coordinate. A sentence that suffers from failure of presupposition is often thought to lack a truth-value (for instance in Strawson, 1950; Keenan, 1969; McCawley, 1969). If we adopt this treatment of presupposition, sentences susceptible to lack of truth-value should have intensions that are undefined at some indices. They might even have intensions that are undefined at *all* indices; a sentence with inconsistent presuppositions should have as its intension the empty function, defined at no index.

Hitherto I have spoken uncritically of 'things'. Things are name extensions and values of name intensions; sets of things are common-noun extensions and values of common-noun intensions; sequences of things are assignment coordinates of indices. Change the underlying set of things and we change the sets of extensions, indices, and Carnapian intensions. What, then, are things? Of course I want to say, once and for all: *everything* is a thing. But I must not say that. Not all sets of things can be things; else the set of things would be larger than itself. No Carnapian intension can be a thing (unless it is undefined at certain indices); else it would be a member of ... a member of itself. We must understand the above definitions of extensions, indices, and Carnapian intensions (and the coming definitions of compositional intensions, meanings, and lexica) as tacitly relativized to a chosen set of things. Can we choose the set of things once and for all? Not quite; no matter what set we choose as the set of things, the system of intensions defined over that set will not provide intensions for certain terms – 'intension', for instance – of the semantic metalanguage corresponding to that choice. Consider the language of this paper (minus this paragraph) with the extension of 'thing' somehow fixed; it is an adequate semantic metalanguage for some languages but not for itself. To do semantics for it, we must move to a second language in which 'thing' is taken more inclusively; to do semantics for that language we must move to a third language in which 'thing' is taken more inclusively still; and so on. Any language can be treated in a metalanguage in which 'thing' is taken inclusively enough; but the generality of semantics is fundamentally limited by the fact that no language can be its own semantic metalanguage (Cf. Tarski, 1936) and hence there can be no universal semantic metalanguage. But we can approach generality as closely as we like by taking 'thing' inclusively enough. For the remainder of this paper, let us proceed on the assumption that the set of things has been chosen, almost once and for all, as some very inclusive set: at least as the universe of some intended model of standard set theory with all the non-sets we want, actual or possible, included as individuals. Let us ignore the sequence of semantic metalanguages that still escape treatment.

In that case there is overlap between things, sets of things, and truth-values. (Not all sets of things can be things, but some should be.) More-over, there is overlap between sets and truth-values if we adopt the common conventions of identifying the truth-values *truth* and *falsity* with the numbers 1 and 0 respectively, and of identifying each natural number with the set of its predecessors. Thus the appropriate extensions and in-tensions for sentences, names, and common nouns overlap. The same function that is the intension of all contradictions is also the intension of the name 'zero' and of the common noun 'round square'. Such overlap, however, is harmless. Whenever we want to get rid of it, we can replace intensions by ordered pairs of a category and an intension appropriate for that category.

IV. INTENSIONS FOR DERIVED CATEGORIES

Turning to derived categories, it is best to foresake extensions and Carna-pian intensions in the interest of generality. Sometimes, for instance, a C/C – that is, an *adjective* – has an extension like that of a common noun: a set of things to which (at a given index) it applies. Probably 'married' is such an *extensional adjective*. But most adjectives do not have exten-sions. What is the set of things to which 'alleged' applies? An alleged Communist is not something which is, on the one hand, an alleged thing and, on the other hand, a Communist.

In general, an adjective takes a common noun to make a new, com-pound common noun; and the intension of the new common noun depends on the intension of the original common noun in a manner deter-mined by the meaning of the adjective. A meaning for an adjective, therefore, is something that determines how one common-noun intension depends on another. Looking for an entity that does what a meaning does, we are led to say that an appropriate intension for an adjective is any function from common-noun intensions to common-noun intensions. In more detail: it is a function whose domain and range consist of functions from indices to sets. Thus the intension of 'alleged' is a function that, when given as argument the intension of 'Communist', 'windshield', or 'chipmunk' yields as value the intension of the compound common noun 'alleged Communist', 'alleged windshield', or 'alleged chipmunk' respec-tively. Note that it would not work to use instead a function from common-noun extensions (sets) to common-noun extensions; for at certain indices 'Communist' and 'Maoist' have the same extension but 'alleged Communist' and 'alleged Maoist' do not – or, at other indices, vice versa.

More generally, let us say that an *appropriate intension for* a $(c/c_1...c_n)$, where $c, c_1, ..., $ and c_n are any categories, basic or derived, is any n-place function from c_1-intensions, ..., and c_n-intensions to c-intensions. That is, it is any function (again in the most general set-theoretic sense) having as its range of values a set of c-intensions, having as its domain of first arguments the set of c_1-intensions, ..., and having as its domain of nth arguments the set of c_n-intensions. A $(c/c_1...c_n)$ takes a c_1 and ... and a c_n and makes a c by concatenation; correspondingly, a $(c/c_1...c_n)$-intension takes a c_1-intension and ... and a c_n-intension as arguments and makes a c-intension as function value. We will call these intensions for derived categories *compositional intensions*. (Intensions resembling some of my compositional intensions are discussed in Kaplan, 1964; in Scott, 1970; and – as appropriate intensions for adjectives and other modifiers – in Parsons, 1968 and Montague, 1970a. The latter discussion is due in part to J. A. W. Kamp.) The general form of the semantic projection rules for an interpreted categorial grammar is implicit in the nature of compositional intensions, just as the general form of the phrase-structure rules is implicit in the nomenclature for derived categories. The result of concatenating a $(c/c_1...c_n)$ with intension ϕ_0, a c_1 with intension ϕ_1, ..., and a c_n with intension ϕ_n is a c with intension $\phi_0(\phi_1...\phi_n)$.

We have considered already the derived category *adjective* C/C. For another example, take the derived category *verb phrase*, S/N.

A verb phrase takes a name to make a sentence. (We rely on the transformational component to change the word order if necessary.) An appropriate intension for a verb phrase – an S/N-intension – is therefore a function from name intensions to sentence intensions. That is, it is a function from functions from indices to things to functions from indices to truth values. The intension of 'grunts', for instance, is that function ϕ whose value, given as argument any function ϕ_1 from indices to things, is that function ϕ_2 from indices to truth values such that, for any index i,

$$\phi_2(i) = \begin{cases} truth \text{ if } \phi_1(i) \text{ is something which grunts at the world and time given by the appropriate coordinates of } i \\ falsity \text{ otherwise.} \end{cases}$$

Applying the projection rule, we find that the sentence 'Porky grunts' is true at just those indices i such that the thing named by 'Porky' at i grunts at the possible world that is the world coordinate of i at the time which is the time coordinate of i. (The appearance of circularity in this account is spurious; it comes of the fact that I am using English to specify the intension of a word of English.)

For another example, take the derived category *adverb* (of one sort), (S/N)/(S/N). An adverb of this sort takes a verb phrase to make a verb phrase; so an appropriate intension for such an adverb – an (S/N)/(S/N)-intension – is a function from verb-phrase intensions to verb-phrase intensions; or, in more detail, a function from functions from functions from indices to things to functions from indices to truth-values to functions from functions from indices to things to functions from indices to truth-values.

I promised simplicity; I deliver functions from functions from functions to functions to functions from functions to functions. And worse is in store if we consider the sort of adverb that modifies ordinary adverbs: the category ((S/N)/(S/N))/((S/N)/(S/N)). Yet I think no apology is called for. Intensions are complicated constructs, but the principles of their construction are extremely simple. The situation is common: look at any account of the set-theoretic construction of real numbers, yet recall that children often understand the real numbers rather well.

In some cases, it would be possible to find simpler intensions, but at an exorbitant cost: we would have to give up the uniform function-and-arguments form for semantic projection rules. We have noted already that some adjectives are extensional, though most are not. The extensional adjectives could be given sets as extensions and functions from indices to sets as Carnapian intensions. Similarly for verb phrases: we may call a verb phrase *extensional* iff there is a function ϕ from indices to sets such that if ϕ_1 is the (compositional) intension of the verb phrase, ϕ_2 is any name intension, ϕ_3 is $\phi_1(\phi_2)$, and i is any index, then

$$\phi_3(i) = \begin{cases} truth \text{ if } \phi_2(i) \text{ is a member of } \phi(i) \\ falsity \text{ otherwise.} \end{cases}$$

If there is any such function ϕ, there is exactly one; we can call it the Carnapian intension of the verb phrase and we can call its value at any index i the extension of the verb phrase at i. 'Grunts', for instance, is an extensional verb phrase; its extension at an index i is the set of things that grunt at the world and the time given by the world coordinate and the time coordinate of the index i. Verb phrases, unlike adjectives, are ordinarily extensional; but Barbara Partee has pointed out that the verb phrase in 'The price of milk is rising' seems to be non-extensional.

There is no harm in noting that extensional adjectives and verb phrases have Carnapian intensions as well as compositional intensions. However, it is the compositional intension that should be used to determine the intension of an extensional-adjective-plus-common-noun or extensional-verb-phrase-plus-name combination. If we used the Carnapian intensions, we would have a miscellany of semantic projection rules rather than the uniform function-and-arguments rule. (Indeed, the best way to formulate projection rules using Carnapian intensions might be to combine a rule for reconstructing compositional intensions from Carnapian intensions with the function-and-arguments rule for compositional intensions.) Moreover, we would sacrifice generality: non-extensional adjectives and verb phrases would have to be treated separately from the extensional ones, or not at all. This loss of generality would be serious in the case of adjectives; but not in the case of verb phrases since there are few, if any, non-extensional verb phrases.

For the sake of generality, we might wish to take account of selection restrictions by allowing a compositional intension to be undefined for some arguments of appropriate type. If we thought that 'green idea' should lack an intension, for instance, we might conclude that the intension of 'green' ought to be a partial function from common-noun intensions to common-noun intensions, undefined for such arguments as the intension of 'idea'. It proves more convenient, however, never to let the intension be undefined but rather to let it take on a value called the *null intension* (for the appropriate category). The null intension for the basic categories will be the empty function; the null intension for any derived category $(c/c_1...c_n)$ will be that $(c/c_1...c_n)$-intension whose value for any combination of appropriate arguments is the null intension for c. Thus the intension of 'green', given as argument the intension of 'idea', yields as value the null intension for the category C. The intension of the adverb 'furiously', given as argument the intension of 'sleeps', yields as value the null intension for the category S/N, and that in turn, given as value any name intension, yields as value the null intension for the category S. (I dislike this treatment of selection restrictions, but provide the option for those who want it.)

It is worth mentioning that my account of intensions for derived categories, and of the corresponding form for projection rules, is independent of my account of intensions for basic categories. Whatever S-intensions and N-intensions may be – even expressions of Markerese or ideas in someone's mind – it still is possible to take S/N-intensions as functions from N-intensions to S-intensions and to obtain the intension of 'Porky grunts' by applying the intension of 'grunts' as function to the intension of 'Porky' as argument.

V. MEANINGS

We have already observed that intensions for sentences cannot be identified with meanings since differences in meaning – for instance, between tautologies – may not carry with them any difference in intension. The same goes for other categories, basic or derived. Differences in intension, we may say, give us *coarse* differences in meaning. For *fine* differences in meaning we must look to the analysis of a compound into constituents and to the intensions of the several constituents. For instance 'Snow is white or it isn't' differs finely in meaning from 'Grass is green or it isn't' because of the difference in intension between the embedded sentences 'Snow is white' and 'Grass is green'. For still finer differences in meaning we must look in turn to the intensions of constituents of constituents, and so on. Only when we come to non-compound, lexical constituents can we take sameness of intension as a sufficient condition of synonymy. (See Carnap, 1947, § 14, on 'intensional isomorphism'; C. I. Lewis, 1944, on 'analytic meaning'.)

It is natural, therefore, to identify meanings with semantically interpreted phrase markers minus their terminal nodes: finite ordered trees having at each node a category and an appropriate intension. If we associate a meaning of this sort with an expression, we are given the category and intension of the expression; and if the expression is compound, we are given also the categories and intensions of its constituent parts, their constituent parts, and so on down.

Perhaps we would thereby cut meanings too finely. For instance, we will be unable to agree with someone who says that a double negation has the same meaning as the corresponding affirmative. But this difficulty does not worry me: we will have both intensions and what I call meanings, and sometimes one and sometimes the other will be preferable as an explication of our ordinary discourse about meanings. Perhaps some entities of intermediate fineness can also be found, but I doubt that there is any uniquely natural way to do so.

It may be disturbing that in our explication of meanings we have made arbitrary choices – for instance, of the order of coordinates in an index. Meanings are meanings – how can we *choose* to construct them in one way rather than another? The objection is a general objection to set-theoretic constructions (see Benacerraf, 1965), so I will not reply to it here. But if it troubles you, you may prefer to say that *real* meanings are *sui generis* entities and that the constructs I call 'meanings' do duty for real meanings because there is a natural one-to-one correspondence between them and the real meanings.

It might also be disturbing that I have spoken of categories without hitherto saying what they are. This again is a matter of arbitrary choice; we might, for instance, take them as sets of expressions in some language, or as sets of intensions, or even as arbitrarily chosen code-numbers. It turns out to be most convenient, if slightly unnatural, to identify categories with their own names: expressions composed in the proper way out of the letters 'S', 'N', 'C' (and whatever others we may introduce later in considering revisions of the system) together with parentheses and diagonal slashes. This does not prevent our category-names from being names of categories: they name themselves. All definitions involving categories are to be understood in accordance with the identification of categories and category-names.

Some might even wish to know what a *tree* is. Very well: it is a function that assigns to each member of the set of nodes of the tree an object said to *occupy* or be *at* that node. The nodes themselves are finite sequences of positive numbers. A set of such sequences is the set of *nodes of* some tree iff, first, it is a finite set, and second, whenever it contains a sequence $\langle b_1...b_k \rangle$ then it also contains every sequence that is an initial segment of $\langle b_1...b_k \rangle$ and every sequence $\langle b_1...b_{k-1}b_k' \rangle$ with $b_k' < b_k$. We regard $\langle \ \rangle$, the sequence of zero length, as the topmost node; $\langle b_1 \rangle$ as the b_1th node from the left immediately beneath $\langle \ \rangle$; $\langle b_1 \ b_2 \rangle$ as the b_2th node from the left immediately beneath $\langle b_1 \rangle$; and so on. We can easily define all the requisite notions of tree theory in terms of this construction.

Once we have identified meanings with semantically interpreted phrase markers, it becomes natural to reconstrue the phrase-structure rules of categorial grammar, together with the corresponding projection rules, as conditions of well-formedness for meanings. (Cf. McCawley, 1968.) Accordingly, we now define a *meaning* as a tree such that, first, each node is occupied by an ordered pair $\langle c\ \phi \rangle$ of a category and an appropriate intension for that category; and second, immediately beneath any non-terminal node occupied by such a pair $\langle c\ \phi \rangle$ are two or more nodes, and these are occupied by pairs $\langle c_0\ \phi_0 \rangle$, $\langle c_1\ \phi_1 \rangle$, ..., $\langle c_n\ \phi_n \rangle$ (in that order) such that c_0 is $(c/c_1...c_n)$ and ϕ is $\phi_0(\phi_1...\phi_n)$.

A meaning may be a tree with a single node; call such meanings *simple* and other meanings *compound*. Compound meanings are, as it were, built up from simple meanings by steps in which several meanings (simple or compound) are combined as sub-trees under a new node, analogously to the way in which expressions are built up by concatenating shorter expressions. We may call a meaning m' a *constituent of* a meaning m iff m' is a subtree of m. We may say that a meaning m is *generated by* a set of simple meanings iff every simple constituent of m belongs to that set. More generally, m is *generated by* a set of meanings (simple or compound) iff every simple constituent of m is a constituent of some constituent of m, possibly itself, which belongs to that set.

We shall in many ways speak of meanings as though they were symbolic expressions generated by an interpreted categorial grammar, even though they are nothing of the sort. The *category of* a meaning is the category found as the first component of its topmost node. The *intension of* a meaning is the intension found as the second component of its topmost node. The *extension at* an index i *of* a sentence meaning, name meaning, or common-noun meaning is the value of the intension of the meaning for the argument i. A sentence meaning is *true* or *false at i* according as its extension at i is *truth* or *falsity*; a name meaning *names at i* that thing, if any, which is its extension at i; and a common-noun meaning *applies at i* to whatever things belong to its extension at i. As we have seen, extensions might also be provided for certain meanings in derived categories such as C/C or S/N, but this cannot be done in a non-artificial, general way.

Given as fundamental the definition of truth of a sentence meaning at an index, we can define many derivative truth relations. Coordinates of the index may be made explicit, or may be determined by a context of utterance, or may be generalized over. Generalizing over all coordinates, we can say that a sentence meaning is *analytic* (in one sense) iff it is true at every index. Generalizing over the world and assignment coordinates and letting the remaining coordinates be determined by context, we can say that a sentence meaning is *analytic* (in another sense) *on* a given occasion iff it is true at every index i having as its time, place, speaker, audience, indicated-objects and previous-discourse coordinates respectively the time, the place, the speaker, the audience, the set of objects pointed to, and the previous discourse on that occasion. Generalizing over the time and assignment coordinates and letting the others (including world) be determined by context, we define *eternal truth* of a sentence meaning *on* an occasion; generalizing over the assignment coordinate and letting all the rest be determined by context, we define simply *truth on* an occasion; and so on.

We also can define truth relations even stronger than truth at every index. Let us call a meaning m' a *semantic variant* of a meaning m iff m and m' have exactly the same nodes, with the same category but not necessarily the same intension at each node, and, whenever a common intension appears at two terminal nodes in m, a common intension also appears at those two nodes in m'. Let us call m' an *s-fixed semantic variant of m*, where s is a set of simple meanings, iff m and m' are semantic variants and every member of s which is a constituent of m is also a constituent, at the same place, of m'. Then we can call a sentence meaning *s-true* iff every s-fixed semantic variant of it (including itself) is true at every index. If s is the set of simple meanings whose bearers we would classify as logical vocabulary, then we may call s-true sentence meanings *logically true*; if s is the set of simple meanings whose bearers we would classify as mathematical (including logical) vocabulary, we may call s-true sentence meanings *mathematically true*. Analogously, we can define a relation of s-fixed semantic variance between sequences of meanings; and we can say that a sentence meaning m_0 is an *s-consequence* (for instance, a *logical consequence* or *mathematical consequence*) of sentence meanings $m_1, \ldots$ iff, for every s-fixed semantic variant $\langle m'_0 \, m'_1 \ldots \rangle$ of the sequence $\langle m_0 \, m_1 \ldots \rangle$ and every index i such that all of $m'_1, \ldots$ are true at i, m'_0 is true at i. (The premises $m_1, \ldots$ may be infinite in number. Their order is insignificant.) These definitions are adapted from definitions in terms of truth in all logically or mathematically standard interpretations of a given language. However, we have been able to avoid introducing the notion of alternative interpretations of a language, since so far we are dealing entirely with meanings.

VI. GRAMMARS RECONSTRUCTED

Our system of meanings may serve, in effect, as a universal base for categorially based transformational grammars. There is no need to repeat the phrase-structure rules of categorial well-formedness as a base component in each such grammar. Instead, we take the meanings as given, and regard a grammar as specifying a way to encode meanings: a relation between certain meanings and certain expressions (sequences of sound-types or of mark-types) which we will call the *representing relation* determined by the grammar. We might just identify grammars with representing relations; but I prefer to take grammars as systems which determine representing relations in a certain way.

If we were concerned with nothing but transformation-free categorial grammars, we could take a grammar to consist of nothing but a *lexicon*: a finite set of triples of the form $\langle e\ c\ \phi \rangle$ where e is an expression, c is a category, and ϕ is an intension appropriate for that category. We may say that an expression e *represents* or *has* a meaning m *relative to* a lexicon **L** iff **L** contains items $\langle e_1\ c_1\ \phi_1 \rangle$, ..., $\langle e_n\ c_n\ \phi_n \rangle$ such that, first, e is the result of concatenating e_1, ..., e_n (in that order), and second, the terminal nodes of m are occupied by $\langle c_1\ \phi_1 \rangle$, ..., $\langle c_n\ \phi_n \rangle$ (in that order).

We could instead have proceeded in two steps. Let us define a (*categorial*) *phrase marker* as a tree having categories at its non-terminal nodes and expressions at its terminal nodes. Then a phrase marker p represents or *has* a meaning m *relative to* a lexicon **L** iff p is obtained from m as follows: given any terminal node of the meaning m occupied by a pair $\langle c\ \phi \rangle$, place below it another node occupied by an expression e such that the item $\langle e\ c\ \phi \rangle$ is contained in the lexicon; then remove the intensions, replacing the $\langle c\ \phi \rangle$ pair at each non-terminal node by its unaccompanied category c. Note that the set of meanings thus representable relative to a lexicon **L** comprises all and only those meanings that are generated by the set of simple meanings of the lexical items themselves; let us call it the set of meanings *generated by* the lexicon **L**.

Next, we define the *terminal string* of a phrase marker *p* as the expression obtained by concatenating, in order, the expressions at the terminal nodes of *p*. Thus we see that an expression *e* represents a meaning *m* relative to a lexicon **L**, according to the definition above, iff *e* is the terminal string of some phrase marker that represents *m* relative to **L**.

In the case of a categorially based transformational grammar, we have not two steps but three. Such a grammar consists of a lexicon **L** together with a *transformational component* **T**. The latter imposes finitely many constraints on finite sequences of phrase markers. A sequence $\langle p_1 \ldots p_n \rangle$ of phrase markers that satisfies the constraints imposed by **T** will be called a (*transformational*) *derivation of p_n from p_1 in* **T**. An expression *e* *represents* or *has* a meaning *m* in a grammar $\langle L\,T \rangle$ iff there exists a derivation $\langle p_1 \ldots p_n \rangle$ in **T** such that *e* is the terminal string of p_n and p_1 represents *m* relative to the lexicon **L**. If so, we will also call *e* a *meaningful expression*, p_n a *surface structure of e*, p_{n-1} and ... and p_2 *intermediate structures of e*, p_1 a *base structure of e*, and *m* a *meaning of e* (all *relative to* the grammar $\langle L\,T \rangle$). However, we will call any phrase marker *p* a *base structure* in $\langle L\,T \rangle$ iff it represents a meaning relative to **L**, whether or not it is the base structure *of* any expression; thus we allow for base structures which are filtered out by not being the first term of any derivation in **T**.

The representing relation given by a grammar $\langle L\,T \rangle$ is by no means a one-to-one correspondence between meanings and expressions. A given expression might be *ambiguous*, representing several different meanings. (If it represents several different but cointensive meanings, however, it might be inappropriate to call it ambiguous; for the common notion of meaning seems to hover between our technical notions of meaning and of intension.) On the other hand, several expressions might be *synonymous*, representing a single meaning. We might also call several expressions *completely synonymous* iff they share all their meanings; synonymy and complete synonymy coincide when we are dealing only with unambiguous expressions. If several expressions represent different but cointensive meanings, we may call them equivalent but not synonymous. If several expressions not only represent the same meaning but also have a single base structure, we may call them not only equivalent and synonymous but also *paraphrases* of one another.

Given a representing relation, all the semantic relations defined hitherto for meanings carry over to expressions having those meanings. (If we like, they may carry over also to the base, surface, and intermediate structures between the meanings and the expressions.) Thus we know what it means to speak, relative to a given grammar and qualified in cases of ambiguity by 'on a meaning' or 'on all meanings', of the category and intension of any meaningful expression; of the extension at a given index of any expression of appropriate category; of the thing named by a name; of the things to which a common noun applies; of the truth at an index, truth on an occasion, analyticity, logical truth, etc. of a sentence; and so on.

We should note an oddity in our treatment of logical truth. A synonym of a logically true sentence is itself a logical truth, since it represents the same logically true meaning as the original. Hence a descendant by synonym-substitution of a logical truth is itself a logical truth if the synonym-substitution is confined to single lexical items in the base structure; but not otherwise. 'All woodchucks are groundhogs' comes out logically true, whereas 'All squares are equilateral rectangles' comes out merely analytic (in the strongest sense).

A transformational component may constrain sequences of phrase markers in two ways. There is the local constraint that any two adjacent phrase markers in a derivation must stand in one of finitely many relations; these permitted relations between adjacent phrase markers are the *transformations*. There may also be global derivational constraints specifying relations between non-adjacent phrase markers or properties of the derivation as a whole. An example is the constraint requiring transformations to apply in some specified cyclic (or partly cyclic) order.

A transformation-free categorial grammar is a special case of a categorially based transformational grammar. It has a transformational component with no transformations or global constraints, so that the derivations therein are all and only those sequences $\langle p_1 \rangle$ consisting of a single phrase marker.

I will not attempt to say more exactly what a transformation or a transformational component is. Mathematically precise definitions have been given (for instance in Peters and Ritchie, 1969), but to choose among these would involve taking sides on disputed questions in syntactic theory. I prefer to maintain my neutrality, and I have no present need for a precise delineation of the class of transformational grammars. I have foremost in mind a sort of simplified *Aspects*-model grammar (Chomsky, 1965), but I have said nothing to eliminate various alternatives.

I have said nothing to eliminate generative semantics. What I have chosen to call the 'lexicon' is the *initial* lexicon. Words not in that lexicon might be introduced transformationally on the way from base to surface, if that seems desirable. It might even be that none of the initial lexical items ever reach the surface, and that all surface lexical items (expressions found at terminal nodes of surface structures) are introduced transformationally within derivations. In that case it would be appropriate to use a standardized initial lexicon in all grammars, and to rechristen my base structures 'semantic representations'. In that case also there might or might not be a level between base and surface at which word-introducing transformations are done and other transformations have not yet begun.

I have also said nothing to eliminate surface semantics. This may seem strange, since I have indeed said that meanings are to be determined by base structures alone. However, I rely here on the observation (Lakoff, 1970, § 3) that surface-structure interpretation rules are indistinguishable from global derivational constraints relating three levels: base structures (regarded as semantic representations), deep structures (an *intermediate* level), and surface structures. Deep structures might be ambiguous; a transformational grammar with base-deep-surface constraints might permit two derivations

$$\langle p_B^1 \cdots p_D \cdots p_S^1 \rangle$$
$$\langle p_B^2 \cdots p_D \cdots p_S^2 \rangle$$

differing at the base and surface but not at the deep level, but it might rule out other derivations of the forms

$$\langle p_B^2 \cdots p_D \cdots p_S^1 \rangle$$
$$\langle p_B^1 \cdots p_D \cdots p_S^2 \rangle.$$

In such a case base structure (and hence meaning) would be determined by deep and surface structure together, but not by deep structure alone. Similarly, we might have constraints relating base structure not only to deep and surface structure but also to structure at various other intermediate levels.

I have said nothing to eliminate a non-trivial phonological component;

but I would relocate it as part of the transformational component. The last few steps of a transformational derivation might go from the usual pre-phonological surface structure to a post-phonological surface structure whence the output expression can be obtained simply by concatenation of terminal nodes.

I have said nothing to eliminate an elaborate system of selection restrictions; but these will appear not as restrictions on the lexical insertions between meanings and base structures but as transformational filtering later on. There will be base structures representing the meanings of such questionable sentences as 'Seventeen eats beans' and 'He sang a pregnant toothbrush'. But these base structures need not be the first terms of any derivations, so these meanings may be unrepresented by sentences. If we like selection restrictions, we might match the lexicon to the transformational component in such a way as to filter out just those meanings that have the null intension.

I have not stipulated that only sentential meanings may be represented; that stipulation could be added if there is reason for it.

In fact, the *only* restriction I place on syntax is that transformational grammars should be categorially based. In other words: a transformational component should operate on a set of categorial phrase markers representing a set of meanings generated by some lexicon. But categorial bases are varied enough that this restriction is not at all severe. I claim that whatever familiar sort of base component you may favor on syntactic grounds, you can find a categorial base (i.e. a suitable part of the system of meanings, generated by a suitable chosen lexicon) that resembles the base you favor closely enough to share its attractive properties. Indeed, with a few preliminary rearranging transformations you can go from my categorial base structures to (notational variants of) more familiar base structures; then you can proceed exactly as before. I shall not marshall evidence for this claim; but I think that the following exploration of alternative categorial treatments of quantification will exhibit the close similarities between these categorial treatments and several alternative familiar base components. If it were necessary to choose between a categorial base that was convenient for semantics and a noncategorial base that was convenient for transformational syntax, I might still choose the former. But I deny the need to choose.

This completes the exposition of my proposed system of categories, intensions, and meanings. Now I shall consider how this system – either as is or slightly revised – might be applied to two difficult areas: the semantics of quantification and the semantics of non-declaratives. The treatments following are intended only as illustrations, however; many further alternatives are possible, and might be more convenient for syntax.

VII. TREATMENT OF QUANTIFICATION AND NOUN PHRASES

Let us consider such expressions as 'a pig', 'most pigs', 'seventeen pigs', 'roughly seventeen pigs', 'some yellow pig', 'everything', 'nobody', and the like. We call these *quantifier phrases* (presupposing that they should belong to a common category). What category in our system is this? What sort of intensions do quantifier phrases have?

Quantifier phrases combine with verb phrases to make sentences: 'Some pig grunts', 'Nobody grunts', 'Roughly seventeen pigs grunt', and the like. Names do this, since the category *verb phrase* is the derived category S/N. But quantifier phrases cannot be names, under our semantic treatment of names, because they do not in general name anything. ('The pig' could be an exception at indices such that exactly one pig existed at the world and time given by the index.) The absurd consequences of treating 'nobody', as a name, for instance, are well known (Dodgson, 1871). If a quantifier phrase combines with an S/N to make an S, and yet is not an N, it must therefore be an S/(S/N).

Except perhaps for one-word quantifier phrases – 'nobody', 'everything', and such – quantifier phrases contain constituent common nouns. These may be either simple, as in 'some pig' or compound, as in 'every pink pig that wins a blue ribbon'. Indeed, we may regard common nouns simply as predicates used to restrict quantifiers. (This suggestion derives from Montague, 1970a.) The expressions 'a', 'the', 'some', 'every', 'no', 'most', 'seventeen', 'roughly seventeen', and so on which combine with common nouns (simple or compound) to make quantifier phrases and which are variously called *quantifiers*, *determiners*, or *articles* must therefore belong to the category (S/(S/N))/C. And modifiers of quantifiers like 'roughly' which combine with certain quantifiers to make quantifiers, must belong to the category ((S/(S/N))/C)/((S/(S/N))/C). Selection restrictions by means of transformational filtering could be used to dispose of quantifiers like 'roughly the'.

The intension of 'some pig' may be taken as that function ϕ from S/N-intensions to S-intensions such that if ϕ_1 is any S/N-intension, ϕ_2 is the S-intension $\phi(\phi_1)$, and i is any index, then

$$\phi_2(i) = \begin{array}{l} \textit{truth} \text{ if, for some N-intension } \phi_3, \phi_3(i) \text{ is a pig and} \\ \text{if } \phi_4 \text{ is } \phi_1(\phi_3) \text{ then } \phi_4(i) \text{ is } \textit{truth} \\ \textit{falsity} \text{ otherwise.} \end{array}$$

The intension of 'some' may be taken as that function ϕ from C-intensions to S/(S/N)-intensions such that if ϕ_1 is any C-intension, ϕ_2 is the S/(S/N)-intension $\phi(\phi_1)$, ϕ_3 is any S/N-intension, ϕ_4 is the S-intension $\phi_2(\phi_3)$, and i is any index, then

$$\phi_4(i) = \begin{array}{l} \textit{truth} \text{ if, for some N-intension } \phi_5, \phi_5(i) \text{ is a member} \\ \text{of } \phi_1(i) \text{ and if } \phi_6 \text{ is } \phi_3(\phi_5) \text{ then } \phi_6(i) \text{ is } \textit{truth} \\ \textit{falsity} \text{ otherwise.} \end{array}$$

I spare you the intension of 'roughly'.

Other intensions might be specified for 'some pig' and 'some' that would differ from these only when a quantifier phrase was applied to a non-extensional verb phrase. If there are no non-extensional verb phrases in English, then the choice among these alternatives is arbitrary.

This treatment of quantifier phrases is motivated by a desire to handle simple sentences involving quantifier phrases as straightforwardly as possible, minimizing the use of transformations. But it raises problems. Quantifier phrases seemingly occur not only as subjects of sentences but also as objects of verbs or prepositions. And in all their roles – as subjects or as objects – they are interchangeable with names. That is why it is usual to have a category *noun phrase* comprising both quantifier phrases and names.

We might try the heroic course of doubling all our object-takers. We could have one word 'loves' which is an (S/N)/N and takes the object 'Petunia' to make the verb phrase 'loves Petunia'; and alongside it another 'loves' which is an (S/N)/(S/(S/N)) and takes the object 'some pig' to make the verb phrase 'loves some pig'. But we need not decide how much we mind such extravagant doubling, since it does not work anyway. It would give us one meaning for 'Every boy loves some girl': the weaker meaning, on which the sentence can be true even if each boy loves a different girl. But the sentence is ambiguous; where shall we get

a stronger meaning, on which the sentence is true only if a certain girl –
Zuleika, perhaps – is loved by all boys? (There are those who do not
perceive this ambiguity; but we seek a treatment general enough to
handle the idiolects of those who do.) The method of doubling object-
takers is a blind alley; rather we must look to the method of variable
binding, routinely used in the semantic analysis of standardly formulated
symbolic logic.

The quantifiers of symbolic logic belong to the category S/NS, taking
a name and a sentence to make a sentence. The name must be a variable;
other combinations could be disposed of by transformational filtering.
For instance, the logician's quantifier 'some' takes the variable 'x' and
the sentence 'grunts x' to make a sentence translatable into English as
'something grunts'. The logician's 'some' has as its intension that function
ϕ from N-intensions and S-intensions to S-intensions such that if ϕ_1 is
the nth variable intension for any number n, ϕ_2 is any S-intension, ϕ_3
is $\phi(\phi_1\phi_2)$, and i is any index, then

$$\phi_3(i) = \begin{cases} truth \text{ if, for some index } i' \text{ that is like } i \text{ except perhaps} \\ \quad \text{at the } n\text{th term of the assignment coordinate,} \\ \quad \phi_2(i') \text{ is } truth \\ falsity \text{ otherwise;} \end{cases}$$

and such that if ϕ_1 is any N-intension that is not a variable intension and
ϕ_2 is any S-intension, then $\phi(\phi_1\phi_2)$ is the null intension. The intension
of the logician's quantifier 'every' is specified similarly, with 'for every
index $i'\ldots$' replacing 'for some index $i'\ldots$'.

It would be troublesome to employ logician's quantifiers in a grammar
for English. In the first place, these quantifiers are unrestricted, ranging
over everything. The base structure of 'Some pig grunts', for instance,
would come out as

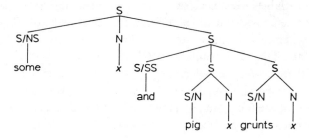

in which there is no constituent corresponding to 'some pig' and in which 'pig' and 'grunts' alike are put into the category S/N. (It was with structures like this in mind that Ajdukiewicz saw fit to omit the category C.) This attempt to dispense with quantifier phrases in favor of unrestricted quantifiers taking compound sentences is clumsy at best, and fails entirely for quantifiers such as 'most' (see Wallace, 1965). In the second place, by having the quantifier itself do the binding of variables, we require there to be bound variables wherever there are quantifiers. We get the unnecessarily complicated base structure

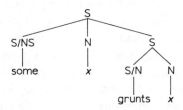

for 'Something grunts', whereas if we had employed quantifier phrases which take verb phrases and do not bind variables, we could have had

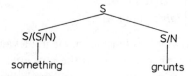

with three constituents instead of six and no work for the transformations to do.

It is not necessary, however, that the quantifier itself should bind variables. We can stick with verb-phrase-taking quantifier phrases of the category S/(S/N), restricted by constituent common nouns in most cases, and bind variables when necessary – but *only* when necessary – by means of a separate constituent called a *binder*: a certain sort of (S/N)/S that takes a sentence and makes an extensional verb phrase by binding a variable at all its free occurrences (if any) in the sentence. To every variable there corresponds a binder. Suppose 'x' is a variable; we may write its corresponding binder as '$\hat{x}$' and read it as 'is something x such that'. (But presumably binders may best be treated as base constituents that never reach the surface; so if the words 'is something x such that' ever appear in a meaningful expression, they will be derived not from an '$\hat{x}$' in base structure but in some other way.) For instance, the following base structure using a binder is equivalent to 'grunts' and might be read loosely as 'is something x such that x grunts'.

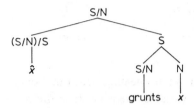

The following is a possible base structure for 'is loved by y'.

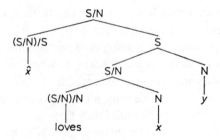

The following might be a base structure for 'Porky loves himself'. (Cf. McCawley, 1969.)

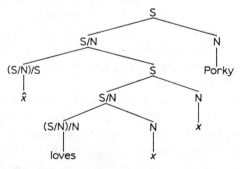

(Provided there is no ambiguity among our variables, we can use them in this way to keep track of coreferentiality, rather than subscripting the

names in

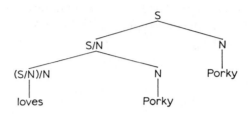

to indicate whether we are dealing with one Porky or two.)

If 'x' has the nth variable intension, then the corresponding binder '$\hat{x}$' has the nth *binder intension*: that function ϕ from S-intensions to S/N-intensions such that if ϕ_1 is any S-intension, ϕ_2 is the S/N-intension $\phi(\phi_1)$, ϕ_3 is any N-intension, ϕ_4 is the S-intension $\phi_2(\phi_3)$, i is any index, and i' is that index which has $\phi_3(i)$ as the nth term of its assignment coordinate and otherwise is like i, then $\phi_4(i) = \phi_1(i')$. It can be verified that this intension justifies the reading of '$\hat{x}$' as 'is something x such that'.

A finite supply of variables and binders, however large, would lead to the mistaken omission of some sentences. To provide an infinite supply by means of a finite lexicon, we must allow our variables and binders to be generated as compounds. We need only three lexical items: one simple variable having the first variable intension; an N/N having as intension a function whose value, given as argument the nth variable intension for any $n \geqslant 1$, is the $(n+1)$th variable intension; and an ((S/N)/S)/N having as intension a function whose value, given as argument the nth variable intension for any $n \geqslant 1$, is the nth binder intension. The first item gives us a starting variable; the second, iterated, manufactures the other variables; the third manufactures binders out of variables. However, we will continue to abbreviate base structures by writing variables and binders as if they were simple.

Variable-binding introduces a sort of spurious ambiguity called *alphabetic variance*. 'Porky loves himself' could have not only the structure shown but also others in which 'x' and '$\hat{x}$' are replaced by 'y' and '$\hat{y}$', or 'z' and '$\hat{z}$', etc. Since different variables may have different intensions, these structures correspond to infinitely many different but cointensive meanings for 'Porky loves himself'. The simplest way to deal with this nuisance is to define an ordering of any such set of meanings and employ transformational filtering to dispose of all but the first meaning in the set (according to the ordering).

Binders have occasionally been discussed by logicians, under the name 'abstraction operators' or 'lambda operators'. (Church, 1941; Carnap, 1958, § 33; Thomason and Stalnaker, 1968.)

Now we are in a position to complete our account of the category S/(S/N) of verb-phrase-taking quantifier phrases, using binders as needed. The base structure for 'Every boy loves Zuleika' may be simply

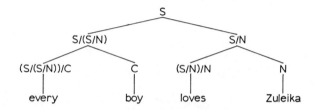

with no unnecessary variable-binding to make work for the transformational component. There is another base structure with variable-binding which we may read roughly as 'Every boy is something x such that x loves Zuleika'; it represents a different but equivalent meaning. We can either let these be another base structure and another (but equivalent) meaning for 'Every boy loves Zuleika' or get rid of them by transformational filtering. The base structure for 'Lothario loves some girl' is

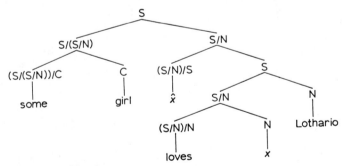

in which the quantifier phrase which is the surface object of 'loves' is treated as subject of a verb phrase obtained by binding the variable which is the base object of 'loves'. To reach an intermediate structure in which the quantifier phrase is relocated as the object of 'loves', we must have recourse to a transformation that moves the subject of a verb phrase made by variable binding into the place of one (the first?) occurrence of the bound variable and destroys the variable-binding apparatus. Note that, if desired, this transformation might apply *beneath* an intermediate level corresponding most closely to the ordinary level of deep structure. The two base structures for 'Every boy loves some girl' are

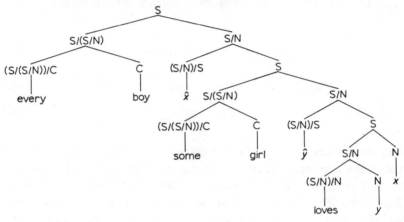

for the weak sense, and

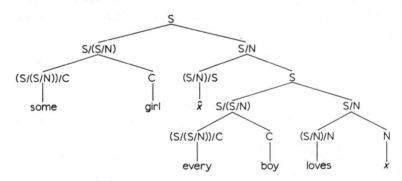

for the strong – Zuleika – sense.

It may be that quantifier-phrase objects should not be abandoned altogether. 'Lothario seeks a girl', in the sense in which it can be paraphrased as 'Lothario seeks a certain particular girl', can have the base structure

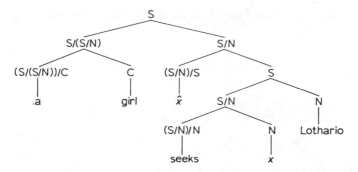

but what about the sense in which any old girl would do? We might give it the base structure

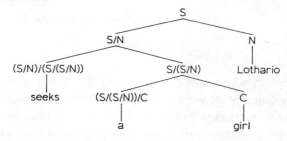

using a second 'seeks' that takes quantifier-phrase objects. The alternative is to let the word 'seeks' be introduced transformationally rather than lexically, as a transformational descendant of 'strives-to-find', so that the base structures would be

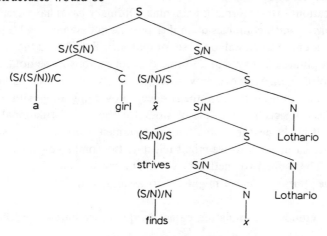

for the sense in which a certain particular girl is sought and

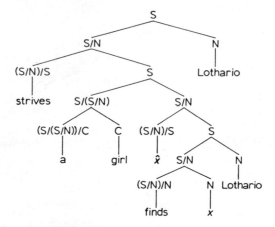

for the sense in which any old girl would do. But it is controversial whether we ought to let words be introduced transformationally in this way; and (as remarked in Montague, 1969) it is not clear how to apply this treatment to 'conceives of a tree'. Perhaps conceiving-of is imagining-to-exist, but perhaps not.

This completes one treatment of quantifier phrases, carried out with no modification of the system I originally presented. It is straightforward from the semantic point of view; however, it might result in excessive complications to transformational syntax. Ordinary bases have a category *noun phrase* which combines quantifier phrases and names; and transformations seem to work well on bases of that sort. By dividing the category of noun phrases, I may require some transformations to be doubled (or quadrupled, etc.). Moreover, my structures involving variable-binding are complicated and remote from the surface, so by doing away with quantifier-phrase objects I make lots of work for the transformational component. It might be, therefore, that this treatment is too costly to syntax. Therefore let us see how we might reinstate the combined category *noun phrase*. There are two methods: we might try to assimilate names to quantifier phrases, or we might try to assimilate quantifier phrases to names.

The method of assimilating names to quantifier phrases proceeds as follows. For every name in our lexicon, for instance 'Porky', we add to our lexicon a corresponding *pseudo-name* in the category S/(S/N). If the intension of the original name 'Porky' is the N-intension ϕ_1, then the intension of the corresponding pseudo-name 'Porky*' should be that function ϕ from S/N-intensions to S-intensions such that for any S/N-intension ϕ_2, $\phi(\phi_2) = \phi_2(\phi_1)$. As a result, a sentence such as 'Porky grunts' can be given either of the base structures

and will have the same intension either way. The category S/(S/N) may now be renamed *noun phrase*. It contains our former quantifier phrases together with our new pseudo-names. It does not contain names themselves. Names are now unnecessary as subjects, but still needed as objects; so the next step is to replace all name-takers except verb phrases by noun-phrase-takers. For instance, the category (S/N)/N of transitive verbs is to be replaced by the category (S/N)/(S/(S/N)) of pseudo-transitive verbs. The intensions of the replacements are related to the intensions of the originals in a systematic way which I shall not bother to specify. Names now serve no further purpose, having been supplanted both as subjects and as objects by pseudo-names; so the next step is to remove names from the lexicon. The category N is left vacant.

Since we have provided for noun-phrase objects for the sake of the pseudo-names, we can also have quantifier-phrase objects and so cut down on variable-binding. For instance, we have

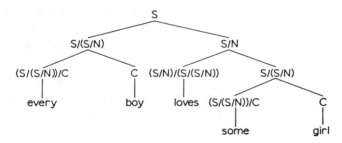

as the base structure for 'Every boy loves some girl' in the weak sense, leaving no work for the transformations. We cannot do away with variable-binding altogether, however. The base structure for 'Every boy loves some girl' in the strong – Zuleika – sense is now

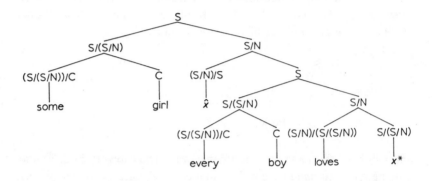

in which the seeming noun-phrase object 'some girl' is treated as subject of a verb phrase obtained by binding the pseudo-variable noun phrase 'x^*' which is the real object of 'loves'. Variables are names, of course, and therefore are replaced by pseudo-names just as any other names are; no change is made, however, in the corresponding binders.

So far we have not departed from the system I presented originally, and we *could* stop here. It is now advantageous, however, to take the step of eliminating the category N altogether and promoting the category *verb phrase* from a derived category S/N to a new basic category VP. Accordingly, the category of noun phrases becomes S/VP; the category of quantifiers becomes (S/VP)/C; the category of transitive verbs becomes VP/(S/VP); and the category which includes binders becomes VP/S.

We can also reopen the question of letting verb-phrase intensions be Carnapian rather than compositional. We rejected this simplification before, principally because it would require a projection rule which was not of our general function-and-arguments form; but that consideration no longer holds after names and verb-phrase-plus-name combinations are done away with. A lesser objection still applies: the simplification only works for extensional verb phrases. If any non-extensional verb phrases exist, they cannot go into our new basic category VP with Carnapian intensions. They will have to go into the category S/(S/VP) instead. The switch to Carnapian intensions for the now-basic verb phrases changes most other intensions in a systematic way which I need not stop to specify.

We turn last to the opposite method, in which quantifier phrases are assimilated to names to give an undivided category of noun phrases. This will require revising the extensions and intensions of names in a manner discussed by Mates (Mates, 1968) and Montague (Montague, 1969 and 1970b).

In the dark ages of logic, a story something like this was told. The phrase 'some pig' names a strange thing we may call the *existentially generic pig* which has just those properties that some pig has. Since some pig is male, some pig (a different one) is female, some pig is pink (all over), and some pig is grey (all over), the existentially generic pig is simultaneously male, female, pink, and grey. Accordingly, he (she?) is in the extensions both of 'is male' and of 'is female', both of 'is pink all over' and of 'is grey all over'. The phrase 'every pig' names a different strange thing called the *universally generic pig* which has just those properties that every pig has. Since not every pig is pink, grey, or any other color, the universally generic pig is not of any color. (Yet neither is he colorless, since not every – indeed not any – pig is colorless). Nor is he(?) male or female (or neuter), since not every pig is any one of these. He is, however, a pig and an animal, and he grunts; for every pig is a pig and an animal, and grunts. There are also the *negative universally generic pig* which has just those properties that no pig has (he is not a pig, but he is both a stone and a number), the *majority generic pig* which has just those properties that more than half of all pigs have, and many more. A sentence formed from a name and an extensional verb phrase is true (we may add: at an index i) if and only if the thing named by the name (at i) belongs to the extension of the verb phrase (at i); and this is so regardless of whether the name happens to be a name like 'Porky' of an ordinary thing or a name like 'some pig' of a generic thing.

This story is preposterous since nothing, however recondite, can possibly have more or less than one of a set of incompatible and jointly exhaustive properties. At least, nothing can have more or less than one of them *as its properties*. But something, a set, can have *any* combination of them *as its members*; there is no contradiction in that.

Let us define the *character* of a thing as the set of its properties. Porkys'

character is that set which has as members just those properties that
Porky has as properties. The various generic pigs do not, and could not
possibly, exist; but their characters do. The character of the universally
generic pig, for instance, is the set having as members just those properties that every pig has as properties.

A *character* is any set of properties. A character is *individual* iff it is a
maximal compatible set of properties, so that something could possess
all and only the properties contained in it; otherwise the character is
generic.

Since no two things share all their properties (on a sufficiently inclusive
conception of properties) things correspond one-to-one to their individual
characters. We can exploit this correspondence to replace things by their
characters whenever convenient. Some philosophers have even tried to
eliminate things altogether in favor of their characters, saying that things
are 'bundles of properties'. (Such a system is proposed as a formal recon-
struction of Leibniz's doctrine of possible individuals in Mates, 1968.)
We need not go so far. We will replace things by individual characters as
extensions of names, and as members of extensions of common nouns.
However, we may keep the things themselves as well, taking them to be
related to their names via their characters. Having made this substitution,
we are ready to assimilate quantifier phrases to names by letting them
also take characters – in most cases, generic characters – as extensions.
'Porky' has as extension Porky's individual character; 'every pig' has as
extension the generic character of the universally generic pig. Even 'nobody' has an extension: the set of just those properties that nobody has.

We revise the system of meanings as follows. Our basic categories are
sentence (S), *noun phrase* (NP), and *common noun* (C). Appropriate extensions for sentences are truth values; appropriate extensions for noun
phrases are characters, either individual or generic; appropriate extensions for common nouns are sets of individual characters. Intensions are
as before: for basic categories, functions from some or all indices to appropriate extensions; for a derived category $(c/c_1...c_n)$, functions from
c_1-intensions, ..., and c_n-intensions to c-intensions. A *name* is an NP that
never has a generic character as its extension at any index. The category
of quantifiers becomes NP/C; the category of verb phrases becomes S/NP.
Object-takers take NP objects which may or may not be names. Some
variable-binding still is required; the two base structures for 'Every boy

loves some girl' are

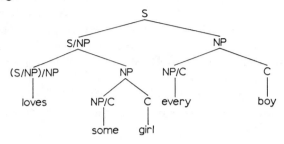

for the weak sense and

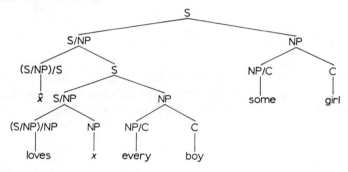

for the strong sense. Variables are names: the *n*th variable intension now becomes that NP-intension that assigns to every index *i* the character at the world coordinate of *i* of the thing that is the *n*th term of the assignment coordinate of *i*. The intensions of binders are revised to fit.

VIII. TREATMENT OF NON-DECLARATIVES

A meaning for a sentence, we said initially, was at least that which determines the conditions under which the sentence is true or false. But it is only declarative sentences that can be called true or false in any straightforward way. What of non-declarative sentences: commands, questions, and so on? If these do not have truth-values, as they are commonly supposed not to, we cannot very well say that their meanings determine their truth conditions.

One method of treating non-declaratives is to analyze all sentences, declarative or non-declarative, into two components: a *sentence radical* that specifies a state of affairs and a *mood* that determines whether the speaker is declaring that the state of affairs holds, commanding that it hold, asking whether it holds, or what. (I adopt the terminology of Stenius, 1967, one recent exposition of such a view.) We are to regard the sentences

> It is the case that you are late.
> Make it the case that you are late!
> Is it the case that you are late?

or more idiomatically

> You are late.
> Be late!
> Are you late?

as having a common sentence-radical specifying the state of affairs consisting of your being late, but differing in their moods: declarative, imperative, and interrogative. They might be given the base structures

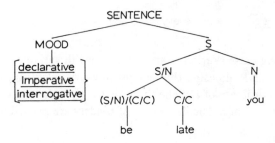

with S now understood as the category *sentence radical*. Different moods will induce different transformations of the sentence radical, leading to the different sentences above. The sentence radical is *not* a declarative sentence. If it is represented on the surface at all, it should be represented as the clause 'that you are late'. All that we have said about sentences should be taken as applying rather to sentence radicals. It is sentence radicals that have truth-values as extensions, functions from indices to truth-values as intensions, and meanings with the category S and an S-intension at the topmost node. We may grant that a declarative sentence is called true iff its sentence radical has the value *truth*; if we liked, we could also call an imperative or interrogative or other non-declarative sentence true iff its sentence radical has the value *truth*, but we customarily do not. Fundamentally, however, the entire apparatus of referential semantics (whether done on a categorial base as I propose, or otherwise) pertains to sentence radicals and constituents thereof. The semantics of mood is something entirely different. It consists of rules of language use such as these (adapted from Stenius, 1967):

Utter a sentence representing the combination of the mood *declarative* with an S-meaning *m* only if *m* is true on the occasion in question.
  React to a sentence representing the combination of the mood *imperative* with an S-meaning *m* (if adressed to you by a person in a suitable relation of authority over you) by acting in such a way as to make *m* true on the occasion in question.

In abstract semantics, as distinct from the theory of language use, a meaning for a sentence should simply be a *pair* of a mood and an S-meaning (moods being identified with some arbitrarily chosen entities).

  The method of sentence radicals requires a substantial revision of my system. It works well for declaratives, imperatives, and yes-no questions. It is hard to see how it could be applied to other sorts of questions, or to sentences like 'Hurrah for Porky!'

  I prefer an alternative method of treating non-declaratives that requires no revision whatever in my system of categories, intensions, and meanings. Let us once again regard S as the category *sentence*, without discrimination of mood. But let us pay special attention to those sentential meanings that are represented by base structures of roughly the following form.

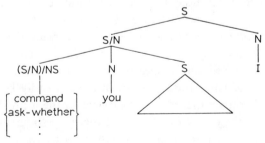

Such meanings can be represented by *performative sentences* such as these.

>I command you to be late.
>I ask you whether you are late.

(See Austin, 1962, for the standard account of performatives; but, as will be seen, I reject part of this account.) Such meanings might also be represented, after a more elaborate transformational derivation, by non-declaratives.

>Be late!
>Are you late?

I propose that these non-declaratives ought to be treated as paraphrases of the corresponding performatives, having the same base structure, meaning, intension, and truth-value at an index or on an occasion. And I propose that there is no difference in kind between the meanings of these performatives and non-declaratives and the meanings of the ordinary declarative sentences considered previously.

It is not clear whether we would classify the performative sentences as declarative. If not, then we can divide sentential meanings into declarative sentential meanings and non-declarative sentential meanings, the latter being represented both by performatives and by imperatives, questions, etc. But if, as I would prefer, we classify performatives as declarative, then the distinction between declarative and non-declarative sentences becomes a purely syntactic, surface distinction. The only distinction among meanings is the distinction between those sentential meanings that can only be represented by declarative sentences and those that can be represented either by suitable declarative sentences (performatives) or by non-declarative paraphrases thereof. Let us call the latter *performative sentential meanings*. I need not delineate the class of performative sentential meanings precisely, since I am claiming that they do *not* need to be singled out for special semantic treatment.

The method of paraphrased performatives can easily be extended to those non-declaratives that resisted treatment by the method of sentence radicals. Not only yes-no questions but other questions as well correspond to performative sentences. The sentences below

>I ask who Sylvia is.
>Who is Sylvia?

for instance, might have a common meaning represented by a base structure something like this.

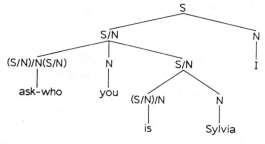

And the sentences

> I cheer Porky.
> Hurrah for Porky!

might have this base structure. (Thus the word 'Hurrah' would be introduced transformationally.)

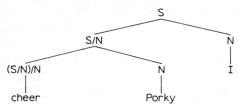

We may classify the sentential meanings represented by these base structures also as performative.

We noted at the outset that non-declaratives are commonly supposed to lack truth-values. The method of sentence radicals respects this common opinion by assigning truth-values fundamentally to sentence radicals rather than to whole sentences. We are under no compulsion to regard a non-declarative sentence as sharing the truth-value of its sentence radical, and we have chosen not to. The method of paraphrased performatives, on the other hand, does call for the assignment of truth-values to non-declarative sentences. The truth-value assigned is not that of the embedded sentence (corresponding to the sentence radical), however, but rather that of the paraphrased performative. If I say to you 'Be late!' and you are not late, the embedded sentence is false, but the paraphrased performative is true because I *do* command that you be late. I see no problem in letting non-declaratives have the truth-values of the performatives they paraphrase; after all, we need not ever mention their truth-values if we would rather not.

So far, I have assumed that performatives themselves do have truth-values, but that also has been denied. (Austin, 1962, Lecture I.) I would wish to say that 'I bet you sixpence it will rain tomorrow' is true on an occasion of utterance iff the utterer *does* then bet his audience sixpence that it will rain on the following day; and, if the occasion is normal in certain respects, the utterer does so bet; therefore his utterance is true. Austin says it is obviously neither true nor false, apparently because to utter the sentence (in normal circumstances) is to bet. Granted; but why is that a reason to deny that the utterance is true? To utter 'I am speaking' is to speak, but it is also to speak the truth. This much can be said in Austin's defense: the truth-values (and truth conditions, that is intensions) of performatives and their paraphrases are easily ignored just because it is hard for a performative to be anything but true on an occasion of its utterance. Hard but possible: you can be play-acting, practicing elocution, or impersonating an officer and say 'I command that you be late' falsely, that is, say it without thereby commanding your audience to be late. I claim that those are the very circumstances in which you could falsely say 'Be late!'; otherwise it, like the performative, is truly uttered when and because it is uttered. It is no wonder if the truth-conditions of the sentences embedded in performatives and their non-declarative paraphrases tend to eclipse the truth conditions of the performatives and non-declaratives themselves.

This eclipsing is most visible in the case of performative sentences of the form 'I state that ____' or 'I declare that ____'. If someone says 'I declare that the Earth is flat' (sincerely, not play-acting, etc.) I claim that he has spoken truly: he does indeed so declare. I claim this not only for the sake of my theory but as a point of common sense. Yet one might be tempted to say that he has spoken falsely, because the sentence embedded in his performative – the content of his declaration, the belief he avows – is false. Hence I do not propose to take ordinary declaratives as paraphrased performatives (as proposed in Ross, 1970) because that would get their truth conditions wrong. If there are strong syntactic reasons for adopting Ross's proposal, I would regard it as semantically a version of the method of sentence radicals, even if it employs base structures that look exactly like the base structures employed in the method of paraphrased performatives.

I provide only one meaning for the sentence 'I command you to be late'. Someone might well object that this sentence ought to come out ambiguous, because it can be used in two ways. It can be used to command; thus used, it can be paraphrased as 'Be late!', and it is true when uttered in normal circumstances just because it is uttered. It can be used instead to describe what I am doing; thus used, it cannot be paraphrased as an imperative, and it is likely to be false when uttered because it is difficult to issue a command and simultaneously say that I am doing so. (Difficult but possible: I might be doing the commanding by signing my name on a letter while describing what I am doing by talking.)

I agree that there are two alternative uses of this and other performative sentences: the genuinely performative use and the non-performative self-descriptive use. I agree also that the non-declarative paraphrase can occur only in the performative use. It still does not follow that there are two meanings. Compare the case of these two sentences.

> I am talking in trochaic hexameter.
> In hexameter trochaic am I talking.

The latter can be used to talk in trochaic hexameter and is true on any occasion of its correctly accented utterance. The former cannot be so used and is false on any occasion of its correctly accented utterance. Yet the two sentences are obviously paraphrases. Whether a sentence can be used to talk in trochaic hexameter is not a matter of its meaning. The distinction between using a sentence to talk in trochaic hexameter or not so using it is one sort of distinction; the distinction between using a performative sentence performatively and using it self-descriptively is quite another sort. Still I think the parallel is instructive. A distinction in uses need not involve a distinction in meanings of the sentences used. It can involve distinction in surface form; or distinction in conversational setting, intentions, and expectations; or distinction of some other sort. I see no decisive reason to insist that there is any distinction in meanings associated with the difference between performative and self-descriptive uses of performative sentences, if the contrary assumption is theoretically convenient.

We may ask to what extent the method of sentence radicals and the method of paraphrased performatives are compatible. In particular: given any sentence that can be analyzed into mood and sentence-radical, can we recover the mood and the sentence-radical intension from the meaning of the sentence according to the method of paraphrased performatives?

We almost can do this, but not quite. On the method of sentence radicals, the difference between the performative and self-descriptive uses of performative sentences *must* be treated as a difference of meanings. So given a performative sentence meaning, we will get two pairs of a mood and a sentence-radical intension corresponding to the two uses. Suppose we are given a performative sentential meaning represented by a base structure like this, for instance.

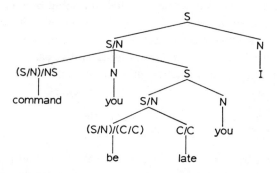

For the self-descriptive use, we do just what we would do for a non-performative sentence meaning: take the mood to be *declarative* and the sentence-radical intension to be the intension of the entire meaning. In this case, it would be the intension corresponding to the sentence radical 'that I command you to be late'. For the performative use, we take the mood to be determined by the (S/N)/NS-intension at node ⟨1 1⟩, and the sentence-radical intension to be the S-intension at node ⟨1 3⟩. In this case, these are respectively the intension of 'command', which determines that the mood is *imperative,* and the S-intension of the embedded sentence meaning, corresponding to the sentence radical 'that you are late'. Note here a second advantage, apart from fineness of individuation, of taking meanings as semantically interpreted phrase markers rather than as single intensions: we can recover the meanings of constituents from the meanings of their compounds.

APPENDIX: INDICES EXPANDED

Indices are supposed to be packages of everything but meaning that goes into determining extensions. Do we have everything? Let me speculate on several expansions of the indices that might prove useful.

First, consider the sentence '*This* is older than *this*'. I might say it pointing at a 1962 Volkswagen when I say the first 'this' and at a 1963 Volkswagen when I say the second 'this'. The sentence should be true on such an occasion; but how can it be? Using the intension of 'this', with its sensitivity to the indicated-objects coordinate, we obtain the intension of the whole sentence; then we take the value of that intension at an index with world and contextual coordinates determined by features of the occasion of utterance. (We generalize over indices alike except at the assignment coordinate; but we can consider any one of these, since the assignment coordinate is irrelevant to the sentence in question.) This procedure ignores the fact that the indicated object changes part-way through the occasion of utterance. So the sentence comes out false, as it should on any occasion when the indicated object stays the same.

On a more extensional approach to semantics, a solution would be easy. We could take the two extensions of 'this' on the two occasions of its utterance and use these, rather than the fixed intension of 'this', to determine the truth-value of the sentence. The intension and the occasion of utterance of the sentence as a whole would drop out. But since the extensions of compounds are not in general determined by the extensions of their constituents, this extensional solution would preclude a uniform treatment of semantic projection rules.

An acceptable solution has been suggested to me by David Kaplan, as follows. Let the indicated-objects coordinate be not just one set of objects capable of being pointed at but an infinite sequence of such sets. Let the indicated-objects coordinate determined by a given occasion of utterance of a sentence have as its nth term the set of things pointed to at the nth utterance of 'this' during the utterance of the sentence so long as n does not exceed the number of such utterances, and let it be the empty set when n does exceed that number. Let there be an infinite sequence of constituents 'this$_1$', 'this$_2$',... with intensions such that 'this$_n$' depends for its extension at an index on the nth term of the assignment coordinate. So that the lexicon will remain finite, let all but 'this$_1$' be compounds generated by iterated application of a suitable N/N to 'this$_1$'. Let all members of the sequence appear as 'this' in surface structure. Use transformational filtering to dispose of all base structures except those employing an initial segment of the 'this'-sequence so arranged that if the subscripts were carried to the surface, they would appear in numerical order without repetition. Thus the only base structure for 'This is older than this' will be

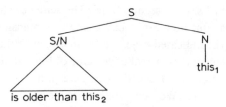

which will be true on occasions of the sort in question.

The solution must be modified to allow for the fact that 'this' is not the only demonstrative; I omit details. Similar difficulties arise, and similar solutions are possible, for other contextual coordinates: time, place, audience, and perhaps speaker.

Second, consider the sentence 'The door is open'. This does not mean that the one and only door that now exists is open; nor does it mean that the one and only door near the place of utterance, or pointed at, or mentioned in previous discourse, is open. Rather it means that the one and only door among the objects that are somehow prominent on the occasion is open. An object may be prominent because it is nearby, or pointed at, or mentioned; but none of these is a necessary condition of contextual prominence. So perhaps we need a *prominent-objects coordinate*, a new contextual coordinate independent of the others. It will be determined, on a given occasion of utterance of a sentence, by mental factors such as the speaker's expectations regarding the things he is likely to bring to the attention of his audience.

Third, consider the suggestion (Kaplan, 1968; Donnellan, 1970) that the extension of a personal name on a given occasion depends partly on the causal chain leading from the bestowal of that name on some person to the later use of that name by a speaker on the occasion in question. We might wish to accept this theory, and yet wish to deny that the intension or meaning of the name depends, on the occasion in question, upon the causal history of the speaker's use of it; for we might not wish to give up the common presumption that the meaning of an expression for a speaker depends only on mental factors within him. We might solve this dilemma (as proposed in Lewis, 1968b) by including a *causal-history-of-acquisition-of-names coordinate* in our indices and letting the intensions of names for a speaker determine their extensions only relative to that coordinate.

Fourth, we have so far been ignoring the vagueness of natural language. Perhaps we are right to ignore it, or rather to deport it from semantics to the theory of language-use. We could say (as I did in Lewis, 1969, Chapter V) that languages themselves are free of vagueness but that the linguistic conventions of a population, or the linguistic habits of a person, select not a point but a fuzzy region in the space of precise languages. However, it might prove better to treat vagueness within semantics, and we could do so as follows. (A related treatment, developed independently, is to be found in Goguen, 1969.)

Pretend first that the only vagueness is the vagueness of 'cool' and 'warm'; and suppose for simplicity that these are extensional adjectives. Let the indices contain a *delineation coordinate*: a positive real number, regarded as the boundary temperature between cool and warm things. Thus at an index i the extension of 'cool' is the set of things at the world and time coordinates of i having temperatures (in degrees Kelvin) less than or equal to the delineation coordinate of i; the extension of 'warm' is the set of such things having temperatures greater than the delineation coordinate. A vague sentence such as 'This is cool' is true, on a given occasion, at some but not all delineations; that is, at some but not all indices that are alike except in delineation and have the world and contextual coordinates determined by the occasion of utterance. But sentences with vague constituents are not necessarily vague: 'This is cool or warm, but not both' is true at all delineations, on an occasion on which there is a unique indicated object, even if the indicated object is lukewarm.

The delineation coordinate is non-contextual. It resembles the assignment coordinate, in that we will ordinarily generalize over it rather than hold it fixed. We may say that a sentence is *true over* a set s of delineations at an index i, iff, for any index i' that is like i except perhaps at the delineation coordinate, the sentence is true at i' if and only if the delineation coordinate of i' belongs to s. Given a normalized measure function over delineations, we can say that a sentence is *true to degree d* at i iff it is true at i over a set of delineations of measure d. Note that the degree of truth of a truth-functional compound of sentences is not a function of the degrees of truth of its constituent sentences: 'x is cool' and 'x is warm' may both be true to degree .5 at an index i, but 'x is cool or x is cool' is true at i to degree .5 whereas 'x is cool or x is warm' is true at i to degree 1.

Treating vagueness within semantics makes for simple specifications of the intensions of such expressions as 'in some sense', 'paradigmatic', '____ish', and '____er than'. The contemporary idiom 'in some sense', for instance, is an S/S related to the delineation coordinate just as the modal operator 'possibly' is related to the world coordinate. The intension of 'in some sense' is that function ϕ such that if ϕ_1 is any S-intension, ϕ_2 is $\phi(\phi_1)$, and i is any index, then

$$\phi_2(i) = \begin{cases} truth \text{ if, for some index } i' \text{ that is like } i \text{ except perhaps} \\ \quad \text{at the delineation coordinate, } \phi_1(i') \text{ is } truth \\ falsity \text{ otherwise.} \end{cases}$$

The comparative '____er than' is a $((C/C)/N)/(C/C)$ having an intension such that, for instance, 'x is cooler than y' is true at an index i iff the set of delineations over which 'y is cool' is true at i is a proper subset of the set of delineations over which 'x is cool' is true at i. It follows that the sun is not cooler than Sirius unless in some sense the sun is cool; but that conclusion seems correct, although I do not know whether to deny that the sun is cooler than Sirius or to agree that in some sense the sun is cool. (This analysis of comparatives was suggested to me by David Kaplan.)

More generally, the delineation coordinate must be a sequence of boundary-specifying numbers. Different vague expressions will depend for their extensions (or, if they are not extensional, for the extensions of their extensional compounds) on different terms of the delineation. More than one term of the delineation coordinate might be involved for a single expression. For instance, the intension of 'green' might involve one term regarded as delineating the blue-green boundary and another regarded as delineating the green-yellow boundary. The former but not the latter would be one of the two terms involved in the intension of 'blue'; and so on around the circle of hues.

BIBLIOGRAPHY

Kazimierz Ajdukiewicz, 'Die syntaktische Konnexität', *Studia Philosophica* **1** (1935) 1–27; translated as 'Syntactic Connexion' in S. McCall, *Polish Logic*, Oxford 1967, pp. 207–231. Part I translated as 'On Syntactical Coherence', *Review of Metaphysics* **20** (1967) 635–647.

J. L. Austin, *How to Do Things with Words*, Harvard University Press, Cambridge, Mass., 1962.

Yehoshua Bar-Hillel, *Language and Information*, Addison-Wesley, Reading, Mass., 1964.

Paul Benacerraf, 'What Numbers Could Not Be', *Philosophical Review* **74** (1965) 47–73.

Rudolf Carnap, *Meaning and Necessity*, University of Chicago Press, Chicago, Illinois, 1947.

Rudolf Carnap, *Introduction to Symbolic Logic*, Dover, New York, 1958.

Rudolf·Carnap, 'Replies and Systematic Expositions', in P. Schilpp, *The Philosophy of Rudolf Carnap*, Open Court, La Salle, Illinois, 1963.

Noam Chomsky, *Aspects of the Theory of Syntax*, M.I.T. Press, Cambridge, Mass., 1965.

Alonzo Church, *The Calculi of Lambda Conversion*, Princeton University Press, Princeton, N.J., 1941.

Donald Davidson, 'Truth and Meaning', *Synthese* **17** (1967) 304–323.

Charles L. Dodgson, *Through the Looking-Glass*, London, 1871.

Keith Donnellan, 'Proper Names and Identifying Descriptions', *Synthese* **21** (1970) 335–358.

Gottlob Frege, 'Über Sinn und Bedeutung', *Zeitschrift für Philosophie und philosophische Kritik* **100** (1892) 25–50; translated as 'On Sense and Reference' in P. T. Geach and M. Black, *Translations from the Philosophical Writings of Gottlob Frege*, Blackwell, Oxford, 1960.

J. A. Goguen, 'The Logic of Inexact Concepts', *Synthese* **19** (1969) 325–373.

David Kaplan, *Foundations of Intensional Logic* (doctoral dissertation), University Microfilms, Ann Arbor, Michigan, 1964.

David Kaplan, 'Quantifying In', *Synthese* **19** (1968) 178–214.

Jerrold Katz and Paul Postal, *An Integrated Theory of Linguistic Descriptions*, M.I.T. Press, Cambridge, Mass., 1964.

Edward Keenan, *A Logical Base for English* (doctoral dissertation, duplicated), 1969.

Saul Kripke, 'Semantical Considerations on Modal Logic', *Acta Philosophica Fennica* **16** (1963) 83–94.

George Lakoff, 'On Generative Semantics' in *Semantics: An Interdisciplinary Reader in Philosophy, Linquistics, Anthropology and Psychology* (ed. by Danny Steinberg and Leon Jakobovits), Cambridge University Press, Cambridge, 1970.

Clarence I. Lewis, 'The Modes of Meaning', *Philosophy and Phenomenological Research* **4** (1944) 236–249.

David Lewis, 'Counterpart Theory and Quantified Modal Logic', *Journal of Philosophy* **65** (1968) 113–126. (1968a).

David Lewis, 'Languages and Language', to appear in the *Minnesota Studies in the Philosophy of Science*. (1968b).

David Lewis, *Convention: A Philosophical Study*, Harvard University Press, Cambridge, Mass., 1969.

John Lyons, 'Towards a "Notional" Theory of the "Parts of Speech"', *Journal of Linguistics* **2** (1966) 209–236.

Benson Mates, 'Leibniz on Possible Worlds' in *Logic, Methodology, and Philosophy of Science III* (ed. by B. van Rootselaar and J. F. Staal), North-Holland Publ. Co., Amsterdam, 1968.

James McCawley, 'Concerning the Base Component of a Transformational Grammar', *Foundations of Language* 4 (1968) 243–269.

James McCawley, 'Semantic Representation', paper presented to a symposium on Cognitive Studies and Artificial Intelligence Research, University of Chicago Center for Continuing Education, March 1969.

Richard Montague, 'Logical Necessity, Physical Necessity, Ethics, and Quantifiers', *Inquiry* 3 (1960) 259–269.

Richard Montague, 'Pragmatics' in *Contemporary Philosophy – La philosophie contemporaine* (ed. by R. Klibansky), La Nuova Italia Editrice, Florence 1968.

Richard Montague, 'Intensional Logic and Some of Its Connections with Ordinary Language', talk delivered to the Southern California Logic Colloquium, April 1969, and to the Association of Symbolic Logic meeting at Cleveland, Ohio, May 1969.

Richard Montague, 'English as a Formal Language I' in *Linguaggi nella società e nella tecnica,* Edizioni di Communità, Milan, 1970. (1970a).

Richard Montague, 'Universal Grammar', *Theoria* 36 (1970). (1970b).

Richard Montague, 'Pragmatics and Intensional Logic', *Synthese* 22 (1970) 68–94 (1970c).

Terence Parsons, *A Semantics for English* (duplicated), 1968.

P. Stanley Peters and R. W. Ritchie, *On the Generative Power of Transformational Grammars*, Technical Report in Computer Science, University of Washington, Seattle, Wash., 1969.

John R. Ross, 'On Declarative Sentences', *Readings in Transformational Grammar* (ed. by R. Jacobs and P. Rosenbaum), Blaisdell, Boston, Mass. (1970).

Dana Scott, 'Advice on Modal Logic' in *Philosophical Problems in Logic: Recent Developments* (ed. by Karel Lambert), D. Reidel Publishing Company, Dordrecht, 1970, pp. 143–173.

Erik Stenius, 'Mood and Language-Game', *Synthese* 17 (1967) 254–274.

P. F. Strawson, 'On Referring', *Mind* 59 (1950) 320–344.

Alfred Tarski, 'Der Wahrheitsbegriff in den formalisierten Sprachen', *Studia Philosophica* 1 (1936) 261–405; translated as 'The Concept of Truth in Formalized Languages' in Tarski, *Logic, Semantics, Metamathematics,* Oxford, 1956.

Richmond Thomason and Robert Stalnaker, 'Modality and Reference', *Noûs* 2 (1968) 359–372.

Bruce Vermazen, review of Jerrold Katz and Paul Postal, *An Integrated Theory of Linguistic Descriptions*, and Katz, *Philosophy of Language*, *Synthese* 17 (1967) 350–365.

John Wallace, 'Sortal Predicates and Quantification', *Journal of Philosophy* 62 (1965) 8–13.

REFERENCE

*This paper is derived from a talk given at the Third La Jolla Conference on Linguistic Theory, March 1969. I am much indebted to Charles Chastain, Frank Heny, David Kaplan, George Lakoff, Richard Montague, and Barbara Partee for many valuable criticisms and suggestions.

BARBARA PARTEE

SOME TRANSFORMATIONAL EXTENSIONS
OF MONTAGUE GRAMMAR*

0. INTRODUCTION

Richard Montague's work on English, as represented in Montague (1970a), (1970b), (1972), represents the first systematic attempt to apply the logician's methods of formal syntax and semantics to natural language. With few exceptions,[1] linguists and logicians had previously been agreed, although for different reasons, that the apparatus developed by logicians for treating the syntax and semantics of artificially constructed formal languages, while obviously fruitful within its restricted domain, was not in any direct way applicable to the analysis of natural languages. Logicians seem to have felt that natural languages were too unsystematic, too full of vagueness and ambiguity, to be amenable to their rigorous methods, or if susceptible to formal treatment, only at great cost.[2] Linguists, on the other hand, emphasize their own concern for psychological reality, and the logicians' lack of it, in eschewing the logicians' approach: linguists, at least those of the Chomskyan school, are searching for a characterization of the class of possible human languages, hoping to gain thereby some insight into the structure of the mind, and the formal languages constructed by logicians appear to depart radically from the structures common to actual natural languages.

Montague's claim, as represented in the title of one of his papers, 'English as a Formal Language', is that English *can* be treated in a natural way within the logical tradition in syntax and semantics. A few remarks about that tradition are in order here. Since Tarski (see, e.g., Tarski (1944)), the concept of truth has played a key role in semantics. It is held that an essential part of the semantic interpretation of any sentence is a specification, given in a metalanguage antecedently understood, of the conditions under which the given sentence is true. Thus an essential part of semantics is the construction of a theory of truth for a language. The mechanism for doing this involves syntax in a fundamental way: first, a set of recursive syntactic rules are given defining the set of *wffs* (well-

Journal of Philosophical Logic 2 (1973) 509–534. *All Rights Reserved*

formed formulas), starting with the smallest, primitive elements and specifying how units of various categories can be combined to form larger units. Then the task of the semantics is to assign interpretations to the smallest units and then to give rules which determine the interpretation of larger units on the basis of the interpretation of their parts. A key feature of this approach is that the part-whole analysis should be the same in the syntax and the semantics; the syntactic analysis should build up larger units from (or equivalently, analyze them into) just those parts on the basis of which the meaning of the larger unit can be determined. (This one-one correspondence between syntactic and semantic structure is not an absolute condition on the construction of formal languages, and some treatments of the semantics of the two standard quantifiers, for instance, violate it;[3] languages constructed in accordance with it are often called 'logically perfect languages').

Note that the logical tradition involves a bottom-up view of both sentence construction and semantic interpretation. In the case of purely context-free phrase structure rules and something like a Katz-Fodor-Postal semantics of the 1963–1965 period, it is easy enough to see a close correspondence between linguistic and logical practice, since *CF*-rules can be equally well interpreted as starting at the bottom (with the lexical units) and applying to build up larger and larger phrases. Then the only gross divergence between the Katz-Fodor view of semantics and that of the logical tradition is in the nature of the output of the semantic rules (see Vermazen (1967)); the idea of a fundamental connection between the syntactic and semantic rules is preserved. But transformational grammar in general has gotten away from that, and semantics was never developed far enough within the 'standard theory' to reach the point of influencing the syntax in any systematic way. What we find now in linguistics are two main approaches which depart radically, in different ways, from the principle of a one-one correspondence between syntactic and semantic rules. One approach, generative semantics, was founded in part on the conviction that semantic and syntactic rules could not be separated in any principled way, and that 'semantic-interpretation' and 'deepest structure' could be identified.[4] The other, interpretive semantics, maintains the distinction between syntactic rules as formation rules and semantic rules as interpretive rules, but does not posit any systematic relation between them.[5]

Within the logical tradition, there are just two criteria of adequacy for syntactic rules: (i) that they define the set of *wffs* of the language (which is not an empirical constraint for constructed languages, unless some independent characterization of the set of *wffs* is already given), and (ii) most importantly, that they provide a basis for the rules of semantic interpretation. To illustrate the consequences of the second condition, consider the long-standing disputes among linguists as to the hierarchical constituency relations within noun phrases containing a determiner, a noun, and a relative clause, e.g., 'the boy who lives in the park'. There have been at least three basically different alternatives suggested in the literature, schematically represented below[6] as (1), (2), and (3).

There are syntactic arguments pro and con each of these structures[7], but semantic arguments have entered in only peripherally, because no systematic attempt was ever made in any of the linguistic treatments to

(1)

(2)

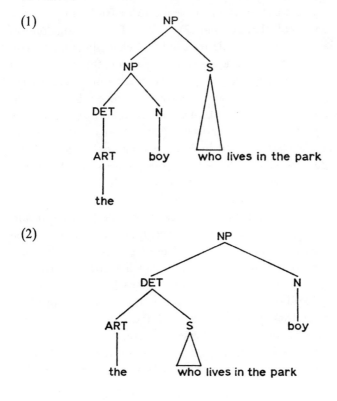

(3)

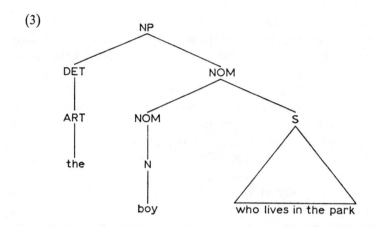

find rules to determine the interpretation of the whole *NP* on the basis of its parts. But the following informal sketch of the relevant semantics[8] shows that a structure like (3) can provide a direct basis for the semantic interpretation in a way that (1) and (2) cannot. The construction has three parts: *the*, a noun, and a relative clause. Each analysis makes two binary subdivisions, and in fact, apart from linear order the three analyses exhaust the possible binary sub-groupings. The semantic consequences of the differences can be seen most clearly by focussing on the interpretation of *the*. Ignoring controversial details, the general principle for interpreting singular phrases of the form *the* α will include an assertion or presupposition that the class denoted by α has one and only one member. The noun *boy* denotes a class (the class of boys), and so does the relative clause *who lives in the park* (the class of entities which live in the park.[9]) Under analysis (3), the two class-denoting phrases are first combined to form a complex class-denoting phrase, which can be interpreted as denoting the intersection of the two classes[10], namely the class of entities which both live in the park and are boys; combining *the* with the results leads to the correct assertion that it is that class that has one and only one member. On analysis (1), on the other hand, *the* is first combined with *boy*, which would lead to an assertion that there is one and only one boy, and only a non-restrictive interpretation of the relative clause could naturally be gotten by combining that assertion with the interpretation of *who lives in the park*. Similarly, the first stage in the interpretation of (2) would lead to an assertion that there is one and only one entity that lives in the park, leaving no natural way to add the interpretation of *boy*. Put another way, the problem with trying to use structure (1) for semantic analysis is that the meaning of the phrase *the boy* is not a part of the meaning of the phrase *the boy who lives in the park*. The problem for structure (2) is analogous. Only by making the major syntactic sub-division between *the* and *boy who lives in the park* can a uniform semantic treatment of *the* be given.[11]

The example just discussed shows that the requirement that semantic interpretation rules correspond structurally to the syntactic rules can put very strong constraints on possible syntactic analyses. This point is worth emphasizing because Montague offers virtually no constraints on syntactic rules themselves; it is only in the connection between syntax and semantics that the grammar is constrained, but that constraint is strong enough that I think it is a serious open question whether natural languages can be so described.

1. MONTAGUE'S 'THE PROPER TREATMENT OF QUANTIFICATION IN ORDINARY ENGLISH'

In this section I will sketch some of the key features of the last (and to a linguist the most interesting) of Montague's three treatments of fragments of English, that in Montague (1972) (henceforth *PTQ*). Since the syntactic rules work bottom-up, I will start with the grammatical categories and the lexicon, then mention the rules most like *CF*-rules, and finally discuss the treatment of quantification. (The fragment also includes relative clauses, about which I will say no more than the few informal remarks above.)

1.0. *Categories and Lexicon*

The categories are defined as in a categorial grammar,[12] though the rules that combine them are not limited to simple concatenation (categorial grammars are a subclass of CF grammars, but Montague's syntax is not.) The two basic categories are t, the category of sentences (t for truth bearing), and e, the category of 'entity-expressions'. The category e seems quite mysterious if one looks only at the syntax, since it turns out that no words or phrases of English are assigned to that category. But it, along with the category t, is used in defining the remaining categories, and in the language of intensional logic into which the English expressions are translated, there *are* expressions of category *e*, and they are interpreted as denoting entities in a straightforward way.

The remaining categories are defined categories; for instance, the category of intransitive verb phrases, abbreviated as *IV* (the linguist's *VP*) is defined[13] as *t/e*: something that could combine with an *e*-phrase (if there were any) to form a *t*-phrase (sentence). In this case, since there are no *e*-phrases in the object language, there is no syntactic rule combining an *IV*-phrase with an *e*-phrase to make a sentence, but the definition nevertheless has consequences in the semantics. The category of common noun phrases, abbreviated *CN*, is defined as *t//e*, another category of the same categorial (henceforth CAT) type as *IV*. (The use of single vs double slashes is simply a device for distinguishing two syntactic categories of the same CAT type; a larger fragment of English might require triple slashes or more.)

The category of term-phrases, abbreviated *T* (the linguist's *NP*) is define das *t/IV*: something that combines with an IV-phrase to make a *t*-phrase (sentence). In this and all the remaining cases, since the constituent categories are non-empty, there are syntactic rules which specify just *how* the constituent categories combine. The following chart gives all the categories of the grammar.

Category	Abbreviation	*PTQ* name	Nearest linguistic equivalent
t	(primitive)	truth-value expression; or declarative sentence	sentence
e	(primitive)	entity expression; or individual expression	(noun phrase)
t/e	IV	intransitive verb phrase	verb phrase
t/IV	T	term	noun phrase
IV/T	TV	transitive verb phrase	transitive verb
IV/IV	IAV	IV-modifying adverb	VP-adverb
t//e	CN	common noun phrase	Noun or NOM
t/t	none	sentence-modifying adverb	same
IAV/T	none	IAV-making preposition	locative, etc., preposition
IV/t	none	sentence-taking verb phrase	V which takes that-COMP
IV/IV	none	IV-taking verb phrase	V which takes infinitive COMP

Most of the categories have both lexical members and derived phrasal members; the category t contains only derived phrases, and the categories t/t, IAV/T, IV/t, and IV/IV contain only lexical members. The complete lexicon for the fragment is presented in the listing below; B_A means 'basic expression of category A'.

$$B_t = \Lambda$$
$$B_e = \Lambda$$
$$B_{IV} = \{\text{run, walk, talk, rise, change}\}$$
$$B_T = \{\text{John, Mary, Bill, ninety}, he_0, he_1, he_2, ...\}$$
$$B_{TV} = \{\text{find, lose, eat, love, date, be, seek, conceive}\}$$
$$B_{IAV} = \{\text{rapidly, slowly, voluntarily, allegedly}\}$$
$$B_{CN} = \{\text{man, woman, park, fish, pen, unicorn, price,}$$
$$\text{temperature}\}$$
$$B_{t/t} = \{\text{necessarily}\}$$
$$B_{IAV/T} = \{\text{in, about}\}$$
$$B_{IV/t} = \{\text{believe that, assert that}\}$$
$$B_{IV//IV} = \{\text{try to, wish to}\}.$$

1.1. *Rules of Functional Application*

The syntactic component of the grammar is a simultaneous recursive definition of the membership of the sets of phrases P_A for each category A, with the set of sentences being the members of P_t. Each syntactic rule has the general form

'If $\alpha_1 \in P_{A_1}$, $\alpha_2 \in P_{A_2}$, ..., $\alpha_n \in P_{A_n}$, then

$$F_i(\alpha_1, ..., \alpha_n) \in P_B\text{'}$$

where F_i is a specification of the syntactic mode of combination of the constituent phrases and B is the category of the resulting phrase. Some of the syntactic functions F_i are simply concatenation or concatenation plus some morphological adjustments and are hence very much like CF-rules; others of the F_i bear more resemblance to transformations. All of the syntactic rules build up larger phrases from smaller ones. The semantic interpretation rules operate in two stages. First, for every syntactic rule there is a corresponding rule of translation into an expression of intensional logic; these rules also apply 'bottom-to-top', paralleling the syntactic derivation, so that the translation of any given sentence into intensional logic is built up via translations of each of its subphrases, starting from the basic expressions. (Most of the basic expressions, e.g., *John*, *walk*, *slowly*, are translated into constants of appropriate categories in the intensional logic; a few, such as *be*, *necessarily*, and he_0, he_1, etc., receive special translations reflecting their special logical roles.) The second stage of the semantic interpretation consists of a possible-worlds semantics defined for the given intensional logic. An independent syntactic characterization of the *wffs* of the intensional logic is given, and the semantic rules for the intensional logic are based on the structure given by those syntactic rules. In some of Montague's earlier work, the possible-worlds semantics was defined directly on the English syntax; the change to two-stage semantics may reflect some measure of agreement with Quine's remarks cited in note 3.

We will concentrate on the relations between the syntactic rules and the rules of translation into intensional logic; the semantics of the intensional logic is developed in a way familiar to logicians and will not be discussed here. Among the syntactic rules there is a subset which relate directly to the CAT definitions, and whose corresponding rules of translation follow a uniform pattern. For every category A/B or $A//B$ there is a syntactic rule of the form (4):[14]

(4)   If $\alpha \in P_{A/B}$ and $\beta \in P_B$, then $F_i(\alpha, \beta) \in P_A$.

For each such rule, the corresponding rule of translation into intensional logic is (5):

(5)   If $\alpha \in P_{A/B}$ and $\beta \in P_B$, and α, β translate into α', β', then $F_i(\alpha, \beta)$ translates into $\alpha'(^\wedge\beta')$.

The notation $^\wedge\beta'$ means 'the intension (or sense) of β''. Thus each member of a complex category A/B is interpreted as denoting a function which takes as argument intensions of expressions of category B; applying that function to that argument gives the interpretation of the resultant A-phrase. For example, the function corresponding to 'rapidly' applied to the sense of 'run' gives the interpretation of 'run rapidly'; the function corresponding to 'in' applied to the sense of the T-phrase 'the park' gives the interpretation of 'in the park'.

Linguists lost interest in CAT grammar when it was shown to be a subcase of *CF*-grammar, since at that time the focus was on pure syntax.

The original point of CAT grammar, however, was to connect syntactic and semantic structure in a certain way. David Lewis (1971) suggests using a pure (i.e. *CF*) CAT grammar for the base component of a transformational grammar. Montague, who has no base component *per se*, makes use of the basic CAT notions in a system of syntactic rules not restricted to *CF* rules, and keeps the close correspondence between syntactic and semantic rules as the central feature of the CAT idea. The CAT rules, which he calls rules of functional application because of their semantic interpretation, do not exhaust the grammar: however, they may be viewed roughly as those rules which define the basic grammatical relations among the parts of simple sentences; there are additional rules for conjunction, relative clauses, quantification, tenses, and negation, to which we now turn.

1.2. *Other Rules of PTQ: Quantification*

To illustrate the workings of the rest of the grammar of *PTQ*, we will describe Montague's treatment of quantification.

Probably the most novel feature of Montague's treatment is that quantifier phrases such as *every man, the unicorn, a woman* are analyzed as term phrases along with *John* and *Mary*. Although such an analysis is not linguistically novel (both sorts have been traditionally called *NP*), it goes against the treatment of quantifier expressions, first suggested by Frege, that opened up the way for the development of quantificational logic and has become standard in logic. The standard logical analysis of, say, *every man runs* would be written as (6):

(6) $(\forall x)(Mx \rightarrow Rx)$.

What looked like a term phrase in the English sentence does not appear as a constituent in the logical expression, but is rather reanalyzed into the whole frame in which '*R*' appears. A proper name, on the other hand, does show up as a simple term-expression in standard logical notation; thus *John runs* would be simply *Rj*.

The way Montague manages a uniform treatment of *every man* and *John* is to interpret both as denoting sets of properties of individual concepts. The individual concept of John is the function which picks out John at each possible world and time. The constant *j* in the intensional logic is of category *e* and simply denotes the individual John (assuming

we have fixed on a particular interpretation of the constants of the intensional logic.) The individual concept of John is denoted by $^\wedge j$, where '$^\wedge$'
means 'intension of'. The term-phrase *John* in the English fragment is not
translated simply as j or as $^\wedge j$, however; it is translated as $\hat{P} P\{^\wedge j\}$, the set
of all properties of the individual concept of John. There is a one-one
correspondence between individuals and the set of all properties of their
individual concepts; the only reason for giving such a 'higher-order' treatment of the proper nouns is that phrases like *every man* can also be interpreted as sets or properties of individual concepts, and in this way the
desired unification of term-phrases can be achieved. The syntactic rule
which creates quantifier phrases is given below as (7):

(7)   If $\alpha \in P_{CN}$, then $F_0(\alpha)$, $F_1(\alpha)$, $F_2(\alpha) \in P_T$, where
$$F_0(\alpha) = every\ \alpha$$
$$F_1(\alpha) = the\ \alpha$$
$$F_2(\alpha) = a/an\ \alpha.$$

The corresponding translation rule is (8).

(8)   If α translates into α', then
$F_0(\alpha)$ translates into $\hat{P}[(\forall x)(\alpha'(x) \to P\{x\})]$
$F_1(\alpha)$ translates into $\hat{P}[(\exists y)((\forall x)[\alpha'(x) \leftrightarrow x = y] \land P\{y\})]$
$F_2(\alpha)$ translates into $\hat{P}[(\exists x)(\alpha'(x) \land P\{x\})]$.

Thus *every man* is interpreted as denoting the set of all properties which
every man has; *the king* as denoting the set of all properties such that
there is a unique entity which is a king and he has those properties; *a fish*
as denoting the set of all properties which some fish has (the union of all
the properties of all the fish there are).

A related innovation of Montague's treatment is that when a term-phrase
and an *IV*-phrase are combined to form a sentence, it is the term-phrase
which is viewed as function and the *IV*-phrase as argument. Thus the
translations of *John runs* and *every man runs* come out schematically as
(9) and (10) respectively:

(9)   *John'* $(^\wedge run')$
(10)   *every man'* $(^\wedge run')$.

What (9) says is that the property of running is in the set of properties of
(the individual concept of) John, which is logically equivalent (at least
given certain of the meaning postulates of *PTQ* regarding the extension-

ality of *run*, etc.) to saying that John has the property of running. Expression (10) says, in a parallel manner, that the property of running is in the set of properties shared by every man, which is likewise equivalent to the usual logical formulation. The ultimate logical interpretations of these sentences are thus just the standard ones; what is new is being able to get to those interpretations from a syntax that assigns proper names and quantifier phrases to the same syntactic category.

In the sentences just discussed, the term-phrases were introduced into the sentence directly by the CAT rules; but they may also be introduced via substitution for free variables, a mechanism necessary to account for ambiguities of scope. The rule for sentence-scope quantification is given in a rough form in (11):

(11)   If $\alpha \in P_T$ and $\phi \in P_t$, then $F_{10,n}(\alpha, \phi) \in P_t$, where $F_{10,n}$ is as illustrated below:

Let α = *every unicorn*, ϕ = *he$_0$ seeks a woman such that she loves him$_0$*

Then $F_{10,0}(\alpha, \phi)$ = *every unicorn seeks a woman such that she loves it.*

What the rule does is combine a term phrase and a sentence (an open sentence in all the non-vacuous cases) with respect to a given free variable in the sentence (the subscript n of the syntactic-operation-schema $F_{10,n}$), by substituting the term phrase for the first occurrence of the variable and appropriate pronouns for the subsequent occurrences. The corresponding translation rule is (12):

(12)   If α, ϕ translate into α', ϕ' respectively, then
$F_{10,n}(\alpha, \phi)$ translates into $\alpha'(\hat{x}_n \phi')$.

This interpretation comes out just like the interpretation of *John runs* or *every man runs* described above, except that instead of the simple property of running we have whatever property of x_n (which corresponds, albeit indirectly, to *he$_n$*) is expressed by the sentence ϕ.

To illustrate the treatment of scope ambiguity we will show two *analysis trees* for sentence (13) below. An analysis tree is a graphic representation of the steps by which a sentence has been constructed (more like a *T*-marker in pre-1965 transformational theory than like a *P*-marker), with each node labelled by an expression and an index indicating the structural operation that was applied to form it, the nodes immediately beneath indicating the expressions from which it was formed. The two analysis trees (13a′) and (13b′) correspond to the interpretations given as (13a) and (13b). The only structural operations labelled in the trees are those that have been presented here.

(13)   A woman loves every man.

(13a) $(\exists x)(\text{woman}(x) \wedge (\forall y)(\text{man}(y) \to \text{loves}(x, y)))$

(13b) $(\forall y)(\text{man}(y) \to (\exists x)(\text{woman}(x) \wedge \text{loves}(x, y)))$

(13a′)

(13b′)

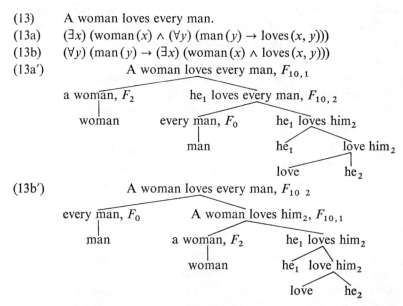

Such trees bear a striking resemblance to the abstract trees found in generative semantic treatments of quantifiers; in particular, a higher position in the tree indicates wider scope, and the quantificational substitution rule is analogous to quantifier-lowering. On the other hand, since the trees are not P-markers, they do not represent constituent structure, and no grammatical relation is said to hold between a quantifier phrase and the sentence with which it is combined. The syntactic rules generate well-formed ('surface') expressions directly without ill-formed 'deeper' structures, with the sole exception of the occurrence of the free variables he_0, he_1 etc. The 'abstractness' which is needed for the semantic rules to correctly interpret the expressions is provided not by a labelled bracketing assigned to the generated expressions themselves (Montague doesn't assign any, although it is a natural extension to make), but by the analysis tree which is in a sense a partly temporal respresentation. For instance, the two analyses of sentence (13) differ not in their parts or the grammatical relations between them, but in the order in which those parts were put together.

This point may be clarified by anticipating the first addition to the system to be proposed in the next section, namely the addition of labelled bracketing. If we assign to each generated expression a labelled bracketing, or *P*-marker, then at each node of the analysis tree there will be a *P*-marker, not simply a string. Then the analogy between an analysis tree and a *T*-marker becomes even stronger: each generated expression is given a *P*-marker which shows its internal constituent structure and to which subsequent syntactic rules may be sensitive, while the analysis tree shows its derivational history, and it is to the latter that the semantic interpretation rules correspond. Note that there is no single level corresponding to 'deep structure' in anybody's sense, since PS-like rules and transformation-like rules are not distinguished and there is no extrinsic rule ordering.

There is much more that could be said about the grammar of *PTQ*, but I want to turn now to some suggestions for extending it to include transformations.

2. TRANSFORMATIONAL EXTENSIONS

2.0. *Introduction*

The fragment Montague chose to develop was semantically a very rich one, including as it did quantification, verbs of propositional attitude, verb-phrase adverbs, *be*, and *necessarily*; but syntactically it was quite simple,[15] and the rules given provide no basis for conjecturing what Montague would have done about such classic constructions as passive sentences, reflexive pronouns,[16] or the *easy-to-please* construction. The rest of the paper is concerned with the question of whether and how such constructions can be accommodated within Montague's framework. I will suggest two additions to the framework itself, labelled bracketing and a 'starred variable convention', additions which seem to me natural and helpful although I have no proof that they are indispensable. With these two general additions and a few grammar-specific departures from the usual ways of stating certain transformations, I will sketch a way to add to Montague's grammar rules for reflexive, passive, 'tough-movement' (= 'easy-to-please'), subject-raising, object-raising, and derived verb phrases in general. I will also discuss some problems raised by apparent dialect differences with respect to various types of scope ambiguity.

2.1. *Labelled Bracketing*

In addition to the generally acknowledged need for labelled bracketing
in the statement of transformational rules, there is some internal evidence
in *PTQ* that the addition of labelled bracketing would be helpful, if not
indispensable.[17] One of Montague's rules adds a subject-agreement
morpheme to the first verb of a verb phrase when the verb phrase is combined with a subject to make a sentence. Thus *John* plus *walk* becomes
John walks. But *PTQ* also contains a verb-phrase conjunction rule, so the
grammar, incorrectly, generates *John walks and talk*, with *talk* instead of
talks. The problem that arises in attempting to correct the agreement rule
is with verb phrases like *try to walk and talk*, which are ambiguous. The
ambiguity shows up in the analysis tree, of course, and can be represented
by labelled bracketing as

$$_{IV}[_{IV}[\text{try to } _{IV}[\text{walk}]] \text{ and } _{IV}[\text{talk}]] \text{ vs } [\text{try to } _{IV}[_{IV}[\text{walk}] \text{ and } _{IV}[\text{talk}]]].$$

A rule sensitive to the bracketing could assign subject-agreement correctly,
giving *John tries to walk and talks* and *John tries to walk and talk*, respectively, while a rule operating only on strings could not make such a discrimination.

I will thus assume that labelled bracketing is a desirable addition to the
theory; as for implementing it, it is straightforward for all the rules which
are analogous to *PS*-rules, and I will just leave open for the time being
the details of what labelled bracketing to assign in cases where the rules
add grammatical morphemes which are not themselves assigned to any
category, or in other ways lead to indeterminacies of bracketing. I assume
that either some general principles can eventually be found to cover such
cases, or the derived structure will have to be determined for each such
rule on the basis of the requirements of subsequent rules, and explicitly
stated (as in current transformational practice, or an idealization thereof.)

2.2. *Semantic Constraint*

The constraint which Montague's theory imposes on the addition of transformational rules is that, as for all syntactic rules, there must be a single
uniform translation rule for each *T*-rule. The translation rule must be
such that the translation of the input expression(s) must occur intact in

the translation of the output; translation rules cannot change the interpretation of expressions which have already been built up by preceding rules. In the case of meaning-preserving transformations, this requirement presents no problem, since the corresponding translation rule will just be the identity mapping. So now that labelled bracketings have been added, any 'purely stylistic' transformations can be added to the grammar in essentially their usual form. (For consistency, they would be worded as follows:

'If $\phi \in P_t$ and ϕ is of the form ..., then ... $\in P_t$,',

where the first '...' would be filled by the structural description and the second by the structural change.)

But the semantic constraint does pose a problem for the statement of rules that involve deletion, such as all the rules which include equi-*NP* deletion, since the translation rules must always preserve what has been built up so far, and can never delete anything. In the rules sketched below, there are two grammar-particular innovations introduced to accommodate rules which have traditionally involved deletion: in the agentless passive, what is usually called agent-deletion is expressed as a rule which syntactically deletes a free variable but semantically adds an existential quantifier over that variable; for derived verb phrases in general, a rule is introduced which syntactically deletes a free variable he_i from subject position but semantically adds an 'abstraction operator' $\widehat{x}_i$ to the translation of the input expression. Thus in both cases the problem is solved by finding a way of interpreting syntactic deletion as semantic addition, and it seems to me that the resulting semantic interpretations are indeed correct. It is of course an open question whether such an approach is the best in the long run, but at least the first major obstacle to synthesizing the two theories has been overcome.

2.3. *Six Transformations*

In this section I sketch, not completely rigorously, rules for reflexivization, passivization, passive agent deletion, tough-movement, subject-raising, and object-rasising. Most of these rules can be stated in essentially their classical forms; I include them primarily to show their interaction with the derived verb-phrase rule presented in Section 2.4 below. Several of the rules are given in two forms, a 'strict form' and a 'loose form', which

I will relate to the questions of conflicting judgments of scope ambiguity.

2.3.1. *Reflexive.*

If $\phi \in P_t$ and ϕ is a simplex sentence[18] of the form α $he_i \, \beta \, him_i \, \gamma$, then $F_{100}(\phi) \in P_t$, where $F_{100}(\phi) = \alpha \, he_i \, \beta \, him_i \, self \, \gamma$.[19]

Example: he_3 sees $him_3 \rightarrow he_3$ sees him_3 self.

Translation rule: identity mapping.

2.3.2. *Passive.*

If $\phi \in P_t$ and ϕ has the form:

(a)   *strict form*: $_t[_T[\alpha]_{IV}[_{TV}[\beta]_T[him_i]\,\gamma]]$
(b)   *loose form*: $_t[_T[\alpha]_{IV}[_{TV}[\beta]_T[\delta]\,\gamma]]$

then $F_{101}(\phi) \in P_t$, where $F_{101}(\phi)$ is:

$$_t[_T \begin{Bmatrix} \text{(a)}\, he_i \\ \text{(b)}\, \delta \end{Bmatrix}]_{IV}[is \, EN_{TV}\,[\beta]\gamma\,[by_T\,[\alpha]]\,]]]$$

Example: John sees $him_2 \rightarrow he_2$ is seen by John.

Translation rule: identity mapping.

2.3.3. *Passive agent deletion.*

If $\phi \in P_t$ and ϕ has the form:

$$_t[_T[he_i]\,_{IV}[is \, EN_{TV}[\beta]\,[by \, him_j]]]$$
then $F_{102}(\phi) \in P_t$, where $F_{102}(\phi)$ is:
$$_t[_T[he_i]_{IV}\,[is \, En_{TV}\,[\beta]]]$$

Example: he_1 is loved by $him_3 \rightarrow he_1$ is loved.

Translation rule: If $\phi \in P_t$ and ϕ translates into ϕ', then $F_{102}(\phi)$ translates into $(\exists x_j)\,\phi'$.

2.3.4. *Tough-movement.*

(In stating this rule I have to make the contrary-to-fact assumption that the fragment already contains a syntactic category *AP* (adjective phrase), a subcategory of adjectives A_E, containing *easy*, *tough*, etc., and infinitive phrases in subject position.)

If $\phi \in P_t$ and ϕ has the form:
$$_t[_{INF}[\beta \, him_i \, \gamma]\,_{IV}[is_{AP}[A_E\,[\alpha]]]]$$
then $F_{103}(\phi) \in P_t$, where $F_{103}(\phi)$ is:
$$_t[_T[he_i]\,_{IV}[is_{AP}\,[A_E[\alpha]]_{INF}\,[\beta \, \gamma]]].$$

Example: to please him_7 is easy $\rightarrow he_7$ is easy to please.

Translation rule: identity mapping

N.B. The above is the strict version; the loose version would have δ in place of him_i.

2.3.5. *Subject raising.* Here I will just indicate the rule by an example. The strict version requires the moved *T*-phrase to be a variable, the loose version does not.

Example: it seems that he$_6$ is happy → he$_6$ seems to be happy
Translation rule: identity mapping.

2.3.6. *Object raising.* Same comments and translation rule as above. John believes that he$_3$ is a fool → John believes him$_3$ to be a fool.

Aside from the question of which constituents are required to be free variables, the only innovation in the rules above is in the treatment of passive agent deletion. There have been two main proposals in the previous transformational literature, one that what is deleted is the word *someone* and the other that it is an 'unspecified *NP*'. I have nothing to say about the latter because its semantic interpretation has never been made explicit, but some comparisons can be made between the treatment above and *someone*-deletion. There is a minor problem with *someone*-deletion in that the deleted agent need not always be animate, but that could be rectified. The problem I am interested in lies in the interpretation of the relative scope of the existential quantifier associated with the deleted agent and any other quantifiers that may occur in the sentence. In the rule as stated above I have only dealt with the subject and object term-phrases, but the treatment could be extended to cover all the term-phrases in the same simplex sentence, or whatever the actual restrictions should be. Consider the following sets of sentences.

(14)   (a) Someone has reviewed all of John's books.
        (b) All of John's books have been reviewed by someone.
        (c) All of John's books have been reviewed.
(15)   (a) Someone caught three fish.
        (b) Three fish were caught by someone.
        (c) Three fish were caught.

Judgments differ as to how many readings the (a) and (b) sentences have, but the (c) sentences are uniformly judged to be unambiguous, with the deleted quantifier having narrower scope than the remaining quantifier. If the (c) sentences were derived from (b) sentences, then those speakers who allow a wide-scope reading for *someone* in the (b) sentences should also do so for the (c) sentences, but they don't. The analysis presented above captures this fact by requiring deletion to occur while both term-phrases are free variables, and existentially quantifying over the deleted variable in the translation of the result. Thus the remaining variable, the derived subject, has to be quantified *after* the deleted variable, and therefore will necessarily be interpreted as having wider scope.

The other matter to be discussed before going on to the derived verb phrase rule is the question of interpretations of scope and the strict vs loose forms of the rules. The sorts of examples we are concerned with here include, for instance the (a)–(b) pairs of sentences (14) and (15) above, and sentences (16a–b) below, which were discussed in Chomsky (1957) and more extensively in Katz and Postal (1964).

(16)   (a) Everyone in this room speaks two languages.
        (b) Two languages are spoken by everyone in this room.

Now although the problem of the order of interpretation of quantifiers has many ramifications and undoubtedly involves a large number of interacting factors,[20] I want to focus on two idealized 'dialects' and their implications for whether the movement rules given above should be restricted to free variables or not. In what I will call the 'loose dialect', the (a)–(b) pairs are fully synonymous, each having two readings. (Factors such as left-right order may make one reading preferred over the other, but I am only concerned with how many readings should be generated at all.) In the 'strict dialect', each sentence has only one reading, with the subject quantifier having wider scope.

For the loose dialect, the unrestricted form of the transformations is a meaning-preserving rule; the active sentence is generated as ambiguous and can be transformed into the passive on either reading. For the strict dialect, constraints will have to be added to block one of the readings of the active sentence, which is generated as ambiguous in Montague's system. One kind of constraint might be an analog to Lakoff's derivational constraints, which could be easily added to Montague's rules (it would represent an extension of the theory, but would be no harder to formulate than for a generative semantics theory); if that were done, it would not be necessary to restrict the individual rules. But what leads me to posit the restriction of movement rules to the movement of free variables is that I suspect there may be a correlation between quantifier scope interpretation and 'dialect differences'[21] in two other phenomena. One is the breaking up of idioms, as in (17) and (18), which some but not all speakers accept:

(17)   Track was kept of the proceedings.
(18)   Little heed was paid to my warnings.

The loose form of the passive rule would permit such sentences while the tight form would not, since the superficial term-phrases *track* and *little heed* should presumably not be allowed to substitute for free variables. The other related phenomenon is opacity: sentence (19a) below has both a specific and a non-specific (or referential and non-referential, or *de re* and *de dicto*) reading, but judgments differ as to whether (19b) is likewise ambiguous or allows only the specific reading.

(19a)   John is looking for a green-eyed woman.
(19b)   A green-eyed woman is being looked for by John.

Again the two forms of the rule would make different predictions: the loose form would give (19b) both of the readings of (19a), while the strict form would predict (19a) to be ambiguous but (19b) to have only a specific reading.

Now *if* (a big if) judgments on these three phenomena were found to correlate strongly, that would suggest that there really might be a difference in people's grammars in whether moved *T*-phrases were restricted to variables or not. Even if matters are not this simple, as they undoubtedly are not, there still might be some psychological reality to both forms of the rules, with the strict form of the rule its fundamental form, providing the main reason why such a rule is in the grammar at all (see especially the next section, where moved free variables are crucially involved in derived verb-phrase formation), and the loose form a 'surface structure analog' of the strict rule, invoked mainly for stylistic variation. This is all much too vague to form an empirical hypothesis of any sort yet, however.

The examples above all dealt with the passive rule, but the same phenomena are to be found in connection with the other rules as well. Consider, for instance, tough-movement: since almost no one interprets (20a) and (20b) as synonymous, it might seem that only the strict form of the rule should be allowed, but the usual interpretation of (21) can be gotten only with the loose form.

(20a)   It is hard to catch every cockroach.
(20b)   Every cockroach is hard to catch.
(21)   A good man is hard to find.

In the case of subject-raising, sentences (22a, b) illustrate the quantifier scope problem and sentences (23a, b) the opacity problem. In my (un-systematic) experience, there are considerable differences of judgment here, plus plenty of 'undecided's'.

(22a)   It seems that some man loves every woman.
(22b)   Some man seems to love every woman.
(23a)   It appears that a unicorn is approaching
(23b)   A unicorn appears to be approaching.

(Montague in *PTQ* accepts (23a) and (23b) as synonymous, with two readings each, although he does not give rules to derive them.)

For object-raising, the data is particularly slippery, partly because there is a third construction whose syntactic relation to the other two is not clear.

(24a)   John believes that a woman robbed the bank.
(24b)   John believes a woman to have robbed the bank.
(24c)   John believes of a woman that she robbed the bank.

While (24a) pretty clearly allows both a specific and a non-specific read-ing, and (24c) only a specific one, (24b) seems to be hard to get clear judgments on. For the loose dialect it should be the case that not only does (24b) share the ambiguity of (24a), but so should (25), the passive of (24b).

(25)   A woman is believed by John to have robbed the bank.

If others share my intuition that it is twice as hard to get a non-refer-ential reading of *a woman* in (25) as in (24b) or a simple passive like (19b), that would be further evidence that this is not really a simple matter of dialect split nor a matter of restrictions on individual rules.

Having reached no conclusions as to the correct version of the rules given above, let us turn to the next section, for which the only crucial thing is that what gets moved *may* be a free variable, which is the case under either formulation.

2.4. *Derived Verb Phrases: Abstraction*

The rule to be given below provides a way to account for the occurrence in verb-phrase conjunction and in infinitives of verb phrases that are not built up directly in the CAT part of the grammar. It will thus allow us to provide for sentences like (26) and (27), which could not be generated in *PTQ*.

(26)   Few rules are both explicit and *easy to read.*

(27)   John wishes *to see himself.*

The rule requires the addition of a syntactic metarule, which is given below.

Derived verb phrase rule. If $\phi \in P_t$ and ϕ has the form $_t[_T[he_i]_{IV}[\alpha]]$, then $F_{104}(\phi) \in P_{IV}$, where $F_{104}(\phi) = \alpha'$, and α' comes from α by replacing each occurrence of he_i, him_i, $him_i self$ by he^*, him^*, $him^* self$ respectively.

Examples: F_{104} (he$_0$ sees him$_0$ self) = see him*self.

$\qquad$ F_{104} (he$_7$ is easy to please) = be easy to please.

Translation rule: If $\phi \in P_t$ and ϕ translates into ϕ', then $F_{104}(\phi)$ translates into $\hat{x}_i \phi'$.

Starred variable convention (syntactic metarule): Whenever any syntactic rule applies to two (or more) arguments such that one is a *T*-phrase and one contains a starred variable, replace all occurrences of the starred variable by pronouns of the appropriate gender.

Example: Mary + try to see him*self → Mary tries to see herself.

The derived verb phrase rule transforms a sentence into a verb phrase; the resulting verb phrase can then be used just like any other verb phrase in building up larger phrases. It can, for instance, enter into verb-phrase conjunction, as in (26); it can serve as a complement to verbs such as *wish* and *try*;[22] it can combine with verb-phrase adverbs. The derived verb phrase rule is incompatible with the usual transformational framework, either standard or generative semantic, since the transformationally derived verb phrase is permitted to recombine with new elements via essentially CF rules. However, it seems to offer a maximally simple way to reconcile the syntactic arguments for deriving certain phrases from whole sentences with the semantic arguments against doing so (as discussed, for instance, in Partee (1970).)

The semantic interpretation of the derived verb phrase makes use of an abstraction operator. If the translation of he_0 *sees* him_0 *self* is $see'(x_0, x_0)$ (a rough approximation to the *PTQ* translation), then the translation of its derivative *see him*self* will be $\hat{x}_0(see'(x_0, x_0))$, i.e. the property of seeing oneself. Since the abstraction operator binds the free variables, there is no further semantic need to keep track of the variables in the underlying sentence; but syntactically the pronouns must be made to agree with whatever term-phrase that property is eventually connected with, and that is the function of the starred variable convention.

The starred variable convention is closely analogous to Rosenbaum's minimum distance principle, except that topographical nearness is replaced by a relation which centers on the analysis tree: the term-phrase that picks up the starred variable is the first term-phrase to be combined as a constituent with the phrase containing the derived verb phrase. If *persuade to* is added to the fragment as *TV/IV*, then *persuade to* would combine with *see him*self* to form a *TV*-phrase *persuade to see him*self*; then the *TV + T-phrase → IV* rule would combine that with *Mary* and the result would be (with appropriate reordering) *persuade Mary to see herself* since the starred variable convention would apply. Richmond Thomason (personal communication) has pointed out that if *promise* is assigned to the category *(IV//IV)/T*, the difference between *promise* and *persuade* will be correctly represented with this starred variable convention; the correct predictions will be made about sentences (28) and (29) below.

(28)   John persuaded Mary to shoot $\begin{Bmatrix} \text{*himself} \\ \text{herself} \end{Bmatrix}$

(29)   John promised Mary to shoot $\begin{Bmatrix} \text{himself} \\ \text{*herself} \end{Bmatrix}$

In conclusion, I will sketch the analysis trees for some sentences whose derivations involve the derived verb phrase rule.

(30)   Every man tries to be found by a woman who loves him

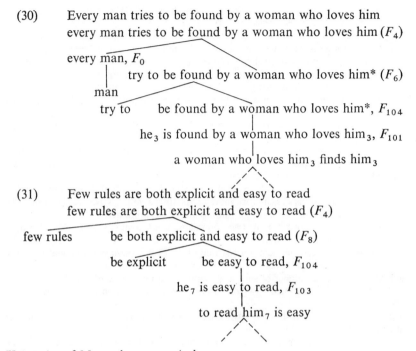

every man tries to be found by a woman who loves him (F_4)

every man, F_0

try to be found by a woman who loves him* (F_6)

man

try to   be found by a woman who loves him*, F_{104}

he$_3$ is found by a woman who loves him$_3$, F_{101}

a woman who loves him$_3$ finds him$_3$

(31)   Few rules are both explicit and easy to read

few rules are both explicit and easy to read (F_4)

few rules   be both explicit and easy to read (F_8)

be explicit   be easy to read, F_{104}

he$_7$ is easy to read, F_{103}

to read him$_7$ is easy

University of Massachusetts at Amherst

NOTES

* This paper is a written version of a talk given in April, 1972, in the Linguistics and Semantics Workshop at the University of Western Ontario. A preliminary version was given in March at the University of Massachusetts at Amherst, and a version was also given at a colloquium at UC San Diego. The first part of the paper, like the first part of the talks, is a condensation of a talk which I gave in various forms and places in the fall and winter 1971–72. A fuller treatment of the same subject can be found in my 'Montague Grammar and Transformational Grammar'. My debts to others in this work are too numerous to list here, but I must at least mention Richmond Thomason, whose suggestions about the abstraction operator helped me get my first ideas about how to accommodate transformations in the Montague framework; Michael Bennett, whose continuing extensions of Montague's work have fertilized and challenged my own; David Kaplan, who has given me constant encouragement and taught me a great deal about philosophy and logic; and of course Richard Montague and Noam Chomsky, without whom I wouldn't have had a starting point. I am also grateful to all the students and other audiences who have given me helpful comments and criticisms, particularly the linguistics and philosophy students in my Montague seminar at UCLA, Winter-Spring, 1972.

[1] The exceptions include the work of Reichenbach (1947) and the exhortation to collaboration made by Bar-Hillel (1954), rebuffed by Chomsky (1955).

[2] "Simplification of theory is a central motive likewise of the sweeping artificialities of notation in modern logic. Clearly, it would be folly to burden a logical theory with quirks of usage that we can straighten. If we were to devise a logic of ordinary language for direct use on sentences as they come, we would have to complicate our rules of inference in sundry unilluminating ways." (Quine (1960), p. 158) As an example: "Our ordinary language shows a tiresome bias in its treatment of time... [T] he form that it takes – that of requiring that every verb form show a tense – is peculiarly productive of needless complications.... Hence in fashioning canonical notations it is usual to drop tense distinctions."

[3] Tarski pointed out to me (pers. communication, 1971) that the substitutional view of quantification, as found in the work of Ruth Barcan Marcus, is an example of a departure from the scheme described above.

[4] Actually, it appears that this principle is being abandoned, and generative semanticists are coming to view their work more as 'abstract syntax', a view that would make their approach compatible with the traditional logical approach.

[5] Some central references for the two approaches are Lakoff (1971), (1972), Chomsky (1971), and Jackendoff (1969).

[6] I am purposely ignoring here the question of the deep structure of the relative clause itself, although that also makes a great difference to the semantics.

[7] For a review of a number of such arguments, see Stockwell et al. (1973).

[8] The semantics here is basically from Montague; the discussion of alternatives is my own.

[9] This view of the semantics of restrictive relative clauses is not unique to Montague; it can also be found in Quine (1960).

[10] The syntactic and semantic details of such an analysis can be found in Montague (1972).

[11] I realize that negative arguments such as those given here against analyses (1) and (2) can never be fully conclusive; the discussion should be construed as a semantic defense of (3) plus a challenge to proponents of (1) or (2) to provide a semantic analysis that supports their syntax. The argument against (2) is weaker than that against (1), since only in (1) is the intermediate constituent called an *NP*.

[12] The originator of categorial grammar was the Polish logician Ajdukiewicz; for exposition see Lewis (1971).

[13] Although in one sense it is correct to speak of the categories as being defined by these specifications, it should be borne in mind that in another sense the categories are defined only implicitly, by the totality of the rules of the grammar.

[14] The two exceptions are *IV* and *CN*, since the set of expressions of category *e* is empty.

[15] The syntactic simplicity was intentional since Montague's interest was in semantics. In the opening paragraph of *PTQ* he says, "For expository purposes the fragment has been made as simple and restricted as it can be while accommodating all the more puzzling cases of quantification and reference with which I am acquainted."

[16] An earlier paper, Montague (1970a), does have a footnote suggesting a treatment of reflexive pronouns to which the one proposed here is almost identical; essentially the same treatment is found in earlier works by generative semanticists. What Montague did not have was a way to generate infinitive phrases containing reflexive pronouns.

[17] The reason I am not prepared to claim that labelled bracketing is indispensable is that in Montague's system rules can, in principle, refer to the derivational history of a

string, and I have no clear cases where that would not suffice. But with labelled bracketing added, one would be free to investigate the possibility of constraining the rules so that only the bracketing, and not arbitrary aspects of the derivational history, could be used by the (syntactic) rules.

[18] This condition needs to be made precise; a first approximation would be to say ϕ contains only one verb (i.e. one basic expression of category IV, TV, IV/t, or $IV//IV$.)

[19] As presented, this rule would have to be obligatory, which would be the first such rule in the grammar. An alternative might be to build reflexivization into the rule that combines subject and verb phrase to make a sentence.

[20] These matters have been discussed extensively in the literature; see, for example, Lakoff (1971) and Jackendoff (1969). Among the factors I think are involved are not only the structural factors of dominance and left-right order, and stress, but also individual differences in 'strength' or 'precedence' among the various quantifiers, and, to complicate matters, non-linguistic judgments of absurdity vs plausibility of the different structurally possible interpretations.

[21] I am very hesitant to call any of these differences dialect differences because I have no conviction that what is going on is to be accounted for in terms of differences in grammatical rules, and I also have no evidence that these 'dialects' are related to speech communities. See Gleitman and Gleitman (1970) for a study of similar problems relating to the interpretation of noun compounds.

[22] We have several choices as to the handling of infinitival complements. The derived verb phrase rule gives appropriate inputs to the PTQ rule which combines *try to* with an *IV*-phrase; or we could add a rule forming infinitives from *IV*-phrases by systematically adding *to* and semantically taking the intension of the *IV*-phrase translation, and let *try* take an infinitive-phrase. We could also let *try* take as complement a sentence with a free variable as subject, with infinitive-formation part of the rule for combining them.

BIBLIOGRAPHY

Bar-Hillel, Yeshoshua: 1954, 'Logical Syntax and Semantics', *Language* **30**, 230–237.

Chomsky, Noam: 1955, 'Logical Syntax and Semantics: Their Linguistic Relevance', *Language* **31**, 36–45.

Chomsky, Noam: 1957, *Syntactic Structures*, The Hague.

Chomsky, Noam: 1971, 'Deep Structure, Surface Structure, and Semantic Interpretation', in Steinberg and Jakobovits, 1971, 183–216.

Gleitman, Lila and Gleitman, Henry: 1970, *Phrase and Paraphrase*, New York.

Harman, Gilbert and Davidson, Donald: 1971, *Semantics of Natural Languages*, Dordrecht.

Hintikka, Jaakko, Moravcsik, Julius, and Suppes, Patrick: 1972, *Approaches to Natural Language*, Dordrecht, 1973.

Jackendoff, Ray: 1969, *Some Rules of Semantic Interpretation for English*, MIT dissertation.

Katz, Jerrold: 1966, *The Philosophy of Language*, New York.

Katz, Jerrold and Postal, Paul: 1964, *An Integrated Theory of Linguistic Descriptions*, Cambridge.

Lakoff, George: 1971, 'On Generative Semantics', in Steinberg and Jakobovits, 1971, 232–296.

Lakoff, George: 1972, 'Linguistics and Natural Logic', in Harman and Davidson, 1971, 545–665.

Lewis, David: 1971, 'General Semantics' *Synthese* **22**, 18–67.

Montague, Richard: 1970a, 'English as a Formal Language', in Visentini *et al.*, 1970, 189–224

Montague, Richard: 1970b, 'Universal Grammar', *Theoria* **36**, 373–398.

Montague, Richard: 1972, 'The Proper Treatment of Quantification in Ordinary English' in Hintikka *et al.*, 1973, 221–242.

Partee, Barbara: 1970, 'Negation, Conjunction, and Quantifiers: Syntax vs Semantics', *Foundations of Language* **6**, 153–165.

Quine, W. V.: 1960, *Word and Object,* Cambridge.

Reichenbach, Hans: 1947, *Elements of Symbolic Logic,* New York.

Steinberg, Danny and Jakobovits, Leon: 1971, *Semantics,* Cambridge, England.

Stockwell, Robert, Schachter, Paul, and Partee, Barbara: 1973, *The Major Syntactic Structures of English,* New York.

Tarski, Alfred: 1944, 'The Semantic Conception of Truth', *Philosophy and Phenomenological Research* **4**, 341–375.

Vermazen, Bruce: 1967, 'A review of Katz and Postal (1964) and Katz (1966)', *Synthese* **17**, 350–365.

Visentini, Bruno, *et al.*: 1970, *Linguaggi nella societa e nella tecnica,* Milan.

RICHMOND H. THOMASON

SOME EXTENSIONS OF MONTAGUE GRAMMAR*

This is an attempt to make intelligible some mechanisms that, when added to the grammatical framework created by Montague, permit the treatment of a variety of English constructions—especially those involving sentence embedding. It introduces an element like the abstraction operator of type-theoretic logics into the syntactic analysis of several kinds of complements, and it develops Montague's program by exploiting strategies of direct decomposition rather than along the transformational lines followed by Partee. I find an elegance in this fragment that makes it extremely attractive, but it remains to be seen to what extent, if any, this feature can be preserved in attempting to encompass more of English.

This paper is a revised version of one that was written in October 1972 and privately circulated. Its purpose was to present the syntactic theory in an informal but readable way. Like that draft, this one sacrifices rigor for intelligibility, and omits a presentation of the semantic component. I mention these things explicitly to avoid conveying the impression that I think that the style of this paper is a model of how to do this sort of grammar. I consider the rigor and explicitness with which Montague presented his syntactic theories, and his unwillingness to indulge in uninterpreted syntax, to be vital elements of his program that should by no means be sacrificed. I hope I managed to conform to them in developing my own theory. But what follows should not be regarded as a full account of the theory; it is only an informal presentation of the syntax. A similar presentation of the semantics is now available for private distribution.

1. LANGUAGES IN GENERAL

The first thing you need to do in making a Montague grammar for a language is to determine the system of grammatical categories. This is done by designating certain indices to represent primitive categories and choosing a collection of complex indices having the form $A/_n B$, where A and B may be any category indices, primitive or complex, and n may be any natural number. In practice the numerical subscripts aren't written—instead, the slashes are repeated. For instance, 'A/B' stands for 'A/$_1$B', 'A//B' for 'A/$_2$B', and so forth.

The fact that a syntactic category is assigned a complex index has nothing to do with the syntactic complexity of phrases that are assigned to that category. A syntactically atomic expression (**who**, for instance, in the fragment presented here) may be assigned to a category which has a quite complicated index. But the indices do provide information about the syntactic role played by these expressions; phrases of category A/$_n$B will combine with phrases of category B to make phrases of category A. (For example, where CN is the index of common nouns, adjectives will be assigned the index CN/CN. From this we know that adjectives, such as **old**, will combine with common nouns, such as **stolen picture**. But we don't know what form the combination will take.) The mode of combination is given by a SYNTACTIC RULE, and these rules may be extremely complex. A syntactic rule must be given for each complex category index; rules corresponding to different categories will in general differ from one another. We allow for different categories—A/B, A//B, etc.—because of the possibility of there being more than one syntactic kind of expression which nevertheless combine with B phrases to make A phrases.

2. CATEGORIAL STRUCTURE OF OUR FRAGMENT

As primitive category indices we choose t and e, corresponding, respectively, to the categories of (open or closed) sentences and of "entity expressions." It will turn out that there are no phrases at all of category e, since—as in Montague (1973)—all noun phrases (or TERMS) are treated as quantifiers. (Why have a syntactic category of e phrases at all, then? Because, though empty syntactically, it has semantic significance. It follows from Montague's semantic framework that, for instance, a phrase of category t/e must denote a function taking senses of entities into truth values.) Table 1 presents the categories of our fragment of English. For each category, it also specifies the set of its "basic expressions." These are the phrases that are assigned to that category by stipulation rather than by syntactic rules. Thus, the table also serves as a lexicon for the fragment. It is, however, only a partial lexicon. In a full, rigorous treatment of the fragment, the lexicon must also give enough information about each basic expression to determine its morphophonemic behavior. For instance, we must be able to infer from the lexicon the inflectional pattern of each basic intransitive verb. Also, of course, the table neglects semantic information.

TABLE 1

Category	Category definition	Syntactic rule no.	Nearest equivalent	Set of basic expressions
t	t		sentence	Λ
e	e		in one sense, none; in another (given meaning postulates), proper names	Λ
AB	t/e	0	none; this is the category of abstracts	Λ
AB/t	AB/t	1	none	$\{that_0, that_1, \ldots\}$
T	t/AB	2	noun phrase	$\{$John, Mary, Bill, he_0, he_1, $\ldots\}$
IV	t/T	3	intransitive, noun-phrase-taking verb phrase	$\{$go, walk$\}$
TV	IV/T	4	1-place transitive, noun-phrase-taking verb phrase	$\{$find, seek, believe, steal, shave, love, resemble$\}$
TTV	TV/T	5	2-place transitive, noun-phrase-taking verb phrase	$\{$give, read$\}$
CN	$t//e$	6	common noun	$\{$man, woman, fish, wife, father, mother, uncle, owner, book, picture, unicorn, centaur$\}$
ACN	CN/CN	7	adjective	$\{$old, large$\}$
ACN/T	ACN/T	8	(one sort of) preposition	$\{$of$\}$
DET	T/CN	9	determiner	$\{$a, the, every, his_0, his_1, $\ldots\}$
INF	$t///e$	10	infinitive phrase	Λ
INF/AB	INF/AB	11	infinitive complementizer	$\{$to$\}$
IV/INF	IV/INF	12	intransitive, infinitive-taking verb phrase	$\{$try, hope, ask, expect, promise$\}$
TV/INF	TV/INF	13	transitive, infinitive-taking verb phrase	$\{$persuade, force, ask, expect$\}$
(IV/INF)/T	(IV/INF)/T	14	transitive, infinitive-taking verb phrase	$\{$promise, ask$\}$
T/t	T/t	15	sentence nominalizer	$\{$that$\}$
ACN/AB	ACN/AB	16	relativizer	$\{$such, who$\}$
IV/ACN	IV/ACN	17	copula	$\{$be$\}$
PP	ACN/TV	18	past participle former	$\{$en$\}$
PP/T	PP/T	19	(one sort of) preposition	$\{$by$\}$

3. SYNTACTIC RULES AND SYNTACTIC STRUCTURE IN GENERAL

For each complex category index A/B there will be a syntactic rule telling how A phrases are constituted from A/B phrases and B phrases. (In the empty case in which there are no B phrases this rule will be vacuous, in that it will have no effect on the phrases generated by the grammar.) In the table, each complex category is assigned a number—the number of the corresponding syntactic rule. Thus, the rule numbered 9 will specify how T phrases (terms or noun phrases) are made from DET phrases (determiners) and CN phrases (common noun phrases). There is no necessity that all the syntactic rules of a language should arise in this way from its categorial structure. But they do, in fact, in this fragment; it is CATEGORIALLY DETERMINED.

Syntactic structure is determined in Montague grammar by trees showing how a phrase has been generated from basic expressions by means of syntactic rules. The following is an example of such an analysis tree, for the T phrase **that John finds a fish**.

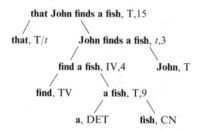

After each phrase follows the index of the category to which it is assigned by the analysis tree and, if the phrase is not assigned lexically to that category, the number of the syntactic rule by which it has been produced. An ANALYZED EXPRESSION is a pair $\langle \alpha, \mathscr{T} \rangle$, where α is an expression and $\mathscr{T}$ is an analysis tree for that expression.

A syntactic rule, in the simplest sort of case, involves a binary function F taking expressions into expressions. If F is the function of the syntactic rule for the category with index A/B, the rule will then specify that for all expressions α and β, if α is an A/B phrase and β is a B phrase then $F(\alpha, \beta)$ is an A phrase. More generally syntactic rules involve partial relations linking analyzed expressions, analyzed expressions, and expressions. Where F is such a relation, the rule will say that for all analyzed expressions $\langle \alpha, \mathscr{T}_0 \rangle$ and $\langle \beta, \mathscr{T}_1 \rangle$, if α is an A/B phrase according to $\mathscr{T}_0$ and β is a B phrase according to $\mathscr{T}_1$, then γ is an A phrase, for all γ such that $F(\langle \alpha, \mathscr{T}_0 \rangle, \langle \beta, \mathscr{T}_1 \rangle, \gamma)$. (Some readers may have noticed a circularity; the definitions of 'analysis tree' and 'syntactic rule' presuppose one another. This circularity isn't vicious; it can easily be done away with.)

4. SYNTACTIC RULES: NOUN PHRASES

This section begins the task of describing the syntactic rules of the fragment. It is at this point that it becomes difficult to preserve both rigorous detail and readability. Here I respond to this problem by allowing the order of exposition to diverge from the numerical order of the rules, and by occasionally giving only examples rather than full definitions. At the end of this paper, there is an Appendix consisting of analysis trees for various phrases. It might be a good strategy to pause occasionally in the sections that follow and glance at the examples in the Appendix.

Here we will discuss the categories T, CN, DET, ACN, ACN/T, and T/t. These constitute a family that is especially important in the formation of noun phrases. A glance at the table of categories shows that determiners combine with common nouns to make terms; thus there must be a syntactic rule showing how, e.g., **the** combines with **old man** to form **the old man**. We'll begin with this rule, number 9. Here the mode of combination is particularly simple: It's mere concatenation—put the determiner to the left of the common noun phrase to make a term—except that morphophonemic alternation of **a[n]** must also be built into the rule. This mode of combination is defined everywhere (any determiner can combine with any common noun phrase), is functional (the mode of combination yields in each case a unique result), and does not depend on the syntactic analyses of the argument expressions. In cases such as this we will use simplified notation and write, e.g., '$F_9(\alpha, \beta) = \gamma$' rather than '$F_9(\langle \alpha, \mathcal{T}_0 \rangle, \langle \beta, \mathcal{T}_1 \rangle, \gamma)$'.

RULE 9:

$$F_9(\alpha, \beta) = \begin{cases} \alpha\ \beta & \text{if } \alpha \text{ is an expression other than } \mathbf{a} \\ & \text{or } \beta \text{ begins with a consonant} \\ \alpha\mathbf{n}\ \beta & \text{if } \alpha \text{ is } \mathbf{a} \text{ and } \beta \text{ begins with a vowel} \end{cases}$$

EXAMPLES:

$F_9(\textbf{every, woman}) = \textbf{every woman}$
$F_9(\textbf{his}_6, \textbf{fish}) = \textbf{his}_6 \textbf{ fish}$
$F_9(\textbf{a, unicorn}) = \textbf{a unicorn}$
$F_9(\textbf{a, old man}) = \textbf{an old man}$

ACN phrases, or adjectives, take common nouns into common nouns. ('ACN' stands for 'ad–common noun'. In general, an ad–A is an A/A.) In this fragment we can say that the positioning of an ACN phrase depends on its length; **old** plus **man** yields **old man**, and **of John** plus **picture** yields **picture of John**. So a first approximation of the syntactic rule for ACN phrases is as follows.

RULE 7:

$$F_7(\alpha, \beta) = \begin{cases} \alpha \beta & \text{if } \alpha \text{ is one word long} \\ \beta \alpha & \text{if } \alpha \text{ is more than one word long} \end{cases}$$

In a larger fragment this approximation would have to be modified in view of examples like **very old woman**. (There is no category in the fragment suitable for **very**.) But this is not why Rule 7 was called an approximation; the formulation just given is inadequate because variable binding can occur in instances of this rule. I want to postpone discussion of variable binding till later; my plan will be to treat only two cases of this phenomenon thoroughly, and to hope that understanding of other cases will follow from this. At this point I will just present some examples that illustrate how variable binding can figure in Rule 7.

A VARIABLE is an expression of the form **he**$_i$, **him**$_i$, **him**$_i$**self**, or **his**$_i$. Two of these forms, **he**$_i$ and **his**$_i$, are introduced in the lexicon. The others are morphologically marked forms of **he**$_i$. When variable binding occurs, these variables lose their subscripts and become anaphorically linked to substantives—terms or common nouns. Now, the syntactic rules of our fragment will eventually generate ACN phrases like **who**$_0$[**is late**] and **whom**$_8$[**John believes that he**$_4$ **seeks**]. These should be regarded as "unsaturated" or unbound relative clauses. Notice that the variable **he**$_0$ does not appear in **who**$_0$[**is late**]; but this ACN does derive syntactically from a sentence, **he**$_0$ **is late**, in which the variable does occur.

Since these are ACN phrases, they will combine with common nouns such as **man** to form common nouns. When this combination takes place, the variable indicated by the subscript on **who[m]** is bound to **man**, resulting in **man who is late** and **man whom John believes that he**$_4$ **seeks**. These examples show that binding involves erasing of brackets and certain numerical subscripts. More is involved when the pronoun that is bound actually occurs in the original expression. Take, for instance, the ACN phrase **who**$_5$[**believes that John seeks him**$_5$]. This combines with **man** to form **man who believes that John seeks him**, and with **woman** to form **woman who believes that John seeks her**. All variables are genderless; they only take on gender in being bound. When **fish** combines with this ACN phrase, Rule 7 generates both of the alternative forms **fish that believes that John seeks it** and **fish which believes that John seeks it**. It is to cope with cases like this that the *F*'s are allowed to be relations. F_7 is defined so that both of the following hold.

F_7(**who**$_6$[**is large**], **fish, fish that is large**)
F_7(**who**$_6$[**is large**], **fish, fish which is large**)

Certain prepositions, such as **of** in **picture of John**, combine with terms to form ACN phrases. The syntactic rule for these ACN/T phrases is simple concatenation, except that when a variable he_i passes through this rule it takes on a case marker and changes to him_i.

RULE 8:

$$F_8(\alpha, \beta) = \begin{cases} \alpha\ \beta & \text{if } \beta \text{ is not a variable} \\ \alpha\ \mathbf{him}_i & \text{if } \beta \text{ is } \mathbf{he}_i \end{cases}$$

EXAMPLES:

$F_8(\mathbf{of, his}_3\ \mathbf{fish}) = \mathbf{of\ his}_3\ \mathbf{fish}$

$F_8(\mathbf{of, he}_{16}) = \mathbf{of\ him}_{16}$

Given a sentence, say **John's father is old**, the syntactic rule associated with **that** (the only T/t phrase generated by our grammar) yields the term **that John's father is old**. This rule couldn't be simpler: Just put **that** to the left of a sentence to make a term.

RULE 15:

$$F_{15}(\alpha, \beta) = \alpha\ \beta$$

EXAMPLE:

$F_{15}(\mathbf{that, every\ fish\ whose\ mother\ is\ large\ is\ large})$
$= \mathbf{that\ every\ fish\ whose\ mother\ is\ large\ is\ large}$

There is no subcategorization of noun phrases in our grammar (into, e.g., "abstract" and "concrete" noun phrases), and it would result in considerable complication to introduce such subcategorization. There is, of course, the consequence that no syntactic restrictions will then be available to prohibit the formation of sentences like **John gives Mary that a woman finds her father**.

This needn't be regarded as a defect. Naturally, such sentences are peculiar, and this peculiarity must be explained; but semantic theory is as able as syntactic theory to accomplish this task. In some cases, I believe it is obvious that a phenomenon is to be explained syntactically, in others that it is to be explained semantically. But there are many phenomena that fall into neither category, and—bearing always in mind that our goal is an entire semantic account of the language—we profit by assigning tasks to various subtheories in a way that makes the whole natural and elegant.

In the case at hand, since the semantic theory will in any event be able to distinguish between the semantic values of nominalized sentences (i.e., propositions) and other kinds of semantic values, it will have the capacity to explain the anomaly of sentences like **that a fish is large believes itself**. For one way in which this can be carried out in an extension of Montague's semantic framework, see Thomason (1972).

5. MORE SYNTACTIC RULES:
VERB PHRASES, SUBJECT–PREDICATE SENTENCES

Here we will discuss the rules for IV, TV, and TTV phrases. If a category of IV-phrase-modifying adverbs (with the index IV/IV) had been included in this fragment, it would have been discussed in this section too. These adverbs and sentence-modifying adverbs (index t/t) were omitted in order to simplify the exposition.

Transitive verbs taking a single object are given the index IV/T, and so will combine with terms to form intransitive verb phrases: Thus, **steal** combines with **a fish**, making **steal a fish**. But there are factors that make the syntactic operation of Rule 4 more complex than mere juxtaposition. First, as in Rule 8, variables must take on a case marking; we want **steal** plus **he$_2$** to yield **steal him$_2$**. Second, phrases like **persuade to$_1$[go]** are treated by this grammar as transitive verbs. When Rule 4 acts on these, the object must be infixed; also there will be variable binding. Thus, **persuade to$_1$[go]** plus **Mary** yields **persuade Mary to go**, and **force to$_5$[persuade his$_5$ father to shave him$_2$]** plus **a woman** yields **force a woman to persuade her father to shave him$_2$**. Third, verbs taking indirect objects generate TV phrases such as **give the book** that also require infixing in Rule 4: **give the book** plus **John** yields **give John the book**.

We will give a simplified formulation of Rule 4 that ignores the second of these factors.

RULE 4:

$$F_4(\alpha, \beta) = \begin{cases} \begin{cases} \alpha\ \beta & \text{if } \beta \text{ is not a variable} \\ \alpha\ \mathbf{him}_i & \text{if } \beta \text{ is } \mathbf{he}_i \end{cases} & \text{if the first word of } \alpha \text{ is a TV} \\ \begin{cases} \alpha_1\ \beta\ \alpha_2 & \text{if } \beta \text{ is not a variable} \\ \alpha_1\ \mathbf{him}_i\ \alpha_2 & \text{if } \beta \text{ is } \mathbf{he}_i \end{cases} & \text{if } \alpha \text{ is } \alpha_1\ \alpha_2, \text{ where } \alpha_1 \text{ is a TTV} \end{cases}$$

EXAMPLES:

$F_4(\textbf{shave, a fish}) = $ **shave a fish**
$F_4(\textbf{seek, he}_i) = $ **seek him$_i$**
$F_4(\textbf{read a large book, Mary}) = $ **read Mary a large book**

This form of Rule 4 also exploits certain limitations of the fragment, such as the fact that **give** is not also classified as a TV.

Intransitive verbs combine with terms to make subject–predicate sentences. In the simplest instances, the term is merely written to the left of the intransitive verb: **eat a fish** plus **Bill** yields **Bill eats a fish**. Here the main verb of the IV has also been changed to its third-person singular present form. In this fragment the main verb of an IV phrase α can be identified as the leftmost word to occur in α; there are no IV phrases like **reluctantly**

go. Thus, **walk** is the main verb of **walk**, **be** the main verb of **be late**, and **persuade** the main verb of **persuade Bill to shave himself**. I presuppose, without stating it explicitly, an inflectional morphology for the verbs of the fragment, from which these verb forms can be gathered.

But there are more complications. Rule 3 is the source of reflexive forms of variables; we want it to generate **he₁ shaves him₁self**, not **he₁ shaves him₁**, from **shave him₁** and **he₁**. Evidently, when an IV phrase combines by Rule 3 with **he$_i$** some of the occurrences of **him$_i$** in that IV phrase become replaced by occurrences of **him$_i$self**. But it would be going too far to say that all such occurrences are changed in this way. We want our fragment to generate sentences like, for instance, **John believes that Mary loves him**, not like **John believes that Mary loves himself**. Therefore, Rule 3 must produce **he₁ believes that Mary loves him₁**, rather than **he₁ believes that Mary loves him₁self**. To distinguish those occurrences of **he$_i$** that should be reflexivized, we will adapt from transformational grammar the generalization that reflexivization can occur only within simplex sentences. In our terms this means that reflexivization is blocked by the embedding of sentences within other phrases. To trace such embeddings in an IV phrase, we must look to its analysis—in other words, the arguments of Rule 3 must be analyzed expressions.

To begin with, take the following analysis of **shave him₁**.

$(\mathcal{T}_0)$

$$\text{shave him}_1, \text{IV},4$$
$$\diagup \qquad \diagdown$$
$$\text{shave, TV} \qquad \text{he}_1, \text{T}$$

According to analysis $\mathcal{T}_0$, the only occurrence of **him₁** in **shave him₁** never traces back to an occurrence in a sentence. Therefore, when $\mathcal{T}_0$ is made part of a larger analysis tree in which **he₁** is made the subject of **shave him₁**, reflexivization occurs, as follows.

$$\text{he}_1 \text{ shaves him}_1\text{self}, t,3$$
$$\diagup \qquad \diagdown$$
$$\text{shave him}_1, \text{IV},4 \qquad \text{he}_1, \text{T}$$
$$\diagup \qquad \diagdown$$
$$\text{shave, TV} \qquad \text{he}_1, \text{T}$$

Now take another analysis.

$(\mathcal{T}_1)$

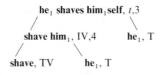

According to analysis $\mathcal{T}_1$, the only occurrence of **him$_3$** in **believe that Mary loves him$_3$** traces back in two steps to an occurrence in a phrase (namely, **Mary loves him$_3$**) that is classified as a sentence by $\mathcal{T}_1$. Therefore when Rule 3 acts on the analyzed phrase, combining it with **he$_3$** to form a sentence, this occurrence of **him$_3$** will not be reflexivized.

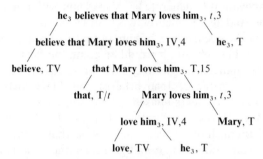

It may happen that both types of occurrences appear in the same IV phrase, as in the following analysis.

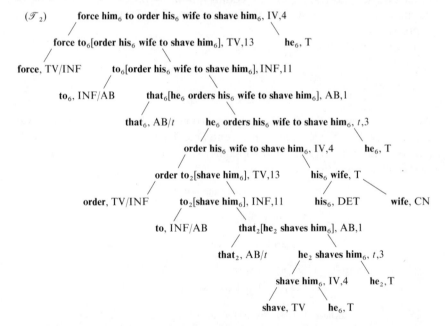

Here the first occurrence of **him$_6$** traces back in one step to an occurrence of **he$_6$** that is introduced as a basic expression. Since this occurrence never developed in $\mathcal{T}_2$ from anything contained in a sentence, it is EXPOSED TO REFLEXIVIZATION and will change to **him$_6$self** when the topmost phrase of

$\mathscr{T}_2$ is combined with **he**$_6$ according to Rule 3. On the other hand, the other occurrence of **him**$_6$ (the one at the extreme right of the IV phrase) does lead back in $\mathscr{T}_2$ to an occurrence in a sentence (namely, the occurrence at the extreme right of **he**$_6$ **orders his**$_6$ **wife to shave him**$_6$). It is therefore SHIELDED FROM REFLEXIVIZATION according to $\mathscr{T}_2$, and will remain unchanged when the topmost phrase of $\mathscr{T}_2$ is combined with **he**$_6$ according to Rule 3, as follows.

he$_6$ **forces him**$_6$**self to order his**$_6$ **wife to shave him**$_6$, $t,3$

/ \

force him$_6$ **to order his**$_6$ **wife to shave him**$_6$, IV,4   **he**$_6$, T

Etc. [as in $\mathscr{T}_2$]

Notice that though Rule 3 is used several times in the analysis $\mathscr{T}_2$, reflexivization can occur in none of these uses of the rule. When **he**$_2$ **shaves him**$_6$ was formed, there were no occurrences of **him**$_2$ in the IV phrase **shave him**$_6$. When **he**$_6$ **orders his**$_6$ **wife to shave him**$_6$ was formed, the only occurrence of **him**$_6$ in the IV phrase **order his**$_6$ **wife to shave him**$_6$ was shielded from reflexivization. (There is indeed an unshielded occurrence of **his**$_6$ in the IV phrase, but we will not allow in this fragment for reflexivization of the possessive form of variables; in English the reflexive form **his own** is optional, anyway.)

Using the concepts of being exposed to and shielded from reflexivization that I have just illustrated, we can now formulate the subject–predicate rule.

RULE 3:

$$F_3(\langle \alpha, \mathscr{T} \rangle, \beta) = \begin{cases} \beta\,\alpha', \text{ where } \alpha' \text{ is the result of first replacing} \\ \text{the leftmost word in } \alpha \text{ by the appropriate} \\ \text{third-person singular tensed form and, in} \\ \text{case } \beta \text{ is } \mathbf{he}_i, \text{ replacing each occurrence of} \\ \mathbf{him}_i \text{ in } \alpha \text{ that is exposed to reflexivization} \\ \text{according to } \mathscr{T} \text{ by an occurrence of } \mathbf{him}_i\mathbf{self} \end{cases}$$

EXAMPLES:

$F_3(\langle \mathbf{go}, \mathscr{T} \rangle, \mathbf{John}) = \mathbf{John\ goes}$,   for any $\mathscr{T}$

$F_3(\langle \mathbf{force\ him}_2\ \mathbf{to\ steal\ a\ fish}, \mathscr{T} \rangle, \mathbf{Bill}) = \mathbf{Bill\ forces\ him}_2\ \mathbf{to}$ **steal a fish**,   for any $\mathscr{T}$

$F_3(\langle \mathbf{seek\ him}_2, \mathscr{T} \rangle, \mathbf{he}_5) = \mathbf{he}_5\ \mathbf{seeks\ him}_2$,   for any $\mathscr{T}$

In each of these examples the analysis of the IV phrase was irrelevant because the other argument of F_3 was not a variable occurring in the IV phrase. But to determine, say, $F_3(\langle$**seek him**$_2$, $\mathscr{T}\rangle$, **he**$_2$) we must specify $\mathscr{T}$. Choose $\mathscr{T}_3$ as follows.

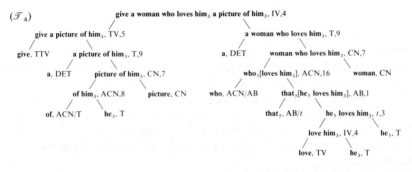

($\mathscr{T}_3$)

Since according to $\mathscr{T}_3$ the only occurrence of **him**$_2$ in **seek him**$_2$ is exposed to reflexivization,

$$F_3(\langle \textbf{seek him}_2, \mathscr{T}_3\rangle, \textbf{he}_2) = \textbf{he}_2 \textbf{ seeks him}_2\textbf{self}.$$

One more example. Let $\mathscr{T}_4$ be the following analysis.

($\mathscr{T}_4$)

give a woman who loves him$_3$ a picture of him$_3$, IV,4

give a picture of him$_3$, TV,5

give, TTV   a picture of him$_3$, T,9

a, DET   picture of him$_3$, CN,7

of him$_3$, ACN,8   picture, CN

of, ACN/T   he$_3$, T

a woman who loves him$_3$, T,9

a, DET   woman who loves him$_3$, CN,7

who$_5$[loves him$_3$], ACN,16   woman, CN

who, ACN/AB   that$_5$[he$_5$ loves him$_3$], AB,1

that$_5$, AB/t he$_5$ loves him$_3$, t,3

love him$_3$, IV,4   he$_5$, T

love, TV   he$_3$, T

According to $\mathscr{T}_4$ the first occurrence of **him**$_3$ in **give a woman who loves him**$_3$ **a picture of him**$_3$ is shielded from reflexivization, while the second occurrence is exposed to reflexivization. Then **he**$_3$ combines as follows with this IV phrase.

$$F_3(\langle \textbf{give a woman who loves him}_3 \textbf{ a picture of him}_3, \mathscr{T}_4\rangle, \textbf{he}_3)$$
$$= \textbf{he}_3 \textbf{ gives a woman who loves him}_3 \textbf{ a picture of him}_3\textbf{self}$$

As usual, I've left out one complication in the statement of Rule 3. It can involve variable binding. I'll illustrate the role of variable binding in the rule with two examples. In both these cases the variable **he**$_2$ is bound to the term **John**.

$$F_3(\langle \textbf{be such that}_2[\textbf{his}_2 \textbf{ wife believes that he}_4 \textbf{ shaves him}_2], \mathscr{T}\rangle,$$
$$\textbf{John}) = \textbf{John is such that his wife believes that he}_4 \textbf{ shaves}$$
$$\textbf{him}, \qquad \text{for any } \mathscr{T}$$

$$F_3(\langle \textbf{promise Mary to}_2[\textbf{read his}_2 \textbf{ father a large book}], \mathscr{T}\rangle, \textbf{John})$$
$$= \textbf{John promises Mary to read his father a large book}, \qquad \text{for}$$
$$\text{any } \mathscr{T}$$

Finally, there is a complication with Rule 3 that has to do with a matter to be discussed in Section 9. The preceding examples make it clear that

Rule 3 will ordinarily change the main verb to the present form; but the official statement of the rule merely reads 'the appropriate third-person singular tensed form'. The reason for this wording is that in one case the verb can take a tense other other than the present. When the IV phrase has the form **be** ζ and the first word of ζ is the past participle of a verb (e.g., ζ is **stolen** or **stolen by a man**) the resulting sentence will have PAST tense, as in the following examples.

$$F_3(\langle \textbf{be stolen}, \mathcal{T} \rangle, \textbf{a fish}) = \textbf{a fish was stolen}, \qquad \text{for any } \mathcal{T}$$

$$F_3(\langle \textbf{be stolen by a man}, \mathcal{T} \rangle, \textbf{a fish}) = \textbf{a fish was stolen by a man}, \qquad \text{for any } \mathcal{T}$$

6. MORE SYNTACTIC RULES: ABSTRACTS AND RELATED PHRASES

Our grammar derives a number of constructions—sentences with bound variables, infinitive phrases, and certain relative clauses—from a category AB of ABSTRACTS. AB phrases are obtained from sentences by designating a variable that has occurrences in that sentence. For instance, in the AB phrase **that$_7$[he$_7$ seeks him$_2$]** the variable **he$_7$** has been distinguished. Abstraction is a familiar device in formal logical calculi; most typically it is used in higher order logics or formal set theory to form names of properties or of sets. There are many reasons for introducing abstraction or a similar mechanism into syntactic theories of English, and these are especially compelling within the framework of Montague grammar. Here I will consider only one example, that of relative clauses using **such that**. Other examples, such as infinitive phrases and relative clauses in **who**, yield similar arguments.

Though Montague himself does not do so, it is desirable to treat the clause **such that he shaves him** in

(1)   **John resembles a man such that he shaves him**

as deriving from an ACN phrase—call it for the moment a **such that** clause—that combines with **man** to form a CN phrase that in turn is made into a term by the determiner **a**. Montague's rule accomplishes this by going from sentences, common noun phrases, and numbers to common noun phrases: e.g., from **he$_1$ shaves him$_2$**, **man**, and 2 to **man such that he$_1$ shaves him**. This not only fails to treat **such that** clauses as adjectives, it gives them no categorial status at all.

Montague's mechanism of pronominalization requires us to attach numerical indices to the clauses themselves, once we have decided to treat

such that clauses as adjective phrases. Thus, for instance,

(2)   **such that$_5$[he$_5$ shaves him$_8$]**

will be a **such that** clause. The square brackets are used only for convenience in stating syntactic rules. But what are the reasons for the subscript? These reasons originate in the behavior of anaphoric pronouns in **such that** clauses. Notice, for example, that (1) is two ways ambiguous. Either **he** can be bound to **John** and **him** to **man**, or **he** can be bound to **man** and **him** to **John**. On the other hand,

(3)   **John resembles a man such that he is old**

is unambiguous, at least with respect to anaphora. The pronoun **he** can be bound only to **man**. Furthermore,

(4)   **Bill believes that John resembles a man such that he shaves him**

is FOUR (rather than six) ways ambiguous, the possibilities for binding being as follows.

Bill	John	man
he		him
him		he
	he	him
	him	he

Finally,

(5)   **Bill tells his father that John resembles a man such that he shaves him**

is 6 (rather than 12) ways ambiguous, assuming that **his** is bound to **Bill**. The possibilities here are as follows.

Bill	his father	John	man
he			him
him			he
	he		him
	him		he
		he	him
		him	he

These data are explained if we assume that **such that** clauses have the form exemplified by (2). The subscript following **that** indicates which variable must be bound by **man** when Rule 7 is applied. The difference between

(2) and

(6)   **such that$_8$[he$_5$ shaves him$_8$]**

is illustrated by the following instance of F_7.

F_7(such that$_5$[he$_5$ shaves him$_8$], man) = man such that he shaves him$_8$

F_7(such that$_8$[he$_5$ shaves him$_8$], man) = man such that he$_5$ shaves him

The sense of (1) in which **he** is bound to **John and him** to **man** will be generated by a **such that** clause like (2). The following analysis (which involves some rules not yet discussed) illustrates how this takes place.

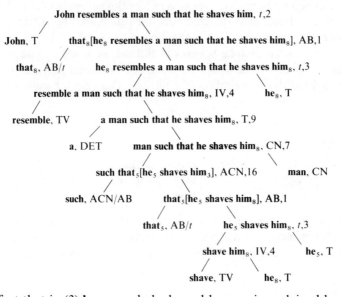

The fact that in (3) **he** can only be bound by **man** is explained by noting that the relative clause must derive from a **such that** clause containing only one variable, say **he$_3$**. (The index of the variable is immaterial and can be chosen arbitrarily.) Then the clause will have the form

(7)   **such that$_i$[he$_3$ is old]**.

A restriction in the syntactic rule for making abstracts will ensure that in (7) i must be 3; we cannot form expressions, like **such that$_9$ [he$_3$ is old]**, that involve vacuous binding of variables. Thus (7) is in fact

(8)   **such that$_3$[he$_3$ is old]**.

But then **man** must bind $\mathbf{he}_3$ when Rule 7 combines it with (8), so there is no possible way of constructing an analysis of

(9) $\mathbf{he}_0$ **resembles a man such that** $\mathbf{he}_0$ **is old**.

And if (9) cannot be generated as a sentence, neither can (3).

The foregoing was only a sketch, designed to indicate the considerations that made me attach subscripts to **such that**, **to**, and **who**. (In a larger fragment, indices might attach to other expressions: the determiner **another**, for instance.) The category of abstracts serves to unify all these cases by providing a single mechanism for designating a variable occurring in a clause. If the expression **that** were omitted from abstracts, they would be formed from sentences by prefixing a number to the result of enclosing the sentence in square brackets. This is very like the customary logical notation for abstracts. I included the **that** because this made the rule for forming **such that** clauses especially elegant, and because there is other evidence (constructions such as **John believes of Bill that he is old** and $\mathbf{he}_8$ **is so large that Mary expects to find him**$_8$, for instance) indicating that **that** is an AB/t phrase in English, as well as a T/t phrase. The rule for constructing abstracts is as follows.

RULE 1:

$$F_1(\alpha, \beta) = \alpha\,[\beta],$$ provided that some variable $\mathbf{he}_i$, $\mathbf{him}_i$ or $\mathbf{his}_i$ occurs in β, where α has the form $\mathbf{that}_i$

The restriction on F_1 blocks, for instance, the formation of a CN phrase **man such that every woman loves a man**. And as noted earlier, it figures in predicting the correct number of ambiguities of (1), (3), (4), and (5).

EXAMPLES:

$F_1(\mathbf{that}_2, \mathbf{he}_5$ **seeks his**$_2$ **father**$) = \mathbf{that}_2[\mathbf{he}_5$ **seeks his**$_2$ **father**$]$

$F_1(\mathbf{that}_6,$ **a man who believes that** $\mathbf{he}_6$ **seeks him finds him**$_6)$
        $= \mathbf{that}_6[$**a man who believes that** $\mathbf{he}_6$ **seeks him finds him**$_6]$

$F_1(\mathbf{that}_4, \mathbf{he}_1$ **gives him**$_2$ **him**$_6)$ is undefined

Since the formation of infinitives is much simpler than that of relative clauses, I'll discuss Rule 11 before Rule 16. An infinitive can't be formed from just any abstract: $\mathbf{that}_1[\mathbf{he}_1$ **seeks a unicorn**$]$ yields $\mathbf{to}_1[$**seek a unicorn**$]$, but **that₁[a unicorn seeks him₁]** can't be permitted to yield an INF. (Note: In the fragment of this paper, neither **that₁[he₁ is sought by a unicorn]** nor the corresponding INF, **to₁[be sought by a unicorn]**, can be formed. An AB phrase **that₁[he₁ was sought by a unicorn]** is generable in the fragment, but it does not give rise to INF phrases; see Section 9 for further discussion of this matter.)

In the present fragment, which lacks sentences like **he₁ might go** and **he₁ goes and Mary seeks him₁**, we can describe the abstracts that yield an INF as having the form **that$_i$[he$_i$ ζ]**. In a more comprehensive fragment, the description would be more complicated.

In building an infinitive the form of the main verb is changed; **is** becomes **be**, **seeks** becomes **seek**. Again, our fragment permits a simple description of the main verb of a sentence having the form **he$_i$** β. It's the first basic verb (i.e. the first basic IV, TV, TTV, IV/INF, TV/INF, (IV/INF)/T, or IV/ACN phrase) to occur in β. Thus, **gives** is the main verb of **he₁ gives a man who he₂ seeks a book** and **forces** is the main verb of **he₈ forces him₅ to go.**

RULE 11:

$$F_{11}(\alpha, \textbf{that}_i[\textbf{he}_i\ \beta]) = \alpha_i\ [\beta'], \quad \text{where } \beta' \text{ is the result of replacing}$$
the first basic verb to occur in β
by its corresponding infinite form

EXAMPLES:

$$F_{11}(\textbf{to}, \textbf{that}_1[\textbf{he}_1\ \textbf{shaves him}_1\textbf{self}]) = \textbf{to}_1[\textbf{shave him}_1\textbf{self}]$$

$$F_{11}(\textbf{to}, \textbf{that}_5[\textbf{he}_5\ \textbf{is stolen}]) = \textbf{to}_5[\textbf{be stolen}]$$

Before proceeding to relative clauses, I should add that I don't believe that Rule 11 would take the preceding form in a fragment giving tense its proper place. In the fragment of this paper verbs are given a finite form (usually the present) by Rule 3, the subject–predicate rule; but this is merely a simplified and not very satisfactory way of making the sentences produced by Rule 3 appear natural.

I would prefer to classify tenses in a category t/t (not, however, the same category as that of sentence-modifying adverbs such as 'almost') and to think of them as binding a temporal variable in the main verb of the sentence to which they apply. This binding would give rise to finite forms. The formation of infinitives would also bind this variable by abstracting it; hence, Rule 11 could not apply to sentences whose main verb was finite, for much the same reason that Rule 1 cannot combine **that**$_i$ with a sentence not containing an i variable. Such a theory would give rise to "sentences" like **John be old**—or perhaps **John be$_t$ old**—but these can be classified with "sentences" like **he$_4$ is old** that contain free variables.

I believe that this approach can be combined with an account of negation and auxiliaries, and that the resulting theory would yield a much more natural treatment of Rule 11. But this is beyond the scope of the present paper.

The following discussion of relative clause formation is rather complicated and tedious, and many readers may wish to go directly to the next section.

There are only two ACN/AB phrases in this fragment, **such** and **who**. **Such** is merely written to the left of an AB phrase to form an ACN phrase. **Who**, however, involves some alteration of the AB phrase that it modifies; the first occurrence of the designated variable of the AB phrase is deleted. Thus, **who$_3$[shaves him$_3$self]** contrasts with **such that$_3$[he$_3$ shaves him$_3$self]**. Also, **who** will assume different forms, according as the first occurrence of the designated variable in the AB phrase has the form **he$_i$**, **him$_i$**, or **his$_i$**. (In this fragment an occurrence of a reflexive form of a variable in an AB phrase cannot precede all other forms of that variable in that phrase.) In the first case, **who** is unaltered, resulting in constructions such as **who$_5$[is old]**. In the second case, **who** may remain unaltered or change to **whom**; we have both **who$_2$[John loves]** and **whom$_2$[John loves]**. In the third case, **who** changes to **whose**. Here there is a further distortion of the AB phrase; we have **whose$_6$[father John seeks]**, not **whose$_6$[John seeks father]**. To characterize the reshuffling that accompanies the placement of **whose**, we must appeal to the analysis of the AB phrase modified by **who**. I won't try to define the relevant notion, that of the expression MODIFIED BY an occurrence of **his$_i$** in an analyzed AB phrase, but will give two examples.

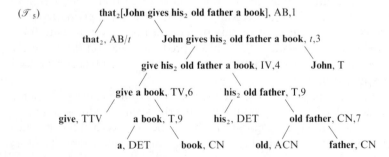

In this analysis, the occurrence of **his$_2$** in the topmost phrase modifies **old father**. What makes it so is the fact that these trace down to a use of

Rule 9 in which **his$_2$** combines with **old father**. The following is a more complicated example.

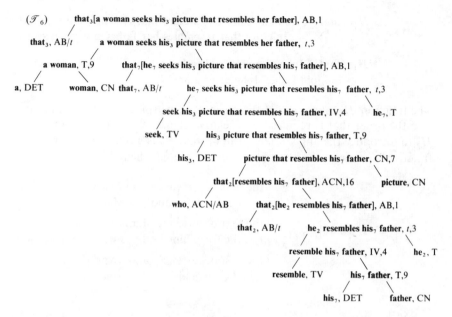

According to $\mathcal{T}_6$ the occurrence of **his$_3$** in its topmost phrase modifies **picture that resembles her father**. This example shows that the expression modified by an occurrence of **his$_i$** need not be a phrase. (The expression **picture that resembles her father** isn't a phrase because it contains the bound pronominal form **her**.)

To simplify the statement of Rule 16, I'll break it down into components and introduce some auxiliary relations H_1 and H_2.

$$H_1(\langle\textbf{that}_i[\beta],\mathcal{T}\rangle) = \begin{cases} i[\beta'], \text{ where } \beta' \text{ is the result of deleting} \\ \text{the first occurrence of an } i \text{ variable in} \\ \beta, \text{ provided that this first occurrence has} \\ \text{the form } \textbf{he}_i \text{ or } \textbf{him}_i \\[6pt] i[\beta_2\beta_1\beta_3], \text{ where } \beta \text{ is } \beta_1\textbf{his}_i\beta_2\beta_3, \, \beta_1 \text{ is} \\ \text{free of } i \text{ variables, and } \beta_2 \text{ is the expres-} \\ \text{sion modified by this occurrence of } \textbf{his}_i \\ \text{according to } \mathcal{T} \end{cases}$$

EXAMPLES:

$$H_1(\langle\textbf{that}_3[\textbf{Mary loves him}_3],\mathcal{T}\rangle) = \;_3[\textbf{Mary loves}], \quad \text{for any } \mathcal{T}$$

$H_1(\langle \text{that}_5[\text{he}_5 \text{ believes that he}_2 \text{ seeks him}_5], \mathscr{T}\rangle)$
$\quad = \,_5[\text{believes that he}_2 \text{ seeks him}_5], \qquad$ for any $\mathscr{T}$

$H_1(\langle \text{that}_3[\text{a woman seeks his}_3 \text{ picture that resembles her father}],$
$\quad \mathscr{T}_6\rangle) = \,_3[\text{picture that resembles her father a woman seeks}]$

$H_1(\langle \text{that }_2[\text{John gives his}_2 \text{ old father a book}], \mathscr{T}_5\rangle)$
$\quad = \,_2[\text{old father John gives a book}]$

The function H_1 takes care of the business of warping the abstract around into the order that is required in a relative clause. We also need a relation H_2 to introduce the appropriate form of **who**. H_2 is a relation rather than a function because of the alternative forms **who** and **whom**.

$$H_2(\text{that}_i[\beta], \gamma) \text{ iff} \begin{cases} \text{the first occurrence of an } i \text{ variable in } \beta \\ \text{has the form } \textbf{he}_i \text{ and } \gamma \text{ is } \textbf{who, or} \\ \text{the first occurrence of an } i \text{ variable in } \beta \\ \text{has the form } \textbf{him}_i \text{ and } \gamma \text{ is } \textbf{who} \text{ or } \textbf{whom, or} \\ \text{the first occurrence of an } i \text{ variable in } \beta \\ \text{has the form } \textbf{his}_i \text{ and } \gamma \text{ is } \textbf{whose} \end{cases}$$

EXAMPLES:

$\quad H_2(\text{that}_5[\text{he}_5 \text{ walks}], \textbf{who})$

$\quad H_2(\text{that}_0[\text{John loves him}_0], \textbf{who})$

$\quad H_2(\text{that}_0[\text{John loves him}_0], \textbf{whom})$

$\quad H_2(\text{that}_7[\text{John steals his}_7 \text{ picture}], \textbf{whose})$

Finally, we state Rule 16.

RULE 16:

$$F_{16}(\alpha, \langle \text{that}_i[\beta], \mathscr{T}\rangle, \gamma) \text{ iff} \begin{cases} \gamma \text{ is } \alpha \textbf{ that}_i[\beta], \text{ provided that } \alpha \text{ is } \textbf{such} \\ \text{for some } \alpha' \text{ such that } H_2(\text{that}_i[\beta], \alpha'), \\ \gamma \text{ is } \alpha' \text{ } H_1(\langle \text{that}_i[\beta], \mathscr{T}\rangle), \text{ provided} \\ \text{that } \alpha \text{ is } \textbf{who} \end{cases}$$

EXAMPLES:

$\quad F_{16}(\textbf{such}, \langle \text{that}_0[\text{he}_0 \text{ shaves him}_0\text{self}], \mathscr{T}\rangle, \textbf{such that}_0[\text{he}_0 \text{ shaves}$
$\quad \text{him}_0\text{self}]), \qquad$ for any $\mathscr{T}$

F_{16}(**who**, $\langle$**that$_2$[he$_2$ shaves him$_2$self]**, $\mathcal{T}\rangle$, **who$_2$[shaves him$_2$self]**),
for any $\mathcal{T}$

F_{16}(**who**, $\langle$**that$_6$[a man seeks him$_6$]**, $\mathcal{T}\rangle$, **who$_6$[a man seeks]**),
for any $\mathcal{T}$

F_{16}(**who**, $\langle$**that$_6$[a man seeks him$_6$]**, $\mathcal{T}\rangle$, **whom$_6$[a man seeks]**),
for any $\mathcal{T}$

F_{16}(**who**, $\langle$**that$_2$[John gives his$_2$ old father a book]**, $\mathcal{T}_6\rangle$,
whose$_2$[old father John gives a book])

F_{16}(**who**, $\langle$**that$_3$[a woman seeks his$_3$ picture that resembles her father]**, $\mathcal{T}_6\rangle$, **whose$_3$[picture that resembles her father a woman seeks]**)

The rules just described take no account of Ross constraints and so generate CN phrases such as **woman whom Mary seeks a man who loves**. But Rodman's paper (in the volume) develops a mechanism for incorporating these constraints within Montague grammar, and this mechanism could easily be adapted to the grammar of the present fragment.

I would add, though, that Rodman's restrictions are not sufficient to account for all cases in which the quantifier scope ambiguities allowed by a fragment seem to exceed those that can in fact be associated with a sentence. For instance, **a woman persuaded Mary to love every man** does not seem to have a reading synonymous with **every man is such that there is a woman who persuaded Mary to love him**. And yet **I know a man who a woman persuaded Mary to love** is grammatical. In this case, uncertainty about the data seems to be as great as the problem of devising a theory that will explain them. I suspect that it will be necessary to find more sophisticated ways of judging and interpreting data concerning scope ambiguity before much progress can be made in this area.

7. SYNTACTIC RULES: VARIABLE BINDING

Rule 2, the rule of quantification, is one of the most important sources of variable binding. In this rule, for instance, **a unicorn** combines with **that$_0$[John wants his$_0$ mother to give him$_0$ a fish]** to form **John wants a unicorn's mother to give it a fish**, and **his$_2$ mother** with **that$_5$[his$_5$ father tries to shave him$_5$]** to form **his$_2$ mother's father tries to shave her**.

When an abstract **that$_i$[β]** is quantified by a term α, then, the result is produced by replacing the leftmost i variable in β by an occurrence of α (or by a possessive form of α if this occurrence has the form **his$_i$**), and the remaining occurrences of i variables in β by

$$\begin{Bmatrix} \textbf{he} \\ \textbf{she} \\ \textbf{it} \end{Bmatrix}$$

according as the gender of α is

$$\begin{Bmatrix} \text{masculine} \\ \text{feminine} \\ \text{neuter} \end{Bmatrix}.$$

The gender of α (which may well be a complex phrase) is determined by the gender of the leftmost basic term or basic common noun to occur in α. We assume that our lexicon gives us the gender of each basic term and each basic common noun.

With J. McCawley, I feel that this assumption is unrealistic. In a more advanced semiotic theory I would expect the lexicon to assign gender only to some nouns, and certainly not to proper names or to common nouns like **neighbor** and **person**. But in the present fragment I assume for simplicity that each basic noun takes a unique gender.

There is some doubt in my mind over which terms have possessive forms. Certainly **John, a man, an old man**, and even **a picture of John** do. Perhaps even **a man who is old** does. But what about **a man who believes that his mother forces a woman to give her father a stolen fish**? I'm undecided as to whether a possessive form of this is bad grammar or bad style. But in any event, the question seems to raise no very significant theoretical issue. Whatever decision one makes can be built into Rule 2, once the decision has been stated in general form.

Variables are terms, and so far we have given no examples to show what happens when Rule 2 combines a variable with an abstract. Nor is this case covered by the sketch we gave of the rule, since variables are inherently without gender. Montague's rule of quantification yields the result of substituting $\textbf{he}_j$ for $\textbf{he}_i$ in β, when it combines $\textbf{he}_j$ with an open sentence β, relative to the variable $\textbf{he}_i$. According to this rule, $\textbf{he}_2$ would combine with $\textbf{that}_0[\textbf{he}_0 \textbf{ goes}]$ to produce $\textbf{he}_2 \textbf{ goes}$, and with $\textbf{that}_6[\textbf{he}_2 \textbf{ seeks him}_6]$ to form $\textbf{he}_2 \textbf{ seeks him}_2$.

In Montague's fragments this rule causes no difficulties that I know of. But when reflexive forms are present it can make trouble. In fact, in the second of the two preceding examples it produced the unwanted expression $\textbf{he}_2 \textbf{ seeks him}_2$, in which the reflexive marker is missing from $\textbf{him}_2$. To avoid such miscarriages I'll introduce a prohibition that is reminiscent of restrictions on "variable collision" in proof theory: A variable $\textbf{he}_j$ can quantify an abstract $\textbf{that}_i[\beta]$ only if there are no occurrences of j variables in β. This restriction works well, as far as I can see, but at present I'm a little uneasy because I have not worked out its ground. I would like to find independent, theoretical reasons for introducing it.

RULE 2:

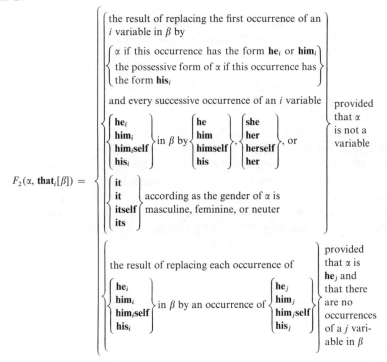

(Note: $F_2(\alpha, \textbf{that}_i[\beta])$ is undefined if α is $\textbf{he}_j$ and there are no occurrences of a j variable in β.)

EXAMPLES:

$F_2(\text{every man, } \textbf{that}_5[\textbf{he}_5 \text{ believes that } \textbf{he}_5 \text{ shaves } \textbf{him}_5\textbf{self}])$
= every man believes that he shaves himself

$F_2(\text{every woman, } \textbf{that}_5[\textbf{he}_5 \text{ believes that } \textbf{he}_5 \text{ shaves } \textbf{him}_5\textbf{self}])$
= every woman believes that she shaves herself

$F_2(\text{every unicorn, } \textbf{that}_5[\textbf{he}_5 \text{ believes that } \textbf{he}_5 \text{ shaves } \textbf{him}_5\textbf{self}])$
= every unicorn believes that it shaves itself

$F_2(\text{every woman, } \textbf{that}_3[\textbf{his}_3 \text{ father believes that he resembles a fish}])$ = every woman's father believes that he resembles a fish

$F_2(\textbf{his}_2 \text{ picture, } \textbf{that}_3[\textbf{he}_3 \text{ was stolen by } \textbf{his}_3 \text{ owner's wife}])$
= his_2 picture was stolen by its owner's wife

$$F_2(\mathbf{he_4}, \mathbf{that_8}[\mathbf{he_8}\ \mathbf{forces\ him_2\ to\ give\ him_8\ him_6}])$$
$$= \mathbf{he_4\ forces\ him_2\ to\ give\ him_4\ him_6}$$

$$F_2(\mathbf{he_4}, \mathbf{that_8}[\mathbf{he_8}\ \mathbf{forces\ him_2\ to\ give\ him_8\ him_4}) \qquad \text{is undefined}$$

I explained earlier that our grammatical mechanism requires us to build variable binding into many syntactic rules. Only syntactic rules that combine a substantive (i.e., a term or a common noun phrase) with other expressions can involve variable binding. In our fragment, among these rules only 2, 3, 4, and 7 actually do so. In general, variable binding involves the erasing of brackets, dropping of subscripts, and introduction of gender. I'll illustrate by discussing Rule 3.

Variable binding occurs in Rule 3 when an IV phrase such as **try to₉[shave him₉self]** combines with a term such as **Mary** to form **Mary tries to shave herself**, or when **be such that₅[he₅ resembles him₂]** combines with **his₈ mother** to produce **his₈ mother is such that she resembles him₂**. This mechanism is added to the statement we gave of Rule 3 on p. 87 by adding to the definition of F_3 a condition that in case α is not a variable and β contains a part having the form $_i[\gamma]$, this part of β must be replaced by γ', where γ' results from γ by replacing each occurrence of a form

$$\left\{\begin{array}{l} \mathbf{he_i} \\ \mathbf{him_i} \\ \mathbf{him_iself} \\ \mathbf{his_i} \end{array}\right\}$$

in γ by

$$\left\{\begin{array}{l} \mathbf{he} \\ \mathbf{him} \\ \mathbf{himself} \\ \mathbf{his} \end{array}\right\}, \quad \left\{\begin{array}{l} \mathbf{she} \\ \mathbf{her} \\ \mathbf{herself} \\ \mathbf{her} \end{array}\right\}, \quad \text{or} \quad \left\{\begin{array}{l} \mathbf{it} \\ \mathbf{it} \\ \mathbf{itself} \\ \mathbf{its} \end{array}\right\},$$

according as the gender of α is masculine, feminine, or neuter. In case α is a variable **he$_j$** and β contains a part having the form $_i[\gamma]$ such that no j variables occur in γ, this part must be replaced by γ', where γ' results by replacing all occurrences of i variables in γ by occurrences of the corresponding j variable.

EXAMPLES:

$$F_3(\langle \mathbf{try\ to_1[go]}, \mathscr{T} \rangle, \mathbf{John}) = \mathbf{John\ tries\ to\ go}, \qquad \text{for any } \mathscr{T}$$

$$F_3(\langle \mathbf{try\ to_3[read\ him_3self\ a\ book]}, \mathscr{T} \rangle, \mathbf{Mary})$$
$$= \mathbf{Mary\ tries\ to\ read\ herself\ a\ book}, \qquad \text{for any } \mathscr{T}$$

$F_3(\langle$**promise him$_7$ to$_6$[persuade him$_2$ to give him$_6$ his$_2$ book],**
$\mathscr{T}\rangle$, he$_5$) = he$_5$ promises him$_2$ to give him$_5$ his$_2$ book,
for any $\mathscr{T}$

$F_3(\langle$**try to$_9$[find him$_4$], $\mathscr{T}\rangle$, he$_4$)**   is undefined, for any $\mathscr{T}$

Reflexivization and variable binding can occur simultaneously in Rule 3. For example, let $\mathscr{T}_7$ be the following analysis of **promise him$_8$ to$_6$[find his$_6$ mother]**.

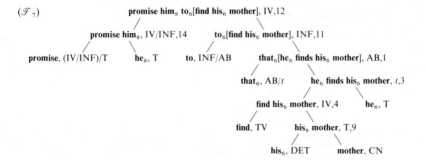

$(\mathscr{T}_7)$

Then $F_3(\langle$**promise him$_8$ to$_6$[find his$_6$ mother], $\mathscr{T}_7\rangle$, he$_8$) = he$_8$ promises him$_8$self to find his$_8$ mother.**

MORE EXAMPLES:

$F_3(\langle$**is such that$_4$[every woman loves him$_4$], $\mathscr{T}\rangle$, every unicorn)**
= every unicorn is such that every woman loves it,
for any $\mathscr{T}$

$F_3(\langle$**is who$_5$[John seeks], $\mathscr{T}\rangle$, Mary) = Mary is who John seeks**

When Rule 3 links an IV phrase requiring variable binding (say, **try to$_3$[shave him$_3$self]**) with a variable (say, **he$_6$**) there is a difference in the way in which the indices in **to$_3$** and **him$_3$self** are treated. The former is removed, the latter is changed to 6. The result is **he$_6$ tries to shave him$_6$self**, not **he$_6$ tries to$_6$ shave him$_6$self**.

This asymmetry is not arbitrary but reflects a difference in function between the indices attached to pronominal forms and those attached to particles like **to**. The latter don't mark "coreference" but serve to distinguish a particular variable in the bracketed expression following the particle, and to show that when the expression in which they occur combines with a substantive, this substantive must interact with that variable and bind it.

Even if the substantive is itself a variable, the indices on particles must be removed as a sign that this binding has occurred.

8. MORE SYNTACTIC RULES: VERBS TAKING
INFINITIVE COMPLEMENTS

First, consider a phrase like **try to$_1$[go]**. It is natural to treat this as an IV phrase. Rule 3 will then yield sentences such as **John tries to go**. **Try**, then, must be classified as an IV/INF phrase, since it combines with INF phrases to form IV phrases. Rule 12 couldn't be simpler.

RULE 12:

$$F_{12}(\alpha, \beta) = \alpha \; \beta$$

EXAMPLES:

$F_{12}($**hope, to$_1$[shave him$_1$self]**$) = $ **hope to$_1$[shave him$_1$self]**

$F_{12}($**expect, to$_1$[be asked to find him$_2$]**
$ = $ **expect to$_1$[be asked to find him$_2$]**

$F_{12}($**promise Mary, to$_3$[find his$_3$ father]**$)$
$ = $ **promise Mary to$_3$[find his$_3$ father]**

Now, take a phrase like **force him$_5$ to go**. (Or should it, perhaps, be **force him$_5$ to$_3$[go]**? I can't choose either of these forms without prejudicing the question I want to discuss, so I'll prejudice it and pick the former.) The syntactic role of **force** must be to combine a T phrase with an INF phrase to form an IV phrase. (Thus, **he$_5$** combines with **to$_1$[go]** to make **force him$_5$ to go**.) This leaves two category indices that could be associated with **force**: (IV/INF)/T or (IV/T)/INF. (Actually there is a third possible index, (IV//T)/INF. I'll discuss this alternative later in connection with participles.) An (IV/INF)/T phrase would take terms into phrases of the same kind as **try**. An (IV/T)/INF phrase would take infinitives into IV/T phrases—that is, into TV phrases.

At first, it may seem that there is little difference between these choices, but this is not so; it affects the way in which INF phrases will be bound in constructions containing the verb **force**. To illustrate this, suppose that α is classified as an (IV/INF)/T phrase and β as a TV/INF phrase. Then we have the following contrasting patterns.

(10)
α **Mary to$_3$[shave him$_3$self], IV,12

α **Mary, IV/INF**   **to$_3$[shave him$_3$self], INF**

α, (IV/INF)/T   **Mary, T**

(11)
β **Mary to shave herself, IV**

β **to$_3$[shave him$_3$self], TV**   **Mary, T**

β, TV/INF   **to$_3$[shave him$_3$self], INF**

In pattern (11), the infinitive phrase has been bound to the term **Mary**; in (10), it has not. Clearly, **force** should conform to the second pattern. This can be seen on semantic grounds: If Bill forces Mary to go it is Mary, not Bill, who is made to go. But there are examples of phrases in English conforming to the other pattern; **promise** is the most striking of these. If Bill promises Mary to go, it is Bill who is obligated to go, not Mary. (Though **promise** is exceptional, it is not the only such verb in English; consider **Bill knows Mary better than to trust her**.) For some speakers, at least, **ask** exhibits syntactic ambiguity between pattern (10) and (11): **John asks his mother to go** is ambiguous as to whether John is asking to go or his mother is being asked to go. Thus, both **John asks his mother to shave him** and **John asks his mother to shave himself** are grammatical. These data are the rationale of the classification of such verbs that is given in the table of categories.

The syntactic rules for TV/INF and for (IV/INF)/T phrases are easily stated.

RULE 13:

$$F_{13}(\alpha, \beta) = \alpha\ \beta$$

RULE 14:

$$F_{14}(\alpha, \beta) = \begin{cases} \alpha\ \beta & \text{if } \beta \text{ is not a variable} \\ \alpha\ \textbf{him}_i & \text{if } \beta \text{ is } \textbf{he}_i \end{cases}$$

EXAMPLES:

$$F_{13}(\textbf{force}, \textbf{to}_7[\textbf{go}]) = \textbf{force to}_7[\textbf{go}]$$

$$F_{14}(\textbf{promise, a woman}) = \textbf{promise a woman}$$

$$F_{13}(\textbf{ask, to}_6[\textbf{shave him}_6\textbf{self}]) = \textbf{ask to}_6[\textbf{shave him}_6\textbf{self}]$$

$$F_{14}(\textbf{ask, he}_6) = \textbf{ask him}_6$$

Together with the other syntactic rules of the fragment, especially Rule 3, which incorporates the mechanism of reflexivization, this account of **force** and **promise** generates the desired patterns of reflexivization in infinitive phrases. The sentences generated by the fragment accord, for instance, with the following data.

(12)   **a woman forces a man to shave** $\left\{\begin{array}{l}\textbf{*him}\\ \textbf{her}\\ \textbf{himself}\\ \textbf{*herself}\end{array}\right\}$

(13)   **a woman promises a man to shave** $\left\{\begin{array}{l}\textbf{him}\\ \textbf{*her}\\ \textbf{*himself}\\ \textbf{herself}\end{array}\right\}$

As an example, I will adumbrate a proof that **a woman forces a man to shave him** is not generated as a sentence in the fragment. The proof is not complete because its various steps presuppose a number of lemmas concerning the way in which certain kinds of phrases must be generated in the fragment, if they are generable at all.

Suppose that **a woman forces a man to shave him** were a sentence. Then **him** must be bound to **a man**, so **a woman forces him**$_1$ **to shave him**$_1$ would be a sentence. But then **force him**$_1$ **to shave him**$_1$ would be an IV phrase. This phrase must come by Rule 4 from a TV phrase **force to**$_i$[**shave him**$_j$] and a term **he**$_1$, where either (*a*) $j = i$, or else (*b*) $j \neq i$ and $i = 1$. The second possibility is ruled out by restrictions on variable binding, since there would then be an occurrence of a 1 variable in the bound phrase. Therefore **to**$_i$[**shave him**$_i$] must be an INF phrase for some i. But then **he**$_i$ **shaves him**$_i$ would be a sentence. And this is impossible, since it would have to come from **shave him**$_i$ and **he**$_i$ by Rule 3. This rule, however, yields the form **he**$_i$ **shaves him**$_i$**self**, where the object has been reflexivized. It follows that **a woman forces a man to shave him** is not a sentence.

9. MORE SYNTACTIC RULES: THE COPULA AND PARTICIPLES

The verb **be** is treated as an IV/ACN phrase in the fragment. This gives IV phrases such as **be old** and **be such that**$_8$[**every woman who loves him**$_8$

expects him$_8$ to love her]. Thus, Rule 3 in turn generates sentences like **a large unicorn is old** and **John is such that every woman who loves him expects him to love her**.

RULE 17:

$$F_{17}(\alpha, \beta) = \alpha\,\beta$$

EXAMPLES:

F_{17}(**be, large**) = **be large**

F_{17}(**be, such that$_1$[he$_1$ shaves him$_1$self]**) = **be such that$_1$[he$_1$ shaves him$_1$self]**

F_{17}(**be, who$_3$[Mary seeks]**) = **be who$_3$[Mary seeks]**

The fact that **stolen** functions as an ACN phrase in **stolen picture** suggests that the morpheme **en** should be treated as an ACN/TV. The syntactic rule for ACN/TV phrases, Rule 13, will therefore combine **en** with **steal** to form the ACN phrase **stolen**. Notice that since **force to$_7$[go]** is also a TV phrase according to our grammar, Rule 13 will also issue in phrases like **man forced to go**. It was to obtain this advantage that verbs like **force** were classified as TV/INF phrases rather than (IV//T)/INF phrases.

Of course, there also are participial adjective phrases making reference to an agent, such as **stolen by John** in **picture stolen by John**. These can't be sensibly treated by classifying **by John** as an ACN/ACN phrase, since this would generate undesirable ACN phrases like **picture old by John**. What is worse, this would also have unacceptable semantic consequences. (If 'buy' and 'sell' were in the fragment, **bought** and **sold** would be rendered semantically equivalent by appropriate meaning postulates on **buy** and **sell**. But **bought by John** and **sold by John** aren't semantically equivalent.) Rather, the "agent" must be inserted before the ACN phrase emerges. The preposition **by** should therefore be regarded as an (ACN/TV)/T phrase; it combines with terms to form phrases of the same semantic type as the morpheme **en**. This yields the following analysis of **picture stolen by John**.

picture stolen by John, CN,7
/ \
stolen by John, ACN,18   picture, CN
/ \
by John, ACN/TV,19   steal, TV
/ \
by, (ACN/TV)/T   John, T

The relevant syntactic rules are as follows.

RULE 18:

$$F_{18}(\alpha, \beta) = \begin{cases} \left\{\begin{array}{l} \beta', \text{ where } \beta' \text{ is the result of} \\ \text{replacing the first basic verb} \\ \text{in } \beta \text{ by its past participle} \end{array}\right\} & \begin{array}{l} \text{provided that} \\ \alpha \text{ is } \textbf{en} \end{array} \\ \left\{\begin{array}{l} \beta'', \text{ where } \beta'' \text{ is the result of} \\ \text{replacing the first basic verb} \\ \text{in } \beta \text{ by its past participle and} \\ \text{inserting } \alpha \text{ immediately after} \\ \text{this past participle} \end{array}\right\} & \begin{array}{l} \text{provided that} \\ \alpha \text{ has the form} \\ \textbf{by } \gamma \end{array} \end{cases}$$

EXAMPLES:

$F_{18}(\textbf{en, force to}_5[\textbf{steal a picture}]) = \textbf{forced to}_5[\textbf{steal a picture}]$

$F_{18}(\textbf{by his}_2 \textbf{ uncle, shave}) = \textbf{shaved by his}_2 \textbf{ uncle}$

RULE 19:

$$F_{19}(\alpha, \beta) = \begin{cases} \alpha\,\beta & \text{if } \beta \text{ is not a variable} \\ \alpha\,\textbf{him}_i & \text{if } \beta \text{ is } \textbf{he}_i \end{cases}$$

EXAMPLES:

$F_{19}(\textbf{by, his}_6 \textbf{ unicorn}) = \textbf{by his}_6 \textbf{ unicorn}$

$F_{19}(\textbf{by, he}_2) = \textbf{by him}_2$

As the following analyses show, Rules 18 and 19 can act together to form passive-like sentences.

(14)

an old man was expected to go, $t,3$

be expected to$_4$[go], IV,17   an old man, T,9

be, IV/ACN   expected to$_4$[go], ACN,18   a, DET   old man, CN,7

en, ACN/TV   expect to$_4$[go], TV,13   old, ACN   man, CN

expect, TV/INF   to$_4$[go], INF

to, INF/AB   that$_4$[he$_4$ goes], AB,1

that$_4$, AB/t he$_4$ goes, $t,3$

go, IV   he$_4$, T

(15)

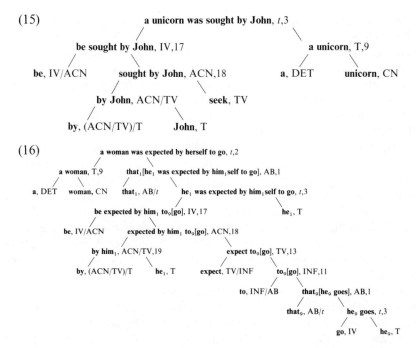

(16)

I thought at first that Rules 18 and 19, in concert with Rules 17 and 3, would precipitate passive constructions without any further fuss. And from a purely syntactic standpoint so they would. From an ACN phrase **stolen by John**, Rule 17 would yield an IV phrase **be stolen by John**, and Rule 3 would then yield **a fish is stolen by John**, if no special clause had been added to this rule concerning the tense of the resulting sentence.

I had an ulterior motive and some independent evidence for arranging things so that Rule 3 will yield **a fish was stolen by John** in this case. First, the ulterior motive: I want to arrange my passive rule so that I can produce a "nonspecific" reading of **a unicorn is expected by John to be found by Mary**, that can be shown semantically equivalent to the corresponding reading of **John expects a unicorn to be found by Mary**. An account of passivization that would generate this passive sentence from an ACN phrase **expected by John to be found by Mary** would render this impossible. (I will not go into the technical reasons for this here.)

Second, the evidence. This has to do with tense—I believe that past tense enters into the attributive uses of the ACN phrases derived by Rule 18. For instance, there is no contradiction in saying 'The car stolen by Bill has been restored to its owner', or 'The report demanded by the Prime Minister is no longer wanted; he has changed his mind', or even 'The lost boy is no longer lost; he was found an hour ago'. Also note that 'man chosen by Mary' agrees much better with 'man who *was* chosen by Mary' than with 'man who *is* chosen by Mary', and 'man forced to shave himself' much better with 'man who *was* forced to shave himself' than with 'man who *is* forced to shave himself'.

My tentative conclusion is that past tense is involved in the semantic interpretation of Rule 18. This doesn't account for all the evidence, but I believe that what remains can be explained by two considerations, both of which can be grounded in independent motivations.

First, there are verb-derived ACNs like 'open'. In general, the semantic relation of such an ACN, β, to the verb γ from which it is derived is this: β expresses a state normally caused by standing in the relation expressed by γ to an "agent." For instance, being open is the state normally caused by opening, and being lost the state normally caused by losing. These ACNs would not be derived by a syntactic rule, but simply listed in the lexicon. (So I am committed to there being a finite number of such ACNs, and in fact I believe there is no such ACN corresponding to TV phrases such as **force to$_6$[go]**.)

A lexical treatment of these verb-derived adjectives is especially welcome in view of the semantic framework that is now available. Intensional logic does not have anything to say about the theory of agency, causality, or normalcy. And the status of these notions in contemporary metaphysics makes it seem desirable to avoid having to explain them within the theory that interprets syntactic rules.

Second, past tense has an indexical element; it does not simply relate to truth at any past time whatever, but to truth at some past time within an interval fixed by the context of utterance. (Partee in her 1973 article has noted this.)

This interval is often understood to be placed close to the time of utterance, and in such cases the use of the past tense suggests that a certain situation has continued, and obtains at the moment of utterance. For instance, if I tell you "I left my wallet at home" without any further qualification, I will give you the impression that I did not go back and get it. So if the past tense enters into the ACNs derived by Rule 18, we can expect similar things to happen with them; and in this way the fact that 'ship expected to arrive' can be used with the same meaning as 'ship that *is* expected to arrive' can be explained without postulating a separate present semantic reading for 'expected to arrive'.

I realize that this discussion is sketchy, informal, and inconclusive. It must remain tentative pending development of an adequate theory of tense and aspect. Nevertheless I regard my conclusion as plausible. As for genuine passives, though I no longer want to use the category ACN/TV to account for them, I would still prefer a categorial rather than a transformational approach. To obtain passives it would only be necessary to generate IV phrases like **be expected to₁[go]** that are not linked by an ACN phrase to the TV phrase from which they are derived.

10. SYNTACTIC RAISING VERSUS SEMANTIC LOWERING

Though this presentation hasn't stressed the matter, it should be evident that the fragment I developed in this paper will provide quite different analyses in many cases where transformational grammar will provide only one derivation, or two derivations differing only with respect to meaning-preserving transformations.

An example that is fundamental to Montague's approach, and will be found in most versions of Montague grammar, is the treatment of sentences like **John loves Mary** as syntactically ambiguous. In the present fragment this sentence has the following two analyses, among others.

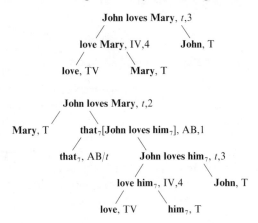

The fact that **John loves Mary** is not perceived as ambiguous is explained by the semantic interpretation: A meaning postulate involving **love** (one that would not apply to **seek**) renders the various analyses of the sentence semantically equivalent.

One of the distinctive, and exciting, things about Montague's approach to natural languages is that in it the semantic component actually performs useful work. In the preceding case it enables us to preserve certain principles regulating the relation between syntactic structure and semantic representation, and at the same time, avoid having to postulate different syntactic categories for **love** and **seek**. (One of these principles is that of the compositionality of semantic interpretation: When a sentence is semantically ambiguous, but this cannot be traced to an ambiguity in any of its lexical constituents, then it is syntactically ambiguous. The other is that when phrases belong to the same syntactic category, their semantic representation will have the same logical type.) Thus, a maneuver in the semantic component allows us to avoid a complication in the syntax.

Reasoning of this sort motivated many of the features of the present fragment, and it differs from other extensions of Montague's fragments in the degree to which this strategy is invoked. One of the most interesting (and controversial) instances concerns constructions that in transformational grammar would involve raising. The present fragment treats **force** and **expect** as syntactic congeners, and the syntactic analyses of (17) and (18) present no structural differences.

(17)   **John forces Mary to find Bill**

(18)   **John expects Mary to find Bill**

One reason why **expect** and **force** are distinguished in transformational syntax is that (18) is synonymous with (20) wheras (17) is not synonymous with (19).

(19)   **John forces Bill to be found by Mary**

(20)   **John expects Bill to be found by Mary**

But both these facts can be explained in purely semantic terms. Here I will do this informally, and with some simplifications. Both **force** and **expect** are interpreted as three-place relations between an entity, an entity, and a property. Sentence (17), for example, is interpreted as saying that John (an entity) and Mary (an entity) stand in a certain relation, say R, to the property of finding Bill. Now, there is no necessity that if the three do stand in the relation R then John, Bill, and the property of being found by Mary will stand in the relation R. In other words, the semantic theory leaves us free to have (17) and (19) nonsynonymous.

By the same token, it leaves us free to have (18) and (20) nonsynonymous; but if we wish we can place a meaning postulate on **expect**, that will make these sentences synonymous. This postulate stipulates that the relation S_1 expressed by **expect** can be characterized by means of a relation, say S_2, between an entity and a proposition. For instance, John, Mary, and the property of finding Bill stand in the relation S_1 if and only if John stands in the relation S_2 to the proposition that Mary will have the property of finding Bill.

Of course, this is only a way of saying that the semantic content of the **expect** taking objects and INF complements reduces to the semantic content of the **expect** taking sentential complements. But the point is, this can be said in the semantic theory. I call this device SEMANTIC LOWERING because a proposition is "lower" on a recognized logical scale than a one-place predicate. In fact, propositions are often treated as zero-place predicates. Many of

Montague's meaning postulates perform various sorts of lowering: They reduce higher semantic values ("higher" along several dimensions, including the predicative hierarchy of type theory and the intensional hierarchy) to lower ones. And these are the postulates that make possible the most striking simplifications in the syntax.

I can't yet claim that this account of raising is superior to the transformational account. In particular, sentences in which the dummy subjects 'there' and 'it' have been raised can only be accomodated by postulating further readings of verbs like **expect**. I am not as reluctant as most transformational grammarians to classify a single word in many syntactic categories, especially when there is an explicable semantic connection between the various readings. But in this case the syntactic rules that would be needed, to the extent that I now understand them, seem unnatural and overcomplicated. So here there is a genuine difficulty.

It comes as a surprise to most transformational grammarians, though, that this seems to be the only difficulty. I hope that even this will be overcome; but whether or not I am successful in doing so, I am encouraged to pursue the line of development marked by this fragment. Montague forged a powerful and elaborate mechanism for employing model-theoretic semantics to simplify the syntax of a semantically based grammar; but he only applied it to a few cases, such as quantification and intensional verbs. We still need to discover exactly what can be done with it.

University of Pittsburgh

APPENDIX

1.

```
              an old old man, T,9
              /            \
        a, DET        old old man, CN,7
                      /           \
                old, ACN        old man, CN,7
                                /        \
                          old, ACN      man, CN
```

2.

```
              picture of a man, CN,7
              /                \
        of a man, ACN,8      picture, CN
        /          \
   of, ACN/T      a man, T,9
                  /      \
              a, DET     man, CN
```

3.

$$
\begin{array}{l}
\textbf{old picture that is large, } CN,7 \\
\quad \diagup \qquad\qquad\qquad\qquad\qquad \diagdown \\
\textbf{who}_3\textbf{[is large], } ACN,16 \qquad\qquad \textbf{old picture, } CN,7 \\
\quad \diagup \qquad\quad \diagdown \qquad\qquad\qquad\qquad \diagup \qquad \diagdown \\
\textbf{who, } ACN/AB \quad \textbf{that}_3\textbf{[he}_3 \textbf{ is large], } AB,1 \quad \textbf{old, } ACN \quad \textbf{picture, } CN \\
\qquad\qquad\qquad \diagup \qquad\qquad \diagdown \\
\qquad\quad \textbf{that}_3\textbf{, } AB/t \qquad \textbf{he}_3 \textbf{ is large, } t,3 \\
\qquad\qquad\qquad\qquad \diagup \qquad\qquad \diagdown \\
\qquad\qquad\qquad \textbf{be large, } IV,4 \qquad \textbf{he}_3\textbf{, } T \\
\qquad\qquad\qquad \diagup \qquad \diagdown \\
\qquad\qquad \textbf{be, } IV/ACN \quad \textbf{large, } ACN
\end{array}
$$

4.

$$
\begin{array}{l}
\textbf{large stolen picture, } CN,7 \\
\quad \diagup \qquad\qquad \diagdown \\
\textbf{large, } ACN \qquad \textbf{stolen picture, } CN,7 \\
\qquad\qquad\qquad \diagup \qquad\qquad \diagdown \\
\qquad\qquad \textbf{stolen, } ACN,18 \qquad \textbf{picture, } CN \\
\qquad\qquad \diagup \qquad\qquad \diagdown \\
\qquad \textbf{en, } ACN/TV \qquad \textbf{steal, } TV
\end{array}
$$

5.

$$
\begin{array}{l}
\qquad \textbf{John finds a man such that he seeks him, } t,2 \\
\qquad \diagup \qquad \diagdown \\
\textbf{John, } T \qquad \textbf{that}_2\textbf{[he}_2 \textbf{ finds a man such that he}_2 \textbf{ seeks him], } AB,1 \\
\qquad\qquad \diagup \qquad\qquad\qquad \diagdown \\
\qquad \textbf{that}_2\textbf{, } AB/t \qquad \textbf{he}_2 \textbf{ finds a man such that he}_2 \textbf{ seeks him, } t,3 \\
\qquad\qquad\qquad\qquad \diagup \qquad\qquad\qquad\qquad\qquad\qquad \diagdown \\
\qquad\qquad \textbf{find a man such that he}_2 \textbf{ seeks him, } IV,4 \qquad \textbf{he}_2\textbf{, } T \\
\qquad\qquad \diagup \qquad\qquad \diagdown \\
\qquad \textbf{find, } TV \qquad \textbf{a man such that he}_2 \textbf{ seeks him, } CN,7 \\
\qquad\qquad\qquad \diagup \qquad\qquad\qquad \diagdown \\
\qquad\qquad \textbf{a, } DET \qquad \textbf{man such that he}_2 \textbf{ seeks him, } CN,7 \\
\qquad\qquad\qquad\qquad \diagup \qquad\qquad\qquad\qquad\qquad \diagdown \\
\qquad \textbf{such that}_5\textbf{[he}_2 \textbf{ seeks him}_5\textbf{], } ACN,16 \qquad \textbf{man, } CN \\
\qquad \diagup \qquad\qquad\qquad \diagdown \\
\textbf{such, } ACN/AB \qquad \textbf{that}_5\textbf{[he}_2 \textbf{ seeks him}_5\textbf{], } AB,1 \\
\qquad\qquad\qquad \diagup \qquad\qquad \diagdown \\
\qquad\qquad \textbf{that}_5\textbf{, } AB/t \qquad \textbf{he}_2 \textbf{ seeks him}_5\textbf{, } t,3 \\
\qquad\qquad\qquad\qquad \diagup \qquad\qquad \diagdown \\
\qquad\qquad\qquad \textbf{seek him}_5\textbf{, } IV,4 \qquad \textbf{he}_2\textbf{, } T \\
\qquad\qquad\qquad \diagup \qquad \diagdown \\
\qquad\qquad \textbf{seek, } TV \qquad \textbf{he}_5\textbf{, } T
\end{array}
$$

6.   John finds a man such that he seeks him, $t,2$
     / \
John, T $that_5[he_5$ finds a man such that he seeks $him_5]$, AB,1
          / \
   $that_5$, AB/t he_5 finds a man such that he seeks him_5, $t,3$
                      / \
            find a man such that he seeks him_5, IV,4 he_5, T
            / \
      find, TV   a man such that he seeks him_5, T,9
                 / \
            a, DET   man such that he seeks him_5, CN,7
                     / \
            such $that_2[he_2$ seeks $him_5]$, ACN,16   man, CN
            / \
      such, ACN/AB $that_2[he_2$ seeks $him_5]$, AB,1
                     / \
                $that_2$, AB/t he_2 seeks him_5, $t,3$
                                   / \
                              seek him_5, IV,4 he_2, T
                              / \
                        seek, TV him_5, T

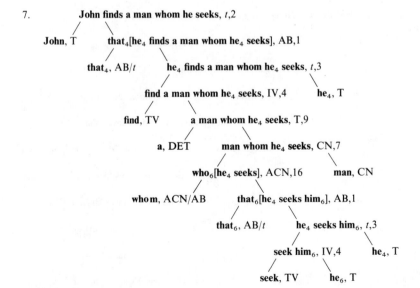

7.   John finds a man whom he seeks, $t,2$
     / \
John, T $that_4[he_4$ finds a man whom he_4 seeks], AB,1
          / \
   $that_4$, AB/t he_4 finds a man whom he_4 seeks, $t,3$
                      / \
            find a man whom he_4 seeks, IV,4 he_4, T
            / \
      find, TV   a man whom he_4 seeks, T,9
                 / \
            a, DET   man whom he_4 seeks, CN,7
                     / \
            $who_6[he_4$ seeks], ACN,16   man, CN
            / \
      whom, ACN/AB $that_6[he_4$ seeks $him_6]$, AB,1
                     / \
                $that_6$, AB/t he_4 seeks him_6, $t,3$
                                   / \
                              seek him_6, IV,4 he_4, T
                              / \
                        seek, TV he_6, T

8.

a man finds a woman whose father shaves him, $t,2$

a man, T   that$_1$[he$_1$ finds a woman whose father shaves him$_1$], AB,1

a, DET   man, CN   that$_1$, AB/t he$_1$ finds a woman whose father shaves him$_1$, $t,3$

find a woman whose father shaves him$_1$, IV,4   he$_1$, T

find, TV   a woman whose father shaves him$_1$, T,

a, DET   woman whose father shaves him$_1$, CN,7

whose$_0$[father shaves him$_1$], ACN,16   woman, CN

who, ACN/AB   that$_0$[his$_0$ father shaves him$_1$], AB,1

that$_0$, AB/t his$_0$ father shaves him$_1$, $t,3$

shave him$_1$, IV,4   his$_0$ father, T

shave, TV   he$_1$, T   his$_0$, DET   father, CN

9.   John tries to believe that Mary loves him, $t,2$

John, T   that$_6$[he$_6$ tries to believe that Mary loves him$_6$], AB,1

that$_6$, AB/t he$_6$ tries to believe that Mary loves him$_6$, $t,3$

try to$_3$[believe that Mary loves him$_3$], IV,12   he$_6$, T

try, IV/INF   to$_3$[believe that Mary loves him$_3$], INF

to, INF/AB   that$_3$[he$_3$ believes that Mary loves him$_3$], AB,1

that$_3$, AB/t he$_3$ believes that Mary loves him$_3$, $t,3$

believe that Mary loves him$_3$, IV,4   he$_3$, T

believe, TV   that Mary loves him$_3$, T,15

that, T/t Mary loves him$_3$, $t,3$

love him$_3$, IV,4   Mary, T

love, TV   he$_3$, T

10.   John expects Bill to try to force Mary to go, *t*,3

        expect Bill to try to force Mary to go, IV,4   John, T

      expect to₁[try to force Mary to go], TV,13   Bill, T

    expect, TV/INF   to₁[try to force Mary to go], INF,11

      to, INF/AB   that₁[he₁ tries to force Mary to go], AB,1

        that₁, AB/*t*   he₁ tries to force Mary to go, *t*,3

   try to force Mary to go, IV,12   he₁, T

  try, IV/INF   to₂[force Mary to go], INF,11

    to, INF/AB   he₂ forces Mary to go, *t*,3

      force Mary to go, IV,4   he₂, T

     force to₃[go], TV,3   Mary, T

   force, TV/INF   to₃[go], INF,11

    to, AB/INF   that₃[he₃ goes], AB,1

     that₃, AB/*t*   he₃ goes, *t*, 3

        go, IV   he₃, T

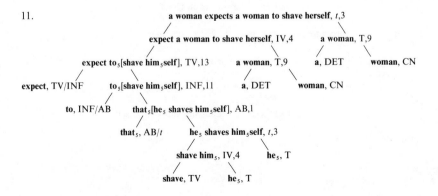

11.   a woman expects a woman to shave herself, *t*,3

     expect a woman to shave herself, IV,4   a woman, T,9

  expect to₅[shave him₅self], TV,13   a woman, T,9   a, DET   woman, CN

expect, TV/INF   to₅[shave him₅self], INF,11   a, DET   woman, CN

   to, INF/AB   that₅[he₅ shaves him₅self], AB,1

    that₅, AB/*t*   he₅ shaves him₅self, *t*,3

      shave him₅, IV,4   he₅, T

      shave, TV   he₅, T

12.

a woman expects a woman to shave her, $t,2$

  a woman, T,9 $that_6[he_6$ expects a woman to shave $him_6]$, AB,1

a, DET   woman, CN $that_6$, AB/t he_6 expects a woman to shave him_6, $t,3$

expect a woman to shave him_6, IV,4 he_6, T

expect $to_2[shave\ him_6]$, TV,13   a woman, T,9

expect, TV/INF $that_2[he_2$ shaves $him_6]$, AB,1   a, DET   woman, CN

$that_2$, AB/t he_2 shaves him_6, $t,3$

shave him_6, IV,4 he_2, T

shave, TV he_6, T

13.

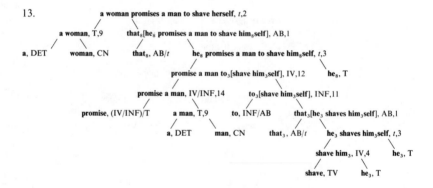

14.

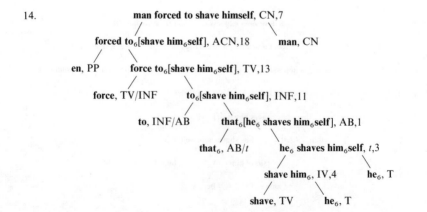

ACKNOWLEDGMENTS

This theory germinated in discussions with Barbara Partee and Robert Stalnaker at a workshop in philosophy of language during the summer of 1971. I am grateful to the Council for Philosophical Studies for sponsoring this workshop. But the theory only emerged in the spring of 1972, when it was presented in talks at the University of Bristol and at Bedford College, of the University of London. Later aspects of my research on this program were supported under NSF Grant GS-40698. And I owe thanks to Allen Hazen for some last-minute revisions.

REFERENCES

Montague, R. The proper treatment of quantification in ordinary English. In J. Hintikka, J. Moravcsik, and P. Suppes (Eds.), *Approaches to Natural Language: Proceedings of the 1970 Stanford Workshop on Grammar and Semantics*. Dordrecht: Riedel, 1973. Pp. 221–242. [Reprinted in R. Thomason (Ed.), *Formal Philosophy: Selected Papers of Richard Montague*. New Haven: Yale Univ. Press, 1974. Pp. 247–270.]

Partee, B. Some structural analogies between tenses and pronouns in English. *Journal of Philosophy*, 1973, **70**, 601–609.

Thomason, R. A semantic theory of sortal incorrectness. *Journal of Philosophical Logic*, 1972, **1**, 209–258.

MICHAEL BENNETT

A VARIATION AND EXTENSION OF A
MONTAGUE FRAGMENT OF ENGLISH

This paper presents and discusses a fragment of English that is a variation and extension of the fragment presented in Montague (1973) (henceforth PTQ). In addition to the syntactic structures originally treated by Montague, this fragment treats adjectival phrases, three-place and other kinds of verbs, the passive voice, sentences involving the dummy subject **it**, and reflexive pronouns. The fragment addresses itself to several issues that cannot be discussed here (see Bennett, 1974). The paper concludes with a discussion of certain related syntactic structures that are not treated in the fragment. It is argued that these structures appear to require syntactic rules that closely resemble some of the standard transformations postulated in recent linguistic theory.

In presenting this fragment I assume an acquaintance with PTQ.

1. THE SYNTAX OF THE FRAGMENT

There are three basic syntactic categories:

    t is the category of declarative sentences.
    CN is the category of common nouns and common noun phrases.
    IV is the category of intransitive verbs and certain other verb phrases.

All of the other syntactic categories are defined in terms of these three. CAT, or the set of CATEGORIES OF THE FRAGMENT, is to be the smallest set X such that (a) t, CN, and IV are in X and (b) whenever A and B are in X, A/B and A//B are also in X.

Besides t, CN, and IV, the following nonbasic syntactic categories are more or less traditional and are exemplified in the fragment:

    T, or the category of terms, is to be t/IV.
    TV, or the category of transitive verbs and certain other verb phrases, is to be IV/T.
    AJ, or the category of adjectives and adjectival phrases, is to be CN/CN.
    IAV, or the category of adverbs and adverbial phrases, is to be IV/IV.

AJP, or the category of adjectival prepositions, is to be AJ/T.

IAVP, or the category of adverbial prepositions, is to be IAV/T.

There are other syntactic categories exemplified in the fragment (since they are not traditional, no special name will be introduced for them):

CN/T is the category of transitive common nouns—phrases that take a term to form a common noun phrase.

TV/T is the category of three-place verbs.

The following syntactic categories are also exemplified in the fragment: IV/t, TV/t, $IV//IV$, $t//IV$, t/t, $(IV//IV)/T$, $(IV/t)/T$, $(t//IV)/T$, $(t/t)/T$, and $((t/t)/T)/T$.

The LETTERS OF THE FRAGMENT are $\mathbf{a}, \mathbf{b}, \ldots, \mathbf{z}$, the blank, (,), #, and *, together with the numerical subscripts $_0, _1, \ldots, _9$. We shall assume that **A** and **a** are the same letter, **B** and **b**, etc. An EXPRESSION OF THE FRAGMENT is any finite concatenation of the letters of the fragment. When two English words are concatenated, they are separated by a blank. For example, **the man** is the finite concatenation $t^\frown h^\frown e^\frown$the blank$^\frown m^\frown a^\frown n$. Subscripts with two or more numerals are assumed to be the finite concatenation of the appropriate numerical subscripts. For example, $_{10}$ is the finite concatenation $_1{}^\frown{}_0$.

By B_A is understood the set of basic expressions for any category A; these sets are characterized as follows:

$B_T = \{$**John, Mary, Bill, Chicago, he$_0$, he$_1$, he$_2$, . . .** $\}$

$B_{CN} = \{$**man, woman, person, god, fish, unicorn, portrait, picture, house, park, conception, story, vision, entity**$\}$

$B_{IV} = \{$**#walk, #talk, #disintegrate, #be**$\}$

$B_{CN/T} = \{$**portrait of, story about, picture of, conception of, vision of**$\}$

$B_{TV} = \{$**#love, #eat, #see, #talk about, #wash, #worship, #build, #find, #form, #be, #have, #seek, #resemble, #avoid, #conceive of**$\}$

$B_{IV/t} = \{$**#believe, #assert, #expect, #prefer, #allege, #wish**$\}$

$B_{TV/T} = \{$**#give, #owe**$\}$

$B_{TV/t} = \{$**#promise, #say**$\}$

$B_{AJ} = \{$**mortal, big, famous, fictional, alleged**$\}$

$B_{IAV} = \{$**rapidly, slowly, voluntarily, almost**$\}$

$B_{IV//IV} = \{$**#try, #wish, #appear, #expect, #prefer, #be eager, #succeed, #fail**$\}$

$B_{t//IV} = \{$**#be easy, #be tough**$\}$

$B_{t/t} = \{$**#appear, #might be, #be true, #be necessary**$\}$

B_{AJP} = {**in, other than**}
B_{IAVP} = {**in, about**}
$B_{(IV//IV)/T}$ = {#**persuade**, #**expect**, #**force**}
$B_{(IV/t)/T}$ = {#**persuade**, #**believe of**}
$B_{(t//IV)/T}$ = {#**be easy**, #**be tough**}
$B_{(t/t)/T}$ = {#**appear**}
B_A = the empty set if A is any category other than those already mentioned

A BASIC EXPRESSION OF THE FRAGMENT is any element of B_A for any category A.

By P_A is understood the set of phrases for any category A. It will be seen that these sets are precisely characterized by the following rules, S1–S35. These rules involve certain auxiliary notions that can be precisely defined in accordance with tradition. The GENDER of an arbitrary member of $B_{CN} \cup B_T$ can be defined by a table, since the relevant set of basic expressions is finite.[1] The INDEFINITE ARTICLE TAKEN by an arbitrary member of $B_{CN} \cup B_{AJ}$ can be defined by a finite table. The rule is roughly that **a** is used before all words beginning with a consonant sound whereas **an** is used before all words beginning with a vowel sound. The THIRD-PERSON SINGULAR SIMPLE PRESENT TENSE FORM of an arbitrary member of $B_{IV} \cup B_{TV} \cup B_{IV/t} \cup B_{TV/T} \cup B_{TV/t} \cup B_{IV//IV} \cup B_{t//IV} \cup B_{t/t} \cup B_{(IV//IV)/T} \cup B_{(IV/t)/T} \cup B_{(t//IV)/T} \cup B_{(t/t)/T}$ can be defined by a finite table. The PAST PARTICIPIAL FORM of an arbitrary member of $B_{TV} \cup B_{IV/t} \cup B_{TV/T} \cup B_{TV/t} \cup B_{(IV//IV)/T} \cup B_{(IV/t)/T}$ can be defined by a finite table.

Syntactic Rules

BASIC RULES

S1. $B_A \subseteq P_A$ for every category A.

S2.   If $\zeta \in P_{CN}$, ζ does not contain an occurrence of $_n$,[2] and $\phi \in P_t$, then $F_{0,n}(\zeta, \phi) \in P_{CN}$, where if a member of B_{CN} occurs in ζ, then

---

[1] It is well known that the notion of the gender of a word is not a purely syntactic one. Sometimes the gender of a word is determined by the context in which it is used. For example, **nurse** might have masculine gender in some contexts but feminine gender in others.

[2] This restriction is designed to rule out unwanted analysis trees (to be explained) such as the following:

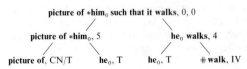

picture of *him₀ such that it walks, 0, 0 → picture of *him₀, 5 / he₀ walks, 4; picture of *him₀, 5 → picture of, CN/T / he₀, T; he₀ walks, 4 → he₀, T / #walk, IV

$F_{0,n}(\zeta, \phi) = \zeta$ **such that** ϕ', and ϕ' comes from ϕ by replacing each occurrence of **he**$_n$, **him**$_n$, or **himself**$_n$ by

$$\begin{Bmatrix} \text{he} \\ \text{she} \\ \text{it} \end{Bmatrix}, \qquad \begin{Bmatrix} \text{him} \\ \text{her} \\ \text{it} \end{Bmatrix}, \qquad \text{or} \qquad \begin{Bmatrix} \text{himself} \\ \text{herself} \\ \text{itself} \end{Bmatrix},$$

respectively, according as the member of B_{CN} that occurs first in ζ is of

$$\begin{Bmatrix} \text{masc.} \\ \text{fem.} \\ \text{neuter} \end{Bmatrix}$$

gender; otherwise $F_{0,n}(\zeta, \phi) = \zeta$ **such that** ϕ.[3]

S3.   If $\zeta \in P_{CN}$, then $F_1(\zeta)$, $F_2(\zeta)$, $F_3(\zeta) \in P_T$, where $F_1(\zeta)$ is **a** ζ or **an** ζ according as the first word in ζ takes **a** or **an**, $F_2(\zeta) = $ **every** ζ, and $F_3(\zeta) = $ **the** ζ.

RULES OF FUNCTIONAL APPLICATION

S4.   If $\alpha \in P_T$ and $\delta \in P_{IV}$, then $F_4(\alpha, \delta) \in P_t$, where $F_4(\alpha, \delta) = \alpha'\delta'$, α' comes from α by deleting all occurrences of $*$, and δ' comes from δ by performing the following operations in order: (*a*) replacing all occurrences of $\#$**not be** by **is not**; (*b*) replacing all remaining occurrences of $\#$**not** by **does not**; (*c*) replacing each remaining occurrence of a word of the form $\#\eta$ or the form $(\#)\eta$ by the third-person singular simple present tense form of $\#\eta$ or $(\#)\eta$, respectively; (*d*) if $\alpha = $ **he**$_n$, replacing all occurrences of $*$**him**$_n$ by **himself**$_n$; (*e*) deleting all parentheses and any remaining occurrences of $*$.

S5.   If $\zeta \in P_{CN/T}$ and $\alpha \in P_T$, then $F_5(\zeta, \alpha) \in P_{CN}$, where (*a*) if $\alpha = $ **he**$_n$, then $F_5(\zeta, \alpha) = \zeta *$**him**$_n$; (*b*) otherwise $F_5(\zeta, \alpha) = \zeta \alpha$.

S6.   If $\delta \in P_{TV}$ and $\alpha \in P_T$, then $F_6(\delta, \alpha) \in P_{IV}$, where (*a*) if either $\delta \in B_{TV}$ or $\delta = \#\eta$ **by**, then (*i*) if $\alpha = $ **he**$_n$, then $F_6(\delta, \alpha) = \delta *$**him**$_n$; (*ii*) otherwise $F_6(\delta, \alpha) = \delta \alpha$; (*b*) otherwise (*i*) if $\alpha = $ **he**$_n$ and δ contains an

[3] A few remarks are in order about the metalanguage in which the syntactic rules are stated. Juxtaposition is serving to indicate concatenation. For example, 'ζ **such that** ϕ' is a metalinguistic abbreviation for '$\zeta \cap$ the blank $\cap$ **such that** $\cap$ the blank $\cap \phi$'. 'F_0,' is to be regarded as denoting a one-place operation that maps the nonnegative integers into two-place structural operations, operations that map ordered pairs of expressions into expressions. Thus the 'n' that appears in '$F_{0,n}$' is a variable ranging over the nonnegative integers. The '$_n$' that appears in '**he**$_n$' is to be regarded as a variable that ranges over certain expressions in the object language: numerical subscripts and finite concatenations thereof. It is intended that in the context of S2, '$_n$' is to be assigned a value that corresponds to the value assigned to 'n' in the natural way.

occurrence of $(*\textbf{him}_n)$, then $F_6(\delta, \alpha) = \delta$ **to himself**$_n$; (ii) if $\alpha = \textbf{he}_n$ and δ does not contain an occurrence of $(*\textbf{him}_n)$, then $F_6(\delta, \alpha) = \delta$ **to** $*\textbf{him}_n$; (iii) if $\alpha \neq \textbf{he}_n$ and δ contains an occurrence of $(*\textbf{him}_n)$, then $F_6(\delta, \alpha) = \delta$ **to** α', where α' comes from α by replacing all occurrences of $*\textbf{him}_n$ by **himself**$_n$; (iv) otherwise $F_6(\delta, \alpha) = \delta$ **to** α.

S7. If $\delta \in P_{IV/t}$ and $\phi \in P_t$, then $F_7(\delta, \phi) \in P_{IV}$, where $F_7(\delta, \phi) = \delta$ **that** ϕ.

S8. If $\delta \in P_{TV/T}$ and $\alpha \in P_T$, then $F_8(\delta, \alpha) \in P_{TV}$, where (a) if $\alpha = \textbf{he}_n$, then $F_8(\delta, \alpha) = \delta\ (*\textbf{him}_n)$; (b) otherwise $F_8(\delta, \alpha) = \delta\ \alpha$.

S9. If $\delta \in P_{TV/t}$ and $\phi \in P_t$, then $F_7(\delta, \phi) \in P_{TV}$.

S10. If $\gamma \in P_{AJ}$ and $\zeta \in P_{CN}$, then $F_9(\gamma, \zeta) \in P_{CN}$, where (a) if γ contains an occurrence of a member of $B_{AJ/T}$, then $F_9(\gamma, \zeta) = \zeta\gamma$; (b) otherwise $F_9(\gamma, \zeta) = \gamma\zeta$.

S11. If $\gamma \in P_{IAV}$ and $\delta \in P_{IV}$, then $F_{10}(\gamma, \delta) \in P_{IV}$, where (a) if γ contains an occurrence of a member of $B_{IAV/T}$, then $F_{10}(\gamma, \delta) = \delta\gamma$; (b) otherwise $F_{10}(\gamma, \delta) = \gamma\delta$.

S12. If $\gamma \in P_{IV//IV}$ and $\delta \in P_{IV}$, then $F_{11}(\gamma, \delta) \in P_{IV}$, where (a) if $\delta = \#\textbf{not}$ η, then $F_{11}(\gamma, \delta) = \gamma$ **not to** η', where η' comes from η by (i) deleting all occurrences of $\#$ and $(\#)$; (ii) if $\gamma = \#v$ and γ contains an occurrence of $(*\textbf{him}_n)$, replacing all occurrences of $*\textbf{him}_n$ in η by **himself**$_n$; (iii) if $\gamma = \#v$, $\gamma \notin B_{IV//IV}$, and γ does not contain an occurrence of $(*\textbf{him}_n)$, replacing all occurrences of $*\textbf{him}_n$ in η by **him**$_n$; and (b) if $\delta \neq \#\textbf{not}$ η, then $F_{11}(\gamma, \delta) = \gamma$ **to** δ', where δ' comes from δ by operations (i)–(iii).

S13. If $\gamma \in P_{t//IV}$ and $\delta \in P_{IV}$, then $F_{12}(\gamma, \delta) \in P_t$, where $F_{12}(\gamma, \delta) = $ **it** γ' **to** δ'; γ' comes from γ by (a) replacing each occurrence of a word of the form $\#\eta$ by the third-person singular simple present tense form of $\#\eta$ and (b) deleting all parentheses and any occurrences of $*$; and δ' comes from δ by performing the following operations in order: (a) if γ contains an occurrence of $(*\textbf{him}_n)$, replacing all occurrences of $*\textbf{him}_n$ in δ by **himself**$_n$ and (b) deleting all parentheses and any occurrences of $\#$, $(\#)$, and $*$.

S14. If $\gamma \in P_{t/t}$ and $\phi \in P_t$, then $F_{13}(\gamma, \phi) \in P_t$, where $F_{13}(\gamma, \phi) = $ **it** γ' **that** ϕ and γ' comes from γ by (a) replacing each occurrence of a word of the form $\#\eta$ by the third-person singular simple present tense form of $\#\eta$ and (b) deleting all parentheses and any occurrences of $*$.

S15. If $\gamma \in P_{AJ/T}$ and $\alpha \in P_T$, then $F_{14}(\gamma, \alpha) \in P_{AJ}$, where (a) if $\alpha = \mathbf{he}_n$, then $F_{14}(\gamma, \alpha) = \gamma \, \mathbf{him}_n$; (b) otherwise $F_{14}(\gamma, \alpha) = \gamma\alpha$.

S16. If $\gamma \in P_{IAV/T}$ and $\alpha \in P_T$, then $F_{14}(\gamma, \alpha) \in P_{IAV}$.

S17. If $\delta \in P_{(IV//IV)/T}$ and $\alpha \in P_T$, then $F_8(\delta, \alpha) \in P_{IV//IV}$.

S18. If $\delta \in P_{(IV/t)/T}$ and $\alpha \in P_T$, then $F_5(\delta, \alpha) \in P_{IV/t}$.

S19. If $\gamma \in P_{(t//IV)/T}$ and $\alpha \in P_T$, then $F_{15}(\gamma, \alpha) \in P_{t//IV}$; where (a) if $\alpha = \mathbf{he}_n$, then $F_{15}(\gamma, \alpha) = \gamma \, \mathbf{for} \, (*\mathbf{him}_n)$; (b) otherwise $F_{15}(\gamma, \alpha) = \gamma \, \mathbf{for} \, \alpha$.

S20. If $\delta \in P_{(t/t)/T}$ and $\alpha \in P_T$, then $F_6(\delta, \alpha) \in P_{t/t}$.

S21. If $\delta \in P_{((t/t)/T)/T}$ and $\alpha \in P_T$, then $F_8(\delta, \alpha) \in P_{(t/t)/T}$.

RULES OF PASSIVIZATION

S22. If $\delta \in B_{TV}$ and neither $\delta = \#\mathbf{be}$, $\delta = \#\mathbf{have}$, nor $\delta = \#\mathbf{resemble}$, then $F_{16}(\delta) \in P_{TV}$, where $F_{16}(\delta) = \#\mathbf{be} \, \delta' \, \mathbf{by}$ and δ' is the past participial form of δ.

S23. If $\delta \in B_{IV/t}$, then $F_{16}(\delta) \in P_{(t/t)/T}$.

S24. If $\delta \in B_{TV/T}$, then $F_{16}(\delta) \in P_{TV/T}$.

S25. If $\delta \in B_{TV/t}$, then $F_{16}(\delta) \in P_{((t/t)/T)/T}$.

S26. If $\delta \in B_{(IV//IV)/T}$, then $F_{17}(\delta) \in P_{(IV//IV)/T}$, where $F_{17}(\delta) = (\#)\mathbf{be} \, \delta'$ **by** and δ' is the past participial form of δ.

S27. If $\delta \in B_{(IV/t)/T}$ and $\delta \neq \#\mathbf{believe \, of}$, then $F_{16}(\delta) \in P_{(IV/t)/T}$.

RULE OF CONJUNCTION AND DISJUNCTION

S28. If $\gamma, \delta \in P_{IV}$, then $F_{18}(\gamma, \delta)$, $F_{19}(\gamma, \delta) \in P_{IV}$, where $F_{18}(\gamma, \delta) = \gamma \, \mathbf{and} \, \delta$ and $F_{19}(\gamma, \delta) = \gamma \, \mathbf{or} \, \delta$.

RULES OF NEGATION

S29. If $\delta \in P_{IV}$ and $\delta \neq \#\mathbf{not} \, \eta$, then $F_{20}(\delta) \in P_{IV}$, where $F_{20}(\delta) = \#\mathbf{not}$ δ' and δ' comes from δ by deleting all occurrences of $\#$ and $(\#)$.

S30. If $\alpha \in P_T$, $\delta \in P_{IV}$, and $\delta \neq \#\mathbf{not} \, \nu$, then $F_{21}(\alpha, \delta) \in P_t$, where (a) if $\delta = \#\mathbf{be} \, \eta$ or $\delta = (\#)\mathbf{be} \, \eta$, then $F_{21}(\alpha, \delta) = \alpha' \, \mathbf{is \, not} \, \eta'$, where α' comes from α by deleting all occurrences of $*$, and η' comes from η by performing the following operations in order: (i) deleting all occurrences of $\#$ and $(\#)$; (ii) if $\alpha = \mathbf{he}_n$, replacing all occurrences of $*\mathbf{him}_n$ by $\mathbf{himself}_n$; (iii) deleting all parentheses and any remaining occurrences of $*$; (b) otherwise $F_{21}(\alpha, \delta) = \alpha' \, \mathbf{does \, not} \, \delta'$, where α'

comes from α by deleting all occurrences of $*$, and δ' comes from δ by performing in order operations (i)–(iii).

S31. If $\gamma \in P_{t//IV}$ and $\delta \in P_{IV}$, then $F_{22}(\gamma, \delta) \in P_t$, where $F_{22}(\gamma, \delta) =$ **it** γ' **to** δ', γ' comes from γ by performing the following operations in order: (a) replacing any occurrence of $\#$**be** by **is not**; (b) replacing any remaining occurrence of a word of the form $\#\eta$ by **does not** η; (c) deleting all parentheses and any occurrences of $*$; and δ' comes from δ by performing the following operations in order: (a) if γ contains an occurrence of $(*$**him**$_n)$, replacing all occurrences of $*$**him**$_n$ in δ by **himself**$_n$ and (b) deleting all parentheses and any occurrences of $\#$, $(\#)$, and $*$.

S32. If $\gamma \in P_{t/t}$ and $\phi \in P_t$, then $F_{23}(\gamma, \phi) \in P_t$, where $F_{23}(\gamma, \phi) =$ **it** γ' **that** ϕ and γ' comes from γ by performing the following operations in order: (a) if $\gamma = \#$**might be**, then replacing γ with **might not be**; (b) replacing any occurrence of $\#$**be** by **is not**; (c) replacing any remaining occurrence of a word of the form $\#\eta$ by **does not** η; (d) deleting all parentheses and any occurrences of $*$.

RULES OF QUANTIFICATION

In order to state the next syntactic rule, it is convenient to give some definitions. The SINGULAR NOMINATIVE TRANSFORM of α is α', where if a member of B_{CN} or B_T other than **he**$_n$ occurs in α, then α' is

$$\begin{Bmatrix} \textbf{he} \\ \textbf{she} \\ \textbf{it} \end{Bmatrix}$$

according as the gender of the member of B_{CN} or B_T other than **he**$_n$ that occurs first in α is

$$\begin{Bmatrix} \text{masc.} \\ \text{fem.} \\ \text{neuter} \end{Bmatrix} ;$$

otherwise $\alpha' = \alpha$. The SINGULAR OBJECTIVE TRANSFORM of α is α', where if a member of B_{CN} or B_T other than **he**$_n$ occurs in α, then α' is

$$\begin{Bmatrix} \textbf{him} \\ \textbf{her} \\ \textbf{it} \end{Bmatrix}$$

according as the gender of the member of B_{CN} or B_T other than **he**$_n$ that occurs first in α is

$$\left\{\begin{array}{l} \text{masc.} \\ \text{fem.} \\ \text{neuter} \end{array}\right\};$$

otherwise $\alpha' = \alpha$. The SINGULAR REFLEXIVE OBJECTIVE TRANSFORM of α is α' where if a member of B_{CN} or B_T other than $\textbf{he}_n$ occurs in α, then α' is

$$\left\{\begin{array}{l} \textbf{himself} \\ \textbf{herself} \\ \textbf{itself} \end{array}\right\}$$

according as the gender of the member of B_{CN} or B_T other than $\textbf{he}_n$ that occurs first in α is

$$\left\{\begin{array}{l} \text{masc.} \\ \text{fem.} \\ \text{neuter} \end{array}\right\};$$

otherwise $\alpha' = \alpha$.

S33. If $\alpha \in P_T$, α contains no occurrences of numerical subscripts,[4] and $\delta \in P_{IV}$, then $F_{24,n}(\alpha, \delta) \in P_{IV}$, where $F_{24,n}(\alpha, \delta) = \delta'$ and δ' comes from δ by performing the following operations in order: (a) replacing the first occurrence, if there is one, of $\textbf{he}_n$, $\textbf{him}_n$, or $*\textbf{him}_n$, whichever is first, by α; (b) replacing any remaining occurrences of $\textbf{he}_n$ by the singular nominative transform of α; (c) replacing any remaining occurrences of $\textbf{him}_n$ or $*\textbf{him}_n$ by the singular objective transform of α; (c) replacing any remaining occurrences of $\textbf{himself}_n$ by the singular reflexive objective transform of α.

[4] This restriction is intended to rule out unwanted analysis trees (to be explained) such as the following:

$$\textbf{he}_1 \textbf{ sees him}_1, 24, 0$$

$\textbf{he}_1$, T $\textbf{he}_0 \textbf{ sees him}_1, 4$

$\textbf{he}_0$, T $\# \textbf{see } *\textbf{him}_1, 6$

$\# \textbf{see}$, TV $\textbf{he}_1$, T

However, the restriction is too strong in that it excludes grammatical sentences such as:

John expects a picture of himself to wash itself

I see no way of weakening the restriction without either allowing ungrammatical sentences into the fragment or horribly complicating the rules.

S34. If $\alpha \in P_T$, α contains no occurrences of numerical subscripts, and $\zeta \in P_{CN}$, then $F_{24,n}(\alpha, \zeta) \in P_{CN}$.

S35. If $\alpha \in P_T$, α contains no occurrences of numerical subscripts, and $\phi \in P_t$, then $F_{24,n}(\alpha, \phi) \in P_t$.

Syntactic rules S1–S35 constitute a simultaneous inductive definition of the sets P_A for any category A. The sets can be explicitly defined as follows. The sets P_A for any $A \in$ Cat are the smallest sets satisfying S1–S35; that is, $\langle P_A \rangle_{A \in CAT}$ is the unique family of sets indexed by Cat such that (a) $\langle P_A \rangle_{A \in CAT}$ satisfies S1–S35 and (b) whenever $\langle P'_A \rangle_{A \in CAT}$ is a family of sets indexed by Cat, if $\langle P'_A \rangle_{A \in CAT}$ satisfies S1–S35, then $P_A \subseteq P'_A$ for all $A \in$ Cat. (It is easy to show that there is exactly one family of sets satisfying these conditions.)

A MEANINGFUL EXPRESSION OF THE FRAGMENT is any element of P_A for any category A.

It is helpful to consider ANALYSIS TREES, which represent derivational histories of nonbasic meaningful expressions. The following is an example:

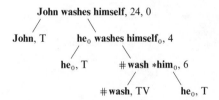

We attach a meaningful expression to each node. In the case that the expression is basic, it is accompanied by its syntactic category. In the case that the expression is nonbasic, it is accompanied by the index of the structural operation *by* which it is obtained, and we place beneath it the expressions *from* which is is obtained in the order in which they appear as arguments of the structural operation in question. It is possible to give a precise characterization of analysis trees, but we shall not do so here.[5] When there would be no confusion, the syntactic categories and the indices of structural operations are sometimes omitted. Occasionally, for the sake of perspicuity, nonbasic expressions are accompanied by their syntactic categories.

In PTQ, syntactic rule S4, which takes a subject and a predicate to form a sentence, is formulated so that only the first verb in the verb phrase is

---

[5] Montague gives such a characterization in a similar context [see "English as a formal language," henceforth EFL (1974, pp. 204–208)].

inflected. The following is an analysis tree in that fragment:

```
        John walks and talk, 4
          /          \
      John       walk and talk, 8
                   /        \
                walk        talk
```

The situation is improved in our fragment by using the marker # to indicate which verbs are to be inflected.[6] The following is an analysis tree in our fragment:

```
          John walks and talks, 4
            /              \
      John, T        #walk and #talk, 18
                      /            \
               #walk, IV        #talk, IV
```

If a verb phrase δ in P_{IV} is modified by a member of $P_{IV//IV}$, then every occurrence of # in δ is deleted. This is illustrated by the following analysis tree:

```
          John tries to walk and talk, 4
            /                   \
      John, T          #try to walk and talk, 11
                        /                \
              #try, IV//IV        #walk and #talk, 18
                                    /            \
                             #walk, IV        #talk, IV
```

The fragment includes a syntactic rule, S29, for negating verb phrases. This is necessary for deriving a sentence like (1), which is not to be confused with (2):

(1)   **John tries not to walk**

(2)   **John does not try to walk**

Sentence (1) has the following analysis tree:

```
          John tries not to walk, 4
            /               \
      John, T         #try not to walk, 11
                       /             \
             #try, IV//IV        #not walk, 20
                                      |
                                  #walk, IV
```

---

[6] The idea of using such a marker was suggested by Barbara Partee.

If a verb phrase δ in P_{IV} is negated, then every occurrence of $\#$ in δ is deleted. This is illustrated by the following analysis tree:

```
        John does not walk and talk, 4
        /                    \
    John, T          # not walk and talk, 20
                              |
                     # walk and # talk, 18
                     /              \
              # walk, IV          # talk, IV
```

Incidentally, S30 is required in addition to S29 in order to assign (3) the reading expressed by (4):

(3)   **a man does not walk**

(4)   **no man walks**

Notice that the fragment allows analysis trees like the following:

```
        *John is not a fish and walk, 21
        /                    \
    John, T          # be a fish and # walk, 18
                     /              \
              # be a fish, 6      # walk, IV
              /         \
        # be, TV      a fish, 1
                         |
                      fish, CN
```

The resulting sentence is ungrammatical.[7] What we want is something like the following:

(5)   **John is not both a fish and walks**

I see no easy way to rectify this problem.

Although Montague treats disjunctive terms in the fragment presented in PTQ, in formulating his syntactic rules he overlooked some of the difficulties that are involved. For example, in PTQ, $F_{10,0}(\textbf{he}_1$ **or** $\textbf{he}_2, \textbf{he}_0$ **loves him**$_0)$ is undefined and $F_5(\textbf{find}, \textbf{he}_0$ **or** $\textbf{he}_1)$ gives the wrong value. It appears that any accommodation of disjunctive terms involves considerable complexity. I do not treat them in this fragment.

2. TRANSLATING THE FRAGMENT INTO INTENSIONAL LOGIC

In this section I show how the fragment translates into Montague's intensional logic. The reader may refer to PTQ for a presentation of the syntax and semantics of this logic.

---

[7] As usual, the asterisk indicates ungrammaticality.

Intuitively, for any syntactic category A, all meaningful expressions in the fragment of category A should translate into expressions of intensional logic of the same type. Accordingly, we introduce a mapping f from the categories of the fragment to the types of intensional logic. Let f be a function that has CAT as its domain and is such that for all A, B $\in$ CAT,

$$f(t) = t,$$
$$f(\text{CN}) = f(\text{IV}) = \langle e, t \rangle,$$
$$f(\text{A/B}) = f(\text{A//B}) = \langle \langle s, f(\text{B}) \rangle, f(\text{A}) \rangle.$$

All of the basic expressions in the fragment, with the exception of #**be** in B_{TV}, #**fail** in $B_{\text{IV//IV}}$, #**might be**, #**be true**, and #**be necessary** in $B_{t/t}$, **other than** in B_{AJP}, and the terms in B_{T}, are translated by constants in intensional logic. The exceptions are given special translations that induce their desired interpretations. For each category A we wish to introduce a function from the basic expressions of category A that do not have a special translation to the constants of intensional logic of type $f(\text{A})$. Accordingly, for every A $\in$ CAT, let g_{A} be a fixed biunique function such that (a) the domain of g_{A} is $B_{\text{A}} - X$, where X is the set, possibly empty, of basic expressions in B_{A} that have a special translation; (b) if $\alpha \in B_{\text{A}}$, then $g_{\text{A}}(\alpha)$ is a member of the set of constants of type $f(\text{A})$; and (c) for every $\text{A}' \in$ CAT that is distinct from A, g_{A} and $g_{\text{A}'}$ have disjoint ranges.[8]

It is convenient to introduce some alternative notation for referring to letters of the intensional logic. Let j, m, b, c be distinct members of the set of constants of type e. Let x, y, z, x_n be the individual variables $v_{1,e}$, $v_{3,e}$, $v_{5,e}$, $v_{2n,e}$, respectively (for any nonnegative integer n). Let p be the proposition variable $v_{0,\langle s,t \rangle}$. Let P, Q be the variables $v_{0,\langle s,\langle e,t \rangle \rangle}$, $v_{1,\langle s,\langle e,t \rangle \rangle}$, respectively, which range over properties of individuals. Let $\mathscr{P}$, $\mathscr{Q}$ be the variables $v_{0,\langle s,\langle \langle s,\langle e,t \rangle \rangle,t \rangle \rangle}$, $v_{1,\langle s,\langle \langle s,\langle e,t \rangle \rangle,t \rangle \rangle}$, respectively, which range over properties of properties of individuals. Let S be the variable $v_{0,\langle s,\langle e,\langle e,t \rangle \rangle \rangle}$, which ranges over two-place relations-in-intension between individuals. Let T be the variable $v_{0,\langle s,\langle e,\langle e,\langle e,t \rangle \rangle \rangle \rangle}$, which ranges over three-place relations-in-intension between individuals. Let U be the variable $v_{0,\langle s,\langle *,\langle e,\langle e,t \rangle \rangle \rangle \rangle}$, where $*$ is $\langle s, \langle \langle s, \langle e, t \rangle \rangle, t \rangle \rangle$, which ranges over three-place relations-in-intension between individuals and properties of properties of individuals. Let W be the variable $v_{0,\langle s,\langle *,\langle e,\langle e,t \rangle \rangle \rangle \rangle}$, where $*$ is $\langle s, t \rangle$, which ranges over three-place relations-in-intension between individuals and propositions. Let X be the variable $v_{0,\langle s,\langle e,\langle *,\langle e,t \rangle \rangle \rangle \rangle}$, where $*$ is $\langle s, \langle e, t \rangle \rangle$, which ranges over three-place

---

[8] In PTQ, Montague considers only one function from the basic expressions to the constants of intensional logic. In this fragment, we are forced to consider a separate function for each nonempty set of basic expressions for some syntactic category because there exist α in both B_{A} and $B_{\text{A}'}$, where $f(\text{A}) \neq f(\text{A}')$, e.g., #**expect** and #**appear**. Condition (c) rules out possibilities such as **man** and #**walk** being assigned to the same constant in intensional logic. In EFL (1974, pp. 193–195) Montague resorts to the same device for the same reason.

relations-in-intension between individuals and properties of individuals. Let Y be the variable $v_{0,\langle s,\langle *,\langle e,\langle e,t\rangle\rangle\rangle\rangle}$, where $*$ is $\langle s, t\rangle$, which ranges over three-place relations-in-intension between individuals and propositions. Let Z be the variable $v_{0,\langle s,\langle e,\langle\langle s,t\rangle,t\rangle\rangle\rangle}$, which ranges over two-place relations-in-intension between individuals and propositions.

Now that we have given the translations for the basic expressions of the fragment (with the exception of those that receive a special translation), it remains to explain how to determine the translation of a nonbasic expression, given the translations of its parts. This is done by giving rules of translation T1–T35, which correspond to syntactic rules S1–S35 respectively. After the translation rules are stated, it will be seen that they define the translation relation for the fragment.

Translation Rules

BASIC RULES

T1. *(a)* For each $A \in$ CAT, if α is in the domain of g_A, then α translates into $g_A(\alpha)$.

   (b) **John**, **Mary**, **Bill**, **Chicago** translate into $\hat{P}P\{j\}$, $\hat{P}P\{m\}$, $\hat{P}P\{b\}$, $\hat{P}P\{c\}$, respectively.

   (c) **he**$_n$ translates into $\hat{P}P\{x_n\}$.

   (d) #**be** in B_{TV} translates into $\lambda\mathcal{P}\lambda x\mathcal{P}\{[\hat{y}x = y]\}$.

   (e) #**fail** translates into $\lambda P\lambda x \urcorner P\{x\}$.

   (f) #**might be** translates into $\hat{p} \urcorner \square \urcorner [{}^{\vee}p]$.

   (g) #**be true** translates into $\hat{p}[{}^{\vee}p]$.

   (h) #**be necessary** translates into $\hat{p}\square[{}^{\vee}p]$.

   (i) **other than** translates into $\lambda\mathcal{P}\lambda Q\lambda x[Q\{x\} \wedge \mathcal{P}\{\hat{y} \urcorner x = y\}]$.

T2. If $\zeta \in P_{CN}$, $\phi \in P_t$, and ζ, ϕ translate into ζ', ϕ', respectively, then $F_{0,n}(\zeta, \phi)$ translates into $\hat{x}_n[\zeta'(x_n) \wedge \phi']$.

T3. If $\zeta \in P_{CN}$ and ζ translates into ζ', then $F_1(\zeta)$ translates into $\hat{P}\vee x[\zeta'(x) \wedge P\{x\}]$, **every** ζ translates into $\hat{P}\wedge x[\zeta'(x) \rightarrow P\{x\}]$, and **the** ζ translates into $\hat{P} \vee x[\wedge y[\zeta'(y) \leftrightarrow y = x] \wedge P\{x\}]$.

RULES OF FUNCTIONAL APPLICATION

T4. If $\alpha \in P_T$, $\delta \in P_{IV}$, and α, δ translate into α', δ', respectively, then $F_4(\alpha, \delta)$ translates into $\alpha'({}^{\wedge}\delta')$.

T5. If $\zeta \in P_{CN/T}$, $\alpha \in P_T$, and ζ, α translate into ζ', α', respectively, then $F_5(\zeta, \alpha)$ translates into $\zeta'({}^{\wedge}\alpha')$.

T6. If $\delta \in P_{TV}$, $\alpha \in P_T$, and δ, α translate into δ', α', respectively, then $F_6(\delta, \alpha)$ translates into $\delta'({}^{\wedge}\alpha')$.

T7. If $\delta \in P_{IV/t}$, $\phi \in P_t$, and δ, ϕ translate into δ', ϕ', respectively, then $F_7(\delta, \phi)$ translates into $\delta'(^\wedge \phi')$.

T8. If $\delta \in P_{TV/T}$, $\alpha \in P_T$, and δ, α translate into δ', α', respectively, then $F_8(\delta, \alpha)$ translates into $\delta'(^\wedge \alpha')$.

T9. If $\delta \in P_{TV/t}$, $\phi \in P_t$, and δ, ϕ translate into δ', ϕ', respectively, then $F_7(\delta, \phi)$ translates into $\delta'(^\wedge \phi')$.

T10. If $\gamma \in P_{AJ}$, $\zeta \in P_{CN}$, and γ, ζ translate into γ', ζ', respectively, then $F_9(\gamma, \zeta)$ translates into $\gamma'(^\wedge \zeta')$.

T11. If $\gamma \in P_{IAV}$, $\delta \in P_{IV}$, and γ, δ translate into γ', δ', respectively, then $F_{10}(\gamma, \delta)$ translates into $\gamma'(^\wedge \delta')$.

T12. If $\gamma \in P_{IV//IV}$, $\delta \in P_{IV}$, and γ, δ translate into γ', δ', respectively, then $F_{11}(\gamma, \delta)$ translates into $\gamma'(^\wedge \delta')$.

T13. If $\gamma \in P_{t//IV}$, $\delta \in P_{IV}$, and γ, δ translate into γ', δ', respectively, then $F_{12}(\gamma, \delta)$ translates into $\gamma'(^\wedge \delta')$.

T14. If $\gamma \in P_{t/t}$, $\phi \in P_t$, and γ, ϕ translate into γ', ϕ', respectively, then $F_{13}(\gamma, \phi)$ translates into $\gamma'(^\wedge \phi')$.

T15. If $\gamma \in P_{AJ/T}$, $\alpha \in P_T$, and γ, α translate into γ', α', respectively, then $F_{14}(\gamma, \alpha)$ translates into $\gamma'(^\wedge \alpha')$.

T16. If $\gamma \in P_{IAV/T}$, $\alpha \in P_T$, and γ, α translate into γ', α', respectively, then $F_{14}(\gamma, \alpha)$ translates into $\gamma'(^\wedge \alpha')$.

T17. If $\delta \in P_{(IV//IV)/T}$, $\alpha \in P_T$, and δ, α translate into δ', α', respectively, then $F_8(\delta, \alpha)$ translates into $\delta'(^\wedge \alpha')$.

T18. If $\delta \in P_{(IV/t)/T}$, $\alpha \in P_T$, and δ, α translate into δ', α', respectively, then $F_5(\delta, \alpha)$ translates into $\delta'(^\wedge \alpha')$.

T19. If $\gamma \in P_{(t//IV)/T}$, $\alpha \in P_T$, and γ, α translate into γ', α', respectively, then $F_{15}(\gamma, \alpha)$ translates into $\gamma'(^\wedge \alpha')$.

T20. If $\delta \in P_{(t/t)/T}$, $\alpha \in P_T$, and δ, α translate into δ', α', respectively, then $F_6(\delta, \alpha)$ translates into $\delta'(^\wedge \alpha')$.

T21. If $\delta \in P_{((t/t)/T)/T}$, $\alpha \in P_T$, and δ, α translate into δ', α', respectively, then $F_8(\delta, \alpha)$ translates into $\delta'(^\wedge \alpha')$.

RULES OF PASSIVIZATION

T22. If $\delta \in B_{TV}$ and δ translates into δ', then $F_{16}(\delta)$ translates into $\lambda \mathscr{P} \lambda x [\mathscr{P}\{[\hat{y}\ \delta'(\hat{P}P\{x\})(y)]\}]$.

T23. If $\delta \in \mathbf{B}_{\mathrm{IV}/t}$ and δ translates into δ', then $F_{16}(\delta)$ translates into $\lambda \mathscr{P} \lambda p[\mathscr{P}\{[\hat{x}\ \delta'(p)(x)]\}]$.

T24. If $\delta \in \mathbf{B}_{\mathrm{TV}/T}$ and δ translates into δ', then $F_{16}(\delta)$ translates into $\lambda \mathscr{P} \lambda \mathscr{Q} \lambda x[\mathscr{P}[\hat{y}\ \delta'(\hat{P}P\{x\})(\mathscr{Q})(y)]\}]$.

T25. If $\delta \in \mathbf{B}_{\mathrm{TV}/t}$ and δ translates into δ', then $F_{16}(\delta)$ translates into $\lambda \mathscr{P} \lambda \mathscr{Q} \lambda p[\mathscr{P}\{[\hat{x}\ \delta'(p)(\mathscr{Q})(x)]\}]$.

T26. If $\delta \in \mathbf{B}_{(\mathrm{IV}//\mathrm{IV})/T}$ and δ translates into δ', then $F_{17}(\delta)$ translates into $\lambda \mathscr{P} \lambda Q \lambda x[\mathscr{P}\{[\hat{y}\ \delta'(\hat{P}P\{x\})(Q)(y)]\}]$.

T27. If $\delta \in \mathbf{B}_{(\mathrm{IV}/t)/T}$ and δ translates into δ', then $F_{16}(\delta)$ translates into $\lambda \mathscr{P} \lambda p \lambda x[\mathscr{P}\{[\hat{y}\ \delta'(\hat{P}P\{x\})(p)(y)]\}]$.

RULE OF CONJUNCTION AND DISJUNCTION

T28. If $\gamma, \delta \in \mathbf{P}_{\mathrm{IV}}$ and γ, δ translate into γ', δ', respectively, then γ **and** δ translates into $\hat{x}[\gamma'(x) \wedge \delta'(x)]$ and γ **or** δ translates into $\hat{x}[\gamma'(x) \vee \delta'(x)]$.

RULES OF NEGATION

T29. If $\delta \in \mathbf{P}_{\mathrm{IV}}$ and δ translates into δ', then $F_{20}(\delta)$ translates into $\hat{x} \neg \delta'(x)$.

T30. If $\alpha \in \mathbf{P}_{\mathrm{T}}$, $\delta \in \mathbf{P}_{\mathrm{IV}}$, and α, δ translate into α', δ', respectively, then $F_{21}(\alpha, \delta)$ translates into $\neg \alpha'(^{\wedge}\delta')$.

T31. If $\gamma \in \mathbf{P}_{t//\mathrm{IV}}$, $\delta \in \mathbf{P}_{\mathrm{IV}}$, and γ, δ translate into γ', δ', respectively, then $F_{22}(\gamma, \delta)$ translates into $\neg \gamma'(^{\wedge}\delta')$.

T32. If $\gamma \in \mathbf{P}_{t/t}$, $\phi \in \mathbf{P}_t$, and γ, ϕ translate into γ', ϕ', respectively, then $F_{23}(\gamma, \phi)$ translates into $\neg \gamma'(^{\wedge}\phi')$.

RULES OF QUANTIFICATION

T33. If $\alpha \in \mathbf{P}_{\mathrm{T}}$, $\delta \in \mathbf{P}_{\mathrm{IV}}$, and α, δ translate into α', δ', respectively, then $F_{24,n}(\alpha, \delta)$ translates into $\hat{y}\ \alpha'(\hat{x}_n[\delta'(y)])$.

T34. If $\alpha \in \mathbf{P}_{\mathrm{T}}$, $\zeta \in \mathbf{P}_{\mathrm{CN}}$, and α, ζ translate into α', ζ', respectively, then $F_{24,n}(\alpha, \zeta)$ translates into $\hat{y}\ \alpha'(\hat{x}_n[\zeta'(y)])$.

T35. If $\alpha \in \mathbf{P}_{\mathrm{T}}$, $\phi \in \mathbf{P}_t$, and α, ϕ translate into α', ϕ', respectively, then $F_{24,n}(\alpha, \phi)$ translates into $\alpha'(\hat{x}_n\phi')$.

If in translation rules T1–T35 we replace the condition that one expression translates into another by the condition that the relation R holds between the two expressions, then the translation relation is the smallest binary relation satisfying T1–T35; that is, the TRANSLATION RELATION OF THE FRAGMENT is the unique binary relation R such that (a) R satisfies T1–T35 and (b) whenever R' satisfies T1–T35, $R \subseteq R'$.

An expression ϕ TRANSLATES IN THE FRAGMENT INTO ϕ' if the ordered pair $\langle \phi, \phi' \rangle$ is a member of the translation relation.

The translation relation is not a function. A meaningful expression of the fragment may translate into more than one expression of intensional logic. This is due to the fact that a meaningful expression can have more than one derivational history. A simple example is the common noun phrase **famous man in Chicago**. The following are two analysis trees for this expression:

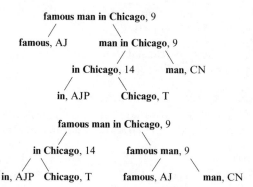

These analysis trees correspond to the expressions of intensional logic (6) and (7), respectively:

(6)   **famous**$'$ ([$^\wedge$**in**$'$ ($\hat{P}P\{c\}$)([$^\wedge$**man**$'$])])

(7)   **in**$'$ ($\hat{P}P\{c\}$)([$^\wedge$**famous**$'$([$^\wedge$**man**$'$])])

Here the primed variants of the basic expressions designate the constants of intensional logic into which the basic expressions are translated.

The interpretations of intensional logic may, by way of the translation relation, be viewed as interpretations of the fragment. However, not all interpretations of intensional logic are appropriate as interpretations of the fragment. In order to reflect certain intuitions about entailment in English, we take as interpretations of the fragment only those interpretations of intensional logic in which the following formulas are true with respect to all, or equivalently some, points of reference.

GUARANTEEING RIGID DESIGNATION

(a) $\vee x \square [x = \alpha]$, where α is j, m, b, or c

GUARANTEEING PROPERTIES CONCERNING EXISTENCE
AND ENTITYHOOD

(b) $\square [\mathbf{entity}'(x) \leftrightarrow \delta(x)]$, where δ translates $\#\mathbf{be}$ in B_{IV}

(c) $\square [\zeta(x) \rightarrow \mathbf{entity}'(x)]$, where ζ translates any member of B_{CN}

(d) $\Box[\gamma(P)(x) \rightarrow \textbf{entity}'(x)]$, where γ translates any member of B_{AJ}

(e) $\Box[\gamma(\mathscr{P})(Q)(x) \rightarrow \textbf{entity}'(x)]$, where γ translates any member of B_{AJP}

GUARANTEEING THE INTERSECTIVE AND SUBSECTIVE PROPERTY

(f) $\Box[\textbf{mortal}'(P)(x) \leftrightarrow [P\{x\} \wedge \textbf{mortal}'([^\wedge \textbf{entity}'])(x)]]$

(g) $\Box[\gamma(\mathscr{P})(Q)(x) \leftrightarrow [Q\{x\} \wedge \gamma(\mathscr{P})([^\wedge\textbf{entity}'])(x)]]$, where γ translates **in** in B_{AJP}, **in** in B_{IAVP}, or **about** in B_{IAVP}

(h) $\Box[\gamma(P)(x) \rightarrow P\{x\}]$, where γ translates **big** or **famous** in B_{AJ}, or **rapidly**, **slowly**, or **voluntarily** in B_{IAV}

GUARANTEEING DEFINITE READINGS

(i) $\vee S \wedge \mathscr{P} \wedge x\Box[\delta(\mathscr{P})(x) \leftrightarrow \mathscr{P}\{\hat{y}[^\vee S](y)(x)\}]$, where δ translates **portrait of** or **story about** in $B_{CN/T}$, or #**love**, #**eat**, #**see**, #**talk about**, #**wash**, #**worship**, #**build**, #**find**, #**form**, or #**have** in B_{TV}

(j) $\vee T \wedge \mathscr{P} \wedge \mathscr{Q} \wedge x\Box[\#\textbf{give}'(\mathscr{P})(\mathscr{Q})(x) \leftrightarrow \mathscr{P}\{\hat{z}\mathscr{Q}\{\hat{y}[^\vee T](z)(y)(x)\}\}]$

(k) $\vee U \wedge \mathscr{P} \wedge \mathscr{Q} \wedge x\Box[\#\textbf{owe}'(\mathscr{P})(\mathscr{Q})(x) \leftrightarrow \mathscr{Q}\{\hat{y}[^\vee U](\mathscr{P})(y)(x)\}]$

(l) $\vee W \wedge \mathscr{P} \wedge p \wedge x\Box[\delta(p)(\mathscr{P})(x) \leftrightarrow \mathscr{P}\{\hat{y}[^\vee W](p)(y)(x)\}]$, where δ translates #**promise** or #**say** in $B_{TV/t}$

(m) $\vee X \wedge \mathscr{P} \wedge Q \wedge x\Box[\delta(\mathscr{P})(Q)(x) \leftrightarrow \mathscr{P}\{\hat{y}[^\vee X](y)(Q)(x)\}]$, where δ translates #**persuade**, #**expect**, or #**force** in $B_{(IV//IV)/T}$, **in** in B_{AJP}, or **in** or **about** in B_{IAVP}

(n) $\vee Y \wedge \mathscr{P} \wedge p \wedge x\Box[\delta(\mathscr{P})(p)(x) \leftrightarrow \mathscr{P}\{\hat{y}[^\vee Y](y)(p)(x)\}]$, where δ translates #**persuade** or #**believe of** in $B_{(IV/t)/T}$

(o) $\vee Z \wedge \mathscr{P} \wedge p\Box[\delta(\mathscr{P})(p) \leftrightarrow \mathscr{P}\{\hat{x}[^\vee Z](x)(p)\}]$, where δ translates #**appear** in $B_{(t/t)/T}$

GUARANTEEING MISCELLANEOUS PROPERTIES

(p) $\Box[\#\textbf{conceive of}' (\mathscr{P})(x) \leftrightarrow \#\textbf{form}'(\hat{P} \vee y[\textbf{conception of}' (\mathscr{P})(y) \wedge P\{y\}])(x)]$

(q) $\Box[\textbf{alleged}'(P)(x) \leftrightarrow \vee y[\textbf{person}'(y) \wedge \#\textbf{allege}'([^\wedge P\{x\}])(y)]]$

(r) $\Box[\#\textbf{believe of}'(\hat{P}P\{y\})([^\wedge Q\{y\}])(x) \leftrightarrow \#\textbf{believe}'([^\wedge Q\{y\}])(x)]$

(s) $\Box[\#\textbf{succeed}'(P)(x) \leftrightarrow [\#\textbf{try}'(P)(x) \wedge P\{x\}]]$

(t) $\Box[\gamma(\mathscr{P})(Q)(x) \leftrightarrow \eta(\mathscr{P})(Q)(x)]$, where γ, η translate **in** in B_{AJP}, **in** in B_{IAVP}, respectively

(u) $\Box[\zeta(x) \rightarrow \textbf{person}'(x)]$, where ζ translates either **man** or **woman**

(v) $\Box[\zeta(\mathscr{P})(x) \rightarrow \gamma(x)]$, where ζ, γ translate either **portrait of** in $B_{CN/T}$, **portrait** in B_{CN}, respectively; **story about** in $B_{CN/T}$, **story** in B_{CN}, respectively; **picture of** in $B_{CN/T}$, **picture** in B_{CN}, respectively; **conception of** in $B_{CN/T}$, **conception** in B_{CN}, respectively; **vision of** in $B_{CN/T}$, **vision** in B_{CN}, respectively; or #**talk about** in B_{TV}, #**talk** in B_{IV}, respectively

(w) $\Box[\#\textbf{resemble}'(\hat{P}P\{y\})(x) \leftrightarrow \#\textbf{resemble}'(\hat{P}P\{x\})(y)]$

(x) $\Box[\#\textbf{force}'(\mathscr{P})(Q)(x) \rightarrow \mathscr{P}\{Q\}]$

(y) $\Box[\textbf{almost}'(P)(x) \rightarrow \neg P\{x\}]$

(z) $\Box[[\gamma(\hat{P}P\{y\})([^\wedge\textbf{entity}'])(x) \;\wedge\; \gamma(\hat{P}P\{z\})([^\wedge\textbf{entity}'])(y)] \rightarrow \gamma(\hat{P}P\{z\})$ $([^\wedge\textbf{entity}'])(x)]$, where γ translates **in** in B_{AJP}

An INDIRECT INTERPRETATION OF THE FRAGMENT is any interpretation of intensional logic for which formulas (a)–(z) are true with respect to all points of reference.

If $\Gamma \cup \{\phi\}$ is a set of formulas of intensional logic, then ϕ is a LOGICAL CONSEQUENCE IN THE FRAGMENT of Γ iff for every indirect interpretation of the fragment $\mathfrak{A}$ and point of reference $\langle i, j\rangle$, if ψ is true with respect to $\mathfrak{A}, i, j$ for all ψ in Γ, then ϕ is true with respect to $\mathfrak{A}, i, j$.

We are concerned primarily with the notion of logical consequence in the fragment rather than with the different notion of logical consequence in intensional logic. Thus, for example, if it is said of two formulas of intensional logic that they are logically equivalent *tout court*, this is to be understood as being logically equivalent in the fragment.

3. DISPENSING WITH INDIVIDUAL CONCEPTS

The fragment presented in PTQ is on the individual concept level; that is, all common noun phrases and intransitive verb phrases have as their extension at a point of reference a set of individual concepts. The point of having individual concepts rather than individuals [as Montague does in the fragment presented in "Universal grammar," henceforth UG] is to be able to treat Partee's puzzles (see PTQ, 1974, pp. 267–268). Individual concepts are introduced in order to treat "extraordinary" common nouns and verbs, such as **temperature** and **rise**. However, Montague raises the "ordinary" common nouns and verbs like **man** and **walk** up to the individual concept level as well. This avoids having a split-level syntax where **man** and **temperature**, for example, are of different syntactic categories. However, this introduces complexity into the semantics by complicating the restrictions on the logically possible interpretations for the fragment. Montague must introduce meaning postulates in order to guarantee "extensionality" with respect to various basic expressions (see PTQ, 1974, pp. 263–265).[9]

In this fragment I drop back to the individual level. By ignoring the Partee puzzles and treating only "ordinary" common nouns and verbs on the

---

[9] I cannot go into detail here, but it is not entirely clear what the purpose is of some of Montague's meaning postulates.

individual level, we avoid extra complications that come with maintaining the individual concept level.[10]

Since our fragment is on the individual level, we can no longer take as the basic syntactic categories e and t as in PTQ (1974, pp. 249–250); it is not possible to give the desired definitions to the categories CN and IV in terms of the categories e and t, given the correspondence that is set up between categories of the forms A/B and A//B and the types of intensional logic. Our solution is to take CN and IV along with t as basic. As a consequence the "mysterious" category e is eliminated (and all of the categories dependent on e)— mysterious because Montague thought that no expression of English, basic or nonbasic, is of this category (Partee 1973, reprinted as pages 51–76. of this volume).

4. THREE-PLACE AND OTHER KINDS OF VERBS

This fragment treats three-place verbs in the manner that Montague (EFL, 1974, p. 191) probably had in mind. Since such verbs have both a direct object and an indirect object, it is natural to regard them as being of syntactic category TV/T:

(8)   **John gives a fish to Mary**

Sentence (8) has the following analysis tree:

```
                John gives a fish to Mary, 4
              /                          \
       John, T              #give a fish to Mary, 6
                                /            \
                     #give a fish, 8        Mary, T
                      /          \
               #give, TV/T      a fish, 1
                                    |
                                 fish, CN
```

---

[10] Maintaining the individual concept level raises the following problem: Since this fragment includes adjectival phrases, we would have to devise some way of ensuring that every "ordinary" common noun phrase has only constant individual concepts in its extension at every point of reference. At present it is not clear to me how this would be done. Incidentally, it is curious that in PTQ, Montague does not require "extensionality" in subject position for any verb phrase resulting from adverbial modification. It seems that such a requirement is correct for a verb phrase like **eat rapidly** but incorrect for one like **rise rapidly**. This bifurcation with respect to **rapidly** rules out introducing a meaning postulate that involves only this adverb in order to ensure that **eat rapidly** is extensional in subject position. It is not clear to me how one ensures that all "ordinary" verb phrases have this property. This is exactly the problem that we face in trying to ensure that all "ordinary" common noun phrases have only constant individual concepts in their extensions.

Sentences closely related to (8) are (9) and (10):

(9)   **John gives to Mary a fish**

(10)   **John gives Mary a fish**

Such sentences are not treated in our fragment. I believe that the most natural way to derive (9) and (10) is by way of a meaning-preserving transformation, say T_0. For example, (9) would have the following derivation:

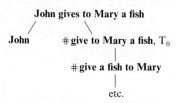

Linguists have postulated a transformation, DATIVE SHIFT, that is similar to T_0.[11] Notice that T_0 should not apply when the direct object is a pronoun variable; otherwise ungrammatical expressions such as (11) are generated:

(11)   ***John eats a fish and gives Mary it**

Not all three-place verbs employ **to**; some employ **for**:

> **John buys a fish for Mary**
> ***John buys a fish to Mary**

For simplicity our fragment treats only three-place verbs that employ **to**.

Montague (EFL, 1974, p. 198, n 12) suggested a test for distinguishing three-place verbs. **give . . . to** and **aim . . . at** are three-place verbs because the indirect object can be a reflexive pronoun:

> **John gives a fish to himself**
> **John aims a fish at himself**

However, **take . . . with**, **pull . . . toward**, and **push . . . away** are not three-place verbs because the "indirect object" cannot be a reflexive pronoun:[12]

> ***John takes the fish with himself**
> ***John pulls the fish toward himself**
> ***John pushes the fish away from himself**

---

[11] The nature of transformations and their status in the Montague framework are discussed in Section 8.

[12] See Chomsky (1965, pp. 146–147). It appears that any adequate treatment of a sentence like the following is somewhat complex:

> **John pulls the fish toward him**

Dowty has a promising approach to such sentences; (see Dowty, pp. 212–256 of this volume).

The fact that (12) is grammatical suggests that **talk about . . . to** is a three-place verb:

(12)   **John talks about Mary to himself**

For some reason (13) seems more natural than (14):

(13)   **John talks to Bill about Mary**

(14)   **John talks about Mary to Bill**

I regard (13) as being derived by way of the transformation T_0. It would have the following derivation:

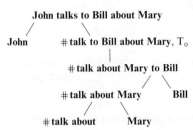

talk about . . . to is anomalous in that (15) is ungrammatical even though (16) and (17) are not:

(15)   ***John talks about Mary to herself**

(16)   **John gives Mary to herself**

(17)   **John talks to Mary about herself**

I have no explanation of this anomaly. The three-place verb **talk about . . . with** does not have this irregularity.

There are intensional three-place verbs:

(18)   **John owes a fish to Mary**

In this fragment (18) has two readings, a definite one and an indefinite one. The first reading asserts that a particular fish is such that John owes it to Mary. The second asserts that John owes any old fish to Mary. **owe** is always definite in its subject and indirect object positions. **give** is not an intensional three-place verb. It is always definite in its subject, object, and indirect object positions.

Another intensional three-place verb is **remind . . . of** with the sense of "cause . . . to think of" rather than "cause . . . to remember." Sentence (19) has an indefinite reading with respect to its indirect object term:

(19)   **John reminds Mary of a fish**

Unlike **owe**, **remind . . . of** is always definite in its subject term and its direct object term.

Our fragment includes verbs of syntactic category TV/t:

(20)   **John promises that Mary walks to a woman**

Sentence (20) has the following analysis tree:

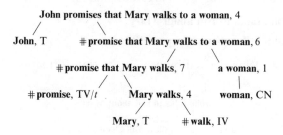

Sentence (20) is unambiguous in the fragment and has only a definite reading with respect to **a woman**. I regard (21) as being derived by way of the transformation T_0:

(21)   **John promises to a woman that Mary walks**

The fragment includes verbs of syntactic category (IV//IV)/T:

(22)   **John expects a woman to walk**

Sentence (22) has the following analysis tree:

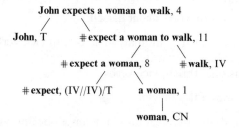

The sentence is unambiguous in the fragment and has only a definite reading with respect to **a woman**. Intuitively it has an indefinite reading as well. I believe that this is due to a transformation; the matter is discussed in Section 8.

Not all verbs of category (IV//IV)/T employ **to**. **see** and **make** are of category (IV//IV)/T and have no such particle:

> **John sees a woman walk**
> **John makes a fish talk**

Our fragment includes verbs of syntactic category (IV/t)/T:

(23)   **John believes of a woman that she walks**

Sentence (23) has the following analysis tree:

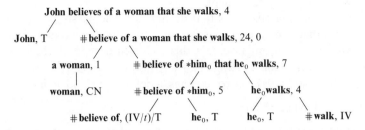

The sentence is unambiguous in the fragment and has only a definite reading with respect to **a woman**. This reading is also assigned to (24):

(24)   **John believes that a woman walks**

It should be noted that the syntax of the fragment allows for a sentence such as (25):

(25)   **John believes of a fish that Mary walks**

This allowance is similar to that which lets in (26):

(26)   **a fish such that Mary walks talks**

Possibly such sentences should be ruled out.

5. THE PASSIVE VOICE

The fragment provides a treatment of the passive voice. Let us consider an example:

(27)   **John finds Mary**

(28)   **Mary is found by John**

Sentence (28) has the following analysis tree in the fragment:

Mary is found by John, 4

Mary, T   #be found by John, 6

#be found by, 16   John, T

#find, TV

#**be found by** is of category TV and is given the following translation in intensional logic, which depends on the translation of #**find**:

$$\lambda \mathcal{P} \lambda x[\mathcal{P}\{[\hat{y} \ \#\textbf{find}'(\hat{P}P\{x\})(y)]\}]$$

This translation is designed in such a way that any two translations of (27) and (28) are logically equivalent.[13]

There are anomalous verbs that do not take the passive form. The syntactic rules that generate the passive form must be formulated to allow for these exceptions. In our fragment this has been done with the verbs #be, #have, and #resemble of category TV (Chomsky, 1965, p. 103).

In the fragment (29) has two readings, a definite one and an indefinite one:

(29)   **John seeks a unicorn**

The definite reading entails that there is a unicorn, whereas the indefinite reading does not. However, in the fragment (30) has exactly one reading, the definite reading:

(30)   **a unicorn is sought by John**

Sentence (30) is not given an indefinite reading. People have differing intuitions on this matter. Keith Donnellan has pointed out that there are contexts that seem to allow for the indefinite reading:

> **although a unicorn is sought by John, no one expects him to find one**

It is interesting that if one excludes from consideration intransitive verb phrases in the passive, such as **be sought by John**, it seems that there are no intransitive verb phrases that allow for an indefinite reading of their subject term.[14] I do not believe sentences such as (31), (32), and (33) contain intransitive verb phrases that refute this observation:

(31)   **a unicorn will be in the park**

(32)   **a unicorn appears to be in the park**

(33)   **a unicorn might be in the park**

I regard the correct treatment of the simple future tense to be something similar to that given in PTQ. There Montague gives a sentence like (31) a reading that does not imply the existence of a unicorn, but **will be in the park** is not considered to be an intransitive verb phrase. Sentences like (32) and (33) are discussed in Section 8.

It is possible in Montague's framework to allow for indefinite readings relative to the subject term. For example, one might want to allow (30) to

---

[13] The fragment guarantees that an active sentence and its passive counterpart are logically equivalent; it does not guarantee that they are synonymous. Presumably the notion of synonymy is not analyzed in Montague's framework. Clearly an active sentence and its passive counterpart are logically equivalent; it is less clear that they are synonymous.

[14] Montague (UG, 1974, p. 244) observed that it is difficult to find an example of a basic intransitive verb with this property.

have an indefinite reading. In UG Montague indicates how this can be done (1974, pp. 243–244). The modification involves redefining the syntactic categories. We take as the primitive categories t, CN and T. We then make the following definition:

IV is $t/$T.

All of the remaining traditional categories are defined as before. The mapping from the categories to the types of intensional logic is a function f that has CAT as its domain and is such that for all A, B $\in$ CAT,

$$f(t) = t,$$
$$f(\text{CN}) = \langle e, t \rangle,$$
$$f(\text{T}) = \langle \langle s, \langle e, t \rangle \rangle, t \rangle,$$
$$f(\text{A}/\text{B}) = f(\text{A}//\text{B}) = \langle \langle s, f(\text{B}) \rangle, f(\text{A}) \rangle.$$

In addition, since most verb phrases intuitively do not allow indefinite readings of the subject term, they will have to be guaranteed this property by adding the appropriate meaning postulates.

Although both #**believe of** and #**persuade** are of category (IV/t)/T, the passive form of #**believe of**, unlike #**persuade**, is not of category (IV/t)/T. The passive of (34) is not (35) but (36):

(34)   **John believes of Mary that she walks**

(35)   ***Mary is believed of by John that she walks**

(36)   **it is believed by John of Mary that she walks**

Sentence (36) is not included in the fragment. It is possible to treat such sentences, but I have not done so for the purpose of simplicity.

Sentence (37) is not included in the fragment:

(37)   **Chicago is given to Mary by John**

I believe that (37) is derived by way of transformation T_0, mentioned in Section 4, as follows:

Possibly transformation T_0, or another transformation that is quite similar, is the source for sentences, which are not in our fragment, such as the following:

> **it is believed that Mary walks by John**
> **Mary is forced to walk by John**
> **Bill is persuaded that Mary walks by John**

Sentences such as (38) and (39) are not included in the fragment:

(38)   **Mary is given by John Chicago**

(39)   **Mary is given Chicago by John**

I regard (38) and (39) as being derived from (40) and (37), respectively, by way of some meaning-preserving transformation that applies to sentences:

(40)   **Chicago is given by John to Mary**

English allows for a passive agent phrase to be omitted when it is **by someone** or **by something**. The following are grammatical sentences:

> **Mary is loved**
> **it is believed that Mary walks**
> **Chicago is given to Mary**
> **Mary is forced to walk**
> **Bill is persuaded that Mary walks**

I believe that such sentences are derived by way of some meaning-preserving deletion transformation.

This treatment of the passive voice suffers from a severe shortcoming. It cannot treat certain combinations of verbs in the passive with adverbs. Intuitively (41) and (42) are logically equivalent:

(41)   **Mary voluntarily loves John**

(42)   **John is loved voluntarily by Mary**

Although the fragment does not include (42), it does include

(43)   **John voluntarily is loved by Mary**

In the fragment (41) and (43) are not equivalent. This is as it should be, since intuitively they make different assertions. Sentence (41) is an assertion about a voluntary act of Mary's. Sentence (43) is an assertion that John voluntarily is the object of Mary's act. However, I can see no way of treating (42) in this framework. It appears that the traditional treatment of the passive voice by way of a transformation can treat (42) but not (43). Partee's approach can accommodate both (42) and (43) (see Partee, 1973).

6. THE DUMMY SUBJECT it

Sentences such as (44) and (45) could be treated by introducing both a proposition level and a property-of-individuals level:

(44)   **that Mary walks is believed by John**

(45)   **to walk is easy for Mary**

The idea is to introduce into a fragment proposition-denoting terms and terms that denote properties of individuals along with common noun phrases and verb phrases that have such entities in their extensions. For example, the following would be an analysis tree for (44):

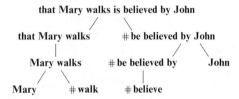

Here **that Mary walks** is a proposition-denoting term that is of a different syntactic category than T, and #**be believed by John** is a proposition-level verb phrase that is of a different syntactic category than IV. However, I believe that sentences (44) and (45) are more properly treated by deriving them from (46) and (47), respectively, by transformations:

(46)   **it is believed by John that Mary walks**

(47)   **it is easy for Mary to walk**

I give my reasons for this view in Section 8.

Both (46) and (47) are included in the fragment. Sentence (46) has the following analysis tree:

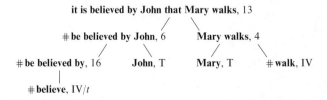

Here #**be believed by John** is a nonbasic expression of category t/t. In the fragment #**appear** is a basic expression of category t/t:

(48)   **it appears that Mary walks**

Sentence (48) has the following analysis tree in the fragment:[15]

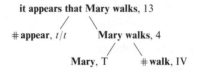

it appears that Mary walks, 13

#appear, *t/t*   Mary walks, 4

Mary, T   #walk, IV

Sentence (47) has the following analysis tree in the fragment:

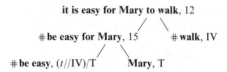

it is easy for Mary to walk, 12

#be easy for Mary, 15   #walk, IV

#be easy, (*t//IV*)/T   Mary, T

Here #**be easy** is a basic expression of category (*t//IV*)/T and #**be easy for Mary** is a nonbasic expression of category *t//IV*. #**be easy** is also a basic expression of category *t//IV*, as in the following analysis tree:

it is easy to walk, 12

#be easy, *t//IV*   #walk, IV

7. REFLEXIVE PRONOUNS

In EFL Montague discusses the problem of accommodating reflexive pronouns (1974, p. 198, particularly n. 12). He states that it would be quite possible to give rules providing for reflexive pronouns, but he declines to do so because of "the rather uninteresting complications that would be involved." In our fragment reflexive pronouns are included by complicating the syntactic rules but without altering the semantics. For example, (49) in PTQ has the same reading as (50) in our fragment:

(49)   **John loves him**

(50)   **John loves himself**

In EFL Montague suggests that reflexive pronouns be introduced by the rules of quantification. Our fragment takes a different approach; certain structural operations reflexivize occurrences of pronoun variables.

---

[15] Wotschke, in Wotschke (1972), was the first to suggest using such a category as *t/t* along with the dummy subject **it** in order to treat a verb like **appear** as in (48).

Structural operation F_4 introduces reflexivization, as exemplified by the following analysis tree:

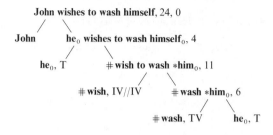

Pronoun variables are marked with an asterisk when they are available for reflexivization. If the subject term is of the form he_n, then F_4 reflexivizes all pronoun variables of the form $*him_n$ that occur in the verb phrase. If the subject term is not of the form he_n, then the relevant pronoun variables are not reflexivized and the asterisks are deleted. The latter case is illustrated by the following analysis tree:

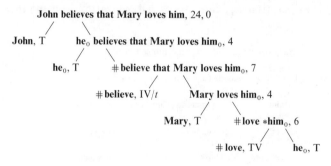

Structural operation F_6 also introduces reflexivization:

#give (Mary) to herself, 24, 0

In this analysis tree F_8 enclosed the direct object in parentheses, since it was of the form he_n. The parentheses enabled F_6 to determine that it should reflexivize the indirect object. The parentheses indicate that $*him_0$ is the entire direct object and not merely a constituent of the direct object, as in the following example:

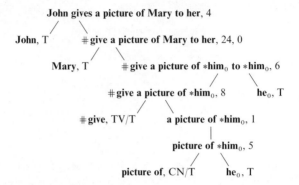

In this analysis tree F_8 did not enclose the direct object in parentheses, since it was not of the form **he**$_n$. The lack of parentheses enabled F_6 to determine that it should not reflexivize the indirect object **he**$_0$ even though *him$_0$ is a constituent of the direct object.

Structural operation F_{11} introduces reflexivization in a manner parallel to F_6:

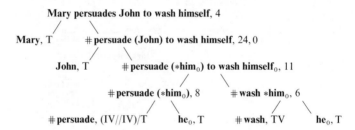

It has been observed that the verbs **force** and **promise** differ in that (51) differs from (53) and (52) from (54) on the matter of whether the bound pronoun is reflexive or not:

(51)   **John forces Mary to wash him**

(52)   **John forces Mary to wash herself**

(53)   **John promises Mary to wash himself**

(54)   **John promises Mary to wash her**

This difference can be explained. Notice that although (51) and (52) are in the fragment, (53) and (54) are not. This is because #**force** is a member of $B_{(IV//IV)/T}$, whereas #**promise** is not. I believe that (53) and (54) are in some way related to, possibly transformationally derived from, the more expanded sentences (55) and (56), respectively:

(55)   **John promises Mary that he will wash himself**

(56)   **John promises Mary that he will wash her**

Notice that (51) and (52) cannot stand in a similar relation to (57) and (58), respectively, since the latter expressions are ungrammatical:

(57)   ***John forces Mary that he will wash him**

(58)   ***John forces Mary that he will wash herself**

In our fragment the objects of adverbial and adjectival prepositions are never reflexive pronouns. The following analysis tree illustrates this feature:

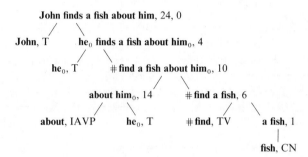

It is still unclear to me how reflexivization interacts with adverbial and adjectival prepositions. Consider **with** in the sense of accompaniment. Intuitively this preposition should be included in B_{IAVP}. When it is used to modify a verb phrase with a transitive verb, it does not take a reflexive pronoun:

> **John takes a pen with him**
> ***John takes a pen with himself**

However, it does take a reflexive pronoun with an intransitive verb:

> **John walks with himself**
> ***John walks with him**

It appears that **in** and **about**, which are included in B_{IAVP} in the fragment, behave in the same way. Sentence (59) seems to be preferable to (60):

(59)   **John walks in himself**

(60)   ***John walks in him**

However, the fragment generates (60) rather than (59). This problem needs further work.

In treating the passive voice along with reflexive pronouns, the syntactic rules had to be complicated in order to treat a certain feature of English. The required complication can be illustrated by an example:

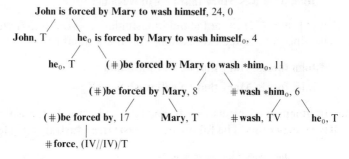

We prefix the passive verbs of category $(IV//IV)/T$ with the marker $(\#)$ rather than $\#$. Thus in the preceding example, when **$(\#)$be forced by Mary** modifies **$\#$wash $*$him$_0$** the marker $(\#)$ signals structural operation F_{11} not to delete the occurrence of $*$ in **$\#$wash $*$him$_0$**. In the following example, when **$(\#)$be forced by $(*$him$_0)$** modifies **$\#$wash $*$him$_0$** the marker $(\#)$ signals structural operation F_{11} not to reflexivize the occurrence of $*$him$_0$ in **$\#$wash $*$him$_0$**:

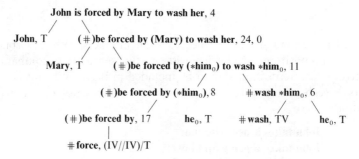

8. **there** AND THE NEED FOR TRANSFORMATIONS

Certain kinds of English sentences appear to be most naturally treated by introducing syntactic rules that closely resemble some of the standard transformations postulated by linguists. It is my impression that these transformations are of a degree of complexity that makes them almost impossible to formulate, even with a modicum of precision, within a reasonable amount of space. In part this is due to there being many exceptions. Yet I am convinced that the only natural way of treating such sentences is by constructing such syntactic rules, and I wish to indicate their character even though this can be done only in a sketchy and imprecise way.

I regard the linguistic facts considered in this section as having the potential to force major revisions in the development given here. This is not to say that such revisions might involve a change in the entailment conditions imposed on sentences by our fragment; I regard my beliefs on this matter as somewhat fixed. Rather, such revisions could involve radical changes in the syntax, the manner in which sentences are derived. More is said about this later.

The need for transformations becomes apparent when one tries to accommodate the word **there** in Montague's framework. Here I have in mind the use of **there** that occurs in sentences asserting existence, as in (61) and (62); this is to be distinguished from the demonstrative use of **there** that is used to indicate a place:

(61)   **there exists a unicorn**

(62)   **there is a unicorn in the park**

How is **there** to be introduced into the derivational history of a sentence? It might be thought that **there** is a lexical item, a basic term in B_T. This is belied by two observations:

1. The following sentences are ungrammatical:

> ***there walks**
> ***John forces there to walk**
> ***John persuades there that Mary walks**

2. If **there** were a term, what would its translation in intensional logic be? It could not be the translation of **an entity**, since the following could be true:

> **there are two unicorns in the park**

A more plausible account is that **there** is a syncategorematic expression that is functioning as a place holder for a term that occurs later in the sentence. This suggests that **there** is introduced by a syntactic rule, as in the following analysis tree for sentence (62):

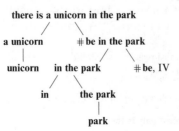

The translation assigned to (62) would be the same as the one given to (63):

(63)   **a unicorn is in the park**

This syntactic rule corresponds to a transformation postulated by linguists called **there** INSERTION. I shall also use this name for our imagined syntactic rule.

It might be thought that **there** INSERTION merely combines a term with an intransitive verb to form a sentence containing **there**. On this view (62) would not be derived as just shown but as follows:

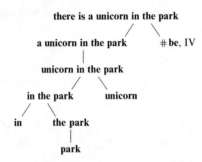

However, this view fails to account for the most natural reading of (64):

(64)   **there are only unicorns in the park**

The proposal requires (64) to be derived as follows:

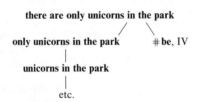

This gives the reading that asserts that everything that exists is a unicorn in the park. Certainly this is a reading for (64). But the approach is unable to assign the most natural reading to (64)—namely, that everything that exists in the park is a unicorn.[16] A similar objection can be made to this

---

[16] Sentence (64) has a third reading, which is expressed by the following:

     all unicorns are in the park

This is probably due to the fact that (64) is structurally similar to the following:

     there are unicorns only in the park

view by considering the following:

(65)   **there landed a bird on the branch**

Sentence (65) should be assigned the reading expressed by (66) and not merely that expressed by (67):

(66)   **a bird landed on the branch**

(67)   **a bird on the branch landed**

It is difficult to formulate **there** INSERTION precisely. There seem to be certain constraints on the terms and verb phrases to which it applies. The following are ungrammatical:

> *there is a unicorn a god
> *there are all unicorns in the park
> *there believes that Mary walks a unicorn

Transformations most naturally explain sentences such as (68) and (69):

(68)   **there appears to be a unicorn in the park**

(69)   **John believes there to be a unicorn in the park**

Sentence (68) seems to have the following derivation:

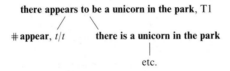

It would be assigned the same translation in intensional logic as that given to the following:

(70)   **it appears that there is a unicorn in the park**

Linguists have called a transformation like T1 SUBJECT-TO-SUBJECT RAISING and **it** REPLACEMENT.

Sentence (69) seems to have the following derivation:

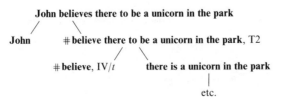

The translation of (69) would‭ be the same as that given to (71):

(71)　　　**John believes that there is a unicorn in the park**

Linguists have called a transformation like T2 SUBJECT-TO-OBJECT RAISING. Transformation T1 accounts for a sentence like (72):

(72)　　　**there is believed by John to be a unicorn in the park**

Sentence (72) has the following derivation:

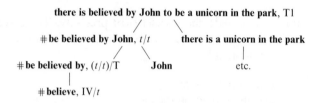

Sentence (72) is not to be confused with (73):

(73)　　　**there is a unicorn believed by John to be in the park**

Sentence (73) is unambiguous and entails the existence of a unicorn. There seem to be two possible sources for (73). It could be elliptic for

(74)　　　**there is a unicorn that is believed by John to be in the park**

Or, if **# be believed by John to be in the park** were a member of P$_{IV}$, which it is not, then (73) could be derived by **there** Insertion as follows:

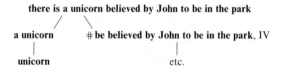

I believe that the verb phrase should be a member of P$_{IV}$; this matter is discussed later.

In the case of certain verbs such as # **prefer** and # **expect**, T2 can introduce **for**:

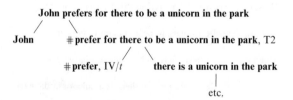

However, there are some verbs that do not take **for**:

*John believes for there to be a unicorn in the park

Possibly a transformation, somewhat similar to T2, introduces **for** into passive constructions, as in the following example:

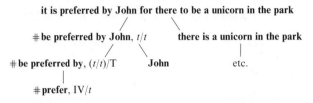

The same transformation might be involved in active constructions such as the following:

be necessary, *t/t* and there is a unicorn in the park

it is necessary for there to be a unicorn in the park

be necessary, *t/t*   there is a unicorn in the park

etc.

As with T2, this transformation will not apply in all cases:

*it is believed by John for there to be a unicorn in the park

Transformations T1 and T2 appear to raise expressions other than **there**. For example, they seem to underlie certain readings for sentences (75) and (76):

(75)   **a unicorn appears to be in the park**

(76)   **John expects a unicorn to be in the park**

Sentences (75) and (76) seem to have the following derivations, respectively:

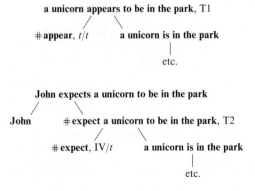

Both (75) and (76) are in our fragment. However, in the fragment they have only readings that entail that a unicorn exists. Intuitively both sentences also have readings that do not entail the existence of a unicorn. I am inclined to account for these readings by way of T1 and T2, as just above.[17]

Both T1 and T2 can raise an occurrence of the dummy subject **it**:

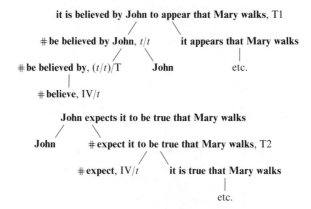

Both T1 and T2 can raise a pronoun variable:

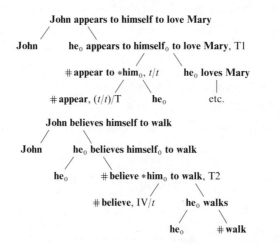

[17] Apparently at one time Montague would have regarded (75) as a sentence having an intransitive verb phrase **appear to be in the park** that allows for a nonreferential reading of its subject term. (See PTQ, 1974, p. 248. This approach is discussed in Section 5.) This idea seems less plausible when one considers the related sentence involving **there**—(68). Montague's approach offers no explanation of (68). The tranformational approach captures the intuition that (68) and (75) are derived, in part, in the same manner and have a reading in common.

T1 can raise the same term more than once:

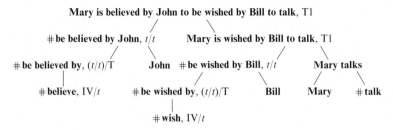

T2 can raise a term that has already been raised by T1, as in the following example:

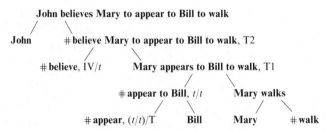

In the case of certain verb phrases such as #**be true** and #**be necessary**, T1 transforms the "adjective" into an "adverb":

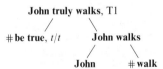

Possibly T1, along with deletion of the passive agent phrase, provides a derivation like the following:

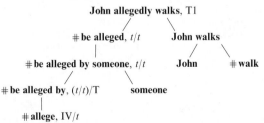

All of the preceding examples illustrating T1 and T2 involve complements in the simple present tense. However, both T1 and T2 can be applied when the complement is in the simple past, the present perfect, or the past perfect tense. It seems that T1 and T2 cannot be applied when the complement sentence is in the simple future or the future perfect tense:

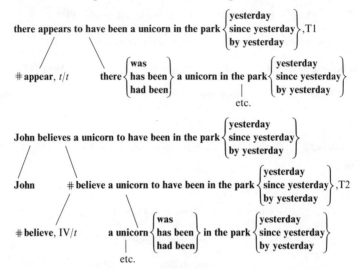

I conjecture that whenever a sentence has an infinitive clause with **have** and a past participle, such as **to have walked**, it is derived transformationally along lines similar to the preceding examples. This is supported by the fact that the following sentences are ungrammatical:

> *John tries to have walked
> *it is easy to have walked
> *John forces Mary to have walked
> *it is easy for Mary to have walked

It appears that another transformation is required in order to treat sentences like (77) and (78):

(77)   **John is easy to please**

(78)   **John is tough for Mary to please**

Sentence (77) seems to have the following derivation:

$$\text{John is easy to please, T3}$$

be easy, $t/\!/\text{IV}$ # please John

please   John

The translation of (77) would be the same as that given to

(79)   **it is easy to please John**

Linguists have called a transformation like T3 **tough** MOVEMENT.

T3 can raise a pronoun variable:

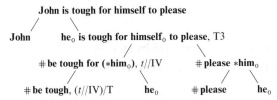

Possibly T3 accounts for sentences such as the following:

a fish is easy to give to Mary
Mary is easy to give a fish to
John is easy to force to wash Mary
Mary is easy to force John to wash
John is easy to persuade that Mary walks

The difficulty in incorporating transformations like T1, T2, and T3 into Montague's framework lies in the fact that they require a "knowledge" of the derivational history of the argument expressions. The transformations appear to be structural operations that take analysis trees as arguments. For example, in order for T2 to derive #**believe a unicorn to be in the park** from #**believe** and **a unicorn is in the park**, T2 must be able to single out the subject of the complement as well as recover the uninflected verb #**be**. It is considerations of this sort that suggests that the syntax might have to be radically revised in order to accommodate transformations.

This framework suggests the need for some meaning-preserving transformations that have not been considered by linguists.[18] Consider sentences (80) and (81):

(80)   **that Mary walks is believed by John**

(81)   **to please John is easy for Mary**

These sentences seem to have the following derivations, respectively:

that Mary walks is believed by John, T4
|
it is believed by John that Mary walks
|
etc.

to please John is easy for Mary, T5
|
it is easy for Mary to please John
|
etc.

---

[18] Emonds seems to be an exception (see Emonds, 1972).

The existence of such transformations is supported by the fact that (82) and (83) are acceptable (where the occurrence of **he** in (82) is a bound pronoun):

(82)   **that he walks is believed by no man**

(83)   **to please herself is easy for no woman**

(I have chosen examples involving a quantifier that is not included in the fragment because it makes the point more clearly than any quantifier in the fragment.) These sentences would have the following derivations, respectively:

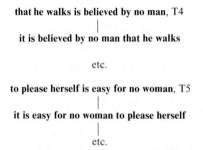

that he walks is believed by no man, T4

|

it is believed by no man that he walks

etc.

to please herself is easy for no woman, T5

|

it is easy for no woman to please herself

|

etc.

Both T4 and T5 can work in combination with T1, as illustrated by the following derivations:

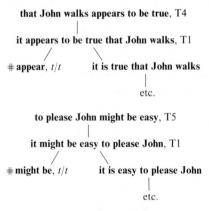

that John walks appears to be true, T4

|

it appears to be true that John walks, T1

/   \

⧣**appear**, t/t **it is true that John walks**

|

etc.

to please John might be easy, T5

|

it might be easy to please John, T1

/   \

⧣**might be**, t/t **it is easy to please John**

|

etc.

T4 cannot raise a complement past a verb like **appear**:

***that John walks appears**, T4

|

it appears that John walks

|

etc.

Unlike T1, T2, and T3, transformations T4 and T5 cannot raise pronoun variables. The following derivations are unacceptable (although the resulting sentences are grammatical, they are assigned inappropriate readings):

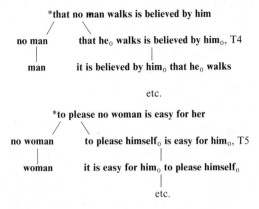

$$\text{*that no man walks is believed by him}$$

no man — that he_0 walks is believed by him_0, T4

man — it is believed by him_0 that he_0 walks

etc.

*to please no woman is easy for her

no woman — to please $himself_0$ is easy for him_0, T5

woman — it is easy for him_0 to please $himself_0$

etc.

I am proposing that (80) and (81) be derived from (84) and (85) by transformations T4 and T5, respectively:

(84)   **it is believed by John that Mary walks**

(85)   **it is easy for Mary to please John**

The standard view in linguistics is just the reverse. Linguists have postulated a transformation, EXTRAPOSITION, that derives (84) and (85) from (80) and (81), respectively. At present I do not prefer this approach. The view requires that (80) and (81) be treated directly. In Section 6, I indicated how this could be done by introducing a proposition level and a property-of-individuals level. But this approach has two drawbacks. The first is that a constraint would have to be introduced to the effect that one cannot quantify certain sentences—certain sentences that have *not* been derived transformationally. Otherwise unacceptable derivations such as the following would be allowed:

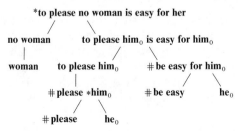

*to please no woman is easy for her

no woman — to please him_0 is easy for him_0

woman — to please him_0 — #be easy for him_0

#please *him_0 — #be easy — he_0

#please — he_0

I find this less congenial than building constraints into the transformations themselves. I am proposing such a constraint for T4 and T5 by requiring that they do not raise pronoun variables.

The second drawback is that we no longer have a natural treatment of sentences (82) and (83); we would still have to provide an explanation of why in these cases the bound pronoun precedes the term that binds it. These are my reasons for regarding the sentences with the dummy subject **it** as fundamental and the related sentences without the **it** as derivative.

In the fragment #**appear** is included in $B_{IV//IV}$, $B_{t/t}$, and $B_{(t/t)/T}$. By including ◁#**appear** in $B_{IV//IV}$ we can explain a puzzle raised in Partee (1968). Suppose that #**appear** is not included in $B_{IV//IV}$. Then (86) and (87) could be derived only by way of T1:

(86)   **John appears to love Mary**

(87)   **Mary appears to be loved by John**

In this case (86) and (87) must be logically equivalent. However, although (86) and (87) seem to have a reading in common, each has, in addition, a reading the other does not have. For example, (86) has the reading that asserts that John has the appearance of loving Mary, but (87) does not have this reading. By including #**appear** in $B_{IV//IV}$ we can account for such readings.

#**appear** is included in both $B_{t/t}$ and $B_{(t/t)/T}$ because it seems that the first #**appear** cannot be analyzed by, or regarded as elliptic for, a construction involving the second #**appear**. For example, (88) is not elliptic for (89).

(88)   **it appears that Mary walks**

(89)   **it appears to someone that Mary walks**

Our fragment, including the proposed transformations, offers no account of the derivations of grammatical sentences such as the following:[19]

> **John walks and is easy to please**
> **John tries to be easy for Mary to please**
> **John forces Bill to be believed by Mary to talk**
> **it is tough to appear to Mary to talk**

The problem stems from the fact that in the fragment #**be easy to please**, #**be easy for Mary to please**, #**be believed by Mary to talk**, and #**appear to Mary to talk** are not members of P_{IV}. Possibly such sentences can be treated by deriving these verb phrases in such a manner that, for example, #**be easy to please** is of category IV and has the translation given to #**be an entity such that it is easy to please it**.

University of Pittsburgh

---

[19] Partee (1968, p. 4) Partee's approach in this volume (pp. 51–76) does account for such sentences.

ACKNOWLEDGMENTS

This paper consists of revised material from my Ph.D. dissertation (Bennett, 1974). The material has had a rather long evolution and many people have influenced the final product. But Barbara Partee and David Kaplan have been major forces. The work was written while I participated in the MSSB Workshop on Syntax and Semantics of Non-Extensional Constructions (funded by NSF) at the University of Massachusetts at Amherst during the summer of 1974.

REFERENCES

Bennett, M. Some Extensions of a Montague Fragment of English. Unpublished doctoral dissertation, University of California, Los Angeles, 1974. [Available from Xerox University Microfilms, Ann Arbor, Michigan, Order Number 74-22,937.]

Chomsky, N. *Aspects of the Theory of Syntax*. Cambridge, Massachusetts: M. I. T. Press, 1965.

Emonds, J. A reformulation of certain syntactic transformations. In S. Peters (Ed.), *Goals of Linguistic Theory*. Englewood Cliffs, New Jersey: Prentice-Hall, 1972.

Montague, R. English as a formal language. In B. Visenti *et al. Linguaggi nella societa e nella tecnica*. Milan: Edizioni di Communità, 1970. Pp. 189–224. [Reprinted in R. Thomason (Ed.), *Formal Philosophy: Selected Papers of Richard Montague*. New Haven: Yale Univ. Press, 1974. Pp. 188–221.]

Montague, R. Universal grammar. *Theoria*, 1970, **36**, 373–398. [Reprinted in R. Thomason (Ed.), *Formal Philosophy: Selected Papers of Richard Montague*. New Haven: Yale Univ. Press, 1974. Pp. 222–246.]

Montague, R. The proper treatment of quantification in ordinary English. In J. Hintikka, J. Moravcsik, and P. Suppes (Eds.), *Approaches to Natural Language: Proceedings of the 1970 Stanford Workshop on Grammar and Semantics*. Dordrecht: Reidel, 1973. Pp. 221–242. [Reprinted in R. Thomason (Ed.), *Formal Philosophy: Selected Papers of Richard Montague*. New Haven: Yale Univ. Press, 1974. Pp. 247–270.]

Partee, B. H. On Some Fundamental Conflicts in the Establishment of Deep Structure Subjects. Unpublished manuscript. University of California, Los Angeles, 1968.

Partee, B. H. Some transformational extensions of Montague grammar. *Journal of Philosophical Logic*, 1973, **2**, 509–534. [Reprinted in this volume, pp. 51–76.]

Wotschke, E. M. Complementation in a Montague Grammar. In R. Rodman (Ed.), *Papers in Montague Grammar*. (Occasional Papers in Linguistics, No. 2.) Los Angeles: University of California, Los Angeles Linguistics Department, 1972.

ROBERT RODMAN

SCOPE PHENOMENA, "MOVEMENT TRANSFORMATIONS," AND RELATIVE CLAUSES

1. INTRODUCTION

In Montague (1973) (henceforth PTQ)[1] rules are given for the production of *such that* (restrictive) relative clauses (e.g., **the man such that he came to dinner**). Whereas Montague's treatment of the semantics of restrictive relative clauses appears to be adequate, the syntax is not. The use of *such that* clauses is confined for the most part to a mathematically oriented mode of speech and should be considered a syntactic manifestation of an argot of English. Therefore one of the tasks of this study is to give the syntactic rules necessary for generating ordinary restrictive relative clauses in English.

It is widely known that there are certain conditions under which an element may not be relativized (cf. Ross, 1967). An adequate grammar of English must provide constraints on the syntax in order to prevent violation of these conditions and forestall the production of ungrammatical sentences. A second objective of this paper, then, is a modification of Montague's syntax, as given in PTQ, to effect these constraints. I will show how in any event the syntax must be modified to account for a certain relationship that obtains between the scope of a quantifier in the head nominal (common noun phrase) of a relative clause and the scope of any quantifier of any element inside that relative clause. I will also demonstrate that such a modification automatically constrains relativization in just the right way. Thus a generalization is captured in a Montague grammar that as yet has not, and perhaps cannot, be captured by any "standard" grammar.

Finally, this study will suggest rules, syntactic and semantic, for the production of nonrestrictive relative clauses in a Montague grammar.

2. RULES OF FORMATION OF RESTRICTIVE RELATIVE CLAUSES

Montague's syntactic rule of restrictive relativization (S3 in PTQ) will be modified to account for the data in (1) and (2):

(1)   a.   **the man who ate a fish**

---

[1] I am assuming familiarity with this work and will make frequent reference to rules that appear in it.

b. **the man that ate a fish**
c. ***the man ate a fish** ($\notin P_T$)

(2)   a. **the fish which a man ate**
b. **the fish that a man ate**
c. **the fish a man ate**

The modification of the rule in (3) is not complete. As more new information is introduced, the rule will be revised accordingly.

(3)   NEW S3: If $\zeta \in P_{CN}$ and $\phi \in P_t$, then $F_{3,n}(\zeta, \phi) \in P_{CN}$, where $F_{3,n}(\zeta, \phi) = \zeta$ **that** ϕ' and ϕ' comes from ϕ by replacing the first occurrence of

$$\begin{Bmatrix} \mathbf{he}_n \\ \mathbf{him}_n \end{Bmatrix}$$

by

$$\begin{Bmatrix} \mathbf{wh-he}_n \\ \mathbf{wh-him}_n \end{Bmatrix}$$

and all further occurrences of $\mathbf{he}_n$ or $\mathbf{him}_n$ by

$$\begin{Bmatrix} \mathbf{he} \\ \mathbf{she} \\ \mathbf{it} \end{Bmatrix} \quad \text{or} \quad \begin{Bmatrix} \mathbf{him} \\ \mathbf{her} \\ \mathbf{it} \end{Bmatrix},$$

respectively, according to the gender of ζ.

It should be noted that translation rule T3 is unaffected by the change.

Three other rules are needed in order to account for (1) and (2). The first of these, which can be thought of as a rule of RELATIVE PRONOUN DELETION, is given in (4):

(4)   S3'—RELATIVE PRONOUN DELETION: If $\phi \in P_{CN}$, then $F_3'(\phi) \in P_{CN}$, where $F_3'(\phi) = \phi'$ and ϕ' comes from ϕ as a result of deleting

$$\mathbf{wh-}\begin{Bmatrix} \mathbf{he}_n \\ \mathbf{him}_n \end{Bmatrix}$$

if it is not preceded by a member of P_{CN}.

When S3' applies, a relative clause results in which the "relative pronoun" is **that**. If the *wh* variable is not deleted by S3', it must be preposed. Rule S3'' in (5) effects *wh* Preposing by replacing the **that** introduced by S3 with the appropriate *wh* word:

(5)   S3''—**wh** PREPOSING: If $\phi \in P_{CN}$, then $F_3''(\phi) \in P_{CN}$, where $F_3''(\phi) = \phi'$ and ϕ' comes from ϕ as a result of replacing the

first **that** in ϕ by the first

$$\mathbf{wh}-\begin{Bmatrix}\mathbf{he}_n \\ \mathbf{him}_n\end{Bmatrix}$$

in ϕ and changing that occurrence of

$$\mathbf{wh}-\begin{Bmatrix}\mathbf{he}_n \\ \mathbf{him}_n\end{Bmatrix} \quad \text{to} \quad \begin{Bmatrix}\mathbf{who} \\ \mathbf{whom}\end{Bmatrix}$$

or **which**, depending on whether the head nominal is of neuter[2] gender.

If both S3′ and S3″ fail to "apply," then the sentence that is being generated will be thrown out. This is not an ad hoc condition that I have added to the grammar because of the (necessary) optionality of Rules S3′ and S3″. It is in fact a result of a convention that is implicit in all of Montague's work, viz., that an expression containing an unbound variable is ill-formed. In this case if a *wh* variable remains—that is, if it is neither deleted by S3′ nor preposed by S3″ and replaced by a *wh* word—then the expression it belongs to is excluded.

The last rule of this group is one that may eventually find broader usage in the grammar. I mean the rule of **that** DELETION, necessary to derive (2c), and quite likely the same rule that relates sentences like **I think that the king is mad/I think the king is mad**. The rule is given in (6):

(6)   S3‴—*that* DELETION: If $\phi \in P_{CN}$, then $F_3{}'''(\phi) \in P_{CN}$, where $F_3{}'''(\phi) = \phi'$ and ϕ' comes from ϕ as a result of deleting the first occurrence of **that**, provided that it is followed immediately by a member of P_T.

Here are a couple of skeletal sample derivations:

(7)
```
          the man who ate a fish, F₁
                  |
          man who ate a fish, F₃″
                  |
          man that wh–he₁ ate a fish, F₃,₁
               /        \
          man          he₁ ate a fish
```

(8)
```
          the fish a man ate, F₁
                  |
          fish a man ate, F₃‴
                  |
          fish that a man ate, F₃′
                  |
          fish that a man ate wh–him₂, F₃,₂
               /        \
          fish          a man ate him₂
```

---

[2] This distinction could be made in Rule S3 or even elsewhere.

3. QUANTIFIER SCOPE

Consider the following data:

(9)   a. **John dates every woman who loves a fish.**
         b. **John has dated a woman who loves every man.**

The grammar given by Montague in PTQ predicts that the sentences in (9) are two ways ambiguous, the ambiguity centering on the relative scopes of the quantifiers **a** and **every**. However, neither sentence actually is ambiguous. In (9a) **every** has wider scope—the sentence is never interpreted semantically as "There exists a single fish such that John dates every woman who loves it." Likewise, no semantic interpretation of (9b) permits there to be more than one woman. The strangeness of (10) punctuates this fact:

(10)   ***Guinevere has a bone that is in every corner of the house.** (cf. **Guinevere has a bone in every corner of the house.**)

Thus the following statement is evidently a fact about English (and perhaps a fact about language) that must be reflected in any adequate grammar of English:

(11)   In a relative clause the element that is relativized always has wider scope than any other element in that relative clause.

In a Montague grammar we capture this important generality by forbidding any variable that appears inside a relative clause to be bound by a quantifier. I propose to do this by introducing a new type of variable called a SUPERSCRIPT R VARIABLE. The following remodified S3 (12) and newly modified S14 (13) will accomplish the change:

(12)   S3 (LATEST VERSION): If $\zeta \in P_{CN}$ and $\phi \in P_t$, then $F_{3,n}(\zeta, \phi) \in P_{CN}$, where $F_{3,n}(\zeta, \phi) = \zeta$ **that** ϕ' and ϕ' comes from ϕ by replacing the first occurrence of

$$\left\{ \begin{array}{l} \mathbf{he}_n \\ \mathbf{him}_n \end{array} \right\}$$

by

$$\left\{ \begin{array}{l} \mathbf{wh\text{--}he}_n \\ \mathbf{wh\text{--}him}_n \end{array} \right\}$$

and all further occurrences of $\mathbf{he}_n/\mathbf{he}_n{}^R$ or $\mathbf{him}_n/\mathbf{him}_n{}^R$ by

$$\left\{ \begin{array}{l} \mathbf{he} \\ \mathbf{she} \\ \mathbf{it} \end{array} \right\} \quad \text{or} \quad \left\{ \begin{array}{l} \mathbf{him} \\ \mathbf{her} \\ \mathbf{it} \end{array} \right\},$$

respectively, according to the gender of ζ, AND ALL OTHER OC-CURRENCES OF $\mathbf{he}_m$ OR $\mathbf{him}_m$, $m \neq n$, ARE CHANGED TO $\mathbf{he}_m^R$ or $\mathbf{him}_m^R$, respectively.

(13)   S14 (MODIFIED):[3] If $\alpha \in P_T$ and $\phi \in P_t$, then $F_{10,n}(\alpha, \phi) \in P_t$, where either (a) α does not have the form $\mathbf{he}_k$: Then $F_{10,n}(\alpha, \phi) = \phi'$ and ϕ' comes from ϕ by replacing the FIRST occurrence of $\mathbf{he}_n$ or $\mathbf{him}_n$ by α and all other occurrences of $\mathbf{he}_n/\mathbf{he}_n^R$ or $\mathbf{him}_n/\mathbf{him}_n^R$ by

$$\begin{Bmatrix} \mathbf{he} \\ \mathbf{she} \\ \mathbf{it} \end{Bmatrix} \text{ or } \begin{Bmatrix} \mathbf{him} \\ \mathbf{her} \\ \mathbf{it} \end{Bmatrix},$$

respectively, according to the gender of α, or (b) $\alpha = \mathbf{he}_k$: Then $F_{10,n}(\alpha, \phi) = \phi'$ and ϕ' comes from ϕ by replacing all occurrences of $\mathbf{he}_n/\mathbf{he}_n^R$ or $\mathbf{him}_n/\mathbf{him}_n^R$ by $\mathbf{he}_k/\mathbf{he}_k^R$ or $\mathbf{him}_k/\mathbf{him}_k^R$, respectively.

The translation rule that corresponds to Rule S14 remains the same.

Let me illustrate the operation of the modified rules by attempting two derivations of (9b). The one in which **every** has wider scope [viz. (15)] will block by the convention, alluded to earlier, that all variables must eventually be bound. The superscript R variable in (15) cannot be bound by Rule S14.

(14)

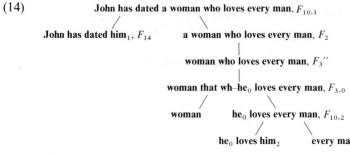

(15)   *John has dated a woman who loves every man

---

[3] Similar changes will of course have to be made in the two other rules of quantification, S15 and S16.

4. RELATIVIZING ELEMENTS OF RELATIVE CLAUSES

The sentences in (16) are ungrammatical. However, (16a) could be generated by the fragment of a grammar given by Montague in PTQ:

(16)   a. *The fish such that John has dated a woman such that she loves it walks.
        b. *The fish which John has dated a woman who loves walks.

In English you cannot relativize an element that belongs to a relative clause, and an adequate grammar of the language must take this into account. As it turns out, the seemingly ad hoc changes made in S3 serve, without need for additional modification, to preclude sentences like (16b) from being generated. Thus the Montague grammar, as I have modified it, claims that the fact that elements of relative clauses cannot be relativized, and the fact that such elements always have narrower scope than the NP head of their relative clause, are somehow related. Whether this claim is empirically justifiable on purely linguistic grounds remains to be seen. If it is, then the kind of grammar advocated by Montague receives empirical support of particular significance, since, as I stated at the outset, no "standard" theory can, to my knowledge, associate two such facts so closely.

In (17) an (unsuccessful) attempt is made to generate (16b):

(17)   *fish that John has dated a woman who loves wh–him_1

DERIVATION BLOCKS (because $him_1{}^R$ cannot be relativized)

fish   John has dated a woman who loves $him_1{}^R$

woman that wh–he_0 loves $him_1{}^R$, $F_{3,0}$

woman he_0 loves him_1

Plainly, then, no element inside a relative clause may be relativized or quantified; that is, superscript R variables are not subject to binding by either the relative clause rule, S3, or the rule of quantification, S14. Note, however, that a superscript R variable is not unbindable—it can be bound by "pronominalization,"[4] as illustrated in (18):

(18)   Bill found a fish and John has dated a woman who loves it, $F_{10,1}$

a fish   Bill found him_1 and John has dated a woman who loves $him_1{}^R$, F_8

---

[4] When a variable falls under the rubric "all further occurrences" (cf. (12) and (13), for example) and is replaced by a pronoun, I consider that operation PRONOMINALIZATION.

5. RELATIVIZING ELEMENTS OF COORDINATE STRUCTURES

Let us now look at sentences that involve the conjoining of term phrases:

(19)　　a. **A soldier shot every woman and every child.**[5]

　　　　b. **Every woman loves a dog or a cat.**

These sentences do not possess the scope ambiguities that Montague's grammatical fragment in PTQ would predict;[6] (19a) and (19b) are only two ways ambiguous, not six ways. The quantifiers in the conjoined structure function as a single unit with respect to scope differences vis-à-vis the subject of the sentence. These facts lead me to reformulate rule S13 along the same lines as S3:

(20)　　S13 (REVISED VERSION): If $\alpha,\ \beta \in P_T$, then $F_9{}'(\alpha, \beta) \in P_T$, where

$$F_9{}'(\alpha, \beta) = \alpha' \begin{Bmatrix} \textbf{or} \\ \textbf{(and)}^7 \end{Bmatrix} \beta'$$

and $\alpha',\ \beta'$ come from α, β by replacing any variable

$$\begin{Bmatrix} \textbf{he}_n \\ \textbf{him}_n \end{Bmatrix}$$

by

$$\begin{Bmatrix} \textbf{he}_n{}^R \\ \textbf{him}_n{}^R \end{Bmatrix}$$

for all n.

This reformulation has the effect of forcing any variable to be quantified or relativized prior to the point in the derivation where the term phrase containing that variable is conjoined to another term phrase. Since the superscript R variables can, as pointed out earlier, be "pronominalized," it is still possible to derive sentences like **the boy believes that Mary saw Bill and him**.

Note that the same results hold if the term phrase–coordinate structure occurs in subject position. The sentences in (21) are only two ways ambiguous:

(21)　　a. **Every dog or every cat loves a woman.**

　　　　b. **A dog or a cat loves every woman.**

---

[5] This sentence does not actually belong to the frequent given in PTQ, but nothing is affected by imagining this slight extension for nonsubject term phrases.

[6] Indeed differences in scope are predicted among elements WITHIN the coordinate structure. Linguistically no such scope ambiguity exists, so a meaning postulate is necessary to eliminate semantic differences that would arise in such a case.

[7] See note 5.

As with the rule of relative clause formation, S3, the changes imposed on S13 are ad hoc to the situation as it has developed so far. However, when it is realized that before the revision made on S13 in (20) the sentences in (22) were generated by the grammar, but that the new S13 blocks the production of such deformities, then the changes appear better motivated:

(22)   a. ***John loves the woman who and the dog walks in the park.**
        b. ***John loves the dog which the woman and walks in the park.**

It is true of English, and indeed of most languages, I suspect, that elements that belong to coordinate structures cannot be relativized. This constraint is captured in Montague's fragment, as I have modified it, as a consequence of changes imposed solely to account for certain facts that obtain with respect to the scope of quantifiers.

6. SOME PROBLEMS

It is natural to try to generalize the modifications made in S13 to the other rules of coordinate structure formation, S11 (t phrase conjunction) and S12 (IV phrase conjunction). In the case of S12, unless my intuitions are mistaken, (23b) does have a scope ambiguity even though (23a) does not:

(23)   a. **Every soldier found a student and shot him.**
        b. **A soldier found every student and shot him.**

I believe (23b) has a preferred reading in which **a soldier** has wider scope, and the superscript R convention can certainly be used to capture that fact, though this is a diluted use of what up to now has been a useful and powerful tool. In any event the generation of (24) must be prevented:

(24)   a. ***The fish that every man finds and loves a woman walks.**
        b. ***The fish that a woman loves every man or seeks walks.**

One can imagine modifying S12 along the lines of S13 [cf. also (26)] so that the sentences in (24) are not generated. Then a very ad hoc change to Rule S16 (which quantifies into IV phrases) would have to be made that would allow that rule to bind a superscript R variable by a term phrase containing **every**.[8]

Problems persist in cropping up when we go to modify S11 in such a way

---

[8] As if that were not bad enough, further modifications have to be made to account for so-called "across-the-board" relativization:

Any woman that every man seeks in the park and finds must be a fanatic lover of squirrels.

as to prevent the generation of sentences like those in (25):

25)   a. ***The man who walks in the park and a woman loves every fish dates Mary.**
       b. ***The woman who the man walks in the park and loves every fish dates Mary.**

Again, we could modify S11 as in (26) to effectively block (25a) and (25b):

(26)   S11 (REVISED): If ϕ and $\psi \in P_t$, then $F_8'(\phi, \psi)$, $F_9'(\phi, \psi) \in P_t$, where $F_8'(\phi, \psi) = \phi'$ **and** ψ' and $F_9'(\phi, \psi) = \phi'$ **or** ψ' and ϕ', ψ' come from ϕ, ψ by replacing any variable

$$\begin{Bmatrix} \mathbf{he}_n \\ \mathbf{him}_n \end{Bmatrix}$$

by

$$\begin{Bmatrix} \mathbf{he}_n^R \\ \mathbf{him}_n^R \end{Bmatrix}$$

for all n.

In effect the new S11 disallows sentential conjunction if at some later point in the derivation quantification or relativization of a variable within a conjunct is to take place. Any binding of variables by the rule of relative clause formation or the rule of quantification must take place within the individual conjuncts prior to the formation of the coordinate structure. In effect I am artificially forcing rule order on the grammar by filtering out (via the "unbounded variable convention") sentences in which rules are executed in the wrong order.

An unfortunate side effect of this innovation is the concomitant blocking of sentences like (27):

(27)   **A man loves the woman and she loves him, too.**

The implication of (27) [and of the ambiguous (23b)] for the work done here so far is that while we must maintain strict control over relativization by means of the superscript R variables, the controls over quantification, which I had originally hoped would parallel all the way down the line the controls over relativization, must in fact be weakened somewhat.

7. NONRESTRICTIVE RELATIVE CLAUSES

The final section of this study concerns itself with nonrestrictive relativization. The kind of data that must be accounted for are exemplified by (28):

(28)   a. **John, who dates a fish, walks in the park.**
        b. **The woman, who Bill loves, seeks a unicorn.**
        c. **John seeks Bill, who has lost a pen.**
        d. **A woman, who Bill dates, loves a unicorn.**

To form a nonrestrictive relative clause, it is necessary to combine a term phrase and a sentence (t phrase) to give a term phrase. The syntactic rule of formation, Rule $S3^{NR}$, is given in (29):

(29) $S3^{NR}$—NONRESTRICTIVE RELATIVE CLAUSE FORMATION: If $\alpha \in P_T$ and $\phi \in P_t$, then $F_{3,n}^{NR}(\alpha, \phi) \in P_T$, where

$$F_{3,n}^{NR}(\alpha, \phi) = \alpha \begin{Bmatrix} \textbf{who} \\ \textbf{which} \end{Bmatrix} \phi',$$

where ϕ' comes from ϕ by deleting the first occurrence of $\textbf{he}_n$ or $\textbf{him}_n$ and replacing all further occurrences of $\textbf{he}_n/\textbf{he}_n^R$ or $\textbf{him}_n/\textbf{him}_n^R$ by

$$\begin{Bmatrix} \textbf{he} \\ \textbf{she} \\ \textbf{it} \end{Bmatrix} \quad \text{or} \quad \begin{Bmatrix} \textbf{him} \\ \textbf{her} \\ \textbf{it} \end{Bmatrix},$$

respectively, according to the gender of α, and by replacing all other occurrences of $\textbf{he}_k$ or $\textbf{him}_k$, $k \neq n$ by $\textbf{he}_k^R$ or $\textbf{him}_k^R$, respectively, and by choosing **who** or **which** according to the gender of α.

In (30) we give a skeletal derivation of (28a):

(30)   John, who dates a fish, walks in the park, $F_{10,4}$

    John, who dates a fish, $F_{3,2}^{NR}$ he$_4$ walks in the park

        John   he$_2$ dates a fish

Note that the syntax of nonrestrictive relative clauses is simpler than that of restrictives in that it is not necessary to introduce *that*; *that* is not a permissible "relative pronoun" in nonrestrictives, as (31) illustrates:

(31)   **The sun,** $\begin{Bmatrix} \textbf{*that} \\ \textbf{which} \end{Bmatrix}$ **was the first god man worshiped, is the dominant element in the superstition of astrology.**

The translation rule $T3^{NR}$ that corresponds to $S3^{NR}$ is given in (32):

(32) $T3^{NR}$—TRANSLATION RULE FOR NON-RESTRICTIVE RELATIVES: If

$\alpha \in P_T$, $\phi \in P_t$, and α, ϕ translate into α', ϕ', respectively, then $F_{3,n}{}^{NR}(\alpha, \phi)$ translates into $\lambda \mathscr{P} \lambda Q[\mathscr{P}\{\hat{x}_n[\phi' \wedge Q\{x_n\}]\}]({}^\wedge \alpha')$

It is important to note that this translation rule reflects the fact that non-restrictives are semantically CONJUNCTIONS. Indeed transformational grammarians have proposed that nonrestrictives be derived from underlying conjunction, so that, for example, (28a), in their view, might come from underlying *John, and John dates a fish, walks in the park* or *John walks in the park and John dates a fish.* In a transformational grammar this approach may be problematic.

Montague grammar, on the other hand, deals with the problem elegantly and in an intuitively satisfying manner. The syntax is straight to the point, with no pretensions of being conjunctive. The conjunctive aspect of the nonrestrictive relative structure—a semantic property—is reflected in the grammar where it should be, viz., in the semantic translation of the syntactic structure. Thus the semantic representation, as it were, of **John, who talks, walks** would, after application of T3^{NR} and appropriate reduction, appear as in (33); (33a) is the translation of the term phrase **John, who walks**, while (33b) is the translation of the entire sentence:

(33)   a. $\lambda Q[\textbf{walk}'({}^\wedge j) \wedge Q\{{}^\wedge j\}]$
        b. $[\textbf{walk}'({}^\wedge j) \wedge \textbf{talk}'({}^\wedge j)]$

One final remark. The data in (34) are not grammatical:

(34) $\begin{Bmatrix} \textbf{Every} \\ \textbf{Some} \\ \textbf{No} \\ \textbf{Any} \end{Bmatrix}$ **man, who is a mammal, walks.**

The restriction seems to be that no term phrase that lacks a unique, identifiable referent can be modified by a nonrestrictive relative clause. The term phrases in (34) either have no referent at all or no unique one. I am not sure how to go about introducing such a notion into a Montague grammar. A (very ad hoc) syntactic solution is possible by restricting α in $S_3{}^{NR}$ from being a term phrase containing the "wrong determiner," but this syntactic approach does not seem to me to be what is happening linguistically, and therefore I will not pursue it.

University of North Carolina

REFERENCES

Montague, R. The proper treatment of quantification in ordinary English. In J. Hintikka, J. Moravcsik, and P. Suppes (Eds.), *Approaches to Natural Language: Proceedings of the*

1970 Stanford Workshop on Grammar and Semantics. Dordrecht: Reidel, 1973. Pp. 221–242.
[Reprinted in R. Thomason (Ed.), *Formal Philosophy: Selected Papers of Richard Montague.*
New Haven: Yale Univ. Press, 1974. Pp. 247–270].

Ross, J. R. Constraints on Variables in Syntax. Unpublished doctoral dissertation, Massachusetts Institute of Technology, 1967. [Available from the Indiana University Linguistics Club,
Bloomington, Indiana.]

ENRIQUE B. DELACRUZ

FACTIVES AND PROPOSITION LEVEL
CONSTRUCTIONS IN MONTAGUE GRAMMAR

In this paper I shall try to modify and extend Montague's treatment of a fragment of English in Montague (1973) (henceforth PTQ) to accommodate factives and to account for some of their semantic and syntactic properties. Since the salient features of this extension of PTQ are motivated largely by the Kiparskys' work on the subject, Kiparsky and Kiparsky (1971), it would be well to consider first the Kiparskys' analysis of factives.

1. THE KIPARSKYS ON FACTIVES

In Kiparsky and Kiparsky (1971) the term FACTIVE is used to denote "predicates" of a certain kind and to distinguish them from predicates of another sort, which they call NONFACTIVE. The terms FACTIVE and NON-FACTIVE are subsequently used, too, to designate sentences built with these predicates. Examples of factive predicates from the Kiparsky list follow:

(1)   a.   **significant, odd, amuse, bother, annoy, surprise**
         b.   **ignore, resent, regret**

Accordingly, the following are considered factive sentences:

(2)   a.   i. **It is significant that John talks.**
            ii. **That John dates Mary is odd.**
           iii. **That John dates Mary bothers Bill.**
         b.   i. **Mary regrets that John talks.**
            ii. **Bill resents that John dates Mary.**

From the nonfactive group, we have the following predicates:

(3)   a.   **likely, seem, appear, happen, turn out**
         b.   **suppose, assert, maintain, think, believe**

In the same vein, the following are nonfactive sentences (henceforth I shall use FACTIVE and NONFACTIVE as short for "factive sentence" and "nonfactive sentence," respectively):

(4)   a.   **It is likely that John dates Mary.**
           It seems that John loves Mary.
           It appears that John walks.

b.   **Bill maintains that John walks.**
     Bill believes that John dates Mary.

One might notice from the preceding examples that the Kiparskys use PREDICATE rather loosely: Their list includes a variety of items from different syntactic categories, a number of which are not really predicates in the sense in which logicians use this term; one cannot just combine them with a term to get a well-formed expression. But this is really of minor importance. What is more important is to notice that predicates from both groups are of the type that can take sentential clauses either as subject, as in (2a) and (4a), or as object, as in (2b) and (4b). The Kiparskys hasten to point out, however, that these structural similarities hold only at the surface level. Factives readily lend themselves to certain transformations involving their embedded sentential clauses, but nonfactives do not allow similar transformations. In particular, the Kiparskys point out that the embedded sentences in (2) can be transformed into gerund clauses without loss of well-formedness; a similar change cannot be effected on the embedded clauses of the sentences in (4) without ill effects:

(5)   a.   **John's dating Mary is odd.**
             John's walking surprises Mary.
        b.   **Bill resents John's dating Mary.**

(6)   a.   ***John's loving Mary seems.**
             *It appears John's walking.
        b.   ***Bill believes John's dating Mary.**

The Kiparskys also notice other differences between factive and nonfactive predicates. In the case of predicates that take sentential clauses as subject, the Kiparskys point out the following differences:

1. Only factive predicates allow the noun **fact** with a sentential complement consisting of a sentence or a gerund to replace the simple *that* clause:

> **The fact that John talks surprises Mary.**
> **The fact of John's talking surprises Mary.**
> ***The fact that John talks is likely.**
> ***The fact of John's talking is likely.**

2. On the other hand, a certain transformation is permissible only on nonfactives. This is the transformation that turns the initial noun phrase of the embedded sentence into the subject of the main sentence and converts the remainder of the embedded sentence into an infinitive clause:

> **It seems that John dates Mary.**
> **John seems to date Mary.**
> **It is odd that John talks.**
> ***John is odd to talk.**

3. The Kiparskys also note that extraposition is optional for verbs in the factive group but obligatory for verbs in the nonfactive group:

That John walks surprises Mary.
*That John walks seems.

For predicates that can take sentential clauses as object, i.e., predicates in (1b) and (3b), the Kiparskys make parallel observations:

1. Only factive predicates can have as their object the noun **fact** with a gerund or a *that* clause.
2. Gerunds can be objects of factive predicates but not freely of nonfactive predicates.
3. Only nonfactives allow the accusative-and-infinitive construction.

The Kiparskys say that factives and nonfactives differ on the semantic level as well. Factives are presuppositional; nonfactives are not. The Kiparskys' exposition on this point, however, leaves much to be desired. They begin by noticing the following:

The force of the *that*-clause is not the same in the two sentences,

It is odd that it is raining (factive)
It is likely that it is raining (nonfactive)

or in the two sentences,

I regret that it is raining (factive)
I suppose that it is raining (nonfactive).

The first sentence in each pair (the factive sentence) carries with it the presupposition 'it is raining.' The speaker presupposes that the embedded clause expresses a true proposition. All predicates which behave syntactically as factives have this semantic property and almost none of those which behave syntactically as non-factives have it [Kiparsky and Kiparsky, 1971, p. 358].

The Kiparskys' way of stating how they consider factives to be presuppositional suggests at least two, possibly three, senses of presupposition, which may be characterized roughly as follows:

1. A sentence p presupposes a sentence p^*.
2. A speaker A of a sentence p presupposes (a proposition) p^*.
3. A predicate (or verb) V presupposes some sentence p^*.

Now each of the last three sentences of the quoted passage suggests a different sense of presupposition. The first suggests sense 1. The second suggests sense 2: The Kiparskys claim here that the speaker of a factive sentence presupposes some proposition p^* that is expressed by the embedded clause of the factive sentence. In the last sentence the Kiparskys seem to be referring to the third sense of presupposition, for they claim here that factive predicates have a semantic property that becomes apparent when these predicates are used in a sentence.

It is easy to see that these three senses are different. In 1, it is THE SENTENCE that has a presupposition (or carries it); in 2, it is THE SPEAKER who makes it; in 3, it is THE USE OF THE PREDICATE itself that carries it. What may have led the Kiparskys to take these three senses of presupposition as one is the way they can be related. Possibly whenever the use of a predicate in a sentence involves a presupposition one could say that the sentence as a whole has or carries a presupposition. And if a sentence carries a presupposition, one might say that whoever asserts it presupposes whatever is presupposed by the sentence. Although it is possible to relate the three senses in this way, they are by no means equivalent, for the converse relations do not always hold. A sentence may be presuppositional, but its having a presupposition may not stem from the use of a certain word or phrase whose use always carries a presupposition. An example is Chomsky's (1971) observation, that the sentence *Einstein lived in Princeton* has a presupposition, i.e., that Einstein is dead. Chomsky traces the presupposition to the tense of the verb. He feels that had the tense been different, as in *Einstein has lived in Princeton*, the presupposition would be absent. The point that is established here is that the presupposition of a sentence cannot always be traced to a word or phrase whose use always involves a presupposition.

The Kiparskys vacillate among these three senses of presupposition throughout their discussion. At one point they remark that the following two sentences are "true instances of presupposition," suggesting sense 1:

(7)   **It is odd that the door is closed.**
        I regret that the door is closed.

They then hasten to add that "the speaker of these sentences presupposes, 'the door is closed'." This remark indicates sense 2. Finally, they shift to sense 3 in proposing that as one "formulates the lexical entries for predicates within the semantics, special consideration must be given to presuppositions." Despite this ambiguity in their use of presupposition, the Kiparskys do point out that the presuppositions of factives behave as expected. Following Strawson, they say that presuppositions remain constant under negation: If a factive sentence p presupposes p^*, its denial, not-p, presupposes p^* as well.

To account for the foregoing semantic and syntactic differences between factives and nonfactives, the Kiparskys propose that factives be viewed as having a deep level source where the NP node has the *that* clause as a complement of the noun *fact*; for nonfactives, they propose that the NP node be viewed as having no head noun. Schematically the hypothesis is represented as follows:

| FACTIVE | NONFACTIVE |

This hypothesis entails that factives like (2a-iii) and (2b-i) have deep level sources like (8) and (9), respectively:

(8)   **The fact that John dates Mary bothers Bill.**

(9)   **Mary regrets the fact that John talks.**

Under the hypothesis (2a-iii) and (2b-i) are derived from (8) and (9), respectively, by a simple *fact* deletion transformation; their gerund forms, (12) and (13), are gotten from (8) and (9) via (10) and (11) and a *fact* deletion transformation:[1]

(10)   **The fact of John's dating Mary bothers Bill.**

(11)   **Mary regrets the fact of John's talking.**

(12)   **John's dating Mary bothers Bill.**

(13)   **Mary regrets John's talking.**

Perhaps this hypothesis does offer an account of the syntactic differences between factives and nonfactives, a point I will discuss later. In view, however, of the ambiguity in their use of "presupposition," it is not evident whether this hypothesis does account for the semantic difference between factives and nonfactives. If the Kiparskys are simply interested in saying that factives are presuppositional in sense 1, their hypothesis does provide an explanation of sorts. I say it is an explanation of sorts because, given a suitable semantic theory, such as the one we shall consider here, one can account for the intuition that factives somehow entail their embedded sentences. This account, however, will show that the semantic relation between a factive sentence and its embedded clause is one of LOGICAL IMPLICATION and not some kind of "presuppositional implication."

Should the Kiparskys make the stronger claim that factives are presuppositional in sense 1 or in sense 2 because they are presuppositional in sense 3, something much stronger than their present hypothesis will be needed. Under their hypothesis it can easily be shown that it is fact ascription,

---

[1] The Kiparskys do not go into the details of how such a transformation rule is formulated.

not the use of a factive predicate, that carries the presupposition.[2] To show that factives are presuppositional because of the use of a factive predicate, the Kiparskys must show that there is something about the use of these predicates that involves a presupposition. What is needed is an hypothesis on factive predicates analogous to the Strawson thesis on the use of definite descriptions. It is unlikely, however, that a similar thesis on factives can be established, since this would involve showing that the use of a factive predicate presupposes the truth of the embedded sentence in the same way that the use of a definite description presupposes the existence of the description's referent. It is easy to find uses of factive predicates where the sentence as a whole does not entail, much less presuppose, its embedded sentential clause; such is the case in the following sentences:

(14)   **The thought that John dates Susan bothers Mary.**

(15)   **The thought that John dates Mary amuses Bill.**

These sentences not only cast doubt on the view that the presuppositionality of factives is due to the use of a factive predicate; they also show that it is fact ascription that involves it. For if one were to replace **thought** in (14) and (15) with **fact**, these sentences would be felt to entail the truth of their embedded clauses. If, therefore, any semantic distinction exists between factive and nonfactive predicates, this distinction cannot be due to presuppositions.

Let us consider now whether the syntactic aspect of the Kiparsky hypothesis is adequate. It is certainly true that, given the difference between the deep structure of factives and nonfactives, it is easy to get the transformational derivatives of these sentences. Aside from this, however, the Kiparskys offer no further justification for positing different deep structures for these sentences. They seem to take for granted as a syntactic fact that the NP node of nonfactives cannot have as its head noun the noun *fact*. But is it syntactic considerations that lead one to regard (16) and (17), for instance, as unacceptable:

(16)   ***The fact that John talks is likely.**

(17)   ***Mary believes the fact that John talks.**

The Kiparskys' belief that factive predicates differ semantically from nonfactives on the matter of presupposition seems to have prevented them

---

[2] Geach (1965) argues that anyone who asserts a sentence like **The fact that John walks surprised Mary** makes two assertions:

1. That John walks is a fact.
2. That John walks surprised Mary.

Of these two assertions, it is the first, not the second, that entails that John walks.

from considering whether the syntactic differences between these predicates derive from semantic differences of another sort. I do not find anything in the syntactic structure of (16) and (17) that patently violates some intuitive phrase structure rule. But if one compares factive and nonfactive predicates with a view to their meanings, it will be felt that factive predicates mean, roughly, those sorts of things that can be said of facts (and events). It is facts, among other things, that can be significant, odd, surprising, or regrettable. There is something about our notion of FACT such that it makes sense to say of a fact that it is odd, significant, surprising, or regrettable. The notion of FACT is also such that it does not make sense to say of a fact that it is likely, sure, or assertable, any more than it makes sense to say of a number that it is colored, light, or rough. The considerations that lead one to regard (16) and (17) as unacceptable grammatically seem to be similar to those that lead one to reject (18):

(18)   *The number nine is bright red.

It is just that being likely is not something that can be said of facts, in the same way that being bright red is not something that can be said of a number. To say that nine is bright red is to make a conceptual confusion of some kind, that of attributing a property that is conceptually alien to our conceptions about numbers. I think a similar confusion underlies (16): Being likely, being sure, being assertable are properties alien to our intuitive conception about facts. That this is the case can be best brought out by considering (16'), a paraphrase of (16):

(16')   That John talks is a fact and it is likely that John talks.

Sentence (16') is by no means ungrammatical, but it does sound incoherent. The case with (17) is somewhat less straightforward, since the confusion that underlies it cannot be brought out without going into an analysis of belief and of the appropriate objects of belief. Still, its unacceptability can be accounted for from semantic considerations.

If the foregoing analysis is correct, it appears that the structural difference between factives and nonfactives does not arise from purely syntactic considerations; instead, it seems to derive from selectional restrictions, i.e., constraints on possible syntactic constructions based on semantic considerations.

In PTQ we do not have an explicit and systematic apparatus for dealing with selectional restrictions. This is a limitation of the framework, but I do not think it is a fundamental one. (Later I shall indicate how certain aspects of the framework can be developed into an apparatus for dealing with certain types of selectional restrictions.) The extension of PTQ that I shall sketch suffers from similar limitations. Thus sentences like (17) will not be excluded from the fragment. What I try to accomplish in extending the framework is to offer an account of the felt semantic properties of factives. In particular, I try to give a formal base for the intuition that there is some logical relation between the factive sentence itself and its embedded sentential clause. In viewing this relation as one of presupposition, the Kiparskys feel that the semantic relation between the factive sentence and its embedded sentential clause cannot be adequately captured in terms of entailment. I claim that this assessment is mistaken; that on the contrary, the semantic relation between a factive sentence and its embedded sentential clause can be analyzed in terms of entailment. To provide this analysis is the purpose of this extension.

2. ACCOMMODATING FACTIVES IN PTQ

To generate representative sentences for factives within the framework, it will be necessary to augment PTQ's vocabulary with the appropriate expressions. This poses a problem of sorts, because an adequate treatment of the semantic properties of factives cannot be obtained by simply supplementing PTQ's vocabulary with the needed expressions. Consider expressions like **John, Mary, the man such that he dates Mary**. These expressions are treated as terms in PTQ. For our purposes we intend to treat expressions like **that John walks, that ninety is rising**, and **that Mary dates Bill** as terms. Semantically, however, the latter group of expressions require a different treatment, unlike the former, they do not denote individual concepts. Philosophers generally think of them as denoting propositions; they are proposition-denoting terms. Similar considerations hold for expressions like **fact, belief**, and **thought**. These expressions are common nouns, as are the expressions **man, woman**, and **fish**. But semantically they differ from the latter in having propositions rather than individual concepts in their extensions.

To obtain the appropriate semantic distinction between these expressions, we extend the framework by adding a set of basic categories that are, in general, parallel to the set of basic categories mentioned in PTQ, together with the appropriate syntactic and translation rules. These rules will, in general, also parallel the rules in PTQ. For convenience and to facillitate reference, I use the terms PROPOSITION LEVEL and INDIVIDUAL CONCEPT LEVEL to distinguish between these two sets of categories. Accordingly, **thought** would be a PROPOSITION LEVEL COMMON NOUN, while **man** would be an INDIVIDUAL CONCEPT LEVEL COMMON NOUN. Similarly, **that John walks** would be a PROPOSITION LEVEL TERM, while **John, every man, ninety** would be INDIVIDUAL CONCEPT LEVEL TERMS. We shall also use a "bar notation" to distinguish between names of categories of different levels that share the same traditional name. For instance, $P_{\overline{CN}}$ will designate the category of proposition level common noun phrases, while P_{CN} will designate the category of individual concept level common noun phrases. It will be recalled that P_{CN} is one of the categories of PTQ. It will be seen that I do not distinguish between factive and nonfactive predicates as the Kiparskys do. When both a factive and a nonfactive predicate appear to belong to the same traditional syntactic category, I classify them thus.

Basic Categories

$B_{\overline{IV}}$ (The set of basic proposition level intransitive verbs, i.e., IV phrases of type $t//t$; this basic category could possibly be empty if it should turn out that a definitive treatment of the passive voice shows that IV phrases in the passive voice are derivable from IV phrases in the active voice. I am not aware of clear-cut examples of basic proposition level IV phrases in the active voice. The Kiparskys would probably put **seem, appear, happen** in this category. This would be ill advised, however, for our framework, because the inclusion of these expressions in this particular category would result in strings like *__that John walks appears__, *__that John walks happens__, *__that John walks seems__. If these verbs MUST be included in the fragment, it would be better to consider them as members of $B_{\overline{IV}//\overline{IV},}$)

$= \{$**be believed**$\}$

$B_{\overline{T}}$ (The set of basic proposition level terms, i.e., terms of type $t/(t//t) = t/\overline{IV}.$)

$= \{$**it**$_0$, **it**$_1$, **it**$_2, \ldots ,$ **it**$_n, \ldots \}$

$B_{\overline{CN}}$ (The set of basic proposition level common nouns, i.e., common nouns of type $t///t.$)

$= \{$**fact, belief, proposition, thought**$\}$

$B_{\overline{IV}/T}$ (The set of basic transitive verbs that take individual concept level terms as object to form proposition level intransitive verbs.)

$= \{$**surprise, bother, annoy, amuse**$\}$

$B_{\overline{IV}/\overline{T}}$ (The set of basic transitive verbs that take proposition level terms to form proposition level intransitive verbs.)

$= \{$**be**$\}$

The member of this category is the identity relation between propositions, in the same way that **be** in $B_{IV/T}$ is the identity relation between individuals. Note that the translation rule for **be** parallels the translation for **be** in PTQ. A cursory comparison of these rules will show that the former holds between propositions while the latter holds between individuals.

$B_{IV/\bar{T}}$ (The set of basic transitive verbs that take proposition level terms as object to form an individual concept level intransitive verb; this category is intended to replace $B_{IV/t}$ of PTQ.)

= {**believe, assert, prove, suppose, deny, regret, resent, ignore**}

$B_{\overline{CN}/\overline{CN}}$ (The set of basic proposition level adjectives.)[3]

= {**true, necessary, significant, odd**}

Notice that we have in this category two factive "predicates" and one nonfactive one. We also include **true** here. By introducing **true** into the object language, we run the risk of allowing some of the semantic paradoxes to creep into the object language. I do not think, however, that we can generate within the fragment those semantic paradoxes that hinge on the introduction of a truth predicate within the object language. We need something else besides a truth predicate to generate these paradoxes, namely, a device for self-reference. So far as I know, the syntax of our fragment does not generate sentences that can refer to themselves.

$B_{\overline{IV}//\overline{IV}}$ (The set of basic proposition level IV-taking verb phrases.)

= {**happen to, appear to**}

$B_{\overline{IV}//\overline{IV}}$ is intended to parallel $B_{IV//IV}$ of **PTQ**. Note that in PTQ, $B_{\overline{IV}//\overline{IV}}$ has only two members, **try to** and **wish to**. We could augment the membership of this category by adding **happen to** and **appear to**, since the following are well-formed:

> **John appears to eat a fish.**
> **Mary happens to eat a fish.**

Happen to and **appear to** are expressions that could occur at two **levels**: the proposition level and the individual concept level. In contrast, notice that it would be ill advised to have "duplicates" of **try to** and **wish to** at the proposition level:

> ***That John runs tries to surprise Mary.**
> ***That John eats wishes to surprise Mary.**

---

[3] Montague does not treat adjectives in PTQ; they are, however, treated in Montague(1970a) The treatment that we adopt here for proposition level adjectives parallels the treatment of adjectives in Montague (1970a).

Syntactic Rules

As mentioned earlier, a majority of the syntactic rules governing proposition level expressions run parallel with those governing individual concept level expressions. Thus we shall not bother to state here those syntactic rules for proposition level expressions that simply mirror syntactic rules for individual concept level expressions in PTQ. It is expected, for instance, that within our augmented fragment there is a rule, say S2′, parallel in formulation to Rule S2 of PTQ, such that when applied to any $\zeta \in P_{\overline{CN}}$ we get expressions like **every** ζ, **the** ζ, and **a** ζ, which are members of $P_{\overline{T}}$. ζ here could be an expression like **belief**. The following rules are exceptions to this norm.

BASIC RULES
S0: If $\phi \in P_t$, then $F_{20}(\phi) \in P_{\overline{T}}$, where $F_{20}(\phi) = $ *that* ϕ.
S3.1: (INDIVIDUAL CONCEPT LEVEL APPOSITION RULE): If $\alpha \in B_T$ and $\zeta \in B_{CN}$, then $F_{21}(\zeta, \alpha) \in P_{\overline{T}}$, provided that whenever α is of the form **he**$_n$, $F_{21}(\zeta, \alpha) = \alpha$; otherwise $F_{21}(\zeta, \alpha) = $ **the** ζ α.
S3.2: (PROPOSITION LEVEL APPOSITION RULE): If $\alpha \in P_{\overline{T}}$ and $\zeta \in B_{\overline{CN}}$, then $F_{22}(\zeta, \alpha) \in P_{\overline{T}}$, provided that whenever α is of the form **that** ϕ, where $\phi \in P_t$, $F_{22}(\zeta, \alpha) = $ **the** ζ α; otherwise $F_{22}(\zeta, \alpha) = \alpha$.

S3.1 and S3.2 are rules that enable us to generate such phrases as **the man John**, **the horse Cannonero**, **the river Thames**, and phrases like **the belief that John walks**, **the thought that Bill dates Mary**, and **the fact that John runs**.

RULES OF FUNCTIONAL APPLICATION
S8.1: If $\beta \in P_{\overline{CN}/\overline{CN}}$ and $\zeta \in P_{\overline{CN}}$, then $F_6(\beta, \zeta) \in P_{\overline{CN}}$, where $F_6(\beta, \zeta) = \beta\zeta$.

This rule enables us to generate phrases like **true belief**, **necessary proposition**, and **significant fact**. Adjectives are not treated in PTQ; but if they were, this rule would parallel the rule for individual concept level common nouns and adjectives.[4]

Translation into Intensional Logic

To translate the PTQ fragment as augmented here, it will be necessary to add to Montague's list of individual concept variables; Thus:

x, y, z, x', y', z', x_n are the individual concept variables $v_{1, \langle s, e \rangle}$, $v_{3, \langle s, e \rangle}$, $v_{5, \langle s, e \rangle}$, $v_{7, \langle s, e \rangle}$, $v_{9, \langle s, e \rangle}$, $v_{11, \langle s, e \rangle}$, and $v_{2n, \langle s, e \rangle}$, respectively.

---

[4] See n. 3, p. 186.

We also require, in addition to the variables and constants of intensional logic mentioned in PTQ, the following variables and their respective types:

1. p, q, r, p', q', r', p_n are proposition variables $v_{1, \langle s, t \rangle}$, $v_{3, \langle s, t \rangle}$, $v_{5, \langle s, t \rangle}$, $v_{7, \langle s, t \rangle}$, $v_{9, \langle s, t \rangle}$, $v_{11, \langle s, t \rangle}$, and $v_{2n, \langle s, t \rangle}$, respectively.
2. K is a variable of type $\langle s, \langle e \langle \langle s, t \rangle, t \rangle \rangle \rangle$, which ranges over two-place relations in intension between individuals and propositions.
3. H is a variable of type $\langle s, \langle \langle s, t \rangle, \langle e, t \rangle \rangle \rangle$, which ranges over two-place relations in intension between propositions and individuals.
4. Q is the variable $v_{0, \langle s, \langle \langle s, t \rangle, t \rangle \rangle}$ which ranges over properties of propositions.
5. $\mathscr{2}$ is the variable $v_{0, \langle s, \langle \langle s, \langle \langle s, t \rangle, t \rangle \rangle, t \rangle \rangle}$, which ranges over properties of properties of propositions.

Translation Rules

The norm for translation rules follows the norm for syntactic rules mentioned earlier. We shall not therefore bother to state those translation rules that simply mirror translation rules in PTQ.

BASIC TRANSLATION RULES

T0: (a) **be** translates into $\lambda \mathscr{2} \lambda p \mathscr{2} \{ \hat{q} [p = q] \}$.
    (b) **proposition** translates into $\hat{p}[p = p]$.[5]
    (c) **it**$_n$ translates into $\hat{Q}[Q\{p_n\}]$.
    (d) If $\phi \in P_t$ and ϕ translates into ϕ', then $F_{20}(\phi)$ translates into $\hat{Q}Q\{^\wedge[\phi']\}$.

T3.1: If $\alpha \in B_T$, $\zeta \in B_{CN}$, and a, ζ translate into α', ζ', respectively, then $F_{21}(\zeta, \alpha)$ translates into α' if α is of the form **he**$_n$; otherwise $F_{21}(\zeta, \alpha)$ translates into

$$\hat{P} \vee y[\wedge x[[\zeta'(x) \wedge \lambda \mathscr{P} \lambda z \mathscr{P} \{ \hat{x}'[^\vee z = {}^\vee x'] \} (^\wedge \alpha')(x)] \leftrightarrow x = y] \wedge P\{y\}].$$

T3.2: If $\alpha \in P_T$, $\zeta \in B_{\overline{CN}}$, and α, ζ translate into α', ζ', respectively, then $F_{22}(\zeta, \alpha)$ translates into α' if α is not of the form **that** ϕ, where $\phi \in P_t$; otherwise $F_{22}(\zeta, \alpha)$ translates into

$$\hat{Q} \vee q[\wedge p[[\zeta'(p) \wedge \lambda \mathscr{2} \lambda r \mathscr{2} \{ \hat{p}'[r = p'] \} (^\wedge [\alpha'])(p)] \leftrightarrow p = q] \wedge Q\{q\}].$$

RULE OF FUNCTIONAL APPLICATION:

T8.1: If $\beta \in P_{\overline{CN}/CN}$, $\zeta \in P_{\overline{CN}}$, and β, ζ translate into β', ζ', respectively, then $F_6(\beta, \zeta)$ translates into $\beta'(^\wedge \zeta')$.

---

[5] The translation we give to **proposition** parallels the translation for **entity** in Montague (1970b). **Entity** is not included in PTQ, possibly because Montague had no use for it in the points he wished to make there.

Meaning Postulates

With the exception of P6′, the following postulates are intended to supplement the stock of meaning postulates in PTQ:

P6′: $\bigvee K \wedge x \wedge \mathscr{Q} \ \square \ [\delta(x, \mathscr{Q}) \leftrightarrow \mathscr{Q}\{\hat{p}K\{\check{}x, p\}\}]$, where δ translates any member of $B_{IV/\overline{T}}$

P10: $\wedge \mathscr{Q} \wedge p \ \square \ [\textbf{true}'(Q)(p) \rightarrow \check{}p]$

P11: $\wedge Q \wedge p \ \square \ [\delta'(Q)(p) \rightarrow Q\{p\}]$, where δ' translates any member of $B_{\overline{CN}/\overline{CN}}$

P12: $\wedge p \ \square \ [\textbf{fact}'(p) \rightarrow \check{}p]$

P13: $\wedge p \ \square \ [\check{}p \rightarrow \textbf{true}'(^\wedge\textbf{proposition}')(p)]$

P14: $\wedge p \ \square \ [\textbf{necessary}'(^\wedge\textbf{proposition}')(p) \leftrightarrow \square \ \check{}p]$

P15: $\wedge Q \wedge p \ \square \ [\textbf{happen to}'(Q)(p) \rightarrow Q\{p\}]$

P16: $\bigvee H \wedge p \wedge \mathscr{P} \ \square \ [\delta'(p, \mathscr{P}) \leftrightarrow \mathscr{P}\{\hat{x}H\{p, \check{}x\}\}]$, where δ translates any member of $B_{\overline{IV}/T}$

Postulate P6′ is a replacement for meaning postulate 6 of PTQ; it guarantees that transitive verbs of type IV/$\overline{T}$ are extensional with respect to subject position. Postulate P16, on the other hand, secures that $\overline{IV}$/T-type transitive verbs are extensional with respect to object position. Postulate 6 of PTQ has to be replaced in view of the change in the treatment of verbs like **believe** and **assert**; this change is discussed in remark A in the following section. Postulate P10 guarantees that anything in the extension of a proposition level common noun that is modified by **true** has the appropriate semantic property. Postulate P11 guarantees that anything in the extension of **true proposition**, **true belief**, **significant fact**, etc. is a proposition, belief, or fact, respectively. Postulate P12 guarantees that any proposition in the extension of fact is true. Postulates P12 and P13 together guarantee that any proposition in the extension of a fact is also in the extension of a true proposition. We could strengthen P12 and P13 by using a biconditional; such a formulation, however, would entail that all true propositions, including tautologies, are facts. But surely it is debatable whether tautologies are facts. Since I do not wish to be drawn into this controversy, the weaker formulation of P12 and P13, which uses only a conditional, is adopted here.

It seems that Montague intended postulate 6 not just to guarantee extensionality of IV/$\overline{T}$-type verbs with respect to subject position but to secure first-order reducibility as well. Postulate P6′ does not satisfy this second function, and neither does P16. To secure first-order reducibility for the expressions covered by P6′ and P16, the following further conditions must be imposed:

P17: $\wedge K \wedge x \wedge p \bigvee M \ \square \ [K\{\check{}x, p\} \leftrightarrow M\{\check{}x\}]$

P18: $\wedge H \wedge p \wedge x \bigvee M \ \square \ [H\{p, \check{}x\} \leftrightarrow M\{\check{}x\}$

Postulate P17 together with P6′ secures that translations of sentences whose main verb is of the type IV/$\overline{T}$ are ultimately equivalent to some first-order formula. Postulates P18 and P16 secure the same result for sentences whose main verb is of the type $\overline{\text{IV}}/\text{T}$.

3. EXAMPLES AND REMARKS ON THE FRAGMENT

A. The grammar we have just discussed does not merely augment the PTQ framework; it also modifies it. In particular, $B_{\text{IV}/t}$ and $P_{\text{IV}/t}$ are replaced by $B_{\text{IV}/\overline{\text{T}}}$ and $P_{\text{IV}/\overline{\text{T}}}$, respectively. This change, although minimal, does simplify the syntax in the following manner. In PTQ verbs like **believe** and **assert** are treated as a special kind of transitive verb in that they take sentences rather than terms as object. To get natural constructions like **believe that John walks** and **assert that John walks**, Montague treats **believe that** and **assert that** as primitive, rather than the more natural **believe** and **assert**. Aside from its unintuitiveness, this treatment seems to introduce unnecessary complications when one compares sentences with these verbs, which are treated in the PTQ fragment, and sentences that are generally viewed as their transformational derivatives. Consider, for instance, (19) and (20):

(19)   **Mary believes that John talks.**

(20)   **That John talks is believed by Mary.**

Sentence (20) is the passive for (19). Linguists generally regard (20) as derived from (19) by some transformation rule. The difficulties attendant upon Montague's treatment of **believe** in PTQ show up when one attempts to incorporate some such transformation rule into the syntax. Since **believe that** is taken as primitive in PTQ, this expression is, in principle, unbreakable or unanalyzable into further expressions. With Montague's treatment of **believe**, the rule that would allow derivation of (20) from (19) would violate this principle, for in (20) we have the **that** of **believe that** deleted or attached to the embedded sentence. This sounds very implausible to me. Rather than trying to justify such a move, it seems more reasonable, in view of the data, to regard **that** in **believes that John talks** as attaching to the sentence rather than to the verb. This is the course adopted in our framework.[6]

B. We have added to the PTQ framework apposition rules S3.1 and S3.1′ and their corresponding translation rules. We can now treat within our framework (given appropriate additions to the vocabulary of the fragment) such constructions as those exemplified by (21) and (22):

(21)   **the horse Cannonero**
        the student Mary

---

[6] This is also the course adopted by Montague (1970b). Since Montague (1970b) is an earlier work, one wonders why Montague decided to adopt a different treatment for **believe** and **assert** in PTQ.

   the man John
   the river Thames
(22) **the thought that Mary walks**
   the fact that John dates Mary
   the proposition that ninety is rising
   the belief that Mary dates John

These expressions are got directly by Rules S3.1 and S3.2, which combine a noun and a term to get a term. Notice that these rules allow us to derive only terms of the form **the** ζ α, where ζ is a noun and α is a term. We cannot, for instance, derive terms like **a horse Cannonero, every student Mary, every proposition that John dates Mary, a fact that John dates Mary.** These terms are of the form **a** ζ α or **every** ζ α, where ζ is a common noun and α is a term. I have decided to exclude terms of this kind from the fragment, since they seem to have an odd ring syntactically. Semantically, however, they are by no means nonsensical, because they can be given the following readings: "a horse such that it is identical with Cannonero," "every student such that she is identical with Mary," "every proposition such that it is identical with the proposition that John dates Mary," etc. In view of the nature of identity, it thus turns out that the above-mentioned terms will denote just those things that are identical with the horse Cannonero, the student Mary, the proposition that John dates Mary, and the fact that John dates Mary, respectively.

If, therefore, we wish to adopt a more general approach and allow expressions of the form **every** ζ α, **and** a ζ α, this can be readily accomplished by revising S3.1, S3.2, T3.1, and T3.2 in the appropriate way.[7]

---

[7] The appropriate revisions are as follows:

S3.1: (INDIVIDUAL CONCEPT LEVEL APPOSITION RULE)
  If $\alpha \in B_T$ and $\zeta \in B_{CN}$, then $F_{21}(\zeta, \alpha) \in P_{CN}$, provided that whenever α is of the form **he**$_n$, $F_j(\zeta, \alpha) = \zeta$; otherwise $F_{21}(\zeta, \alpha) = \zeta \alpha$.

S3.2: (PROPOSITION LEVEL APPOSITION RULE)
  If $\alpha \in P_T$ and $\zeta \in B_{CN}$, then $F_{22}(\zeta, \alpha) \in P_{CN}$, provided that whenever α is of the form **that** ϕ, where $\phi \in P_t$, $F_{22}(\zeta, \alpha) = \zeta \alpha$; otherwise $F_{22}(\zeta, \alpha) = \zeta$.

T3.1: If $\alpha \in B_T$, $\zeta \in B_{CN}$, and α, ζ translate into α', ζ', respectively, then $F_{21}(\zeta, \alpha)$ translates into ζ' if α is of the form **he**$_n$; otherwise $F_{21}(\zeta, \alpha)$ translates into

$$\hat{x}[\zeta'(x) \wedge \lambda \mathcal{P} \lambda y \mathcal{P}\{\hat{z}[^\vee y = {}^\vee z]\}(^\wedge \alpha')(x)].$$

T3.2: If $\alpha \in P_T$, $\zeta \in B_{CN}$, and α, ζ translate into α', ζ', respectively, then $F_{22}(\zeta, \alpha)$ translates into ζ' if α is not of the form **that** ϕ, where $\phi \in P_t$, otherwise $F_{22}(\zeta, \alpha)$ translates into

$$\hat{P}[\zeta'(p) \wedge \lambda \mathcal{Q} \lambda q \mathcal{Q}\{\hat{r}[q = r]\}(^\wedge [\alpha'])(p)].$$

Under this approach the rules generate a common noun phrase of the form $\zeta \alpha$, where ζ is a common noun and α is a term. The desired term phrases, **every** $\zeta \alpha$, **a** $\zeta \alpha$, **the** $\zeta \alpha$, are gotten from $\zeta \alpha$ by an application of S3 itself and/or the parallel rule at the proposition level.

To illustrate how the present apposition rule works, consider a possible derivation tree, (24), for (23):

(23)   **The horse Cannonero runs.**

(24)   The horse Cannonero runs

                        /   \

    the horse Cannonero [by S3.1]   run

                /   \

            horse   Cannonero

That the translation rule corresponding to S3.1 gives us the desired result may be gleaned by considering the logical structure of (25), the translation of (24′) in intensional logic:

(25) $\vee y[\wedge x[[\mathbf{horse'}(x) \wedge c = {}^{\vee}x] \leftrightarrow x = y] \wedge \mathbf{run'}(y)]$

Example (25) entails (26) and (27) via the usual instantiation rules:

(26) $\mathbf{horse'}({}^{\wedge}c)$

(27) $\mathbf{run'}({}^{\wedge}c)$

Thus the semantic interpretation for (24) captures our intuition that (23) should entail that Cannonero is a horse and that Cannonero runs. Notice that although (23) entails that Cannonero runs, (28):

(28)   **Cannonero runs.**

is syntactically independent of (23); i.e., (28) and (23) do not come from a common syntactic source.

C. Recall that under the Kiparskys' analysis (29) is the deep structure source of (30); (30) is gotten from (29) via a *fact* deletion transformation:

(29)   **The fact that John walks surprises Mary.**

(30)   **That John walks surprises Mary.**

Although they do not explicitly say so, I think they regard (29) and (30) to be synonymous. Within our framework it is possible to treat both (29) and (30). However, the treatment we have for (29) and (30) does not relate them syntactically. Instead, they are generated independently. Semantically, however, (29) and (30) parallel (23) and (28): (29) entails (30), as evidenced by the structure of (31) and (32), the translations of (29) and (30), respectively:

(31) $\vee q[\wedge p[[\mathbf{fact'}(p) \wedge p = {}^{\wedge}[\mathbf{walk'}({}^{\wedge}j)]] \leftrightarrow p = q] \wedge \mathbf{surprise'}(q, \hat{P}P\{{}^{\wedge}m\})]$

(32) $\mathbf{surprise'}({}^{\wedge}[\mathbf{walk'}({}^{\wedge}j)], {}^{\wedge}\hat{P}P\{{}^{\wedge}m\})$

Notice that (31) entails (33) in the same way that (24) entails (26):

(33) $\mathbf{fact'}({}^{\wedge}[\mathbf{walk'}({}^{\wedge}j)]$

Given (33), we know by meaning postulate P12 that **walk'**$(^\wedge j)$ is true. The interpretation of (29) thus captures the intuition that (29) entails that John walks.

It is evident from the foregoing that our treatment of (29) and (30) differs from the Kiparskys' in one more respect. Since the Kiparskys treat (29) and (30) as synonymous, (30), for them, has a reading that entails (29). We do not have such a reading for (30) in our framework. Sentence (30) is thus nonpresuppositional for us. I shall indicate shortly some reasons for wanting to have a nonpresuppositional reading for (30).

In this fragment, as in PTQ, the favored analysis for definite descriptions is Russell's. Thus for the fragment the negative of factive sentences—more precisely, the negative of their deep level source—is ambiguous, depending on whether the definite description is analyzed as having a primary occurrence ("wide scope") or not. For instance, the negative of (29), which is (34), will have two distinct readings, (36) and (38), corresponding to analysis trees (35) and (37):

(34)   **The fact that John walks does not surprise Mary.**

(35)   **The fact that John walks does not surprise Mary**

                  /   \

   the fact that John walks   **it$_0$ does not surprise Mary**

                            / \

                         it$_0$ **surprise Mary**

                                etc.

(36) $\vee q[\wedge r[[\mathbf{fact'}(r) \wedge r = {}^\wedge[\mathbf{walk'}(^\wedge j)]] \leftrightarrow r = q] \neg \mathbf{surprise'}(q, \hat{P}P\{^\wedge m\})]$

(37)   **The fact that John walks does not surprise Mary**.

               / \

   the fact that John walks   **surprise Mary**

(38) $\neg \vee q[\wedge r[[\mathbf{fact'}(r) \wedge r = {}^\wedge[\mathbf{walk'}(^\wedge j)]] \leftrightarrow r = q] \wedge \mathbf{surprise'}(q, \hat{P}P\{^\wedge m\})]$ (This does not entail **fact'**$(^\wedge[\mathbf{walk}(^\wedge j)])$.)

If (34) has (35) as its analysis tree, its semantic interpretation, (36), would entail (33). Sentence (34) would thus entail that John walks. We therefore have an interpretation of (29) and of (34) where each entails that John walks. Since these particular entailments seem to be the basis for calling (29) presuppositional, we can now claim to have captured within the framework our logical intuitions on (29) and on factives in general.

It might be argued that since our treatment does not relate (29) and (30) syntactically, we cannot claim that our account of the semantic properties of (29) accounts for the semantic properties of (30) when (30) is used in ordinary discourse. Yet it is an account of the semantic properties of (30) as used in ordinary discourse that is wanting, not an account of the semantic properties of (29).

Now insofar one claims that:

1. Sentence (30) is a transformational derivative from (29), and
2. Sentence (30) is synonymous with (29)

I think we are justified in claiming that we have an account for the semantic properties of (30), for all that the preceding claims amount to, in more naïve terms, is the claim that (30) is elliptic for, or short for, (29).

The foregoing argument leaves some loose ends, though, since there now seem to be two versions of (30). One version, call it (30K), is that version which is synonymous with and derived from (29) and is presumably the one that occurs in ordinary everyday discourse. Another version, call it (30M), is the version treated in the framework; it is syntactically independent of (29) but presumably has no counterpart in ordinary everyday discourse. So it appears that within our framework we may claim to have captured the semantic properties of sentences like (30K) via their deep level paraphrase only at the price of having to recognize sentences like (30M), which are not exemplified in ordinary discourse.

However, this is not quite how things are. The Kiparskys are right in pointing out that (30) has a reading having the same force as (29). Still, I do not think one can maintain that this is the only reading for (29) and that (30) occurs only in contexts where it has the same force as (29). To see how this is so, let us shift to more natural examples. Consider the following situation. John and Bill are close associates in a project that has become controversial, and John is under some political pressure to resign. John himself has at various times considered such a possibility in Bill's presence, and one day one of the men involved in the project reports to Bill that John has resigned although, unknown to Bill, John has in fact not resigned. Considering the close association between the two men, it is certainly possible for Bill to react to the report by exclaiming "What a regrettable thing to do!" Now, given this context, it seems that an observer can describe Bill's reaction truly with (39):

 (39) **Bill regrets that John resigned.**

Or, if he were in on the whole affair, the observer could say (40):

 (40) **Believing John to have resigned, Bill regrets that John resigned.**

Situations like this are perhaps unusual, but they certainly are not odd. One can easily imagine a parallel situation where an utterance of (41) would be appropriate:

(41)   **Believing every student to have passed, Mary was surprised that every student passed.**

The occurrence of a factive sentence in contexts like (40) and (41) shows that factives do not always have the force of the-fact-that-ϕ sentences.[8]

Turning now to our previous examples, (29) and (30), it appears that our treatment of (30) as syntactically independent of (29) in the fragment is an advantage, rather than a defect, of the framework. With it we are able to capture semantically the force of factive sentences when they occur in contexts such as (40) and (41).[9]

---

[8] A philosopher who seems to share the Kiparskys' intuitions on some factive predicates is Unger (1972), who argues that a sentence like (i) entails (ii):

(i)   **John regrets that it is raining.**

(ii)   **It is raining.**

He also claims that similar entailments hold for sentences whose main verb is one of the following: **recognize, remember, notice, observe, realize, reveal**, etc. Unger's reasons for believing that (i) entails (ii) are of course different from the Kiparskys'. If I understand Unger's argument correctly, the basis for the entailment is this: A necessary condition for John to regret or, for that matter, to notice, recognize, remember, realize, etc. that Mary runs, is that John knows that Mary runs:

> . . . We might say that here our verb entails *its* knowledge sentence. For, owing to the meaning of 'noticed,' if John noticed there were tables, it follows that John knew there were tables.

Now I think Unger's observations on sentences with main verbs, such as **remember, recognize, realize, notice**, etc., are accurate in general. For these are verbs that designate various kinds of cognitive acts. **Regret**, however, is not a verb that designates a cognitive act. Unger's intuitions about regret are, I think, mistaken. **Regret** is more like **fear** in that one's feelings of regret may be unfounded the same way one's fears may be unfounded. One could regret, feel regretful, that it is raining simply on the basis of a belief that it is raining. It could turn out that one was mistaken about this, and at a later time one could discover that one was indeed mistaken about the weather, but this discovery cannot erase the fact that at an earlier time one did feel regret when one believed otherwise. One therefore can assert (i) truly even if it is not raining, since all that is necessary for (i) to be true is that John FEEL REGRET that it is raining—presumably because he believes it is raining.

[9] We cannot quite make the stronger claim that we have a full treatment for (40) and (41) because the framework does not have the apparatus for treating the past tense; we also do not have the necessary transformational rules. But if these requirements are waived, a treatment of (40) and (41) is possible via their deep level sources, (40') and (41'):

(40')   **Bill believes that John resigns and Bill regrets that John resigns.**

(41')   **Mary believes that every student passes and that every student passes surprises Mary.**

These can be treated within the framework once the vocabulary is appropriately augmented by **student, pass**, and **resign**.

D. I mentioned earlier that certain aspects of Montague's framework can be developed into an apparatus for dealing with certain types of selectional restriction. Recall that in PTQ categories of the types A/B and A//B are regarded as playing the same semantic but different syntactic roles. Semantically, for instance, intransitive verb phrases and common noun phrases receive the same treatment, but syntactically these phrases differ in the obvious way. Clearly this arrangement can be reversed. One may also have two distinct categories of expressions, where both categories have the same syntactic roles but each requires different semantic interpretations. The latter arrangement is explored in this study via the distinction of levels. We use it to guarantee that certain expressions that are traditionally classified as terms, common nouns, transitive verbs, etc. are treated as such in the syntax while receiving semantic interpretations that differ from certain other expressions also treated in the syntax as terms, common nouns, etc.

Although the distinction between proposition level expressions and individual concept level expressions was introduced to meet a problem of semantic interpretation, the distinction has a desirable by-product. Notice that within our framework we cannot, for instance, generate expressions like (42) and (43):

(42)   *Mary asserts John.

(43)   *Mary dates that John runs.

despite the fact that **assert** and **date** are transitive verbs and **John** and **that John runs** are terms. This is because **assert** and **date** have different syntactic types. **Assert** can take only a proposition level term as object, while **date** takes only individual concept level terms as objects. Thus the distinction between levels also functions as a filter on certain possible constructions whose unacceptability stems from selectional considerations.

The distinction between levels clearly cannot be expected to filter out all constructions that one might want to reject on selectional considerations, but it can be used to filter out certain constructions. To illustrate its possibilities consider how infinitives might be added to the fragment. One way to treat infinitives is to regard them as nonbasic terms that are members of the category $P_{\bar{T}}$, generated by the following rule:

If $\zeta \in P_{IV}$, then $F_{30}(\zeta) \in P_{\bar{T}}$, where $F_{30}(\zeta) = $ **to** ζ.

With this rule **to date Mary** would come from **date Mary**. Given this treatment of infinitives, one could go on to introduce categories of transitive verbs, intransitive verbs, common nouns, etc. concerning infinitives in the same manner as the various categories for proposition level expressions are introduced. Possibly **like** would be of the category $B_{IV/\bar{T}}$, so given the appropriate rules, one could generate a sentence like (44) but not (45):

(44)   **John likes to date Mary.**

(45)   ***John likes that Mary walks.**

A more interesting possibility is to use the distinction between various levels to predict which transformations are allowable on certain verbs. Consider the following sentences:

(46)   **John believes that Mary walks.**

(47)   **John believes Mary to walk.**

(48)   **John believes Mary.**

Sentence (46) is generally regarded as a possible source of (47); the Kiparskys say that (47) comes from (46) by some "accusative-and-infinitive-construction transformation." It is debatable whether (48) should be considered as coming from (47) or as coming from another syntactic source. It seems best to regard (48) as derivable independently of either (46) or (47). Suppose now that the PTQ framework is extended in such a way that we have **believe** in two categories, say, **believe**$_1$ in $B_{IV/\bar{T}}$ and **believe**$_2$ in $B_{IV/T}$. With the usual rules we can now generate (46) and (48). Suppose, further, that within the fragment we have a transformation rule, say, the accusative-and-infinitive construction; this rule would allow us to derive (47) from (46). But notice that we cannot allow this rule to apply to all sentences whose main verb is a member of $B_{IV/\bar{T}}$, for if we did, strings like (49) would be derivable too:

(49)   ***John regrets Mary to walk.**

It is in limiting the application of the accusative-and-infinitive construction transformation that the distinction between levels may be of some use. The transformation rule could be formulated in such a way that it would apply to sentences whose main verb is a member of $B_{IV/\bar{T}}$ only if there is a similar entry for the verb in the category $B_{IV/T}$. With this restriction the transformation would apply to (46), since **believe** occurs at two levels, IV/$\bar{T}$ and IV/T; but it would not apply to (50):

(50)   **John regrets that Mary walks.**

for regret is found at only one level, as evidenced by (51):

(51)   ***John regrets Mary.**

One then could not derive (49) from (50) via the transformation.

It is interesting to note that the Kiparskys consider factivity/nonfactivity as the criterion for determining whether the accusative-and-infinitive construction transformation should apply to sentences like (46) and (49). Notice that this criterion breaks down when applied to verbs of cognition like **know** and **remember**. The Kiparskys would consider these verbs factive. Thus by their criterion the transformation would not apply to sentences where these verbs occur. Yet intuitively it seems to be the case that (52) and (53) come from (54) and (55) via the accusative-and-infinitive construction transformation:

(52)   **Bill knows John to be bald.**

(53)   **Bill remembers John to be bald.**

(54)   **Bill knows that John is bald.**

(55)   **Bill remembers that John is bald.**

By my criterion, on the other hand, (52) and (53) can be shown to be transformational derivatives of (54) and (55) via the transformation, since **know** and **remember** are not just in the category IV/$\overline{\text{T}}$ but also in the category IV/T, as indicated by the following locutions:

(56)   **Bill knows John.**

(57)   **Bill remembers John.**

E. In summary, I have tried to account for the key semantic properties of factives within the framework of PTQ by adding to this framework higher-level expressions and the corresponding syntactic and translation rules. My analysis of the meanings of factive predicates indicates that it would be a mistake to regard these predicates as presuppositional predicates, i.e., presuppositional in sense 3, for there seems to be nothing in their meaning to indicate that their use always involves a presupposition. In the case of factive sentences, I have indicated that it is equally misleading to regard these sentences as presuppositional in sense 1. For the logical properties that seem to mark these sentences as presuppositional have been shown to be analyzable in terms of entailment. Factives are not presuppositional if by that term is meant that factives have certain logical properties that cannot be adequately captured in terms of entailment.

This leaves us with the question of whether factives are presuppositional in sense 2. When the Kiparskys refer to factive sentences as being presuppositional in this sense, they indicate that whoever utters or asserts a factive sentence makes a presupposition of some sort. But how does one determine whether a sentence is such that anyone who utters or asserts it makes a presupposition? What, for instance, is the difference between a speaker making a presupposition and a sentence having a presupposition?

Until these points are clarified the question of whether factives are pre-suppositional in this last sense cannot be fruitfully considered. It seems best to postpone consideration of this question to another work.

University of California, Los Angeles

ACKNOWLEDGMENTS

I am indebted to Michael Bennett and Barbara Partee for discussions and suggestions.

REFERENCES

Chomsky, N. Deep structure, surface structure, and semantic interpretation. In D. D. Steinberg and L. A. Jakobovits (Eds.), *Semantics: An interdisciplinary reader in philosophy, linguistics, and psychology.* Cambridge: Cambridge Univ. Press, 1971. Pp. 183–215.

Geach, P. T. Assertion. *Philosophical Review,* 1965, **64,** 449–465

Kiparsky, P., and Kiparsky, C. Fact. In D. D. Steinberg and L. A. Jakobovits (Eds.), *Semantics: An interdisciplinary reader in philosophy, linguistics, and psychology.* Cambridge: Cambridge Univ. Press, 1971. Pp. 345–369.

Kaplan, D., "DThat," Unpublished manuscript (1972), Philosophy Department, UCLA.

Montague, R. English as a formal language. In B. Visenti *et al., Linguaggi nella societa e nella tecnica.* Milan: Edizoni di Communità, 1970. (a)

Montague, R. Universal grammar. *Theoria,* 1970, **36,** 373–398. (b)

Montague, R. The proper treatment of Quantification in English. In K. J. J. Hintikka, J. M. Moravcik, and P. C. Suppes (Eds.), *Approaches to natural language.* Dordrecht: Reidel, 1973. Pp. 221–242.

Unger, P. Propositional verbs and knowledge. *The Journal of Philosophy,* 1972, **69,** 301–312.

DAVID R. DOWTY

MONTAGUE GRAMMAR AND THE
LEXICAL DECOMPOSITION OF CAUSATIVE VERBS

1. INTRODUCTION

The theories of the syntax and semantics of natural language proposed by Montague and like-minded logicians (e.g., Lewis, 1972; Cresswell, 1973) share two important methodological premises with the school of American linguistics known as generative semantics: (*a*) that no "serious" theory of the syntax of a natural language can be constructed apart from a semantic theory of that language and (*b*) that the analysis of the semantics of natural language is best approached through the existing theoretical framework of mathematical logic.

Recently it was observed by Peters (in a talk at the Institute for Advanced Study in May 1973) that despite apparently contradictory claims about the domain of the "syntactic" component there appear to be significant similarities between generative semantics and the version of Montague's theory that appears in "The Proper Treatment of Quantification in Ordinary English" (henceforth PTQ) when the overall organization of the two theories is considered.

The grammar of PTQ provides for (*a*) the specification of the set of well-formed sentences of a fragment of English, (*b*) the specification of the set of well-formed formulas of a certain artificial language, (*c*) a procedure for mapping sentences of English onto formulas of the artificial language, and (*d*) a model-theoretic interpretation of the formulas of the artificial language.

Generative semantics can be described as providing for (*a*) the specification of the set of well-formed sentences (i.e., SURFACE STRUCTURES) of English, (*b*) the specification of the set of well-formed formulas (LOGICAL STRUCTURES) of a certain artificial language (NATURAL LOGIC), and (*c*) a procedure for mapping formulas of the artificial language onto surface structures. Note that this mapping is claimed to be bidirectional (cf. Lakoff, 1971, pp. 236, 237), so it supposedly matters little whether we consider it a mapping from logical structures to surface structures or vice versa. Though no mention of (*d*)—which would be a model theory for natural logic—is to be found in the more familiar generative semantics literature, some generative semanticists have acknowledged that a model theory for natural logic is desirable. Tentative formulations of such a model theory have been made in Keenan (1972) and, for a different set of problems, in Dowty (1972).

Peters' observation about the parallel structure of the two theories leads immediately to the question of what real differences there are between them. Could one construct an "upside-down generative semantics theory" as an extension of PTQ? In such a theory the formulas of intensional logic would play the role of logical structures; the formal interpretation of the intensional logic would play the role of the interpretation of the logical structures; the translation relation of PTQ would correspond in part to the derivational constraints of generative semantics; and the syntax of PTQ would correspond roughly to the more superficial aspects of the derivational process, such as lexical insertion rules and morphological "spelling out" rules, etc.[1] In fact carrying out such a construction would probably be a quick way of finding out whether there are any conflicts or significant differences between the two theories, where these differences lie, and whether any empirically decidable issues might be involved.[2] For example, though generative semanticists claim to have arguments that the mapping of logical structures onto surface structures must be accomplished by "rules of syntax" and not "rules of semantic interpretation," these arguments were directed against the Fodor–Katz–Jackendoff notion of semantic interpretation, and it will be interesting to see what force, if any, they will turn out to have against the rich semantic theory Montague used.

Unfortunately such a direct comparison of the two theories immediately encounters two obstacles:

1. There exists no representative formalization of generative semantics explicit enough to be compared with PTQ at the level of rigor at which the latter theory is constructed. (In fact Peters' suggestion was that the PTQ theory might be useful as a guide to producing a rigorous formalization of generative semantics.)

---

[1] This analogy cannot be pushed too far, of course. Though the syntactic functions of PTQ often do correspond to "surface" syntactic rules in generative semantics (e.g., they perform number agreement, gender agreement, and case marking, and they determine surface word order) and the translation rules for basic expressions are like the generative semanticists' lexical insertion rules "in reverse," there is apparently no real counterpart in generative semantics to the syntactic rules of PTQ (as distinct from the syntactic functions), nor to the translation rules associated with these. The syntax of surface structure is only derivatively defined in generative semantics (as a result of the derivational constraints applied to logical structures), not independently defined as in PTQ (though the existence of surface structure constraints somewhat qualifies this statement), and even if there were such an independent surface syntax, there appears to be nothing approaching a strict homomorphism from surface structures into logical structures (or vice versa), as there is in the translation relation of PTQ.

[2] Conversely, there would be some theoretical interest in constructing an "upside-down PTQ theory," a theory in which well-formed formulas of the intensional logic of PTQ are mapped onto sentences of English; such a construction is being carried out by Goodman at Ohio State University (Goodman, in preparation).

2. Despite a number of recently proposed extensions to Montague's original fragment of English, the class of syntactic and semantic problems treated in Montague grammar is still quite small compared to that which has been investigated by generative semanticists (not to mention transformationalists in general); in particular, most of the crucial classes of sentences and semantic problems on which the major claims of generative semantics rest have not yet been treated in Montague grammar.

These claims might conveniently be divided into three areas: the treatment of quantification (including bound pronouns, scope ambiguities, de dicto/de re ambiguities, etc.), the lexical decomposition hypothesis, and the treatment of pragmatics (including indexical expression, presuppositions, the abstract performative analysis, etc.).

In the first area the situation is the clearest. In the treatment of quantification I believe that the claims made by generative semanticists about the proper logical analysis of sentences do not really conflict with the PTQ analysis; and to the extent that the derivational procedures differ in the two theories I think the PTQ analysis is more satisfactory and certainly more explicit. [The first reformulation of the PTQ theory given by Cooper and Parsons (pages 311–362 in this volume) nicely brings out the close parallel between the generative semanticists' transformation QUANTIFIER LOWERING and quantification rules S14–S16 of PTQ.]

The greatest potential disagreement will lie in the third area, of course, and I will have nothing more to say about this topic.

It is with the LEXICAL DECOMPOSITION HYPOTHESIS that I am concerned in the rest of this paper, in the hope that this discussion will serve as a useful first step in making an explicit comparison of the two theories possible. In Section 2, I outline a general procedure for reconstructing arbitrary lexical decomposition analyses of verbs as extensions of the PTQ theory along the "upside-down generative semantics" analogy mentioned earlier, illustrating this procedure in Section 3 by converting the generative semantics analysis of causative transitive verbs from Dowty (1972) into an extension of PTQ. In Section 4, I discuss a class of sentences (involving ambiguities produced by adverbs) that have been cited as independent motivation for lexical decomposition; and in Section 5, I provide treatments of various kinds of syntactically complex causative phrases in which the adverb ambiguities are automatically accounted for. In Section 6, I consider the more difficult problem of how to account for these ambiguities when they appear with simple lexical causatives, and here I provide two additional methods of approaching the ambiguity problem. In the final section, I offer some tentative proposals for a general theory of derivational morphology within the PTQ framework. My goal in presenting these analyses is not to argue for the correctness of the details of any of them (which would be pointless, since they touch on so many unresolved issues within this theoretical framework) but to illustrate the many possibilities as well as some difficulties that Montague's theory presents us with in dealing with the problems surrounding lexical decomposition.

2. MCCAWLEY'S "PREDICATE-RAISING" TRANSFORMATION
AND PREDICATE ABSTRACTION IN PTQ

2.1. *The Decomposition of Causatives in Generative Semantics*

It was long ago observed by transformationalists that the morphological and semantic parallels among sets of sentences like (1)–(3) suggest a transformational relationship:

(1)   **The door was open.**

(2)   **The door opened.**

(3)   **John opened the door.**

Yet (1)–(3) cannot be derived from the SAME deep structure if transformations preserve meaning. Comparing (2) and (3) with their paraphrases, (4) and (5), respectively, G. Lakoff (1965) proposed that the deep structures of (2) and (3) should include the deep structure of (1) as a proper subpart, together with an "abstract" verb BECOME or verbs BECOME and CAUSE, which were deleted (or "incorporated") by a transformation.

(4)   **The door became open.**

(5)   **John caused the door to become open.**

Later, Gruber (1967) and J. McCawley (1968) noticed that there were other triads of sentences having exactly the same semantic relationship among them as (1)–(3) but in which there was not a common verb stem:

(6)   **Harry was not alive.**

(7)   **Harry died.**

(8)   **John killed Harry.**

In order to generalize Lakoff's treatment of (1)–(3) to cover such examples, Gruber and McCawley proposed that in the derivation of such sentences the "choice" of verb in surface structure be "postponed" until the abstract verbs had been condensed into a single main verb. Thus McCawley's derivation of (8) went as follows: The structure underlying (8) [which is rechristened the LOGICAL STRUCTURE or SEMANTIC REPRESENTATION of (8)] would be (9):

(9)

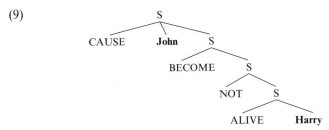

Successive applications of a transformation McCawley called PREDICATE RAISING would convert (9) first into (10), then into (11), then into (12):

(10)

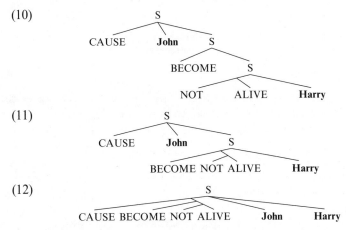

(11)

(12)

At this stage a transformation ("late lexical insertion transformation") replaces the tree dominating the four abstract verbs with the "lexical" verb **kill**, giving (13):

(13)

```
            S
    ┌───────┼───────┐
  kill    John    Harry
```

Finally, appropriate reordering transformations give sentence (8) (the past tense having been omitted from discussion for simplicity).

What I wish to call attention to with this example is the striking parallel between the role played in McCawley's analysis by Predicate Raising together with late lexical insertion and the role played in PTQ by the device of abstraction as used in giving complex translations of single words of English into intensional logic. In both cases the result is to allow a word of English to be related to an arbitrarily complex logical expression while maintaining at both levels correct syntactic characterizations of the expressions involved.

2.2. *The Procedure for Reconstructing Lexical Decomposition Analyses in PTQ*

Thus in principle it should be possible to "reproduce" any proposed lexical decomposition analysis in the PTQ grammar as follows:

CASE I: Suppose that the logical structure of a sentence with an intransitive verb is (14), which is converted into (15) by applications of Predicate Raising (where $OP_1 \ldots OP_n$ and $Pred_i$ are "atomic predicates" of generative semantics):

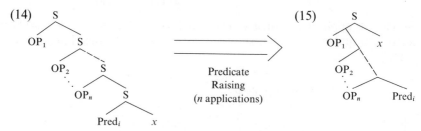

and then undergoes the lexical insertion transformation that replaces the accumulation of operators with $Verb_i$. In the corresponding PTQ grammar the intransitive verb $Verb_i$ will be given the complex translation rule in (16):

(16) $Verb_i$ translates into $\hat{x}[OP_1 \ldots OP_n[Pred_i(x)] \ldots]$.

Of course the success of this procedure will depend on whether (*a*) care is taken that the operators $OP_1 \ldots OP_n$ and $Pred_i$ are assigned to the appropriate logical types of the intensional logic of PTQ such that the formula in (16) is a well-formed expression and is of the appropriate type to serve as the translation of an IV phrase, and (*b*) appropriate truth conditions for $OP_1 \ldots OP_n$ and $Pred_i$ can be stated relative to the intensional model in such a way that all the appropriate entailments can be accounted for that motivated the decomposition in (14) in the first place.

CASE II: Suppose that the logical structure of a sentence with a transitive verb is (17), which is converted into (18) by Predicate Raising and then undergoes the lexical transformation that inserts the transitive verb $Verb_j$:

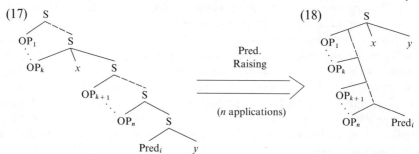

Then in a PTQ grammar *Verb_j* will be assigned a translation as in (19):

(19)   *Verb_j* translates into
$\lambda \mathcal{P} \lambda x \mathcal{P}\{\hat{y}[OP_1 \ldots OP_k(x, OP_{k+1} \ldots OP_n[Pred_i(y)] \ldots) \ldots]\}$.

(Again, the requirements mentioned for Case I must be observed.)

3. THE LEXICAL DECOMPOSITION OF CAUSATIVES IN PTQ

The ideas for the semantics of CAUSE and BECOME presented here are discussed in more detail in Dowty (1972); a complete discussion will have to be deferred to a later article (Dowty, in preparation). Briefly, the proposal (based on a discussion by von Wright) is that a causative sentence like (20) has the entailments (21)–(24):

(20)   **John opened the door** (at time *t*).

(21)   The door was not open (just before *t*).

(22)   The door was open (at, or just after, *t*).

(23)   John acted or was involved in some event (at *t*).

(24)   If John had not done what he did, the door would not have come to be open (at *t*), if all else about the situation had remained the same.

A pattern of entailments such as (20)–(24) is in fact characteristic of a large class of verbs (to be more precise, of complete verb phrases) in English called ACCOMPLISHMENT VERBS in Vendler (1967) and Dowty (1972), and these entailments may be taken as a criterion (but by no means the only criterion) for membership in that class.

The claim made in Dowty (1972) was that in a generative semantics theory a sentence such as (20) should be associated with the logical structure in (25), which is to be understood as representing a logical formula in which **John** and **the door** are terms, **open** and the unspecified verb represented by the triangle are one-place (stative) predicates, BECOME is a one-place sentence operator, and CAUSE is a two-place sentence connective:

(25)

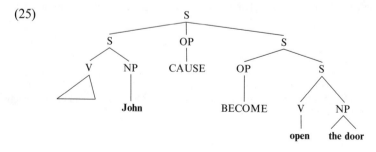

Semantically, BECOME is to be interpreted as a special kind of tense operator (which asserts that a formula is now true but was false at the previous moment); CAUSE is a sentence connective interpretable within the semantics proposed by Stalnaker for his conditional logic: ϕ CAUSE ψ is the case in some world i iff ϕ and ψ are the case in i and in that possible world which is most similar to i except that $\neg\phi$ is the case, $\neg\psi$ is also the case.

In order to formalize these notions within the PTQ theory, it will be necessary to make the following additions to the intensional logic and intensional model of PTQ.

3.1. *Additions to PTQ Semantics*

1. Add to the recursive definition of MEANINGFUL EXPRESSION:
    If ϕ, $\psi \in \text{ME}_t$, then [BECOME ϕ], [ϕ CAUSE ψ] $\in \text{ME}_t$.
2. Add to the semantic apparatus of PTQ a SELECTION FUNCTION f that assigns to each wff ϕ and each $i \in I$ a member $f(\phi, i)$ of I. [Intuitively $f(\phi, i)$ is to be that i' most like i with the (possible) exception that ϕ is the case. See Stalnaker (1968), Stalnaker and Thomason (1970), and Lewis (1973a) for details.]
3. Add to the definition of an INTERPRETATION the following:
    a. If $\phi \in \text{ME}_t$, then [BECOME ϕ]$^{\mathfrak{A}, i, j, g}$ is 1 if and only if $\phi^{\mathfrak{A}, i, j, g}$ is 1 and $\phi^{\mathfrak{A}, i, j', g}$ is 0 for some $j' < j$, and for all j'' such that $j' < j'' < j$, $\phi^{\mathfrak{A}, i, j'', g}$ is 0.
    b. If $\phi, \psi \in \text{ME}_t$, then [$\phi$ CAUSE ψ]$^{\mathfrak{A}, i, j, g}$ is 1 if and only if [$\phi \wedge \psi$]$^{\mathfrak{A}, i, j, g}$ is 1 and [$\neg\psi$]$^{\mathfrak{A}, f(\neg\phi, i), j, g}$ is 1.

3.2. *Comments on the Semantic Additions*

Lewis (1973b) has published a counterfactual semantic theory of causation that is similar to the preceding but embodies a number of refinements that allow it to avoid many of the objections that my original analysis is subject to. I definitely consider Lewis' treatment preferable, but since causation per se is not the subject of this study and since what follows does not depend on any details of either analysis, (but only on the assumption that SOME satisfactory account of the truth conditions for [ϕ CAUSE ψ] can be given), I have retained my earlier formulation on account of its expository simplicity.[3]

---

[3] The reader seriously interested in this problem should, in any case, consult Lewis' article and not judge the viability of counterfactual analyses on the basis of the simple version given here. My remaining qualms about the counterfactual analysis involve the problem Lewis calls CAUSAL SELECTION; an excellent discussion of this issue has been given by Abbott (1974). An earlier idea of mine about how to solve this (discussed by McCawley, 1976) unfortunately turns out to be inadequate.

I have treated CAUSE syntactically as a sentence connective, whereas McCawley treated it as a relation between individuals and sentences (or propositions?). For arguments within the generative semantics theory that the former treatment is preferable, see Geis (1973) and Dowty (1972).

It has been suggested to me that it may ultimately be preferable to treat CAUSE as a two-place predicate on events rather than a sentence connective. I have chosen to retain the sentence connective analysis for the present because (a) it is simpler to deal with the truth conditions from conditional logic in this way and (b) I wish to leave open the possibility that this analysis can be made general enough to encompass sentences like (26)–(28), yet no "events" in the usual sense are involved here:

(26)　**Mary's living nearby causes John to prefer this neighborhood.**
[cited in Fillmore (1971)]

(27)　**The failure of universal instantiation in line three makes the proof invalid.**

(28)　**A kangaroo is a marsupial because it has a pouch.**

Note that English has a causal sentence conjunction *because* (though the ordinary order of its arguments is the opposite of that of CAUSE as given earlier) which connects sentences expressing events as well as stative and definitional relationships such as those in (26)–(28).

The interpretation given here to [BECOME ϕ], while simple to state, likewise suffers from some problems. A more satisfactory, but also more complicated, semantic account of [BECOME ϕ] is given in Dowty (in preparation).

3.3. *Complex Translations versus Meaning Postulates*

There are actually two methods available within the PTQ theory by which verbs like **kill** or **open** could be semantically "decomposed": (a) Complex translations of such verbs could be assigned by special translation rules (as Montague did for the words **be** and **necessarily**, or (b) these verbs could be given a regular translation into the constants **kill'** and **open'**, and meaning postulates could be added requiring that certain relationships hold between these constants and other formulas in all admissible models (as Montague did for the translation of **seek**).

According to the first method, the transitive verb **open** (member of B_{TV}) could be given the special translation rule in (29), in which M, as in PTQ, is a variable of type $\langle s, \langle e, t \rangle \rangle$ and **open'** is of type $\langle \langle s, e \rangle, t \rangle$ and is intended to "represent"[4] the translation of the predicative adjective **open**:

(29)   **open** translates into

$$\lambda \mathcal{P} \lambda x \mathcal{P}\{\hat{y}[\vee M[M\{^{\vee}x\} \text{ CAUSE } [\text{BECOME } [\textbf{open}'(y)]]]]\}.$$

Likewise, **kill** would be assigned a complex translation by (30):

(30) **kill** translates into

$$\lambda \mathcal{P} \lambda x \mathcal{P}\{\hat{y}[\vee M[M\{^{\vee}x\} \text{ CAUSE } [\text{BECOME } [\neg \textbf{alive}'(y)]]]]\}.$$

Here **alive**′ represents the translation of **alive** and is of type $\langle\langle s, e\rangle, t\rangle$. Given these rules, (20) and (8) will have translations equivalent to (31) and (32), respectively (ignoring the past tense):

(31) $\vee y[\wedge x[\textbf{door}'(x) \leftrightarrow x = y] \wedge \vee M[M\{j\} \text{ CAUSE } [\text{BECOME } [\textbf{open}'(y)]]]]$.

(32) $\vee M[M\{j\} \text{ CAUSE } [\text{BECOME } [\neg\textbf{alive}'(^{\wedge}h)]]]$

In these translations existential quantification on the individual property variable M has been employed because the meanings of the verbs in question do not specify the kind of activity that produces the result—e.g., one can open a door by leaning against it, kicking it open, pressing a remote control button, etc. The same applies to **kill**, but of course this is not true of all accomplishment verbs. For example, the activities that bring about the

---

[4] Of course adjectives do not occur at all in the PTQ grammar. In this study I have assumed for the sake of simplicity that extensional adjectives (in predicate position at least) are of the same semantic category as IV phrases and CN phrases (but presumably of a different syntactic category, say $t///e$), so that **he**$_5$ **is open** would translate into **open**$'(x_5)$, etc. Montague, following a theory developed by himself, Terence Parsons, and J. A. W. Kamp, considered adjectives to denote functions from properties to sets—hence, of the syntactic category CN/CN in the PTQ notation (cf. Montague, 1970a, b). This category is syntactically appropriate for adjectives in attributive position and affords a correct semantic treatment for "intensional" adjectives in phrases such as **former senator** and **alleged communist**, but leaves the occurrence of adjectives in predicate position completely unexplained. These occurrences must now apparently be analyzed as "elliptical" attributive occurrences; e.g., **The door is open** will be analyzed semantically along the lines of "The door is an open entity"; cf. Montague (1970a) for a treatment of this sort.

Though it could be argued on the basis of syntactic as well as semantic peculiarities of the two kinds of adjectives that one might as well have TWO syntactic categories of adjectives, this question is too complicated to discuss here and remains an open one for the time being. The only relevant point is that the choice between these two treatments only trivially affects the analyses in this study. Only extensional adjectives occur in these constructions, and an expression denoting a set of individual concepts can always be "recovered" from the translation of a CN/CN by applying the latter to the universal property "entity"; i.e., **open**$'(^{\wedge}$**entity**$')$, etc. can be substituted for **open**′, etc. wherever it occurs.

existence of a picture are specified in the two accomplishment sentences **John drew a picture** and **John painted a picture**. The use of a variable in this position corresponds to the "unspecified predicate" represented by the triangle in the generative semantics analysis in (25).

Of course it may be objected that not every property of individuals is a property of being involved in some event, whereas only events are causes; if so, it would be easy enough to modify translations like these by replacing M with an appropriately restricted abstract property mentioning an event, once a mechanism for referring to events in the intensional logic has been settled upon.

According to the second method, the translations of **kill, open**, etc. would be simple constants of intensional logic of the appropriate type, and meaning postulates such as (33) and (34) would be added to the existing list of postulates (here I use **open″** as the translation of the transitive verb **open**, and **open′**, as before, to represent the translation of the predicative adjective **open**):

(33) $\Box[\textbf{kill′}(x, \mathscr{P}) \leftrightarrow \mathscr{P}\{\hat{y}[\lor M[M\{^\lor x\} \text{ CAUSE } [\text{BECOME } [\lnot \textbf{alive′}(y)]]]]\}]$

(34) $\Box[\textbf{open″}(x, \mathscr{P}) \leftrightarrow \mathscr{P}\{\hat{y}[\lor M[M\{^\lor x\} \text{ CAUSE } [\text{BECOME } [\textbf{open′}(y)]]]]]\}]$

Under this method the translations of (20) and (8) would still be logically equivalent to (31) and (32), respectively, and there are no semantic consequences of choosing one method rather than the other.

However, one option the meaning postulate method offers that the complex-translation method does not is the possibility of weakening the biconditional to a conditional, e.g.:

(35) $\Box[\textbf{kill′}(x, \mathscr{P}) \to \mathscr{P}\{\hat{y}[\lor M[M\{^\lor x\} \text{ CAUSE } [\text{BECOME } [\lnot \textbf{alive′}(y)]]]\}]$

This is of interest because the objection most frequently raised to generative semanticists' lexical decomposition analyses on grounds of empirical adequacy is that, though a sentence with one of these verbs may always entail its "decomposed" English paraphrase, the converse may not be the case. For instance, **kill** may always entail **cause to become not alive**, but not vice versa; (36) may entail (37), but (37) may not always entail (36), etc.:

(36)   **John persuaded Harry to leave.**

(37)   **John caused Harry to come to intend to leave.**

If such objections are valid, then the causative entailments of accomplishment verbs might still be capturable through the use of weakened meaning postulates like (35), yet the analysis will escape the objection.[5]

Making this move might strike some as very questionable, however. "Lexical decomposition," after all, is often intuitively thought of as the process of unpacking the meaning of a word into a finite configuration of, as it were, "primitive semantic building blocks" that together determine its entire meaning. These building blocks, "atomic predicates," as the generative semanticists call them, are frequently supposed to be language universal. A meaning postulate like (35) seems to assert, speaking impressionistically, that "cause to become not alive" is a part of the meaning of **kill** but not all of it: What else it might involve we are not told.

In actuality it is as yet quite unclear that all the words of a natural language (or all natural languages) will yield themselves to exhaustive decomposition into expressions formed out of some small set of semantic primitives. My point is that, regardless of the outcome of this question, there is a valuable and immediate purpose that such analyses as (33) or (35) serve, that of capturing a large and important class of entailment relations between sentences [e.g., (20)–(24)] that we at present have no other way of dealing with in a semantically precise way. I suggest that an appropriate strategy of research in word semantics would be to gradually enlarge the set of entailments that can be captured between pairs of sentences involving certain classes of words, rather than going after the "whole meaning" of any word all at once. Montague's PTQ, with its two-step semantic interpretation, seems to provide an excellent framework in which to carry out such research, offering as it does a semantic explicitness not to be found in other existing linguistic theories. If subsequent research justifies the claim that operators

---

[5] The advantage of choosing a meaning postulate over a complex translation rule to "decompose" a verb turns out to be analogous to an advantage that may be gained by choosing to relate certain pairs of sentences semantically through meaning postulates rather than deriving one from the other by a transformation. If we relate two sentences by transformation, then we are forced to predict their synonymy. However, if we relate them by meaning postulate, we always have the option of weakening the biconditional in the meaning postulate affecting them to a conditional, should the facts of the language require it. To cite a familiar example (cf. Postal, 1973, where it is attributed it to William Cantrall), sentences (i) and (ii) are allegedly related by the transformation RAISING TO SUBJECT POSITION, yet they are apparently not quite synonymous:

(i)   **It struck me that Julius Caesar was honest.**
(ii)   **Julius Caesar struck me as honest.**

Sentence (ii) clearly entails (i), but probably not conversely. A semantic account of the relation between these sentences (along the lines of Thomason, 1974) could describe such an asymmetric entailment relationship, whereas a transformational account could not. Parallel nonsynonymous examples could be constructed for the transformations TOUGH MOVEMENT, PASSIVE, RAISING TO OBJECT POSITION, and RICHARD—cf. Rogers (1974) for a description of the latter.

such as CAUSE, BECOME, etc. deserve special theoretical status as language universals, then so much the better. But in the meantime these operators can be regarded by skeptics as a mere technical convenience for capturing entailment relations.

4. THE ADVERB ARGUMENT FOR PREDICATE RAISING
AS A SYNTACTIC RULE

Generative semanticists have not been content to cite only semantic justification for lexical decomposition analyses, however, but claim also to have found independent syntactic arguments that prelexical syntactic transformations must be appealed to, rather than merely rules of semantic interpretation. We would expect such arguments to offer prima facie evidence against the kind of analysis I am presenting here. The strongest such argument, which I call the "adverb argument," involves an ambiguity found with certain temporal sentence adverbials such as **again, temporarily, for an hour, for a few minutes**, etc., and **until tomorrow, until Thursday**, etc. when they occur in sentences with accomplishment verbs.[6] An example of this ambiguity is (38) (cited by McCawley and attributed to Robert I. Binnick):

(38)   **The sheriff of Nottingham jailed Robin Hood for four years.**

Sentence (38) is ambiguous among two or three types of readings, which I shall call the INTERATIVE READING, the DURATIVE READING, and, for lack of a better term, the INTERNAL READING. These readings are loosely paraphrasable as (39)–(41):

(39)   ITERATIVE READING: *On multiple occasions during a period of four years it was the case that the sheriff of Nottingham brought it about that Robin Hood was in jail.*

(40)   DURATIVE READING: *The sheriff of Nottingham spent four years bringing it about that Robin Hood was in jail.*

(41)   INTERNAL READING: *The sheriff of Nottingham brought it about that for four years Robin Hood was in jail.*

I am not interested in the question of how the difference between the durative and iterative readings is to be analyzed or even in the question of whether

---

[6] Ambiguities with adverbs other than temporal adverbs have also been cited in this kind of argument, such as **carefully** and **almost**. See footnote 8 for discussion of **almost**.

there is a genuine ambiguity between these two readings but only in the distinction between these readings, on the one hand, and the internal reading, on the other. For my purposes I need only make the assumption that on the iterative (and/or durative) reading(s) the adverbial phrase is a sentence modifier (member of $P_{t/t}$ in PTQ).

Intuitively one can characterize the iterative (durative) reading as one in which the adverb limits the time of the action described by the verb, whereas the internal reading is one in which the adverb limits the time of the RESULT of that action. Thus it is quite plausible, under a decomposition analysis of causatives, that the iterative/durative reading of (38) has been assigned the logical structure in (42) in generative semantics, whereas the internal reading is assigned the structure in (43):

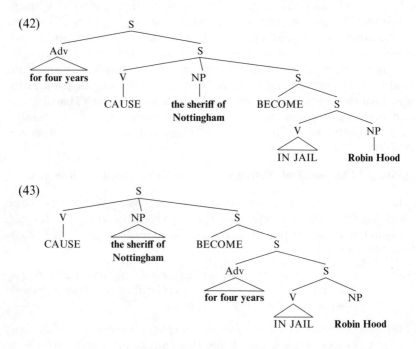

With the adverb **again** the situation is even clearer. Here the durative/iterative distinction does not arise (because **again** is a point-in-time adverb), and one can properly speak of an EXTERNAL versus an INTERNAL reading of **again**. The external reading of **again** entails that the subject has performed the action on the object at least once before, but the internal reading entails only that the object has been in the result state at least once before and not that the subject (or anyone else) has performed that act on it earlier. Thus, to cite a familiar example of an internal reading of **again**:

(44)   **All the king's horses and all the king's men couldn't put Humpty-Dumpty together again.**

does not, on the intended reading, entail that anyone had put Humpty-Dumpty together on an earlier occasion but merely that Humpty-Dumpty had been "together" once before.

With both types of adverbs the external–durative/iterative reading is strongly preferred (to the complete exclusion of the internal reading for most speakers) when the adverb appears in sentence-initial position:

(45)   **For four years the Sheriff of Nottingham jailed Robin Hood.**

(46)   **Again John glued the broken plate together.**

Sentence (45) has the reading in (42), and (46) entails[7] that John has glued the plate at least once before. Particularly telling are examples like (47), cited in McCawley (1971):

(47)   **John left his bicycle at Bill's house until tomorrow.**

where the future time adverbial **until tomorrow** would be incompatible with the past tense of the verb **left** were it not for the possibility of the internal reading paraphrasable as "At some time in the past John performed an action that caused (allowed) it to be the case that his bicycle came to be at Bill's house for a period of time lasting until tomorrow." Compare (48), which does not contain an accomplishment verb and therefore does not allow the internal reading, and (49), where the internal reading is difficult because of the initial position of the adverbial:

(48)   *****John stayed in his room until tomorrow.**

(49)   *****Until tomorrow John left his bicycle at Bill's house.**

It must be mentioned that the generative semantics account of the derivations of sentences with internal readings from logical structures like (43) is not without its difficulties. In the derivation of sentence (38) from (43), the subtree CAUSE–BECOME–**in**–**jail** must be replaced by the verb **jail**, yet in order for Predicate Raising to give rise to this subtree it is necessary to get the adverbial **for four years** "out of the way" by some

---

[7] Actually the sentence adverb **again** presupposes as well as entails that the sentence it is attached to was true on an earlier occasion. I will continue to make this simplification, as the distinction does not affect the issues I am concerned with here.

means or other, or else the subtree CAUSE–BECOME–for–four–years–in– **jail** would arise, and this would not allow **jail** to be inserted. The means proposed for this is the transformation ADVERB RAISING, which would make the adverbial a constituent of the highest clause. Such a transformation would be completely ad hoc, as it is completely unmotivated (and quite possibly unmotivatable) from independent data.[8]

For the purposes of this study, the essentials of the adverb argument are as follows:

1. It is (implicitly) claimed that the ambiguity between the durative/ iterative and internal readings of adverbs like **again**, **for an hour**, etc. is definitely not due to an ambiguity in the meaning (or syntactic category) of each adverb; rather,

---

[8] The only argument I have seen to the effect that Adverb Raising is independently motivated is Morgan's (1969) argument based on (i) and (ii):

(i)   **John almost drank all his milk.**
(ii)   **John drank almost all his milk.**

Sentence (i) is claimed to be ambiguous, having the reading expressed by (ii) as one of its readings. Therefore it is assumed that there is a transformation optionally converting (ii) to (i), dubbed Adverb Raising. From the fact that (iii) is likewise felt to be ambiguous (actually multiply ambiguous):

(iii)   **John almost killed Harry.**

it is argued that Adverb Raising must have applied here also to produce one of its readings; hence, it has applied "prelexically."

These claims seem to me to be very weak for at least three reasons:

1. It is very doubtful that **almost** in (i) and (ii) is of the category sentence adverb, since it (like **only** and **even**) invariably occurs attached to a term phrase, IV phrase, or adjective and does not occur where sentence adverbs usually occur in English, i.e., at the beginning or end of sentences.

2. If there is a transformation converting (ii) to (i), then here it only moves **almost** within a verb phrase, whereas under the generative semantics analysis of (iii) the transformation would have to move it from a lower to a higher clause. But generally sentence adverbs must be prohibited from moving from an embedded clause to a higher clause. For example, (iv) cannot be a transformational variant of (v):

(iv)   **John promised on Tuesday to leave for New York.**
(v)   **John promised to leave on Tuesday for New York.**

3. I do not think it has been convincingly shown that (i) is really ambiguous between two readings; perhaps it is merely vague with respect to an indefinite number of possibilities, one class of which happens to be expressed by (ii).

2. The ambiguity arises according to whether the adverb has the whole sentence or a part of the logical structure of the verb as its scope; therefore

3. Any theory that does not recognize that single surface verbs are syntactically complex at a more abstract syntactic level cannot appropriately account for this scope ambiguity of adverbs.

I will now turn to the question of whether these adverb ambiguities can be accommodated within the modified PTQ framework, and the degree to which such an accommodation, if possible, would be compatible with the argument outlined earlier. I will not discuss verbs like **kill** and **open** immediately, but proceed indirectly, first discussing a class of causative constructions called FACTITIVES by traditional grammarians, NEXUS OBJECT by Jespersen (1924), but more familiar to many linguists as the HAMMER FLAT construction. This digression will bring out the limits imposed by the PTQ theory more clearly; moreover, the topic has independent relevance for the lexical decomposition question.

5. THE ADVERB ARGUMENT AND

THE FACTITIVE CONSTRUCTION

5.1. *The Factitive Construction*

Sentences such as (50)–(53) have attracted the attention of generative semanticists recently [cf. Green(1970, 1972); McCawley (1971); Dowty (1972)] as well as Jespersen:

(50)   **John hammered the metal** $\begin{cases} \textbf{flat.} \\ \textbf{smooth.} \\ \textbf{shiny.} \end{cases}$

(51)   **John wiped the surface** $\begin{cases} \textbf{clean.} \\ \textbf{dry.} \\ \textbf{smooth.} \end{cases}$

(52)   **Mary wrenched the stick** $\begin{cases} \textbf{free.} \\ \textbf{loose.} \end{cases}$

(53)   **Mary shot him dead.**

Semantically these sentences intuitively involve a subject that performs an act or activity with respect to an object; the sentence-final adjective expresses a state that the object comes to be in as a result of the activity performed by the subject.[9] They contain accomplishment verb phrases, according to all the tests in Vendler (1967) and Dowty (1972) (though, as we shall see, they do not necessarily contain accomplishment verbs as such). Most of the concern has been with the question of why this construction is not fully productive. That is, why do sentences such as (50)–(53) sound perfectly normal while sentences such as (54)–(57) sound odd, though they seem to conform to the same syntactic and semantic patterns (cf. Green (1972), from which I have taken these examples):

(54)   ?John hammered the metal $\begin{cases} \text{beautiful.} \\ \text{safe.} \\ \text{tubular.} \end{cases}$

(55)   ?John wiped the surface $\begin{cases} \text{damp.} \\ \text{dirty.} \\ \text{stained.} \end{cases}$

(56)   ?She wrenched the stick $\begin{cases} \text{broken.} \\ \text{tight.} \end{cases}$

(57)   ?She shot him $\begin{cases} \text{lame.} \\ \text{paranoid.} \\ \text{wounded.} \end{cases}$

No clear criterion for predicting the differences between (50)–(53) and (54)–(57) has been found, yet any attempt to claim that (50)–(53) are "frozen idioms" of some type must contend with the existence of the paradigm in (58):

(58)   He $\begin{cases} \text{painted} \\ \text{colored} \\ \text{dyed} \\ \text{etc.} \end{cases}$ it $\begin{cases} \text{green.} \\ \text{ochre.} \\ \text{alizarine crimson.} \\ \text{Fabulous Fuchsia.} \\ \text{etc.} \end{cases}$

which involves a potentially unlimited class of sentences, as any color terms whatsoever may appear in it (existing or invented), or any combination of

---

[9] Not all sentences of the form noun phrase–verb–noun phrase–adjective follow this semantic pattern (cf. Green, 1970); the other two main types are exemplified by **Mary found John alone**, where the final adjective expresses a temporary property the individual denoted by the direct object possessed at the time of the event denoted by the verb, and **Mary considers John obnoxious**, where the adjective expresses a belief or attitude possessed by the individual denoted by the subject. The latter two classes of sentences would of course have to be produced by rules other than those I discuss in this work.

them, and any verb having to do with coloring may be used. For the moment I will make the assumption that the rule responsible for producing this type of sentence is to be unrestricted and that sentences like (54)–(57) are to be excluded by pragmatic or stylistic considerations, if at all. I believe the careful observer will find that native speakers of English occasionally produce certain sentences of this form in casual conversation that would sound as odd as (54)–(57) in isolation, yet sound normal in the context of the discourse. In Section 7 I return to the question of whether the rules for these sentences are "rules of the lexicon" or "rules of syntax."

5.2. An Analysis of the Factitive Construction in the PTQ Grammar

The first derivation of factitive sentences that I propose here involves a DERIVED CATEGORY RULE, by which I mean a syntactic rule that takes a formula containing a free variable plus possibly some other phrase and gives a derived phrase of some category other than "sentence" as its output. The example of this type of rule in PTQ is the relative clause rule, which takes a formula with a free variable plus a common noun as its input and gives a derived common noun as its output. Examples of such rules in extensions to PTQ are (a) Thomason's proposal for deriving infinitive phrases [Thomason (1974b); actually this is a two-stage process involving creation of an "abstract" from a formula with a free variable, and subsequent creation of an infinitive from the abstract]; (b) Partee's derived verb phrase rule, which creates a derived P_{IV} from a formula with a free variable in subject position (cf. Partee, 1973, reprinted in this volume, pages 51–76); and (c) Delacruz' rule for *that* clauses, which produces a term phrase denoting a proposition from a sentence (though here no free variable is involved (cf. Delacruz, 1972, reprinted in this volume, pages 177–200).

In the present case the rule must take a transitive verb (for example, **hammer**) plus a formula of a certain form with a free variable (for example, **he₄ is flat**), and give a derived transitive verb (member of P_{TV}) as output (in this case **hammer flat**). The rule would look something like S30:

S30: If $\alpha \in P_{TV}$, $\phi \in P_t$, and ϕ has the form **he**$_n$ **is** γ, then $F_{30,n}(\alpha, \phi) \in P_{TV}$, where $F_{30,n}(\alpha, \phi) = \alpha \, \gamma$.

[Again I am making the simplifying assumption that the grammar produces sentences such as **he₅ is flat** with translations **flat**$'(x_5)$, etc.; cf. footnote 4.]

The translation rule corresponding to S30 will be responsible for providing the "causative meaning" of the construction:

T30: If α translates into α' and ϕ translates into ϕ', then $F_{30,n}(\alpha, \phi)$ translates into

$$\lambda \mathscr{P} \lambda x \mathscr{P}\{\hat{x}_n[\alpha'(x,\hat{P}[P\{x_n\}]) \text{ CAUSE [BECOME } [\phi']]]\}$$

Under this analysis a sentence such as (59) would have an analysis tree like (60) and would have a translation equivalent to (61):

(59)   **Mary shakes John awake.**

(60)

(61)   **shake′**$_*(m, j)$ CAUSE[BECOME[**awake′**$_*(j)$]]]

In (61) it has been assumed that **shake′** and **awake′** are subject to the meaning postulates for extensional first-order reducibility. The translation in (61) entails that Mary shakes John, that John was not awake earlier but now is, and that if Mary had not shaken John at this particular time, he would not have awakened, all else being the same.

There would of course be simpler ways of deriving these sentences syntactically. For example, the adjective **awake** might be combined directly with the transitive verb **shake**. My reason for considering a derivation in which **he₃ is awake** is an intermediate stage is that the factitive sentences allow internal readings of adverbs [as shown by (62)], and the analysis I have proposed will automatically give the internal as well as external readings in a way compatible with the adverb argument:

(62)   **John dozed off once during the lecture, but Mary quickly shook him awake again.**

If we assume that **again** is a sentence modifier (member of $P_{t/t}$) that can be placed at the end as well as the beginning of the sentence it modifies, then sentences such as **he₃ is awake again** will be produced, and these can undergo S30 as specified. Thus two readings for **Mary shakes John awake again** will be produced as specified in the analysis trees in (63) and (64), which have the translations in (65) and (66), respectively:

(63) (EXTERNAL)

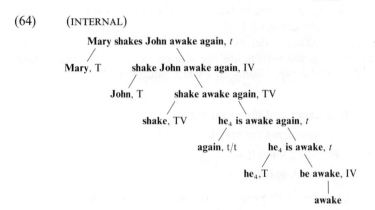

(64) (INTERNAL)

(65) $\textbf{again}'(\char94[\textbf{shake}'_*(m, j)\ \text{CAUSE}[\text{BECOME}[\textbf{awake}'_*(j)]]])$

(66) $\textbf{shake}'_*(m, j)\ \text{CAUSE}[\text{BECOME}[\textbf{again}'(\char94[\textbf{awake}'_*(j)])]]$

If the meaning of **again** is explained by the meaning postulate in (67):[10]

(67) $\Box[\textbf{again}'(p) \leftrightarrow [\char94^{\vee}p \land H[\neg\ ^{\vee}p \land H[\,^{\vee}p]]]]$

then (63) will entail that Mary shook John at an earlier time, whereas (64) will have only the weaker entailment that John had been awake at an earlier time.

The careful reader will have observed that a word order change is necessary in all these sentences with derived transitive verb phrases, or else sentences like ***Mary shakes awake John** will be produced rather than **Mary**

---

[10] To see why the negated middle conjunct is needed in the right half of the meaning postulate for **again**, it is only necessary to consider the difference between **John is still here** and **John is here again**.

shakes John awake. What is called for is a modification in the syntactic function, F_5, that combines transitive verb phrases with their objects. In fact the appropriate modification is found in the corresponding syntactic rule, S3, in Montague (1970a). It is argued in Dowty (in preparation) that this modification is justified by sentences treated in transformational grammar by transformations such as COMPLEX NP SHIFT, PARTICLE SHIFT, EXTRAPOSITION FROM NP, and others.

I turn next to some other syntactic constructions of English whose semantics closely parallels that of the factitive construction.

5.3. *The Factitive Construction with Transitive Absolute and Intransitive Verbs*

A fact that escaped the generative semanticists but was noted by Jespersen is that certain sentences exist that appear to be of the same syntactic and semantic class as those under discussion, but in which the apparent direct object of the transitive verb is not the semantically "real" object. That is, sentence (68), of the type discussed earlier, entails (69), but (70) does not entail (71):

(68)   **John hammered the metal flat.**

(69)   **John hammered the metal.**

(70)   **John drank himself silly.**

(71)   **John drank himself.**

There are also cases with prepositional phrases (see Section 5.4) that exhibit the same problem:

(72)   **John read himself to sleep.**

(73)   **The king ate himself to death.**

Jespersen notes that there are certain metaphorical expressions that have this property if their literal meanings are considered:

(74)   **John ate his father out of house and home.**

(75)   **He drank the officers under the table.**

Moreover, there are also cases where the basic verb involved is always INTRANSITIVE in isolation [examples from Jespersen (1924, p. 311)]:

(76)   **John slept himself sober.**

(77)   **John bowed her into an armchair.**

(78)   **A lovers eyes will gaze en eagle blinde.** (Shakespeare)

In fact ALL the sentences in (70) and (72)–(78) can and should be treated as derived from intransitive verbs. Whereas transformational grammar usually treats transitive absolute verbs (**John drank**) as derived from transitives (**John drank something**) by a transformation called INDEFINITE OBJECT DELETION, it can be argued on various grounds [cf. Dowty (in preparation)] that in the PTQ theory it is better to simply enter such verbs in the category B_{IV} as well as in B_{TV}, appealing to a meaning postulate to correctly express the meaning of the transitive absolutes. Making this move will enable us to subsume (70) and (72)–(78) under a single rule, S31, which is exactly like S30 except for taking a B_{IV} rather than a B_{TV} as input:

S31: If $\alpha \in P_{IV}$, $\phi \in P_t$, and ϕ has the form **he**$_n$ **is** γ, then $F_{30,n}(\alpha, \phi) \in P_{TV}$, where $F_{30,n}(\alpha, \phi) = \alpha\gamma$.

Likewise, its translation rule is parallel to T30:

T31: If α translates into α' and ϕ translates into ϕ', then $F_{30,n}(\alpha, \phi)$ translates into

$$\lambda \mathscr{P} \lambda x \mathscr{P}\{\hat{x}_n[\alpha'(x) \text{ CAUSE [BECOME } [\phi']]]\}$$

Thus (70) would have the translation in (79):

(79)   [**drink**$'_*(j)$ CAUSE[BECOME[**silly**$'_*(j)$]]]]

Translation (79) entails that John drank, and that his drinking made him silly, but does not entail that he drank himself.[11]

5.4. *Prepositional Phrases Expressing "Goal"*

It was noted in Dowty (1972) and Vendler (1967) that a verb phrase that is NOT an accomplishment verb phrase can be turned into an accomplishment verb phrase by the addition of certain prepositional phrases. Thus (80) does not have an accomplishment verb phrase [according to all the tests in Dowty (1972)], but (81) does:

(80)   **John drove the car.**

(81)   **John drove the car** $\begin{cases} \textbf{into the garage.} \\ \textbf{to the office.} \end{cases}$

---

[11] The suggestion that both these rules exist raises the possibility that some sentences might be ambiguous between readings produced by each of the rules, inasmuch as some verbs of English are ambiguously transitive or intransitive. Partee has supplied the sentence **The carpenters were pounding John deaf**, which does in fact exhibit this ambiguity.

(Intuitively an accomplishment verb phrase describes an action that produces a specifiable result state or has a "natural end point.") Such sentences as (81) can be produced by Rules S30 and T30 (with the correct entailments, I believe), with a couple of modifications. First, it will be necessary to assume that the grammar produces sentences of the form **he$_n$ is in the garage**, **he$_n$ is at the office**, etc., where the phrases **is in the garage**, etc. are IV phrases. I will not attempt to give the details here, but I assume that this could be done in a way parallel to what I suggested for sentences like **he$_n$ is flat**. That is, the prepositions **in**, **on**, **at**, etc. as they occur here would be assigned to a category $(t///e)/T$.

The syntactic rule for factitive sentences would then be modified as follows:

S30: (MODIFIED VERSION): If $\alpha \in P_{TV}$, $\phi \in P_t$, and ϕ has the form **he$_n$ is** γ, then $F_{30,n}(\alpha, \phi) \in P_{TV}$, where $F_{30,n}(\alpha, \phi) = \alpha\gamma$. Exception: If γ has the form

$$\begin{Bmatrix} \textbf{in} \\ \textbf{on} \\ \textbf{at} \end{Bmatrix} \zeta,$$

then

$$F_{30,n}(\alpha, \phi) = \alpha \begin{Bmatrix} \textbf{into} \\ \textbf{onto} \\ \textbf{to} \end{Bmatrix} \zeta.$$

Sentence (81) would have the analysis tree in (82):

(82)

```
                    John drives the car into the garage, t
                   /                        \
           John, T         drive the car into the garage, IV
                          /                       \
                the car, T        drive into the garage, TV (by F₃₀.₂)
                                 /                    \
                          drive, TV          he₂ is in the grage, t
                                            /              \
                                        he₂        be in the garage, IV
                                                  /              \
                                         in, (t///e)/T     the garage, T
                                                                |
                                                            garage, CN
```

The translation of (82) would entail that John drives the car and that the car comes to be in the garage as a result of John's driving it.

5.5. *Derived Intransitive Accomplishment Verb Phrases*

If we decide to include derived transitive verb phrases with the prepositions **into, onto, to**, etc. under the domain of the causative rule, then we are bound to consider also the possibility that the intransitive verb phrases in (83), (84), and (85) should be given a similar analysis:

(83)   **John walked onto the stage.**

(84)   **Mary waltzed into the room.**

(85)   **Sam swam to the boat.**

From (83) we have the entailments that John was not on the stage before walking, that he was on the stage after he walked, and that if he had not walked at that particular time under those particular circumstances, he would not have come to be on the stage.[12]

Such sentences might be produced by yet another variant of S30, which I call S32. This rule would have the same syntactic function as the modified S30 (namely, $F_{30,n}$) and would differ only in that it would take an INTRANSITIVE verb and a sentence as its input and give a derived INTRANSITIVE verb as output. If we call such a rule S32, then its corresponding translation rule, T32, is as follows:

T32:   If α translates into α' and ϕ translates into ϕ', then $F_{30,n}(\alpha, \phi)$ translates into $\hat{x}_n[\alpha'(x_n)\text{CAUSE}[\text{BECOME}[\phi']]]$.

This variant would predict the existence of derived intransitive causatives consisting of verb plus adjective (as well as verb plus prepositional phrase); if such exist, they may be phrases such as **fall flat** and **stand up tall**, but I find this somewhat doubtful.

Since transitive verb phrases become intransitive verb phrases once a term phrase has been attached, it might be questioned whether it is neces-

---

[12] Some readers may balk at this step because it seems quite peculiar to paraphrase (83) as "John's walking caused it come about that John was on the stage." Of course, postulating (32) does not obligate me to claim that this IS an acceptable paraphrase of (83), since CAUSE is not after all the translation of the English word **cause**; rather, the "meaning" of CAUSE is at this point neither more nor less than the formal interpretation I have assigned it, and this in fact seems unobjectionable when applied to (83)–(85) via T32. Nevertheless if it turns out that causation is not the appropriate relation between activity and result state in (83)–(85), then 'CAUSE' in T32 can be replaced by some weaker connective. For example, we might replace it by ' $\wedge$ ', though this seems on the other hand to be too weak to capture the intuitively felt connection between activity and result. However, such a modified T32 might be appropriate for Fillmore's (1974) sentences **Mary wore a green dress to the party** and **John read a newspaper all the way to Chicago**. Thus I will leave it as an interesting but open question whether some intermediate analysis can be found that could treat both Fillmore's examples and (83)–(85) by the same rule.

sary to have both S30 and S32 rather than get by with only the rule for intransitive verb phrases. Both are needed, however, because of the semantic difference between the two.[13] In the case of transitive verb modification with a locative phrase, it is the location of the entity denoted by the OBJECT that is asserted to have changed position (cf. **John threw the letter into the wastebasket**); whereas with intransitive verb modification, it is the location of the entity denoted by the SUBJECT that changes, regardless of whether a transitive or intransitive basic verb is involved (cf. **John walked to Times Square**, **John rode the subway to Times Square**). Facts about transportation in the real world cause the distinction to be somewhat blurred, however. For instance, it might be claimed that the sentence **John drove his car to Boston** is really semantically ambiguous between the two types of readings, though in the actual world one reading could hardly be true without the other being true as well. That is, you cannot get yourself to Boston by driving your car without getting your car there as well, any more than you can get your car to Boston by driving it there without simultaneously getting yourself there too.

Unfortunately not quite all locatives of goal can be treated by these rules; Fillmore's (1974) examples **Mary wore a green dress to the party** and **John read the newspaper all the way to Chicago** resist this treatment because there is no causal connection between the activity and the change of position (but cf. footnote 12).

5.6. *Other Related Syntactic Constructions*

There are a couple of other causative constructions in English that resemble the preceding in their syntactic and semantic properties, yet it is not clear that they would require an exactly parallel analysis in a synchronic grammar of modern English.

The first of these follows the pattern subject–verb–object–common noun phrase and is exemplified by **They elected Bill president**, **John appointed Mary director of the project**, etc. But because the class of verbs that participate in this is small and semantically restricted (it includes **nominate**, **designate**, **make** (in one sense), **name**, etc.), and because these verbs are semantically elliptical when they occur WITHOUT the common noun phrase (rather than denoting an irresultative activity), it might be best to treat them simply as members of a basic category TV/CN.

---

[13] I must hedge on this point, however, because (*a*) I have no clear-cut example of a single sentence that must be considered ambiguous between the two readings, and (*b*) if there are no such examples, then it may yet be possible to get away with only intransitive verb modification by using a meaning postulate for prepositional phrases with **into**, **onto**, and **to** that makes the entailment of subject result state versus object result state dependent on the particular verb being modified. Further discussion of this problem will be deferred to Dowty (in preparation).

Certain instances of the verb–particle construction have the same pattern of causative entailments as the factitive sentences; consider (86)–(88):

(86)   **John turned the switch off.**

(87)   **John took the garbage out.**

(88)   **John chased the dog away.**

For instance, (86) entails that John turned the switch, that the switch came to be off, and that John's action caused the switch to come to be off. Yet in other instances of verb-plus-particle constructions the particle does not literally express a result state (cf. **clean up, dry out, put off**), and in others even the verb gives little clue to the meaning (cf. **egg on, touch off, rule out**). Perhaps the best statement is that this construction might represent a productive semantically regular causative rule at an earlier stage of the language but that the construction is not typically compositional in meaning today.

6. THE ADVERB ARGUMENT AND LEXICAL CAUSATIVES

I am now ready to return to the discussion of basic (or "lexical") verbs that are already accomplishments without the addition of any prepositional phrase, adjective, or other type of complement, e.g., **kill, build, open, hide**, etc. What I hope became clear from the discussion of the factitive construction and other related sentences is that the adverb argument can be accounted for in the PTQ grammar only if an intermediate stage in the derivation of each accomplishment verb phrase occurs in which a phrase of the category "sentence" is produced. Only in this way could the adverbs **again, for an hour**, etc. have the proper scope for the internal readings to be produced. In all the cases discussed in Section 5, it was more or less plausible for me to indulge in enough "abstract syntax" to resurrect sentences such as **he$_i$ is flat** out of the derivational history of the sentences in question. It would be slightly less plausible to resurrect **he$_i$ is in jail** from **The Sheriff jailed Robin Hood**.

But the situation is quite different with simple sentences like (89):

(89)   **John hid the money again.**

Here the verb **hide** is not even morphologically related to a stative verb meaning "not visible" (or some such meaning). Yet (89) seems to allow the internal reading of **again**, as can be more clearly seen from (90):

(90)   **John found $10,000 buried in his backyard, but he quickly hid it again.**

Thus we have encountered a rather serious dilemma. If we continue with
the type of analysis presented in the preceding sections, then it seems we
must now analyze sentences like (90), when the adverb has the internal
reading, as having a complex syntactic derivation from something on the
order of **John caused it that the money was again not visible**. This of course
would mean nothing less than accepting the generative semantics claim
that "lexical decomposition" is a matter of syntactic transformation rather
than semantic interpretation after all.

There seem to me to be three kinds of positions one could take with
respect to this dilemma:

1. One could accept the generative semanticists' conclusion that the
adverb ambiguities offer real evidence for syntactic rules that compress
complex sentences into single verbs.

2. One could take the position that the basic semantic analysis the generative semanticists have given to these sentences is completely wrong and
the question of ambiguity does not arise.

3. One could accept the claim that a genuine syntactic ambiguity is involved, but search for a second SURFACE syntactic analysis of the crucial
sentences within the PTQ theory to which the appropriate second semantic
interpretation can be given.

The second position could be interpreted in two ways. It is claimed either
that the intuitive judgments of speakers of English about these sentences
are simply faulty or else that the ambiguity resides in the meaning (but not
the syntactic category) of a single word and hence is not a "syntactic"
ambiguity at all. Both these positions fail to take into account the facts
that the ambiguity is lost if the adverb is moved to the beginning of the
sentence (though this operation otherwise preserves synonymy), that in the
case of **again** the two readings characteristically have different stress patterns,
and that the occurrence of a future time adverb in a past tense sentence
would be paradoxical were it not for this analysis. Of course one cannot
rule out the possibility that a simple solution to these problems will turn
up someday, but for now we seem to be stuck with the generative semantics
explanation of them, or else we must ignore them altogether.

The third position is viable and interesting from the point of view of
Montague grammar precisely because one of its greatest advantages (as well,
some will no doubt claim, as one of its greatest disadvantages) is that it
allows us to multiply syntactic categories at will (hence, multiply the possible
analyses we could give of what grammatical relationships exist in any given
sentence), and gives us a ready-made semantic category for any new syntactic category we conjure up. Thus if we are willing to abandon the implicit

generative semantics assumption in the adverb argument that neither adverb nor verb is contributing to the ambiguity by belonging to more than one category, we immediately have two ways of attacking the problem: entering the adverbs in a second category or entering the verbs in a second category. This step should not be unexpected; whereas generative semantics has historically been quite parsimonious in the grammatical categories it admits, Montague grammar seems destined to postulate a plethora of them. (Of course both of these alternatives avoid the need for the generative semantics transformation Adverb Raising.)

6.1. A Reanalysis of the Adverb Ambiguity as an Ambiguity between Sentence Adverb and Verb Phrase Adverb

In PTQ, Montague provided for both sentence adverbs (members of $P_{t/t}$) and verb phrase adverbs (members of $P_{IV/IV}$), and the motivation for this distinction has recently been examined in some detail by Stalnaker and Thomason (1973). A plausible suggestion, then, would be that adverbs with internal readings are functioning as verb phrase adverbs, whereas adverbs with external readings are the homophonous sentence adverbs. This would offer a natural account of why internal readings are not present when the adverb appears in sentence-initial position.

It should be recognized immediately, however, that this move does not in itself provide a solution to the problem of internal readings. Rather, it is necessary to furnish an explanation of WHY the paraphrase relationship exists between pairs such as (91) and (92):

(91)   **John opened the door for a few minutes.**

(92)   **John brought it about that for a few minutes it was the case that the door was open.**

It is not, after all, a general property of verb phrase adverbs with causative verbs that there exists a paraphrase with a homophonous sentence adverb:

(93)   **John opened the door carefully.**

(94)   ***John brought it about that it was carefully the case that the door was open.**

To reply that **for a few minutes** is a verb phrase adverb that happens to have a sentence adverb analog in English, whereas **carefully** does not, is to beg the question of what the precise semantic relationship between (91) and (92) is. Obviously a meaning postulate is needed that makes the relationship between (91) and (92) precise.

Moreover, the ambiguity between the internal and other readings appears only with accomplishment verbs, not with states and nonresultative activities. Sentence (95) is not ambiguous the way (96) is, and (97) is not ambiguous the way (98) is (though it has the durative–iterative ambiguity):

(95)   **John saw the door again.**

(96)   **John opened the door again.**

(97)   **John drove the car for an hour.**

(98)   **John parked the car for an hour.**

The meaning postulate needed here must therefore distinguish between verbs that entail that some particular result came about and those that do not; the verb phrase adverb reading must be defined only for those verbs that do entail a result state. These requirements will be satisfied by (99), where **again''** is the translation of the verb phrase adverb **again** (and is therefore of type $\langle\langle s, \langle\langle s, e\rangle, t\rangle\rangle, \langle\langle s, e\rangle, t\rangle\rangle\rangle$); **again'** is the translation of the homophonous sentence adverb (of type $\langle\langle s, t\rangle, t\rangle$); M is a variable of type $\langle s, \langle e, t\rangle\rangle$; and p is of type $\langle s, t\rangle$:

(99) $\bigwedge x \bigwedge M \bigwedge p \; \Box \, [\textbf{again}''(\hat{z}[M\{^\vee z\}\text{CAUSE}[\text{BECOME}[^\vee p]]])(x) \leftrightarrow$
$M\{^\vee x\}\text{CAUSE}[\text{BECOME}[\textbf{again}'(p)]]]$

Note that this meaning postulate is applicable to causatives in which the entity denoted by the subject undergoes the change of state (cf. (83)–(85) and T32) as well as those in which the entity denoted by the object undergoes the change of state.[14]

6.2. *Accounting for the Adverb Ambiguity by Reanalyzing the Verb*

The second way of circumventing the adverb argument is to claim that the ambiguity we are observing is due to the fact that the verbs involved, rather than the adverbs, belong to more than one syntactic category. Whereas in the former analysis we could use a second category already employed in the

---

[14] Whereas (99) would be applicable to lexical causatives that are "decomposed" by means of either a complex translation rule or a meaning postulate with a biconditional connective, it would not be directly applicable in cases where we have assigned only the weaker conditional meaning postulates such as (35). We would still be able to get the appropriate entailments, however, if we replaced (99) by (i):

(i) $\bigwedge x \bigwedge P \bigwedge M \bigwedge p \Box[[\textbf{again}''(P)(x) \wedge \Box[P\{x\} \rightarrow M\{^\vee x\}\text{CAUSE}[\text{BECOME}[^\vee p]]]$
$\rightarrow M\{^\vee x\}\text{CAUSE}[\text{BECOME}[\textbf{again}'(p)]]]$

This might turn out to be so strong as to produce undesirable entailments as well, but so far I am not sure whether there are any; cf. Dowty (in preparation).

grammar ($B_{IV/IV}$), for this analysis we must appeal to a new verb category, the best choice being $B_{TV/(t/t)}$—"something that combines with a sentence adverb to give a transitive verb." Thus the internal reading of **John opens the door again** will be produced syntactically by first combining the "new" verb **open** with **again** to form the transitive verb **open again**, then combining this with **the door**, etc. The translation rule for such a verb **open** would be (100), in which R is a variable of type $\langle s, f(t/t)\rangle$, that is, $\langle s, \langle\langle s, t\rangle, t\rangle\rangle$:

(100)   **open** translates into

$$\lambda R\lambda\mathscr{P}\lambda x\mathscr{P}\{\hat{y}[\vee M[M\{^\vee x\}\text{CAUSE}[\text{BECOME}[^\vee R(^\wedge[\textbf{open}'(y)])]]]]\}$$

In this analysis it is predicate abstraction on the sentence-operator variable R that allows the adverb to modify "a part of" the meaning of the verb; the combination **open again** would literally have the translation in (101), and this, in turn, is logically equivalent to (102), where the adverb is in the desired internal position:

(101)
$$\lambda R\lambda\mathscr{P}\lambda x\mathscr{P}\{\hat{y}[\vee M[M\{^\vee x\}\text{CAUSE}[\text{BECOME}[^\vee R(^\wedge[\textbf{open}'(y)])]]]]\}(^\wedge\textbf{again}')$$

(102) $\lambda\mathscr{P}\lambda x\mathscr{P}\{\hat{y}[\vee M[M\{^\vee x\}\text{CAUSE}[\text{BECOME}[\textbf{again}'(^\wedge[\textbf{open}'(y)])]]]]\}$

Given the PTQ system, this is all a perfectly straightforward consequence of the decision to use the syntactic category $\text{TV}/(t/t)$.

6.3. *Evaluating the Three Analyses of the Adverb Argument*

The first treatment of the adverb argument (that is, the treatment in Sections 5.2–5.5 in which an intermediate sentence is first produced, then reduced) was initially appealing because it automatically produced both adverb readings without any extension of the grammar whatsoever. Its disadvantages were (*a*) that it required a more complicated syntactic treatment of the factitive of constructions than would be needed otherwise and (*b*) that it had the fatal flaw of not being extendable to lexical causatives.

Both the second and third treatments are open to the objection that they require postulating homophonous and semantically similar lexical items of two different syntactic categories, whereas our intuitions lead us to believe that only a single "word" is involved. Whatever the force of this objection, it will certainly not apply to this analysis alone, for such duplication of lexical items in multiple categories seems endemic to Montague's theory. Had Montague treated conjunctions lexically rather than grammatically, for example, **and** and **or** would appear in three syntactic categories, since they conjoin sentences, term phrases, and verb phrases. The method of dealing with verb complementation begun in PTQ and extended in Thomason (1974) requires that verbs be entered in as many categories as they take complement types. However we may choose to think of Montague's syntactic categories intuitively, they definitely do not correspond to the eight or so traditional "parts of speech" but to much finer subcategories. If we wanted to define supercategories of Montague's categories that conform to these intuitions, we could do so; for example, we might want a supercategory VERB that encompasses B_{IV}, B_{TV}, $B_{IV//IV}$, $B_{IV/t}$, etc. But this would be hardly different from Chomsky's (1965) treatment of categories involving the devices of complex symbols and contextual features, since this too is a device for collapsing several distinct categories into one. And under this proposal the question of whether a lexical entry for a verb that has two mutually exclusive contextual features is really one lexical entry or two becomes almost purely a terminological one.

The second treatment (involving ambiguous adverbs) might be claimed to involve a certain artificiality in the treatment of **again**, etc. as verb phrase modifiers. For the meaning postulate in (99) affecting these adverbs makes clear that these "verb phrase modifiers" merely act as a signal that their sentence adverb counterparts are modifying a proposition that is semantically entailed but not syntactically expressed in the sentence. (I have no idea at present whether to regard this criticism as a serious one or not.)

The third treatment avoids this last criticism, since the adverb is a sentence modifier in both cases. And the new verbs postulated (members of $B_{TV/(t/t)}$) do not seem open to a parallel objection, since they have translations exactly like their counterparts in B_{TV} except that a "hole" has been left in their translations that the adverb will slip into.

The third treatment, on the other hand, has a serious defect not shared by the second. Lauri Karttunen has pointed out to me that there are sentences with two adverbials, such as (103), that allow for BOTH adverbials to have internal readings; i.e., (103) has a reading that does not entail that John has hidden the money before, nor that his act or acts of hiding the money lasted for a two-week period:

(103)   **John hid the money again for two weeks.**

The third treatment makes no provision for a second internal adverb; to treat (103) in parallel fashion, we would have to make a maneuver such as adding yet a third verb **hide**, of category $B_{(TV/((t/t)/(t/t)))}$, and at this point the plausibility of the third treatment diminishes rapidly. The second treatment, however, classifies the internal adverb as an "ad-phrase"; hence, it predicts the possibility of iterated internal modification. (In Bloomfieldian terms the second treatment describes the internally modified verb phrase as an EN-DOCENTRIC CONSTRUCTION, the third treatment as an EXOCENTRIC CON-STRUCTION.) And in fact the second treatment can assign exactly the right interpretation to sentences such as (103) (though this is complicated and may require the revised version of (99) found in footnote 14).

On the whole, the second treatment encounters much less serious difficulties than either the first or the third. If it were adopted into a grammar in order to handle internally modified lexical causatives, then it would also automatically produce internal readings for factitive phrases, such as **hammer the metal flat**, regardless of how these composite phrases were derived. In other words, there would be no reason why we should not then take the step of simplifying Rules S30–S32 drastically by omitting the intermediate stage in which a sentence is produced. That is, **hammer** could be combined directly with **flat** to produce the transitive verb **hammer flat**, and the prepositions **into**, **onto**, **to**, etc. could be entered as basic expressions in the categories $B_{(TV/TV)/T}$ and $B_{(IV/IV)/T}$.[15] (Trying to eliminate the first treatment in favor of the third would, on the other hand, require the "factitive" rule to be dupli-

---

[15] The simplified rules will now read as follows:

S30 (REVISED): If $\alpha \in P_{TV}$ and $\beta \in B_{t///e}$, then $F_6(\alpha, \beta) \in P_{TV}$, where $F_6(\alpha, \beta) = \alpha\beta$.

T30 (REVISED): If α translates into α' and β translates into β', then $F_6(\alpha, \beta)$ translates into

$$\lambda\mathscr{P}\lambda x\mathscr{P}\{\hat{y}[\alpha'(x, \hat{P}[P\{y\}]) \text{ CAUSE [BECOME } [\beta'(y)]]]\}$$

S31 (REVISED): If $\alpha \in P_{IV}$ and $\beta \in B_{t///e}$, then $F_6(\alpha, \beta) \in P_{TV}$.

T31 (REVISED): If α translates into α' and β translates into β', then $F_6(\alpha, \beta)$ translates into

$$\lambda\mathscr{P}\lambda x\mathscr{P}\{\hat{y}[\alpha'(x) \text{ CAUSE [BECOME } [\beta'(y)]]]\}$$

S32 (REVISED): If $\alpha \in P_{IV}$ and $\beta \in B_{t///e}$, then $F_6(\alpha, \beta) \in P_{IV}$.

T32 (REVISED): If α translates into α' and β translates into β', then $F_6(\alpha, \beta)$ translates into $\hat{x}[\alpha'(x)\text{CAUSE[BECOME}[\beta'(x)]]]$.

We could have retained a more complex syntactic function like F_{30} in Rules S30–S32, making the rules produce **hammer into the floor** from **hammer** plus **in the floor**, etc. as well as **hammer flat** from **hammer** plus **flat**. However, it is just as simple to enter **into**, **onto**, **to**, etc. as basic expressions rather than deriving them from **in**, **on**, **at**, etc. by the preceding rules. (To exclude prepositional phrases from S30–S32, I have mentioned $B_{t///e}$ rather than $P_{t///e}$.) A sample translation rule for such a basic item **into** (actually a pair of them) is given in (i) and (ii), where the translation of **into** still involves the translation of **in**: Here $\mathscr{R}$ is of type $\langle s, f(TV)\rangle$ and both $\mathscr{P}$ and $\mathscr{Q}$ are of type $\langle s, f(T)\rangle$:

(i)   **into** (member of $B_{(TV/TV)/T}$) translates into

$$\lambda\mathscr{P}\lambda\mathscr{R}\lambda\mathscr{Q}\lambda x\mathscr{Q}\{\hat{y}[\,{}^{\vee}\mathscr{R}(x, \hat{P}[P\{y\}) \text{ CAUSE [BECOME } [\text{in}'(\mathscr{P})(y)]]]\}.$$

(ii)   **into** (member of $B_{(IV/IV)/T}$) translates into

$$\lambda\mathscr{P}\lambda P\lambda x[P\{x\}\text{CAUSE[BECOME[in}'(\mathscr{P})(x)]]].$$

However, in other languages such as Finnish the corresponding stative locative expressions and change-of-location expressions are syntactically realized by particular case endings rather than prepositions. For Finnish it would be necessary to retain a complicated syntactic function for S30–S32, namely, one changing the inessive, adessive, or essive case ending on β to the illative, allative, or translative, respectively (as well as other case changes). Otherwise the syntactic rule and translation would be the same as for English.

cated so as to produce derived phrases in the category $P_{TV/(t/t)}$ as well as in P_{TV}.)

It should be clear already that I find none of the three analyses overwhelmingly convincing as they stand. But rather than attempting to argue for any particular solution to the problem of internal readings, I have attempted to show only that (a) there are syntactic analyses of internal readings available within the PTQ theory that avoid the generative semanticists' conclusion from the adverb argument, and (b) determining which of these (or other) alternatives is most satisfactory appears to be a complicated task to which this work will serve only as a preliminary exploration.

7. SYNTACTIC RULES OR RULES OF DERIVATIONAL MORPHOLOGY?

It is still somewhat controversial in present linguistic theory whether or not operators such as CAUSE and BECOME are really necessary in analyzing the meaning of basic lexical causatives, but I think it cannot be denied that such operators (or semantically equivalent theoretical constructs) have a place in a language-universal theory of DERIVATIONAL MORPHOLOGY. One natural language after another exhibits morphological processes for producing new causative and inchoative verbs out of adjectives, nouns, and noncausative and noninchoative verbs. English has not only such obvious causative suffixes as -ize and -ify for making causative verbs from adjectives but also less obvious processes such as a rule for making locative causatives from nouns denoting containers or locations, a process that does not add any affix at all. By this process we have verbs such as **box**, **crate**, **bag**, **sack**, **bottle**, **file**, **package**, etc., meaning "cause to be in a NOUN."

It is for this reason that I find the factitive construction particularly intriguing. If such derived transitive verbs as **hammer flat**, **wipe clean**, etc. are formed by a syntactic rule, then this is the only case I know of where operators such as CAUSE and BECOME must be invoked in the interpretation of a syntactic (rather than morphological) formation rule of English. This must be the case because the causative semantic relation between activity verb (e.g., **hammer**) and result adjective (e.g., **flat**) cannot be attributed to the meaning of either of these constituents as they appear in isolation but must be introduced by the translation of the syntactic rule itself.

On the other hand, we noted that certain combinations following this pattern sound odd (e.g., ?**hammer tubular**, ?**wipe damp**) for no apparent reason. Should we not conclude from this that the verb-plus-adjective combinations should be regarded as unitary (though polymorphemic) basic expressions, just as verb-plus-particle combinations are? If so, then these combinations must have their origin in rules of derivational morphology of some sort, and we can retain the generalization that CAUSE and BECOME belong to the domain of derivational morphology alone, and not to syntax as well.

There are (at least) two criteria one might wish to use to separate rules of syntax from rules of derivational morphology:

1. The ways that the elements are concatenated must be different in the two processes in order to distinguish word boundaries from morpheme boundaries. The difference can be observed from phonological as well as syntactic phenomena. (There must be certain exceptions to this if we want to maintain that, say, verb-plus-particle combinations are products of derivational morphology.)

2. Whereas speakers of the language freely apply syntactic rules within the limits of the grammar to form ever-novel phrases and sentences, rules of derivational morphology are employed only sporadically and cautiously unless the speaker is aware that the combination has already been used by others and is "a part of the language." (I am unsure to what degree this caution is language universal and to what degree it is due, in our present speech community, to the tyranny of the dictionary and the influence of prescriptive grammar.)

Nevertheless I would argue not only that knowledge of rules of derivational morphology and the semantic correlates of these rules plays an important role in the child's acquisition of his vocabulary but also that it is a part of any speaker's knowledge of his language that potential, if not yet "legitimate," forms exist and that he can therefore understand the approximate meanings of unfamiliar or newly coined words as long as they conform to familiar morphological patterns.

That children actually make use of such rules in some form or other is easy to demonstrate from language acquisition studies of young children who go through periods in which they produce a large number of derived words that do not exist in the adult language but conform semantically and phonologically to the pattern set by marginally productive processes in the adult language. For example, Bowerman (1974) discusses a child who adopted such rules between the ages of two and four. Presumably on the basis of sentences such as **The stick broke**, **John broke the stick** and **The door opened, John opened the door** in adult speech, the child postulated a rule deriving causative transitives from noncausative intransitives[16] and proceeded to produce utterances such as **Daddy go me around** (in a situation where it was clear that she meant "Daddy, make me go around"), **I come it closer so it won't fall**

---

[16] This theoretical description of Bowerman's data is my own, of course, and not necessarily one that Bowerman would agree with. (I feel that the conclusions Bowerman draws do not conflict with the kind of treatment I am proposing, however.)

("make it come closer"), **I gonna just fall this on her** ("make this fall on her, drop this on her"), etc., as well as rules deriving causative transitive verbs from adjectives (**Unstuck it**, "make it not stuck"), particles (**Down your little knee**, "make your little knee go down"), and transitive verbs (cf. the discussion of Comrie's work in Section 7.1).

I think one can view the rather heated controversy that took place in the late 1960s between the lexicalists and the generativists (and centered to a great degree on derivational morphology) in retrospect and see that both sides had good reasons for holding the positions that they did. The lexicalists, Chomsky in particular, pointed out that it was not really desirable to lump morphological processes together with the syntactic rules because of the situation pointed out earlier—the sharp difference in productivity between the two processes. The generativists, I believe, felt that the semantic relationships involved in morphological processes were an interesting and important part of linguistic description, and were unhappy about relegating such matters to semantic interpretation, given the vague and undeveloped notion of "semantic interpretation rule" that was current in linguistic theory at the time. Moreover, they could present arguments that the very same kind of "deep grammatical relations" were involved within morphological formations as those the lexicalists cited in arguing for transformations at the macro-syntactic level. In order to describe such phenomena, then, they invoked the only theoretical device that was well developed in the linguistic theory of the time, the syntactic transformation.

What I would like to suggest is that Montague's theory may provide a way of satisfying both types of concerns by making it possible to have a major formal and functional distinction between syntactic and morphological rules, yet using the same semantic apparatus for both types of rules.

Under this tentative proposal for a theory of derivational morphology,[17] the first formal distinction between syntactic and morphological rules would be in the type of expression they each produce. Whereas syntactic rules combine or transform PHRASES (members of the sets P_A for $A \in Cat$) to produce other phrases, rules of derivational morphology would combine or transform BASIC EXPRESSIONS (members of the sets B_A for $A \in Cat$) into other basic expressions. For example, a hypothetical morphological rule for forming causative transitive verbs out of stative intransitive verbs would be (104):

(104)   If $\alpha \in B_{IV}$, then $F_m(\alpha) \in B_{TV}$, where $F_m(\alpha) = \alpha + $ Affix.
         Translation: If α translates into α', then $F_m(\alpha)$ translates into
         $\lambda \mathscr{P} \lambda x \mathscr{P} \{ \hat{y} [\vee M [M \{ ^\vee x \} CAUSE[BECOME[\alpha'(y)]]]] \}$.

AFFIX here stands for the phonological spelling out of the causative affix

---

[17] All discussion of morphology in this study applies only to derivational affixes; inflexional morphology (e.g., case endings, gender agreement on pronouns, person and number agreement on verbs, etc.) is presumably handled entirely by syntactic rules.

(prefix, suffix, or null morpheme): + is the morpheme boundary. Note that this affix would not appear separately as a basic expression and would consequently represent a BOUND MORPHEME. For the morphological rule (if it is that) producing **hammer flat**, some distinctive means of affixation must be assumed so that subsequent syntactic rules will treat it as two words, whereas compounds like **blackboard** are treated as one.

In the second place, such a morphological rule need not be treated as a part of the (synchronic) grammar of a language proper but could, rather, be thought of as a means for modifying the grammar by enlarging its lexicon.[18]

Note that I do not suggest that the adoption of such "extragrammatical" rules of word formation would make it unnecessary to include morphologically complex words (together with their translations) as basic expressions. (Hence, this would be a LEXICALIST theory of derivational morphology.) There would of course be a certain amount of redundancy in such a treatment, since the phonological forms and translations of certain words would be listed "in the lexicon" as well as predicted independently by morphological rule. Some linguists may object to this idea in principle, but I believe it would be desirable for two reasons: It could account for an English speaker's judgment that, for example, *beautify* is an actual English word meaning "make beautiful," whereas *uglify* is not a word of English, though it is clearly a possible word and would obviously mean "make ugly" if it were a word. An even more compelling reason for separate lexical entries is that as soon as a new morphological formation is established it may acquire a specialized or new meaning not predictable from the translations of its subparts and the morphological translation rule. In such cases the morphological translation rule would supply the speaker of the language with only a rough approximation of the correct meaning of the complex word, the "real" interpretation being obtainable only from independent definition or contextual information. In extreme cases the rule might serve the speaker of English as little more than a mnemonic aid for remembering the meaning of a new word.

Because a natural language speech community is made up of similar but not quite identical idiolects and because the lexicon at any given historical stage of a language bears traces of various word formation processes from its past in varying degrees, it is not implausible that one speaker may learn a certain series of words via a rule of word formation while the next speaker learns them individually without ever noticing such a rule. If such structural inconsistency actually exists among speakers of the "same" language, then it seems pointless to insist on a theory of grammar that requires us to pick a unique "correct" grammatical description with respect to such details.

---

[18] This view of the extragrammatical status of rules of word formation seems to be similar to that expressed in Halle (1973), where it is motivated largely by phonological considerations. However, Halle's theoretical proposals are not necessarily compatible with mine.

I suggest this extragrammatical treatment of derivational morphology for derivational processes that are only partially or sporadically productive; at present I can see no reason why fully productive morphological processes that are also perfectly regular semantically should not be identified with syntactic rules, except possibly for the manner of concatenation. Once again, I think we probably should not expect to be able to distinguish a partially or almost fully productive morphological process from a syntactic process in every case. For this reason I do not feel obliged to lose a lot of sleep worrying whether the factitive rule is really a syntactic rule or a morphological rule; the semantics of such phrases could be described in essentially the same way under either analysis. However, the question of whether the operators CAUSE and BECOME are ever justified outside of the semantics of word formation makes the status of the factitive rule have some theoretical interest, and I think that the factitive construction, the productive verb-plus-particle constructions, and related constructions in languages other than English deserve much closer study. (A more explicit formalization of a word formation theory for Montague grammar is given in Dowty, 1975.)

7.1. Derived Causative Rules for
   Comrie's "Paradigm Case"

As a final and somewhat hypothetical illustration of the possibility of writing rules for derived morphological (and/or syntactic) causative verbs in the PTQ framework, I will propose rules for Comrie's PARADIGM CASE of causative constructions (Comrie, 1976).

In his interesting and valuable cross-linguistic study of causative constructions in a large number of natural languages, Comrie is concerned with the syntax of causative sentences derived from noncausative intransitive, transitive, and three-place verbs. Comrie conceives of the problem in transformational terms; that is, he assumes that the underlying structure of all such derived causatives consists of a sentence with a noncausative verb embedded in a higher sentence with a (possibly abstract) verb CAUSE and a subject denoting the "agent" or instigator of the causation. In the surface structure the causative element and embedded verb are fused into a single verb, there is no longer an embedded sentence, and the subject of CAUSE in underlying structure becomes the surface structure subject. The problem, then, is what to do with the embedded subject noun phrase that is necessarily "displaced" by this operation. As a background against which to discuss the way various languages solve this problem for the various types of embedded verbs, Comrie sets up what he calls the PARADIGM CASE (to which few languages correspond exactly but from which all languages differ minimally); this is described as follows:

1. If the embedded verb is intransitive, then the embedded subject becomes a direct object in surface structure (cf. the way the embedded subject in **John brought it about that the window broke** corresponds to the direct object in **John broke the window**).
2. If the embedded verb is transitive, the embedded subject becomes an indirect object.
3. If the embedded verb is a three-place verb—i.e., already possesses a subject, object, and indirect object—then the embedded subject assumes another oblique case or becomes the object of a preposition. Put in a more general form, the paradigm case requires that the embedded subject move down the accessibility hierarchy (i.e., the hierarchy *subject–direct object indirect object–oblique case*) to the first "vacant" position. (Comrie devotes the bulk of his work to discussing the various exceptions to the paradigm case, the most common of these being that the embedded subject is simply deleted in surface structure or else "doubles" some case already represented; I have nothing to offer concerning these doublings.)

In order to treat these processes as an extension of PTQ, I will have to have some theory of case, but I will offer only a rudimentary version of such a theory at present. PTQ already provides a definition of SUBJECT (any P_T that is combined with a P_{IV} to make a P_t) and DIRECT OBJECT (any P_T that is combined with a P_{TV} to make a P_{IV}). It has already been suggested that verbs that take indirect objects be entered in the category $B_{TV/T}$ (giving a definition of INDIRECT OBJECT as any P_T that is combined with a $P_{TV/T}$ to make a P_{TV}). For the four-place verbs I will simply extend the pattern that has already been set up and enter these as $B_{(TV/T)/T}$, giving a definition of the "oblique case" (i.e., whatever case is in fourth position on the accessibility hierarchy) as any P_T that is combined with a $P_{(TV/T)/T}$ to make a $P_{TV/T}$. Case endings on the term phrases would then be introduced by the syntactic functions of the corresponding rules of functional application—e.g., the function for combining a P_{TV} with a P_T would introduce the accusative case marking, the function for combining a $P_{TV/T}$ with a P_T would introduce the dative case, etc.—or these functions might sometimes introduce prepositions rather than case endings. Note that the accessibility hierarchy is now simply defined by the ORDER in which the various term phrases combine with a multiplace verb. Of course a great deal of work would be needed to turn this into a viable case theory for any language (we might wonder, for example, what to do with a verb that obligatorily takes a dative but no accusative, such as German *folgen*), but it will do for my purposes here.

It is now quite simple to state rules for Comrie's paradigm case as operations (whether morphological or syntactic) on verbs rather than on sentences. In (105)–(107), F_c is CAUSATIVE VERB FORMATION and will of course differ from language to language: For some languages (e.g., French) it will involve concatenating a verb that normally means "cause," but for other languages (e.g., Turkish) it involves attaching a causative suffix. In the translations of (105)–(107), $\mathscr{P}$, $\mathscr{Q}$, and $\mathscr{S}$ are all variables of type $\langle s, f(T) \rangle$, and to aid in the decipherment of these translations I have adopted the impromptu and nonessential notational convention that $\mathscr{P}$ represents the position of the direct object, $\mathscr{Q}$ the position of the indirect object, and $\mathscr{S}$ the position of the oblique case term phrase:

(105)   Producing transitive causative verbs from intransitives: If $\alpha \in B_{IV}$, then $F_c(\alpha) \in B_{TV}$.
Translation: If α translates into α', then $F_c(\alpha)$ translates into
$\lambda \mathscr{P} \lambda x \mathscr{P} \{ \hat{y} [\vee M[M\{^\vee x\} CAUSE[\alpha'(y)]]]\}$

(106)   Producing three-place causative verbs from transitives: If $\alpha \in B_{TV}$, then $F_c(\alpha) \in B_{TV/T}$.
Translation: If α translates into α', then $F_c(\alpha)$ translates into
$\lambda \mathscr{Q} \lambda \mathscr{P} \lambda x \mathscr{Q} \{ \hat{y} [\vee M[M\{^\vee x\} CAUSE[\alpha'(\mathscr{P})(y)]]]\}$

(107)   Producing causative four-place verbs from three-place verbs: If $\alpha \in B_{TV/T}$, then $F_c(\alpha) \in B_{(TV/T)/T}$.
Translation: If α translates into α', then $F_c(\alpha)$ translates into
$\lambda \mathscr{S} \lambda \mathscr{Q} \lambda \mathscr{P} \lambda x \mathscr{S} \{ \hat{y} [\vee M[M\{^\vee x\} CAUSE[\alpha'(\mathscr{Q})(\mathscr{P})(y)]]]\}$

Languages discussed by Comrie that have (105) as a productive rule are Sanskrit, Italian, Ewenki, Hungarian, Tagalog, French, Hindi, Punjabi, Persian, German, Dutch, Turkish, Mongolian, Finnish, Georgian, Songhai, and Swahili; cf. Comrie (1975). Languages that have (106) are Hindi, Persian, French, Dutch (in restricted form), Turkish, Georgian, Songhai, Tagalog, Punjabi, Italian, and Mongolian. Languages with (107) include Hindi, Italian, Turkish, Punjabi, French, German, Dutch, Japanese, Finnish, and Hungarian. Many of these languages have other syntactic realizations of these causatives as well as the versions produced by these rules, e.g., ones in which some case is "doubled."

One of the most common deviations from the paradigm case, according to Comrie, is that in which one of the term phrases of the embedded sentence is simply deleted in the causative sentence, the embedded subject almost always being the one deleted. This can be handled easily enough by a derived causative verb rule similar to those given earlier except that an existentially quantified variable is introduced in the translation rule. For example, Finnish would have a rule like (108) for producing causative transitive verbs:

(108) If $\alpha \in B_{TV}$, then $F_c(\alpha) \in B_{TV}$

Translation: If α translates into α', then $F_c(\alpha)$ translates into
$\lambda \mathscr{P} \lambda x \vee y \vee M[M\{^\vee x\}\text{CAUSE}[\alpha'(\mathscr{P})(y)]]$.

Note that in such a rule the derived causative verb is of the same syntactic category as the original verb. This suggests at least the possibility that this kind of rule (unlike the earlier ones) could be iterated, and in fact such iteration (meaning "cause somebody to cause somebody to . . . do VERB") is possible in Finnish and Turkish at least.

I must stress the hypothetical nature of these rules, since many more details would have to be supplied before any of them could be incorporated into even a small fragment of a grammar for any of the languages Comrie discusses. For example, I have not mentioned the problems of word order. What I have intended to show is that we do not have to resort to a transformation operating on complex sentences to account for the complex syntactic and semantic relationship between causative and noncausative sentences that Comrie describes, but that these relationships can be "encoded" into the translation of the causative verb itself, and this translation is, in turn, statable in terms of the translation of the noncausative verb.

This possibility of treating causativization as an operation (whether considered morphological or syntactic) on verbs rather than sentences is of particular interest in the light of recent research by Aissen (1974) and Newmeyer (1974). On the basis of her study of causatives in Turkish, French, and a few other languages, Aissen reached the startling conclusion that if there is a transformation fusing a noncausative verb with a verb CAUSE in a higher sentence (a transformation she calls VERB RAISING), then this transformation must be precyclic, since cyclic transformations must be prohibited from applying in any embedded sentence where Verb Raising later applies in the matrix sentence. Newmeyer, on the basis of parallel but largely different arguments, claimed that McCawley's prelexical transformation, Predicate Raising, must likewise be precyclic. However, the existence of precyclic transformations has not previously been accepted by most transformational grammarians, so Aissen's and Newmeyer's results appear to require a major complication in the theory of transformational grammar.

If causativization is an operation on verbs rather than sentences, however, then the possibility of a syntactic rule applying on the embedded sentence does not arise, since there is in fact no such sentence in the syntactic derivation of the causative structures; hence, there is no need to postulate precyclic transformations for this case. The decomposition of lexical causatives via the translation relation likewise solves the cyclicity problem for Newmeyer's cases.

Though Comrie does not appear to claim any language-universal (or psychologically innate) status for his paradigm case, close comparison of his paradigm with Bowerman (1974) tempts one to speculate about it. Though English offers a child pairs like intr. **break**/tr. **break** and **warm** (adj.)/**warm** (v.) as a possible basis for postulating rules making transitive causative verbs from intransitive verbs and adjectives, I am not aware of any such pairs of transitive verb/causative three-place verb that would offer a child the basis for postulating a rule like (106). (Though pairs like **give**/**have** and **feed**/**eat** exist that may have this semantic relationship, I have noticed no such pairs where the two are morphologically related as well). Nevertheless Bowerman's subject produced the sentences **You turn me a somersault** ("You make me turn a somersault") and **I'm gonna guess it to him** ("I'm gonna make him guess it"), which look suspiciously as if they were produced by Comrie's rule for derived three-place causatives (the "embedded subject" appearing as indirect object, in both English syntactic realizations of indirect object) with the same morphological function that the child is using at this stage for all other causatives (i.e., the identity mapping). If these sentences do not derive from syntactic patterns exemplified in adult speech, then where do they come from?

8. CONCLUSION

In this study I have outlined syntactic and semantic treatments of three different forms of causative expressions in natural languages: lexical causatives, syntactically derived causatives, and morphologically derived causatives. Though produced syntactically in completely different ways, these three kinds of causatives are given quite similar translations into intensional logic and, hence, similar interpretations induced by these translations. It can be argued that this treatment satisfies any generalization about semantic properties these constructions have in common and is, therefore, sufficient to counter any arguments based on selectional restrictions, synonymy or entailment relations, or intuitively perceived "deep grammatical relations" to the effect that these constructions must come from similar deep structures.

As the adverb argument appears to be the strongest independent motivation for syntactic lexical decomposition, I have attempted to show that there are alternative treatments of this phenomenon available within the PTQ theory that are, if not completely satisfactory, no more problematic than the generative semantics account of the ambiguity. Moreover, the treatment of lexical decomposition in the translation procedure seems to have certain advantages over a transformational treatment, such as greater syntactic and semantic explicitness, the possibility of handling one-way entailments as well as mutual entailments between sentences and their decomposed paraphrases, and the avoidance of precyclic transformations.

A broader purpose of this work is to illustrate a general procedure for formalizing and testing the insights of generative semantics analyses by converting them into extensions of PTQ. I hope that this demonstration will stimulate interest in applying this procedure to other topics. Though I have used only causatives and inchoatives as examples in this study, it should take only a little imagination to see how this treatment could be extended to other decomposition analyses, such as Psych Movement verbs, the various types of nominalizations, and various nominal compounds.

Finally, I hope this study has helped point up a number of methodological questions that research in Montague grammar will have to confront sooner or later. For example, how many of the infinitely many potential syntactic categories should we allow ourselves to use, and what should be the criteria for introducing a new one? Is a "weird" category like $B_{TV/(t/t)}$ to be regarded as undesirable in a PTQ extension, and if so, precisely what is the criterion for weirdness? To what degree should homophonous lexical items in different syntactic categories be tolerated? What counts as a "legitimate" meaning postulate, and what counts as ad hoc? Given the power and flexibility of the semantic theory, how does one decide in general between a syntactic and a semantic analysis of a particular problem when both are feasible? If a mechanism for enlarging the lexicon is to be postulated, then what criteria can be used to distinguish a morphological from a syntactic process?

Ohio State University and The Institute for Advanced Study

ACKNOWLEDGMENTS

The ideas for this work were developed during the 1973 MSSB Advanced Research Workshop on Formal Pragmatics of Natural Language and during the 1974 MSSB Advanced Research Workshop on the Syntax and Semantics of Non-Extensional Constructions. Work on this study has also been supported in part by fellowships from the American Council of Learned Societies and the Institute for Advanced Study. I would like to thank the participants of both workshops for their many comments and suggestions, which played a large part in shaping my ideas, and I would like to thank Stanley Peters especially for a number of technical as well as conceptual suggestions. Needless to say, none of these people will agree entirely with my proposals, and I am responsible for remaining errors.

REFERENCES

Abbott, B. Some problems in giving an adequate model theoretic account of CAUSE In Fillmore *et al.* (Eds.), *Berkeley Studies in Syntax and Semantics*. Berkeley: Univ of California, Berkeley, 1974.

Aissen, J. Verb raising. *Linguistic Inquiry*, 1974, **V**, 325–366.

Bowerman, M. Learning the structure of causative verbs: A study in the relationship of cognitive, semantic and syntactic development. *Papers and Reports on Child Language Development* No. 8, Stanford University, 1974. Pp. 142–178.

Comrie, B. The syntax of causative constructions: Cross-language similarities and divergences. Paper presented at The University of Southern California Causative Festival, Los Angeles, California, May 2–3, 1974. [To appear in M. Shibatani (Ed.), Syntax and Semantics VI: The Grammar of Causative Constructions. New York: Academic Press, 1976.]

Cresswell, M. J. *Logics and languages*. London: Methuen, 1973.

Delacruz, E. Factives and proposition level constructions in a Montague grammar. In R. Rodman (Ed.), *Papers in Montague Grammar*. Los Angeles: Univ. of California Press, 1972. [Reprinted as pages 177–200 of this volume.]

Dowty, D. R. Studies in the logic of verb aspect and time reference in English. (*Studies in Linguistics, No. 1*) Austin, Texas: University of Texas, Department of Linguistics, 1972.

Dowty, D. R. Toward a semantic Theory of word-formation in Montague Grammar. In S. Schmerling (Ed.), *Texas Linguistic Forum*. Austin, Texas: Univ. of Texas Department of Linguistics, 1975.

Dowty, D. R. Two Theories of Semantic Description: Word Meaning and Syntax in Generative Semantics and in Montague Grammar. In preparation.

Fillmore, C. Some problems for case grammar. In Report on the 22nd Annual Round Table Meeting on Linguistics and Language Studies. Washington, D. C.: Georgetown Univ. Press, 1971.

Fillmore, C. Golden Anniversary Lecture to the Linguistic Society of America, July 25, 1974.

Geis, J. E. Subject complementation with causative verbs, In B. B. Kachru *et al.* (Eds.), *Issues in Linguistics: Papers in Honor of Henry Renee and Kahane*. Urbana, Illinois: Univ. of Illinois Press.

Goodman, F. *A PTQ Generative Grammar*. In preparation.

Green, G. M. How abstract is surface structure? In Campbell *et al.* (Eds.), *Papers from the Sixth Regional Meeting of the Chicago Linguistic Society*. Chicago: Univ. of Chicago Press, 1970.

Green, G. M. Some observations on the syntax and semantics of instrumental verbs. In Peranteau *et al.* (Eds.), Papers from the Eighth Regional Meetings of the Chicago Linguistic Society. Chicago: Univ. of Chicago Press, 1972.

Gruber, J. *Functions of the Lexicon in Formal Descriptive Grammars*. Bloomington: The Indiana University Linguistics Club, 1967.

Halle, M. Prolegomena to a theory of word formation. *Linguistic Inquiry*, 1973, **IV**, 3–16.

Jespersen, O. *The Philosophy of Grammar*. Originally published in 1924; republished New York: Norton, 1965.

Keenan, E. L. On semantically based grammar. *Linguistic Inquiry*, 1972, III, 413–462.

Lakoff, G. *On the Nature of Syntactic Irregularity*. New York: Holt, 1967. [Written in 1965.]

Lakoff, G. On generative semantics. In D. Steinberg and L. Jakobvits (Eds.), *Semantics: An Interdisciplinary Reader in Philosophy, Linguistics, and Psychology*. Cambridge: Cambridge Univ. Press, 1971.

Lewis, D, *Counterfactuals*. Cambridge, Massachusetts: Harvard Univ. Press, 1973. (a)

Lewis, D. Causation. *The Journal of Philosophy*, 1973, **70**, 556–567.

McCawley, J. Lexical insertion in a transformational grammar without deep structure. In Darden et al. (Eds.), *Papers from the Fourth Regional Meetings of the Chicago Linguistics Society*. Chicago: Univ. of Chicago Press, 1968.

McCawley, J. Pre-lexical syntax. In O'Brien, (Ed.), *Report of the Twenty-Second Annual Round Table Meeting on Linguistics and Language Studies*. Washington, D.C.: Georgetown Univ. Press, 1971

McCawley, J. Remarks on what can cause what. Paper presented at the University of Southern California Causative Festival, Los Angeles, California, May 2–3, 1974. [To appear in M. Shibatani (Ed.), *Syntax and Semantics VI: The Grammar of Causative Constructions*. New York: Academic Press, 1976.]

Montague, R. English as a formal language. In B. Visenti *et al.*, *Linguaggi nella Societa e nella Tecnica*. Milan: Edizioni di Communità, 1970. (a) [Reprinted in R. Thomason (Ed.), *Formal Philosophy: Selected Papers of Richard Montague*. New Haven: Yale Univ. Press, 1974.]

Montague, R. Universal grammar. *Theoria*, 1970, **36**, 373–398. (b) [Reprinted in R. Thomason (Ed.), *Formal Philosophy: Selected Papers of Richard Montague*. New Haven: Yale Univ. Press, 1974. Pp. 189–224.]

Montague, R. The proper treatment of quantification in ordinary English. In J. Hintikka, J. Moravcsik, and P. Suppes (Eds.), *Approaches to Natural Language: Proceedings of the 1970 Stanford Workshop on Grammar and Semantics*. Dordrecht: Riedel, 1973. Pp. 221–242. [Reprinted in R. Thomason (Ed.), *Formal Philosophy: Selected Papers of Richard Montague*. New Haven: Yale Univ. Press, 1974. Pp. 247–270.]

Morgan, J. On arguing about semantics. *Papers in Linguistics*, 1969, **1**, 49–70.

Newmeyer, F. J. The precycling nature of Predicate Raising. Paper presented at the University of Southern California Causative Festival, Los Angeles, California, May 2–3, 1974. [To appear in M. Shibatani (Ed.), *Syntax and Semantics VI: The Grammar of Causative Constructions*. New York: Academic Press, 1976.]

Partee, B. H. Some transformational extensions of Montague grammar. *Journal of Philosophical Logic*, 1973, **2**, 509–534. [Reprinted in this volume, pp. 51–76.]

Postal., P. *On Raising*. Cambridge, Massachusetts: M. I. T. Press, 1973.

Rogers, A. A trans-derivational constraint on *Richard*. In La Galy *et al.* (Eds.), *Papers from the Tenth Regional Meeting of the Chicago Linguistic Society*. Chicago: Univ. of Chicago Press, 1974.

Stalnaker, R. A theory of conditionals. In Rescher (Ed.), *Studies in Logical Theory*. London: Blackwell, 1968.

Stalnaker, R., and Thomason, R. A semantic analysis of conditional logic. *Theoria*, 1970, **36**, 32–42.

Stalnaker, R., and Thomason, R. A semantic theory of adverbs. *Linguistic Inquiry*, 1973, **IV**, 195–220.

Thomason, R. Introduction. In R. Thomason (Ed.), *Formal Philosophy: Selected Papers of Richard Montague*. New Haven: Yale Univ. Press, 1974. (a)

Thomason, R. Some complement constructions in Montague grammar. In La Galy (Ed.), *Papers from The Tenth Regional Meetings of the Chicago Linguistic Society*. Chicago: Univ. of Chicago Press, 1974. (b)

Vendler, Z. *Linguistics in Philosophy*. Ithaca, New York: Cornell Univ. Press, 1967.

C. L. HAMBLIN

QUESTIONS IN MONTAGUE ENGLISH

In a paper [8] that must surely be regarded as a milestone in formal linguistics[1], Richard Montague constructed a complete syntactic and semantic theory of a formal language that "may reasonably be regarded as a fragment of ordinary English." Taking as building bricks basic linguistic items of the categories *proper name* (prn), *formula* (fml), *one-place verb* (1vb), *two-place verb* (2vb), *common noun* (cmn), *adformula* (adf), *adverb* (adv) and *adjective* (adj)[2], he gives rules for concatenation of these into non-basic items of the same categories and, in parallel, the recursive definition of *denotations* of non-basic items in terms of those of the basic ones. Let '$D_{prn}(a)$' mean 'the denotation of a, taken as a proper name', and similarly '$D_{fml}(a)$', '$D_{1vb}(a)$' and so on. (This multiplicity of denotation-functions is necessary because a word may be meaningful in more than one category; for example 'orange' may be either a colour-adjective or a common noun denoting a fruit.) The denotation $D_{prn}(a)$ of a proper name a is an individual; and the denotation $D_{fml}(a)$ of a formula a is a proposition, in turn identified (as commonly in logic) with a set of possible universes. The denotations of items of other categories are *functions*; thus:

> the denotation $D_{1vb}(a)$ of a one-place verb a is a function that maps individuals on to propositions. (The idea is that the denotation of the one-place verb 'walks' is the function that maps the individual Mary on to the proposition that Mary walks, the individual Rover on to the proposition that Rover walks, and so on.)

> the denotation $D_{2vb}(a)$ of a two-place (that is, transitive) verb a is a function that maps pairs of individuals on to propositions. (The two-place verb 'walks' maps the pair consisting of Mary and Rover on to the proposition that Mary walks Rover.)

> the denotation $D_{cmn}(a)$ of a common noun a, like that of a one-place verb, is a function that maps individuals on to propositions.

---

[1] I have chosen to discuss [8] rather than his comprehensive paper [11] because it works out particular proposals in detail on the side of language, as distinct from logic. Some remarks on what is new in the later paper appear below.

Montague's disturbing death in 1971 was felt as a loss by all who knew his work and were following with interest the direction of his thought.

[2] The notation of this article is mine, not Montague's.

Foundations of Language **10** (1973) 41–53. *All rights reserved.*

(The denotation of 'man' maps John on to the proposition that John is a man.)

the denotation $D_{adf}(a)$ of an adformula a is a function that maps propositions on to propositions. (Adformulae are items such as 'not' and 'necessarily' that modify whole formulae.)

the denotation $D_{adv}(a)$ of an adverb a is a function that maps denotations of one- or two-place verbs on to denotations of one- or two-place verbs respectively.[3]

the denotation $D_{adj}(a)$ of an adjective a is a function that maps denotations of common nouns on to denotations of common nouns.

The rules of construction of the language, syntactic and semantic together, can now be stated as follows.[4] Concatenation is indicated by '⌢' and single quotes are equivalent to Quinean corners.

1. RULES CORRESPONDING TO FUNCTIONAL APPLICATION

(1)   If a is a proper name and b a one-place verb, $a⌢b$ is a formula and
$$D_{fml}(a⌢b) = D_{1vb}(b)[D_{prn}(a)]$$
Example: 'Mary walks'. The semantic rule says that the denotation of the whole is the result of operating on the denotation of a (of 'Mary') with that function that is the denotation of b (of 'walks').

(2)   If a and b are proper names and $c⌢d$ is a two-place verb, where c is a basic two-place verb and d is possibly null, $a⌢c⌢b⌢d$ is a formula and
$$D_{fml}(a⌢c⌢b⌢d) = D_{2vb}(c⌢d)[D_{prn}(a), D_{prn}(b)]$$
Examples: 'Mary walks Rover', 'Mary walks Rover rapidly'. In the latter case 'walks rapidly' is a non-basic two-place verb and the object is inserted after the basic part of it.

(3)   If a is an adformula and b a formula,
(i) if a is 'not' and b does not end with 'not', $b⌢a$ is a formula;
and if a is not 'not', $a⌢b$ is a formula;

---

[3] Montague distinguishes *ad-one-verbs* from *ad-two-verbs,* but remarks that the categories in practice coincide.
[4] In giving an exposition of Montague's formal language I have been guided partly by the fact that many readers would appreciate one that is as simple as possible. (Montague's symbolism is uncompromising.) So I have omitted some rules that can be taken for granted, and slightly fudged some issues such as the denotations of variables. The reader who objects must tackle Montague's paper for himself.

(ii) $D_{fml}(c) = D_{adf}(a)[D_{fml}(b)]$

where c is the formula specified in (i).

Examples: 'necessarily Mary walks Rover', 'Mary loves John not'. The archaic negation idiom is simpler than the modern one (though the latter could be specified if desired) and the avoidance of iteration of 'not' has a further rationale in avoiding some kinds of ambiguity in case of simultaneous negation in embedded clauses.

(4)   If a is an adverb and b a one-place verb, or a two-place verb other than 'is', $b{\frown}a$ is a one- or two-place verb respectively and

$$D_{1vb}(b{\frown}a) = D_{adv}(a)[D_{1vb}(b)]$$
$$D_{2vb}(b{\frown}a) = D_{adv}(a)[D_{2vb}(b)]$$

Examples: 'sleeps soundly', 'loves passionately'. Adverbial modification of 'is' apparently does not occur in English.

(5)   If a is an adjective and b a common noun,

(i)   if a is one word long $a{\frown}b$ is a common noun, and if a is more than one word long $b{\frown}a$ is a common noun;

(ii) $D_{cmn}(c) = D_{adj}(a)[D_{cmn}(b)]$

where c is the common noun specified in (i).

Examples: 'big dog', 'man in Havana', 'man over six feet tall'. The adjectives permitted in the language must be of a rather restricted kind, excluding "indexical" adjectives such as 'former' and "quantificational" ones such as 'three'; and others that would require different treatment.

2. Rules of quantification for formulae

As a structural expedient it is convenient to permit individual variables 'v_0', 'v_1',... to count as proper names; and there is further no reason why these variables should not occur as parts of items of other categories: Montague lists 'brother of v_0' as a basic common noun, 'v_0 believes that' as a basic ad-formula and 'in v_0' and 'with v_0' as basic adverbs and adjectives. It may be assumed that proper names are eventually substituted for variables. The denotation of any item containing variables is not a constant, but a function of an *allocation* of individuals as the denotations of the variables. In the case of the following rules for quantification we are required to consider the set of all possible such allocations.

Up to this point the syntactic parts of the rules have been consistent with formulation in a context-free grammar; but the rules that follow introduce an element of context-sensitivity.

(6)   Let $a⌢b⌢c$ be a common noun, where b is the first basic common noun that occurs in it, and a and c may be null. If d is a formula containing a variable v, and e is the result of replacing v at its first occurrence with 'every'$⌢a⌢b⌢c$ and at later occurrences if any with 'that'$⌢b$,

    (i) e is a formula;

    (ii) $D_{fml}(e)$ is the intersection of the sets of universes
$$- D_{cmn}(a⌢b⌢c)[D_{prn}(v)] \cup D_{fml}(d)$$
for all possible allocations to $D_{prn}(v)$.

Examples: from the common noun 'bird' and the formula 'v_0 flies' we can get 'every bird flies'; and from 'tall man in Amsterdam' and 'v_3 loves a woman such that that woman loves v_3' we can get 'every tall man in Amsterdam loves a woman such that that woman loves that man'. The semantic rule says that if we consider all possible allocations to the variable v, the denotation of the end-formula e is that proposition that is true if every such individual either does not yield a true proposition when taken as an argument of $D_{cmn}(a⌢b⌢c)$, or does satisfy the formula d.

(7)   As (6), with 'a' or 'an' in place of 'every' (depending on whether the following word begins with a consonant or a vowel), and with clause (ii) replaced by

    (ii) $D_{fml}(e)$ is the join of the sets of universes
$$D_{cmn}(a⌢b⌢c) [D_{prn}(v)] \cap D_{fml}(d)$$
for all possible allocations to $D_{prn}(v)$.

Examples: substitute 'a' for 'every' in examples in (6).

(8)   As (6), with 'the' in place of 'every', and with clause (ii) replaced by

    (ii) When the individual α is allocated to $D_{prn}(v)$ let σ_α be the set of universes $D_{cmn}(a⌢b⌢c)[\alpha]$ less any universes that would be members of the corresponding set on any other allocation than α. $D_{fml}(e)$ is the set of universes
$$\sigma_\alpha \cap D_{fml}(d)$$
for all possible such allocations α to $D_{prn}(v)$.

Examples: substitute 'the' for 'every' in examples in (6). This is Russellian definite description, but Montague seems to be the first to point out the parallel between 'the' and quantifiers in English.

3. RULES OF QUANTIFICATION FOR COMMON NOUNS

Montague gives separate rules, which we many omit in virtue of their close parallel with those just stated, for the case in which the scope of the quantification is a common noun rather than a formula. Example: from 'man such that that man loves v_4' we may get 'man such that that man loves every woman'.

4. RULE OF RELATIVE CLAUSES

(9)   Let $a\frown b\frown c$ be a common noun, where b is the first basic common noun occurring in it and a and c may be null. If d is a formula containing a variable v and e is the result of replacing v at all occurrences with 'that'$\frown b$,

(i) $a\frown b\frown c\frown$'such that'$\frown e$ is a common noun;

(ii) $D_{cmn}(f)$, where $f = a\frown b\frown c\frown$'such that'$\frown e$, is the function such that

$$D_{cmn}(f)[D_{prn}(v)] = D_{cmn}(a\frown b\frown c)[D_{prn}(v)] \cap D_{fml}(d)$$

for every possible allocation to $D_{prn}(v)$.

Example: from 'tall woman in Amsterdam' and 'v_0 loves v_1' get 'tall woman in Amsterdam such that that woman loves v_1'.

5. RULE OF PREDICATIVE ADJECTIVES

(10)   If a is a proper name and b an adjective, $a\frown$'is'$\frown b$ is a formula, and

$$D_{fml}(a\frown\text{'is'}\frown b) = D_{adj}(b)[\phi][D_{prn}(a)]$$

where ϕ is that function whose value, for any individual argument, is the set of all possible universes. Here ϕ is the denotation of the common noun 'entity'; $D_{adj}(b)[\phi]$ is accordingly the denotation of the common noun $b\frown$'entity' (or 'entity'$\frown b$, if b is more than one word long); and this is in turn a function of $D_{prn}(a)$. In effect $a\frown$'is'$\frown b$ is synonymous with $a\frown$'is a'$\frown b\frown$ 'entity' (or $a\frown$'is an entity'$\frown b$).

6. SEMANTIC RULES FOR PARTICULAR ITEMS

The word 'entity' is an example of a word with special semantic properties, and Montague specifies explicitly that 'not' should have the properties of negation, thus

$$D_{adf}(\text{'not'})[x] = U - x$$

and that 'is' as a two-place verb should have the properties of identity, and that 'necessarily' should have those of Leibnizian necessity, that is, truth in all possible universes. This completes the rules for the language.

Because of ambiguities, the rules do not attach a unique denotation to every formula. For example, 'every man loves a woman' can derive from 'v_0 loves a woman' by (6), or from 'every man loves v_1' by (7), and has different denotations in the two cases. In general a unique denotation attaches only to a "reading" of a formula, that is, to a tree that gives an analysis of it.

7. MONTAGUE'S ENVISAGED EXTENSIONS

Montague says ([8], p. 189):

I have restricted myself to a very limited fragment, partly because there are portions of English I do not yet know how to treat, but also for the sake of simplicity and the clear exposition of certain basic features. It is already known how to extend the treatment rather widely in various directions, and some of the extensions will be sketched in Part II of this paper; ...

and later (p. 221):

Certain extensions, comprehending larger portions of English (for instance, indexical or context-dependent portions), will be given in Part II; and still wider extensions are known.

But Part II, it seems, was never written. If we want to guess what might have been in it we must turn to Montague's other writings. In [9] and [10] he was concerned particularly with what he called "intensional logic": a consequent proposal for a syntax and semantics of verbs taking a propositional object, such as 'believe', 'assert', 'deny', 'know', 'prove', was worked out in some detail in [11]. Elsewhere [7] he formulated a rather general semantic model to deal with tenses, certain indexical terms such as demonstratives and personal pronouns, modal and deontic terms, and "inductive logic", namely, the probability calculus. It is not difficult to imagine that with patience in the working out of detail these terms and theories could be incorporated in the language we have been describing. But two considerations make it likely that much of ordinary English would never find its way into Montague's program.

The first can be hung on the remark ([8], p. 189):

Like Donald Davidson I regard the construction of a theory of truth – or rather, of the more general notion of truth under an arbitrary interpretation – as the basic goal of serious syntax and semantics; ...

The reference is to Davidson's paper [4] and is in a context of criticism of "the developments emanating from the Massachusetts Institute of Technology". This criticism is more than just, but in setting his goal merely as a "theory of truth" Montague has unnecessarily limited his terms of reference. What of the many uses of natural language for purposes incidental to, or with other goals than, the embodiment of truth, as in questions? commands, requests, advice? greetings, promises, exhortations? And what of the variant kinds even of declarative utterance such as the satirical, vicarious, jocular?

Secondly, something can be deduced from Montague's use of the word "pragmatics". At the beginning of [10] he refers to Bar-Hillel's suggestion (in [1]) that pragmatics concern itself with indexical exprsssions, and says that

> ... pragmatics should at least initially follow the lead of semantics – or its modern version, model theory – which is primarily concerned with the notions of truth and satisfaction ... though here we should speak about truth and satisfaction with respect not only to an interpretation but also to a context of use.

I do not want to involve Bar-Hillel or Davidson in the defence of positions stated on their behalf. (For some discussion see the remarks of Bar-Hillel [2] – and also those of Cohen [3] – to the symposium to which Montague's paper was directed.) It seems to me important, however, to defend pragmatics from this weakened interpretation. (Or, which amounts to the same thing, to affirm or reaffirm that a much wider conception of language should be taken than that currently adopted by most logicians and even theoretical linguists.) Pragmatics is the study of the *use* (not just reference) of language of all kinds; or, if it is not, we need a new name for the study that complements syntax and semantics. Montague's "pragmatics" would be better classed as a special part of semantics.

In what follows, this paper is a contribution to semantics too, and is without prejudice to any program of study of pragmatics proper.[5] But it represents a part of semantics that Montague, perhaps because of his conception of the field, has not dealt with in this connection. The study of *questions* leans out to pragmatics in the sense that someone who thinks the exclusive purpose of language is to state truths may be led by it to think again. But it is remarkable that it is possible to produce a semantics (or model theory) of questions, and that this dovetails surprisingly neatly with Montague's own semantics of statements.

8. EXTENSION TO QUESTIONS

The basic interrogative words of English nearly all fit more or less neatly into Montague's categories. Thus 'who' (or 'whom') and 'what', with a qualification to be noted later, are interrogative proper nouns, in the sense that they take the same positions in sentences as proper nouns do; 'what' may also do duty in standard compounds as one-place verb ('does what'), two-place verb ('does what to'), adjective ('of what kind') and even common noun (as in 'what is Rover', or with 'a' as in 'Rover is a what'). The terms 'how', 'when'

---

[5] Such as that to which my [6] is a contribution.

and 'where' can stand on their own feet as adverbs, though they also have
synonyms with 'what'. Only 'why' seems to lead us outside the bounds of
Montague English (and we shall ignore it in what follows). Most importantly,
there are also interrogative quantifiers; since for example 'what man' (or
'which man') may take the same positions as 'every man', 'a man' and 'the
man'.

Although standard English word-order places the interrogative word or
phrase (or the main one, if there are more than one) first, with inversion of
the verb, there is no real need for an order different from that appropriate to
indicatives.[6] So let us assume that no special rules about word-order are
needed. It now seems that to introduce questions into Montague English *all*
we need to do syntactically is supplement the vocabulary with interrogative
terms. Ordinary yes-no questions can be incorporated by the use of 'is it the
case that' as a prefix. This can be treated as a species of adformula, though it
must be distinguished from the others since it cannot be preceded by
them.

So let us turn to semantics. Here we must make some departure, since although we are inclined to class 'who' and 'what' with proper names we cannot by any stretch regard them as denoting individuals. But there is a simple
alternative: they *can* be regarded as denoting *sets* of individuals, namely
the set of humans and the set of non-humans respectively. This does not
mean, of course, that the formula 'who walks' asserts that the set of human
individuals walks: we must modify other stipulations in sympathy. We shall
need to regard 'who walks' as itself denoting a set, namely, the set whose
members are the propositions denoted by 'Mary walks', 'John walks',...
and so on for all individuals. Pragmatically speaking a question sets up a
choice-situation between a set of propositions, namely, those propositions
that count as answers to it.

It would be possible to make semantic rules for interrogatives quite
separately from those for indicatives. But a unified set of rules can be constructed quite simply if indicatives are regarded as equivalent to one-alter-
native or Hobson's-choice interrogatives.[7] All we need to do is to resolve to
say that an indicative proper name such as 'Mary' stands not for the individual Mary but for the set whose sole member is Mary; that 'Mary walks'
stands not for the proposition that Mary walks but for the set whose sole
member is this proposition; and so on. The discomfort some might feel at
saying that proper names such as 'Mary' denote not individuals but unit sets

---

[6] In many languages, for example all Melanesian ones, word-order is always that of the
corresponding indicative and there is not even a distinct inflexion.
[7] I do not feel impelled to apologise for having elsewhere [5, 6] given an account of questions different from this one. Either account is tenable.

can be alleviated by alteration of our terminology to speak of *denotation-sets* rather than *denotations*.

So let us write 'E_{prn}', 'E_{fml}',... for functions forming the denotation-sets of linguistic items of the various categories, indicative or interrogative. In the case of indicatives we shall have

$$E_{prn}(a) = \{D_{prn}(a)\}$$
$$E_{fml}(a) = \{D_{fml}(a)\}$$

and so on.

In formulating semantic rules we shall need the operation of forming a set whose members are the result of operating with members of a given set of functions on members of a given set. So let us write

$$E_{1vb}(b)\text{'''}E_{prn}(a)$$

for the set whose members are the result of operating with members of the denotation-set of the one-place verb b on members of the denotation-set of the proper name a.[8] If a and b are indicative the denotation-sets are one-membered and the operation yields a one-membered result, the denotation-set of the indicative formula $a\frown b$. If either $E_{prn}(a)$ or $E_{1vb}(b)$ is multimembered the result will in general be multimembered.

We are now in a position to set down a complete set of syntactic-semantic rules for the language as supplemented with questions, in parallel with those above and containing them as special cases. It will not be necessary here to state them all, but several will be given for the purpose of illustration and in order to make some special points.

(1Q)   If a is a proper name and b a one-place verb, $a\frown b$ is a formula and
$$E_{fml}(a\frown b) = E_{1vb}(b)\text{'''}E_{prn}(a).$$
Examples: 'Mary walks rapidly', 'who sleeps', 'John does what', 'who does what'. This is a generalisation of (1).

Rule (2) needs some recasting. Let us redefine the denotation of a two-place verb as a function from individuals to denotations of one-place verbs. Now the rule may read:

(20)   If a is a proper name and $b\frown c$ is a two-place verb, where b is a basic two-place verb and c may be null, $b\frown d\frown c$ is a one-place verb (where $d = a$ except that if a is 'who', d is 'whom') and
$$E_{1vb}(b\frown d\frown c) = E_{2vb}(b\frown c)\text{'''}E_{prn}(a).$$

---

[8] Formally $a\text{'''}b = \mathrm{Df}\{c: (\exists d\varepsilon a, e\varepsilon b)(c = d(e))\}$. We might call $a\text{'''}b$ the *joint image* of b by a: it is the union of the set of images $d\text{''}b$ of b by members d of a.

Examples: 'loves John', 'walks what', 'does what to Rover', 'does what to whom'. Besides easing the symbolic formulation this version of the rule has the effect, which a precise parallel of (2) would not have, of making the denotation of a formula such as 'Mary walks Rover' a member of the denotation-set of 'Mary does what', and this is of some importance when we come to consider the answer-relation.

Now let us define the denotation-set of the adformula 'is it the case that'. The denotation-set of 'is it the case that'$^\frown a$ must have as members just the denotation of a and the denotation of the negation of a; hence

$$E_{adf}(\text{'is it the case that'}) = \{I, D_{adf}(\text{'not'})\}$$

where I is the identity function. Now we can write:

(3Q)   If a is an adformula and b a formula that does not begin with 'is it the case that', (i) if a is 'not' and b does not end with 'not', $b^\frown a$ is a formula; and if a is not 'not', $a^\frown b$ is a formula;
(ii) $E_{fml}(c) = E_{adf}(a)^{\,\prime\prime\prime}E_{fml}(b)$
where c is the formula specified in (i).
Examples: 'John sleeps not', 'is it the case that it rains', 'is it the case that necessarily it rains not', 'is it the case that John does what'. Perhaps the last of these is unacceptable and 'is it the case that' should be prefixable only to indicatives, but I leave this decision to the reader.

A dilemma arises concerning whether we want 'John sleeps not' (for example) to count as an answer to 'John does what'. If 'not' can only be an adformula, 'sleeps not' is not a one-place verb and its denotation is not a member of the denotation-set of 'does what'. But if in turn we allow 'not' to count as an adverb so that 'sleeps not' may be a verb, we risk another kind of ambiguity, since if the 'not' in 'John reads every book not' may be either adformula or adverb the meaning may be either that John does not read every book or that John non-reads every book, that is, reads no book. I think this dilemma must be taken by the horns, and reveals a defect in Montague's rules. We *should* allow 'not' to count also as an adverb and remind ourselves that the resulting ambiguity is not uncommon in ordinary English. A supplementary definition of $D_{adv}(\text{'not'})$ is required but no further change in the rules is needed [9] and in simple cases such as 'John sleeps not' the alternative parsings give identical denotations.

Rules (4)–(9) can be adapted straightforwardly, and (10) needs only minor

[9] Except possibly a rule for word-order among adverbs.

reformulation consequent on the recasting of (2). We may add a rule for the use of 'what' as a quantifier:

(11Q)   As (6) with 'what' in place of 'every' and clause (ii) replaced by:
(ii) For given allocation $\{\alpha\}$ to $E_{prn}(v)$ let σ_α be the set of intersections of members of $E_{cmn}(a\frown b\frown c)$'''$\{\alpha\}$ with members of $E_{fml}(d)$. $E_{fml}(e)$ is the join of the sets σ_α generated by the possible allocations $\{\alpha\}$.

Examples: 'what dog walks with Mary', 'John loves what tall woman in Amsterdam such that that woman loves whom'. The semantic rule says for example that the members of the denotation-set of 'what dog walks with Mary' are the propositions that Rover is a dog and walks with Mary, that Fido is a dog and walks with Mary, and so on for all possible individuals. None of these propositions implies that uniquely one dog walks with Mary (as would be the case with members of the denotation-set of the different question 'what dog is the dog such that that dog walks with Mary').

In one respect this rule is controversial. We would like to think that the phrase 'what dog' could be treated as an interrogative proper name denoting the set of *dogs*, and that 'what dog walks with Mary' has as answers just the set '*x* walks with Mary' where '*x*' is the name of a *dog*. But the composition of the set of dogs does not necessarily remain constant from universe to universe: in some universes Rover may be a horse, and Mary herself a dog. I have taken the attitude that when someone answers 'what dog walks with Mary' with 'Rover' he states not merely that Rover walks with Mary but also implicitly that Rover is a dog, and hence that he states the conjunction. The distinction between assertion and presupposition, if it is to be invoked to resolve the issue, requires pragmatic treatment or, at least, a major elaboration of the model.

Now that 'what human' and 'what non-human' (but do we not need common noun negation for the latter?) can be introduced by (11Q), we no longer need 'who' and 'what' as interrogative proper-nouns; and what we have just said reveals, in any case, the weakness of this conception. Moreover 'who' and 'what' are sometimes used with reflexive pronouns, and need to be analysed as quantificational. Although there are cases in which these complications do not arise, we should suffer no loss in regarding 'who' and 'what' as synonyms of 'what human' and 'what non-human' respectively, so that the language contains no basic interrogative proper names.

The identification of statements with one-answer questions has one paradoxical result. It may occasionally happen that the denotation-set of a phrase has only one member in spite of the fact that the phrase contains interrogatives. For example, 'what entity is an entity' (though not a question one would commonly want to ask) has as members the denotations of 'x is an entity and is an entity' for all x; but these are all identical, being equivalent to the set U. Hence the denotation-set of 'what entity is an entity' is one-membered, and the apparent interrogative is really an indicative. I leave it to the reader to decide whether this disturbs him enough to make him want to reject the theory.

9. SYNTAX OF THE ANSWER-RELATION

Semantically, an answer to a question on a given reading is any statement whose denotation-set on a suitable reading is contained in that of the question. But there might also be syntactic requirements to the effect that the verbal form of the answer be more or less directly related to that of the question. For example one might stipulate that answers be obtainable from questions by direct substitution of indicative terms for basic interrogative ones (with suitable arrangements for quantificational and yes-no questions).

We cannot insist that *basic* indicative terms be substituted for basic interrogative ones, for there may be no suitable ones in the language; and, on the other hand, it is necessary that the semantic requirement be retained as well, to exclude tautological answers (such as the answer 'a dog such that that dog barks barks' to 'what dog barks'). These problems are, however, easy of solution in a number of logically satisfactory ways. It seems also possible to provide an appropriate analysis of abbreviated answers such as 'yes' and 'Rover'.

I conclude that there is no difficulty in incorporating most kinds of English question in Montague's language; and that the adjustments required to achieve this incorporation raise a number of issues relevant to the formulation of the language.

University of New South Wales

BIBLIOGRAPHY

[1] Bar-Hillel, Yehoshua, 'Indexical Expressions', *Mind* **63** (1954), 359–79.
[2] Bar-Hillel, Yehoshua, 'Communication and Argumentation in Pragmatic Languages', in *Linguaggi nella società e nella tecnica* (Bruno Visentini *et al.*) Milan, Edizioni di Comunità, 1970, pp. 269–84.
[3] Cohen, L. Jonathan, 'What is the Ability to Refer to Things, as a Constituent of a Language-Speaker's Competence?' in *Linguaggi nella società e nella tecnica* (Bruno Visentini *et al.*), Milan, Edizioni di Comunità, 1970, pp. 255–68.
[4] Davidson, Donald, 'Semantics for Natural Languages', in *Linguaggi nella società e*

nella tecnica (Bruno Visentini *et al.*), Milan, Edizioni di Comunità, 1970, pp. 177–88.

[5] Hamblin, C. L., 'Questions', *Australasian Journal of Philosophy* 36 (1958), 159–68.

[6] Hamblin, C. L., 'Mathematical Models of Dialogue', *Theoria* 37 (1971), 130–55.

[7] Montague, Richard, 'Pragmatics', in *Contemporary Philosophy – La philosophie contemporaine* (ed. by R. Klibansky), Florence, 1968, pp. 102–22.

[8] Montague, Richard, 'English as a Formal Language', in *Linguaggi nella società e nella tecnica* (Bruno Visentini *et al.*), Milan, Edizioni di Comunità, 1970, pp. 189–223.

[9] Montague, Richard, 'On the Nature of Certain Philosophical Entities', *Monist* 53 (1969), pp. 161–94.

[10] Montague, Richard, 'Pragmatics and Intensional Logic', *Dialectica* 24 (1970), pp. 277–302; also in *Synthese* 22 (1970), pp. 68–94.

[11] Montague, Richard, 'Universal Grammar', *Theoria* 36 (1970), pp. 373–98.

M. J. CRESSWELL

THE SEMANTICS OF DEGREE

This paper presents possible-worlds semantics for comparative constructions in English. In particular, a unified treatment is given of comparatives involving adjectives, mass nouns, and numerical comparisons. The paper is not "Montague grammar" in the strict sense of expounding or developing Montague's own work, but it shares two important features: (*a*) It is based on possible-worlds semantics, and (*b*) it aims to make the underlying formal language as close as possible to the surface.[1] It in fact uses the procedure and terminology I adopted in Cresswell (1973), though I have taken pains to make the paper self-contained, and at certain points I reject analyses I once favored and present alternative ones.

In Section 1 I set out the formal languages I want to put forward as underlying natural languages, and summarize their semantic framework. Section 2 is the heart of the paper and presents a detailed semantic analysis of comparative adjectives. Section 3 discusses mass nouns and plurals; Section 4 looks at the metaphysics that underlie comparisons; Section 5 takes up the relation between the underlying formal language of comparatives and their surface form; and Section 6 lists a few problem cases, with tentative suggestions for the solution of some of them.

1. λ-CATEGORIAL LANGUAGES

This section is a summary of material from Part II of Cresswell (1973). For those familiar with that work the only difference here is that I treat propositions simply as sets of possible worlds rather than as sets of "heavens," and I avoid any explicit reference to contexts of use.[2]

We first need the notion of a SYNTACTIC CATEGORY. For the purposes of this paper, there are two basic categories—0 of SENTENCE and 1 of NAME. Given categories $\tau, \sigma_1, \ldots, \sigma_n$, then $\langle \tau, \sigma_1, \ldots, \sigma_n \rangle$ is the category of a FUNCTOR that makes an expression of category τ out of expressions of category $\sigma_1, \ldots, \sigma_n$, respectively.

---

[1] An example of an approach that satisfies (a) but does not pretend to satisfy (b) is to be found in Lewis (1972).

[2] Propositions need to be something more elaborate than sets of possible worlds for two reasons: first, because of context dependence (discussed later), and second, because of functors that represent propositional attitudes to logically equivalent propositions. This area is very obscure to me (see Cresswell, in prep.) and, I suspect, to others also e.g., Partee (1973).

We can now define a λ-CATEGORIAL LANGUAGE $\mathscr{L}$ as follows: Where σ is a syntactic category, F_σ is the (finite) set of SYMBOLS of category σ.

In addition, there is, for each category σ, a denumerably infinite set X_σ of variables (in the logician's sense)[3] of category σ and a "logical" symbol λ (called the ABSTRACTION OPERATOR) that is not in any category. E_σ denotes the set of simple or complex expressions of category σ and is made up as follows, where $\sigma, \tau, \sigma_1, \ldots, \sigma_n$ are any categories:

(1.1) $F_\sigma \subseteq E_\sigma$

(1.2) If $\sigma = \langle \tau, \sigma_1, \ldots, \sigma_n \rangle$ and $\delta \in E_{\langle \tau, \sigma_1, \ldots, \sigma_n \rangle}$, $\alpha_1 \in E_{\sigma_1}, \ldots,$ $\alpha_n \in E_{\sigma_n}$, then $\langle \delta, \sigma_1, \ldots, \sigma_n \rangle \in E_\tau$.

(1.3) If $\alpha \in E_\tau$, and $x \in X_\sigma$, then $\langle \lambda, x, \alpha \rangle \in E_{\langle \tau, \sigma \rangle}$.

(An expression of the latter kind is called an ABSTRACT.)

In an expression of the form $\langle \delta, \alpha_1, \ldots, \alpha_n \rangle$, the order of $\alpha_1, \ldots, \alpha_n$ is important but the position of δ is not. In a well-formed functorial expression, there is only one expression that can be the functor, and we could write, e.g., $\langle \alpha_1, \ldots, \alpha_n, \delta \rangle$ or $\langle \alpha_1, \delta, \ldots, \alpha_n \rangle$. From time to time it is convenient to make use of this freedom (Cresswell, 1973, p. 78f).

For semantics we have a function $\mathbf{D}$ that associates with each syntactic category the things that can be the values of expressions in that category. $\mathbf{D}_0$ is the domain of PROPOSITIONS, and in this paper a proposition is A SET OF POSSIBLE WORLDS.[4] $\mathbf{D}_1$ is the domain of "things" and should be as inclusive as possible. Where $\sigma = \langle \tau, \sigma_1, \ldots, \sigma_n \rangle$, $\mathbf{D}_\sigma$ is a set of partial functions from $\mathbf{D}_{\sigma_1} \times \cdots \times \mathbf{D}_{\sigma_n}$ into $\mathbf{D}_\tau$. That is, if $\omega \in \mathbf{D}_\sigma$, then for appropriate

$$a_1 \in \mathbf{D}_{\sigma_1}, \ldots, a_n \in \mathbf{D}_{\sigma_n}, \qquad \omega(a_1, \ldots, a_n) \in \mathbf{D}_\tau.$$

I am sorry to have to inflict so much set theory at a blow, but the paper requires it and a full exposition would take too long. Set theory is a good thing to learn anyway. Readers who want more amplification of my own approach can refer to Cresswell (1973).

(1.4) A VALUE ASSIGNMENT V to the symbols of $\mathscr{L}$ is a function such that where $\alpha \in F_\sigma$, $V(\alpha) \in \mathbf{D}_\sigma$.

Because λ-categorial languages have variables and allow binding, we need, in addition, a value assignment to the variables. Let N be the set of

---

[3] VARIABLES are symbols that go in quantifiers or abstracts (see, e.g., Cresswell, 1973, p. 81). I mention this point because "variables in syntax" seems to mean something quite different.

[4] Some motivation for treating propositions as sets of possible worlds will be found in Cresswell (1973, p. 24f), see also Montague (1969) and Stalnaker (1972). We are, as noted, ignoring context dependence. Some remarks on the metaphysics of $\mathbf{D}_0$ and $\mathbf{D}_1$ are given in Cresswell (1973, Chapters 3, 7). Possible worlds are put to philosophical use in Montague (1969).

functions v such that where $x \in X_\sigma$, $v(x) \in \mathbf{D}_\sigma$. Where $a \in \mathbf{D}_\sigma$, $(v, a/x)$ is the function like v for all arguments except that $(v, a/x)(x) = a$.

We may show how V induces an assignment to all expressions of $\mathscr{L}$. Let $V_v(\alpha)$ mean "the value induced by V to the expression α, with respect to the assignment v to the variables"; V_v is defined as follows:

(1.5) If $\alpha \in F_\sigma$, then $V_v(\alpha) = V(\alpha)$.

(1.6) If $x \in X_\sigma$, then $V_v(x) = v(x)$.

(1.7) If $\alpha = \langle \delta, \alpha_1, \ldots, \alpha_n \rangle$, then where $\omega = V_v(\delta)$, $V_v(\alpha) = \omega_\delta(V_v(\alpha_1), \ldots, V_v(\alpha_n))$.

(1.8) If $\alpha = \langle \lambda, x, \beta \rangle$ and $\beta \in E_\tau$, then $V_v(\alpha)$ is the function $\omega \in \mathbf{D}_{\langle \tau, \sigma \rangle}$ such that for any $a \in \mathbf{D}_\sigma$, $\omega(a) = V_{(v, a/x)}(\beta)$.

We assume the usual distinction between FREE and BOUND variables. In the expression $\langle \lambda, x, \alpha \rangle$ any x that occurs in α will be bound. A variable that is not bound will be FREE. (The occurrence of x after the λ of course counts as neither bound nor free.) An expression without free variables is called CLOSED. The value assigned to closed expressions does not depend on the assignment to the variables. If α is closed and v and μ are any assignments to the variables, then $V_v(\alpha) = V_\mu(\alpha)$. We frequently write simply $V^+(\alpha)$ in such a case. (The $+$ is to show that it is an induced assignment to the complex expression α, uniquely determined by the assignment V to the finite number of symbols of $\mathscr{L}$.)

Where $\mathbf{W}$ is the set of all possible worlds, $\mathbf{D}_0 \subseteq \mathscr{P}\mathbf{W}$. That is, the domain of propositions is a subset (possibly but not necessarily a proper subset) of the set of all sets of possible worlds—which is just another way of saying that propositions are sets of possible worlds. If $a \in \mathbf{D}_0$ (i.e., if $a \subseteq \mathbf{W}$) and $w \in \mathbf{W}$, then to say that a is TRUE IN w is to say that $w \in a$. Where α is a sentence of $\mathscr{L}$ (i.e., $\alpha \in E_0$ and contains no free variables), α is true in w under V iff $w \in V^+(\alpha)$.

Because our domains include partial functions, there are many expressions that will not be defined. This kind of semantic anomaly must of course be clearly distinguished from grammatical ill-formedness. Only well-formed expressions are candidates for semantic oddness in λ-categorial languages.

In Section 5 I say something about the relation between λ-categorial and natural languages, and I have said a good bit about it elsewhere (Cresswell, 1973; in press). What we do is represent the symbols of $\mathscr{L}$ by English words printed in boldface type and then try to get expressions, sometimes called λ-DEEP STRUCTURES, that look as though they could become English sentences with a bit of tinkering. In this particular work I am concerned more with the underlying semantic structure than with the tinkering. There have been a number of recent syntactic studies of the comparative in English, and I have made use of some of these (Doherty and Schwartz, 1967; Hale, 1970; Lees, 1961; Smith, 1961).[5] One in particular has guided much of my analysis, and that is Bresnan (1973). In Section 5 of this study, I discuss the relation between my λ-deep structures and her underlying structures.

Beginning with names (category 1) and sentences (category 0), we can produce symbols in certain other categories that look a bit like various parts of speech. For instance, intransitive verb expressions (whether simple or complex) look as though they should be treated as one-place predicates. This means that they make sentences out of names, which means that they are in category $\langle 0, 1 \rangle$. (Transitive verb expressions are in category $\langle 0, 1, 1 \rangle$, and so on). Another class of expression in category $\langle 0, 1 \rangle$ is the class of common count nouns, whether simple or complex. Because they must be distinguished from intransitive verb expressions, Montague (1973, p. 223) has assigned them a different category. We might indicate this category by $\langle\langle 0, 1 \rangle\rangle$. Expressions in category $\langle\langle 0, 1 \rangle\rangle$ would still make sentences out of names, but they would be syntactically distinct from expressions of category $\langle 0, 1 \rangle$. However, in this study we shall not make such a distinction. In Cresswell (1973) the category 2 was introduced, with $\mathbf{D}_2 = \mathbf{D}_{\langle 0, 1 \rangle}$; but I am now inclined to think that this was a mistake. I now believe that it is the function of the principles that relate the λ-deep structures and the sentences of ordinary language to distinguish nouns and verbs.

The meaning of common count nouns can be illustrated by **man**:

(1.9) $V(\mathbf{man})$ is the function $\omega \in \mathbf{D}_{\langle 0, 1 \rangle}$ such that for any $a \in \mathbf{D}_1$, a is in the domain of ω iff a is a physical object in some $w \in \mathbf{W}$; and for any $w \in \mathbf{W}$, $w \in \omega(a)$ iff a is a man in w.[6]

---

[5] At the time this work was written I had not seen Seuren (1973) and had had to rely on Borowski (1973). What Seuren's article shows is, in effect, that if the basic primitive for an adjective like **tall** is taken as 'x is tall to degree at least y' then my **er than** can be expressed in terms of the concepts of ordinary quantification theory. For we can then say things like 'there is a degree u such that Bill is tall to degree at least u but it is not the case that Ophidia is long to degree at least u'. If one's aim is to make the object language look as much like quantification theory as possible, rather than as close to the surface as possible, then Seuren's analysis must be preferred to mine. Otherwise the issue must turn on how strong Seuren's (1973) syntactic arguments on pages 532–537 that there is an underlying negative in comparisons are felt to be. (I find myself agreeing with about half of Seuren's data.)

[6] These semantic "rules" frequently provoke a charge of circularity. My reply is always that I am not attempting to teach anyone the meaning of English words. I assume that he understands English because English is the metalanguage of the paper. $V(\mathbf{man})$ is a (set-theoretical) function of a certain kind, and if the analysis is correct, it is that function, however our English metalanguage serves to pick the function out. Those who think that rules like $V(\mathbf{man})$ are circular seem to be making the impossible demand that we write articles on semantics without using a language.

I am taking the analysis of the semantics of common count nouns and intransitive verbs to be relatively unproblematic. I would hope at least that if I am wrong, the error will not affect what I say in this work. There is one obvious respect in which the semantics is not adequate as it stands, and this is that the meaning of nouns frequently depends on such things as the temporal context. In the case of **man**, there is perhaps the temptation to say once a man always a man (but is even this so certain?). However, in the case of a word like **widow**, we have to know not only what world is involved but also what point of time. Logicians have spoken of things like moments of time as "contextual indices." Another index is an utterer index, so that:

(1)   **I am hungry.**

could be said to be true for u at time t in world w iff u is hungry at time t in world w. Most of the semantics we go on to present ought to make reference to contextual indices, but it is in every case clear how it should be done, and we shall simply enjoy the relative simplicity afforded by forgetting about contexts of use. (It is in the analysis of features such as tenses and pronouns that context dependence becomes vital; vide (Cresswell, 1973, Chapters 11, 12). In what follows, a world w can always be thought of as a world at a particular moment of time. This will take care of a great deal of the more important kinds of context.)

Another simplification is to treat names as expressions of category 1. In Cresswell (1973 p. 130f) it was argued that an important syntactic category is that of NOMINAL. Nominals are in category $\langle 0, \langle 0, 1 \rangle \rangle$ and contain, as well as names, expressions that underlie phrases like:

(2)   **at least one person present**

(3)   **no philosopher**

(4)   **the saggy baggy elephant**

The need for nominals was argued in Cresswell (1973), but the questions we are currently interested in can be discussed without the irrelevant complexity they introduce.

2. COMPARATIVE ADJECTIVES

The approach adopted in Cresswell (1973) by me and in Montague (1970, p. 394) by Montague, and by other logicians besides, takes the attributive use of adjectives to be prior to their predicative use. In this we differ not only from almost all linguists (at least as far as my reading goes) but also, I suspect, from most philosophers. Indeed I am coming to think that a great many philosophical puzzles have been generated by the taking of expressions like:

(5)   **is red**

as paradigmatic instances of predicates.[7] Be that as it may, adjectives are here treated as noun modifiers. In Cresswell (1973) they are treated as being of category $\langle\langle 0, 1\rangle, \langle 0, 1\rangle\rangle$. One of the main tasks of this study is to refine the analysis given there in such a way as to give a semantically coherent account of comparatives. In so doing we shall also discover some important semantic features of mass nouns and the collectivizing function of plurals.

When we make comparisons we have in mind points on a scale. The scale can be represented by a relation, and the points on the scale by the field of that relation. (A relation in set theory is a set of ordered pairs; the FIELD of a relation is the set of all things that are related in one direction or another to something else.) Where $>$ is a relation we denote its field by $\mathscr{F}(>)$:

(2.1)   A DEGREE (of comparison) is a pair $\langle u, > \rangle$, where $>$ is a relation and $u \in \mathscr{F}(>)$.

The $>$ is heuristic, in order to suggest the direction of the comparison. It is tempting to think of $>$ as at least a partial ordering (i.e., a transitive and antisymmetric relation); whether it should be strict or not or total or not seems unimportant, and perhaps we should even be liberal enough not to insist on transitivity and antisymmetry (Wheeler, 1972, p. 319).

We suppose that in phrases like:

(6)   **a tall man**

(7)   **a very tall man**

(8)   **a much too tall man**

(9)   **a taller man**

the underlying semantic concept is:

(10) x–**much tall man**

where x is a degree of tallness. In fact I am going to regard the word *much* as a surface marker that signals the underlying degree variable (Bresnan, 1973, p. 277f). On this analysis $\langle$**tall, man**$\rangle$ becomes in effect a two-place

---

[7] When I first read Prior (1955) and (1957), I used to think it strange that he read ϕx as "$x\phi$'s" rather than "x is ϕ." I am only now beginning to see the deep philosophical wisdom of that reading.

predicate with (roughly) the meaning of:

(11) x **is a man who is tall to degree** y

We want to give a semantics for **tall** that applies to any count noun to which it is applied. On this view **tall** is of category $\langle\langle 0, 1, 1\rangle, \langle 0, 1\rangle\rangle$ and has the following semantics:

(2.2) $V(\textbf{tall})$ is a function $\zeta \in \mathbf{D}_{\langle\langle 0, 1, 1\rangle, \langle 0, 1\rangle\rangle}$ such that where $\omega \in \mathbf{D}_{\langle 0, 1\rangle}$, ω is in the domain of ζ iff ω is a property whose domain contains only physical objects. For any $a, b \in \mathbf{D}_1$ in the domain of $\zeta(\omega)$, and any $w \in \mathbf{W}$, $w \in \zeta(\omega)(a, b)$ iff $w \in \omega(a)$ and $b = \langle u, > \rangle$, where $>$ is the relation whose field is the set of all v such that v is a spatial distance, and $\langle v_1, v_2\rangle \in >$ iff v_1 is a greater distance than v_2, and u is the distance between a's extremities in w, and in the case of most c's such that $w \in \omega(c)$ this distance will typically be vertical.

It must be constantly borne in mind that semantic "rules" like (2.2) are for purposes of illustration only. This study is not trying to tie down the English meaning of **tall** but only to show the kind of thing that should represent it in a λ-categorial base for English. I would not go so far as Wheeler (1972 p. 319) and describe the study of the meanings of actual words as "physics" rather than "semantics," but I would agree with him that an investigation into the logical structure underlying a natural language is not concerned primarily with getting the details of the meanings of particular words absolutely correct. Nevertheless the closer one can come, the more illuminating the examples will be.

I think a few words should be said about (2.2). The early part of the clause says something about the kinds of things that could be in the domain of the function. Where an expression is made up out of a functor whose arguments have as their meanings something that is not in the domain of the meaning of the functor, then the whole expression lacks a value. Thus in this case the phrase:

(12)   *a tall idea[8]

would not have a value. This means that semantic anomalies do not require that any "feature theory" be present in the syntax. Example (12) will be perfectly well-formed but semantically anomalous. In the illustrations throughout the rest of this work, the domains of the functors will have to

---

[8] Since reading Householder (1973) on asterisks (see also Bar Hillel, 1971 and Weydt, 1973, p. 578), I venture to use them with some trepidation. An asterisk means that there is something odd about the sentence. In each case I shall try to explain what sort of oddness I think it is, and why I think it a sort of oddness. An asterisk does NOT mean that the sentence is ungrammatical.

be suitably restricted. It is, however, tedious to mention this most of the time, and we shall always assume that when we say things like "for ANY $a \in \mathbf{D}_1$" or "or ANY $\omega \in \mathbf{D}_{\langle 0, 1 \rangle}$" what we really mean is "for any appropriate a (or ω)."

The difference between **tall** and **long** is that **tall** usually applies to distances measured vertically and from the ground up, though of course one can find out how tall a man is by measuring him lying down. I do not think (2.2) has by any means captured all these nuances (e.g., that the distance between the extremities, in the case of something like a man, will have to be measured when he is stretched out and not curled up, and so on), but it will certainly do for our purposes. **Long** can also be used to measure temporal distances. We shall examine this use in (4.3).

We can now introduce the symbol for the comparative. We shall write it as **er than**. For the present we shall regard it as a single symbol in category $\langle 0, \langle 0, 1 \rangle, \langle 0, 1 \rangle \rangle$, but there is no reason why a transformation cannot regard it as two symbols and separate the two parts on the way to the surface.

The problem facing most analyses of **er than** is that the comparison scales used vary from adjective to adjective. That is, if we define **er than** by means of distances, then it may be all right for:

(13)   **Bill is taller than Arabella.**

but it will not do for:

(14)   **Bill is uglier than Arabella.**

The advantage of our approach is that the terms of the **er than** supply the comparison scale: $\langle \alpha, \textbf{er than}, \beta \rangle$ essentially means that the degree of α is higher than the degree of β on the scale that is common to the meaning of α and β.

(2.3) $V(\textbf{er than})$ is the function $\zeta \in \mathbf{D}_{\langle 0, \langle 0, 1 \rangle, \langle 0, 1 \rangle \rangle}$ such that where ω and $\omega' \in \mathbf{D}_{\langle 0, 1 \rangle}$, ω and ω' are in the domain of ζ only if they are functions whose domains consist entirely of degrees. For any $w \in \mathbf{W}$, $w \in \zeta(\omega, \omega')$ iff there is an a and a b such that $\omega \in \omega(a)$ and $w \in \omega'(b)$, and for any such a and b there is some relation $>$ and some u_1 and u_2 in $\mathscr{F}(>)$, and $a = \langle u_1, > \rangle$ and $b = \langle u_2, > \rangle$ and $u_1 > u_2$.

The generality of the analysis proposed here may be seen from a detailed discussion of:

(15)   **Bill is a taller man than Ophidia is a long snake.**

I have chosen this example because most logicians who have tried to analyze comparatives (Wheeler, 1972, p. 318; Wallace, 1972; Rennie, 1974, pp. 146–151) have stayed with such examples as:

(16)   **Bill is a taller man than Tom.**

If we can analyze (15), then we can regard (16) as a shortened version of:

(17)   **Bill is a taller man than Tom is a tall man.**

Snake is a count noun, and its semantics ought to be obvious; and something was said about the semantics for **long** in the discussion of (2.2). The important thing is that **tall** and **long** both involve the same scale.

A plausible λ-deep structure for (15) would seem to be:

(18) $\langle\langle\lambda, x, \langle$**Bill**, $\langle$**tall, man**$\rangle, x\rangle\rangle$, **er than** $\langle\lambda, x, \langle$**Ophidia**, $\langle$**long, snake**$\rangle, x\rangle\rangle\rangle$[9]

(In this sentence $\langle$**tall, man**$\rangle$ and $\langle$**long, snake**$\rangle$ are in category $\langle 0, 1, 1\rangle$ and are placed between their arguments; the first arguments are **Bill** and **Ophidia**, respectively, and the second argument is the variable x.)

Let us now see how (18) should be evaluated semantically. We first obtain, for an assignment v to the variables:

(19) $V_v(\langle$**Bill**, $\langle$**tall, man**$\rangle, x\rangle)$

Now $V_v($**Bill**$) = V($**Bill**$) = $ Bill, and $V_v(x) = v(x)$. Suppose that $v(x)$ is b; then (19) becomes:

(20) $V_v(\langle$**tall, man**$\rangle)(V_v($**Bill**$), V_v(x)) = V_v(\langle$**tall, man**$\rangle)($Bill, $b)$

Further,

$$V_v(\langle\textbf{tall, man}\rangle) = V_v(\textbf{tall})(V_v(\textbf{man})) = V(\textbf{tall})(V(\textbf{man}))$$

This means that (19) $= V($**tall**$)(V($**man**$))($Bill, $b)$. Where $V($**man**$)$ is ω and $V($**tall**$)$ is ζ, then (19) $= \zeta(\omega)($Bill, $b)$. By (2.2), $w \in \zeta(\omega)($Bill, $b)$ iff Bill is a man in w and b is a pair $\langle u, >\rangle$ and $>$ is the "greater than" relation with respect to length, and u is the distance between Bill's extremities in w, and this distance is typically vertical.

This means that:

(21) $V^+(\langle\lambda, x, \langle$**Bill**, $\langle$**tall, man**$\rangle, x\rangle\rangle)$

is the ω such that $w \in \omega(a)$ iff $a = \langle u, >\rangle$, where u is Bill's height in w (i.e., the typically vertical distance between his extremities) and Bill is a man in w.

---

[9] $\langle\lambda, x, \langle$**Bill**, $\langle$**tall, man**$\rangle, x\rangle\rangle$ can be read as **is an x such that Bill is an x-tall man**. In Cresswell (1973) one analysis of *wh* questions presented them as predicates. With the addition of the symbol **how** by analogy with the **who**^{q} of Cresswell (1973, p. 237$\rangle$, $\langle\lambda, x, \langle$**Bill**, $\langle$**tall, man**$\rangle$, $x\rangle\rangle$ might well be what underlies *How tall is Bill?* (cf. Lees 1961, p. 176).

By analogous reasoning we discover that:

(22) $V^+(\langle \lambda, x, \langle \textbf{Ophidia}, \langle \textbf{long, snake} \rangle, x \rangle \rangle)$

is the function ω' such that $w \in \omega'(b)$ iff $b = \langle v, > \rangle$, where v is Ophidia's length in w and Ophidia is a snake in w.

It is important that the $>$ involved in both **tall** and **long** is, despite their differences in meaning, the same relation.

Now $V^+((18)) = V(\textbf{er than})(\omega, \omega')$

(where ω and ω' are as described earlier), and by (2.3), $V(\textbf{er than})$ is the function ζ such that $w \in \zeta(\omega, \omega')$ iff there are an a and b such that $w \in \omega(a)$ and $w \in \omega'(b)$ and for any such a and b, $a = \langle u, > \rangle$ and $b = \langle v, > \rangle$, $u > v$. In the particular case we have in mind, this will be true iff the distance that is Tom's height in w exceeds the distance that is Ophidia's length. That is, (18) will be true in w iff Tom is taller than Ophidia is long.

This sentence will also entail that Tom is a man and Ophidia a snake, because (2.3) requires that for (18) to be true in w, there must be some a such that $w \in \omega(a)$, and also that there is some b such that $w \in \omega'(b)$; and as we saw in our discussion of (21) and (22), the former entails that Tom is a man in w and the latter that Ophidia is a snake.[10]

---

[10] The semantics also provides a natural explanation for why, although:

(i)   **Bill is the father of Arabella or Clarissa.**

means (on its most natural interpretation):

(ii)   **Either Bill is the father of Arabella or Bill is the father of Clarissa.**

yet:

(iii)   **Bill is taller than Arabella or Clarissa.**

does not mean (at least not usually):

(iv)   **Bill is taller than Arabella or Bill is taller than Clarissa.**

but means, rather:

(v)   **Bill is taller than Arabella and Bill is taller than Clarissa.**

These points have been noticed by Jennings [13]. The underlying structure is:

(vi) $\langle \langle \lambda, x, \langle \textbf{Bill}, \langle \textbf{tall, man} \rangle, x \rangle \rangle, \textbf{er than}, \langle \lambda, x, \langle \langle \textbf{Arabella}, \langle \textbf{tall, woman} \rangle, x \rangle, \textbf{or,}$
        $\langle \textbf{Clarissa}, \langle \textbf{tall, woman} \rangle, x \rangle \rangle \rangle$

And this will be true if for any u that is Bill's height and v that is Arabella's height or Clarissa's height, $u > v$.

This example is possible because we have allowed the functions in the domain of V(**er than**) to be true of more than one degree. However, the members of their domains are still all degrees and, further, always degrees involving the same comparison scale. Lees (1961, p. 175) notes the

This semantics also explains why:

(23)   *Bill is a taller man than Tom is a clever man.

though perfectly grammatical, is semantically anomalous. For **clever** will induce its own "degrees of cleverness" scale, and **er than** works only when its terms have the same scale:

(2.4) $V($**clever**$)$ is the function $\zeta \in \mathbf{D}_{\langle\langle 0, 1, 1\rangle, \langle 0, 1\rangle\rangle}$ such that for $w \in \mathbf{W}$, $\omega \in \mathbf{D}_{\langle 0, 1\rangle}$, and $a, b \in \mathbf{D}_1$: $w \in \zeta(\omega)(a, b)$ iff $w \in \omega(a)$ and $b = \langle u, >\rangle$, where $>$ is a greater than relation among degrees of cleverness, and $u \in \mathscr{F}(>)$, and u is the degree of a's cleverness in w.

The reason (23) is semantically anomalous is that we would end up with a $\langle u_1, >_1 \rangle$ and a $\langle u_2, >_2 \rangle$, where $>_1$ and $>_2$ would not be the same relation. One would be a relation among heights and the other a relation

---

semantic deviance of sentences like:

(vii)   *I know him better than she doesn't.

The reason for this deviance, on our account, would be that an expression like:

(viii) $\langle \lambda, x, \langle \mathbf{not}, \langle \mathbf{Bill}, \langle \mathbf{tall, man}\rangle, x\rangle\rangle\rangle$

would denote a function ω whose domain will include things that are not degrees. ω would thus not be in the domain of $V($**er than**$)$. And even the degrees in its domain can involve many different comparison scales (see Green, 1970).

More complicated cases pose no SEMANTIC problems. Thus examples (23) and (24) of Smith (1961 p. 352):

John has a bigger car than Bill has.

and

George climbed a higher mountain than Everest.

become (ix) and (x):

(ix) $\langle\langle \lambda, x, \langle\langle \lambda, y, \langle \mathbf{John, has}, y\rangle\rangle, \mathbf{a}, \langle \lambda, z, \langle z, \langle \mathbf{big, car}\rangle, x\rangle\rangle\rangle\rangle$, **er than**, $\langle \lambda, x,$
$\langle\langle \lambda, y, \langle \mathbf{Bill, has}, y\rangle\rangle, \mathbf{a}, \langle \lambda, z, \langle z, \langle \mathbf{big, car}\rangle, y\rangle\rangle\rangle\rangle\rangle$

(We assume that **has** is in category $\langle 0, 1, 1\rangle$ and **a** is in category $\langle 0, \langle 0, 1\rangle, \langle 0, 1\rangle\rangle$ with the semantics attributed to it in Cresswell (1973, p. 136). It occurs here between the arguments:

(x) $\langle\langle \lambda, x, \langle\langle \lambda, y, \langle \mathbf{George, climbed}, y\rangle\rangle, \mathbf{a}, \langle \lambda, y, \langle y, \langle \mathbf{high, mountain}\rangle, x\rangle\rangle\rangle\rangle$,
er than, $\langle \lambda, x, \langle \mathbf{Everest}, \langle \mathbf{high, mountain}\rangle, x\rangle\rangle\rangle\rangle$

(We take **climbed** as a complete unit because tense is not our present concern.) In these representations **er than** is the main operator, and if we regard it as a conjunction, the analysis we propose is one of those Smith rejects (p. 353f). However, her objection is in terms of the simplicity of the deletion and order changes, and it is not clear to me whether it still applies when the base structure is in a λ-categorial language. Some other examples of this kind are given in Doherty and Schwartz (1967, p. 908).

among degrees of cleverness, and the semantics for **er than** provides for no way of comparing the two.[11]

Our underlying semantic concept for **tall** was in fact "x-much tall." But of course we have sentences like:

(24)   **Bill is a tall man.**

What seems to be meant in a case like this is something like:

(25)   **Bill is taller than the average man.**

I propose to treat the 'tall' in (24) as composed of two symbols, **pos** and **tall**. **tall** satisfies (2.2), while **pos** conveys the "er than the average———."

pos (for positive, as opposed to comparative) is in category $\langle\langle\langle 0, 1\rangle$, $\langle 0, 1\rangle\rangle$, $\langle\langle 0, 1, 1\rangle$, $\langle 0, 1\rangle\rangle\rangle$. This looks very complicated, but all it means is that **pos** makes an ordinary noun modifier, say, $\langle$**pos**, **tall**$\rangle$, out of a modifier like **tall**.[12]

(2.5) $V(\textbf{pos})$ is the function η in $\mathbf{D}_{\langle\langle\langle 0, 1\rangle, \langle 0, 1\rangle\rangle, \langle\langle 0, 1, 1\rangle, \langle 0, 1\rangle\rangle\rangle}$ such that where $\zeta \in \mathbf{D}_{\langle\langle 0, 1, 1\rangle, \langle 0, 1\rangle\rangle}$, $\eta(\zeta)$ is the following function: For any $\omega \in \mathbf{D}_{\langle 0, 1\rangle}$ and $a \in \mathbf{D}_1$ and $w \in \mathbf{W}$, $w \in \eta(\zeta)(\omega)(a)$ iff $w \in \omega(a)$ and there is exactly one b such that $\zeta(\omega)(a, b)$; and for that b, $b = \langle u, >\rangle$ (for some $>$ and $u \in \mathscr{F}(>)$) and u is toward the top of the scale determined by $>$ when restricted to those v such that for some c, $w \in \zeta(\omega)(c, \langle v, >\rangle)$ and $w \in \omega(c)$.

Let us see how (2.2), (2.3), and (2.5) combine to give us a value for:

(26) $\langle\langle$**pos**, **tall**$\rangle$, **man**$\rangle$

In this case, if we let $V(\textbf{tall})$ be ζ, $V(\textbf{man})$ be ω, and $V(\textbf{pos})$ be η, then $V^+(26) = \eta(\zeta)(\omega)(a)$, and (2.2), (2.3), and (2.5) give us that $w \in \eta(\zeta)(\omega)(a)$ iff a is a man in w and there is exactly one b such that $b = \langle u, >\rangle$ and $>$ is the greater than relation over spatial distances, and u is the distance between a's extremities in w, and u is towards the top of the scale determined by $>$ when restricted to those v that are the heights of c's who are men in w.

---

[11] The comparison scales mentioned in the text have all been independent of the noun being modified. The following examples show that this need not always be so:

(i)   **This is a more effective ashtray than a saucer.**
(ii)   ***This is a more effective ashtray than Bill is an effective manager.**

Obviously degrees of "effectiveness" depend on what sort of thing is being stated to be effective.

[12] See Vennemann (1973, p. 8). Perhaps the meaning of $\langle\langle$**pos**, **tall**$\rangle$, $\alpha\rangle$ is better captured by "tall enough to make it sensible to distinguish it from other α's." A meaning of this kind is very context dependent, but perhaps it gives some clue to why **pos** has a null surface realization. Wheeler (1972, p. 315f) takes as the semantic primitive a relation between an individual and a set. Roughly, **tall**, for Wheeler, means "x is tall by comparison with the set α." He is then able to analyze x **is taller than** y as "x is tall by comparison with $\{y\}$." Wheeler's treatment is ingenious, but it does not seem to me able to deal with x **is taller than** y **is high.**

The phrase *top end* alludes simply to the metaphor by which we speak of u_1 being "higher than" u_2^* iff $u_1 > u_2$. There is a certain amount of vagueness about this metalinguistic statement, but that is all to the good because the definiendum is likewise vague. What the rules amount to in the case of (26) is that to be a tall man is, in effect, to be taller than the average man. This explains why (16) does not entail that Bill is a tall man (Vennemann, 1973, p. 8f).

$\langle$**pos, tall**$\rangle$ is realized on the surface simply as 'tall'.

The superlative seems best treated by a symbol **est** in category $\langle\langle 0, 1\rangle$, $\langle 0, 1, 1\rangle\rangle$:

(2.6) $V(\textbf{est})$ is the function ζ such that for $\omega \in \mathbf{D}_{\langle 0, 1, 1\rangle}$ and $a \in \mathbf{D}_1$ and $w \in \mathbf{W}$: $w \in \zeta(\omega)(a)$ iff there is a unique b such that $w \in \omega(a, b)$ and $b = \langle u, >\rangle$, and for any c and d such that $w \in \omega(c, d)$, $d = \langle v, >\rangle$ for some v and either $u = v$ or $u > v$.

If we apply this to *tallest spy*, we have:

(27) $V^+(\langle\langle\textbf{tall}, \textbf{spy}\rangle, \textbf{est}\rangle)$

$V^+(\langle\textbf{tall}, \textbf{spy}\rangle)$ is the $\omega \in \mathbf{D}_{\langle 0, 1, 1\rangle}$ such that $w \in \omega(a, b)$ iff a is a spy in w and a is tall to degree u, where $b = \langle u, >\rangle$. Thus $w \in V^+(27)$ iff a is a spy in w such that the degree u to which a is tall is greater than the degree to which any other spy in w is tall.

In this semantics **est** modifies whole phrases. In obtaining the surface sentence it would have to be attached to the adjective. It is semantically plausible to have *est* modifying complex expressions, since in a sentence like:

(28) **The tallest spy in Australasia is not in New Zealand.**

the **est** would seem to modify the whole:

(29) **tall spy in Australasia**

Bresnan (1973, p. 277) notes certain other locutions that seem to correspond to **er than**. We can have:

(30) **as tall as**

(31) **so tall (that)**

(32) **too tall (to)**

(33) **that tall**

We shall give a semantics for (30) by taking **as as** as a single symbol of category $\langle 0, \langle 0, 1\rangle, \langle 0, 1\rangle\rangle$. (It splits as it gets toward the surface.) Examples (31)–(33) are a little more complicated, involving, as they seem to, references to human purposes and other matters beyond the scope of this paper.

(2.7) $V(\textbf{as as})$ is the function ζ such that for ω and $\omega' \in \mathbf{D}_{\langle 0, 1\rangle}$, and $w \in \mathbf{W}$: $w \in \zeta(\omega, \omega')$ iff there is an a and b such that $w \in \omega(a)$

and $w \in \omega'(b)$; and for any such a and b, $a = \langle u_1, > \rangle$ and $b = \langle u_2, > \rangle$ and either $u_1 > u_2$ or $u_1 = u_2$.

The point is that Bill is as tall as Tom iff he is either taller than Tom or the same height as Tom. The modifier *exactly* would require that $u_1 = u_2$ and would not allow $u_1 > u_2$.

Another distinction we must capture is that between:

(34)   **Bill is taller than Arabella.**

and:

(35)   **Bill is taller than six feet.**

We shall for the present treat **six feet** as a single symbol in category 1 and let $V(\textbf{six feet})$ be a particular degree, viz. $\langle u, > \rangle$, where $>$ is the relation ordering lengths and u is the length of six feet. Thus (35) is:

(36) $\langle\langle \lambda, x, \langle \textbf{Bill}, \langle \textbf{tall}, \textbf{man} \rangle, x \rangle\rangle, \textbf{er than}, \textbf{six feet} \rangle$

and of course:

(37)   **Bill is six feet tall.**

is even simpler, viz. (with the functor following its arguments):

(38) $\langle \textbf{Bill}, \textbf{six feet}, \langle \textbf{tall}, \textbf{man} \rangle \rangle$

If **six feet** is the name of $\langle u, > \rangle$, then it cannot also be the name of $\langle u, < \rangle$. This may provide an explanation for:

(39)   *****Bill is six feet short.**

3. MASS NOUNS AND PLURALS

Our approach to mass nouns assumes that the underlying semantic primitive of a word like **water** is a two-place predicate with some such meaning as:

(40) x **is an amount of water of volume** y[13]

[13] This is not quite right, since many mass nouns seem able to be measured in several different ways, e.g., by both weight and volume. The meaning would have to supply several scales, and either the linguistic or the pragmatic context would select one of them. Mass nouns can of course be modified by adjectives. The λ-categorial expression underlying Parson's **blue styrofoam** (1970, p. 364) would be:

(i) $\langle\langle \textbf{blue}, \langle \lambda, x, \langle \textbf{styrofoam}, x, y \rangle\rangle\rangle, x, z \rangle$

which would mean, roughly:

(ii) x **is** y-**much styrofoam of** z **degree of blueness**

Because there are two degrees involved, we can explain the ambiguity in:

(iii)   **more blue styrofoam**

water is in category $\langle 0, 1, 1 \rangle$, and its semantics is as follows:

(3.1) $V(\textbf{water})$ is the function ω such that for a, $b \in \mathbf{D}_1$ and $w \in \mathbf{W}$:
         $w \in \omega(a, b)$ iff $b = \langle u, > \rangle$, where $>$ is the greater than relation
         with respect to volumes, and $u \in \mathscr{F}(>)$ and u is the volume of
         a in w and a is water in w.

We want to analyze a sentence like:

(41)   **More water ebbs than mud flows.**

(This example, like so many that are candidates for formalization, is slightly
unnatural because we want the irrelevant parts, in this case the verb phrases,
to be as short as possible. The use of **ebbs** and **flows** rather than longer,
albeit more natural, expressions corresponds to the use of "cop-out triangles"
in phrase markers.) We take (41) to be something like:

(42)   **The degree of the totality of ebbing water is greater than the**
        degree of the totality of flowing mud.

We introduce a symbol **tot** to mean "the degree of the totality of." **tot** is
in category $\langle \langle 0, 1 \rangle, \langle 0, 1, 1 \rangle, \langle 0, 1 \rangle \rangle$, and:

(3.2) $V(\textbf{tot})$ is the function ζ such that for $\omega \in \mathbf{D}_{\langle 0, 1, 1 \rangle}$ and $\omega' \in \mathbf{D}_{\langle 0, 1 \rangle}$
         and $w \in \mathbf{W}$: $w \in \zeta(\omega, \omega')(a)$ iff there is a b such that $w \in \omega'(b)$
         and $w \in \omega(b, a)$, and $a = \langle u, > \rangle$ (for some $u \in \mathscr{F}(>)$, for some
         $>$), and for any c and d such that $w \in \omega'(d)$ and $w \in \omega(d, c)$,
         $c = \langle v, > \rangle$ for some v and either $u = v$ or $u > v$.

What $V(\textbf{tot})$ means is that a is the degree of the greatest part of whatever
satisfies both ω and ω' in w. So if $V(\textbf{water}) = \omega$ and $V(\textbf{ebbs}) = \omega'$, then:

(43) $V^+(\langle \textbf{tot}, \textbf{water}, \textbf{ebbs} \rangle)$

is the a such that $a = \langle u, > \rangle$, where $>$ is the greater than relation with
respect to volume, and any amount of ebbing water not equal to u is less
in volume than u (which means that u is the volume of the totality of ebbing
water).

We can now formalize (41) as:

(44) $\langle \langle \textbf{tot}, \textbf{water}, \textbf{ebbs} \rangle, \textbf{er than}, \langle \textbf{tot}, \textbf{mud}, \textbf{flows} \rangle \rangle$

We assume here that the $>$ that will form part of the meaning of **mud** is
the same $>$ as the one that forms part of the meaning of **water**, viz., "greater
than" ranging over volumes. This means that the **er than** of (44) is the very
same symbol as the one introduced for adjectives, whose semantics is
captured by (2.3).

We shall later examine in more detail just how the surface sentence in (41) might be obtained from (44). At present we observe that **much** will be brought in as a signal of a degree and **er much** will be realized as *more*. **tot water** and **tot mud** will be realized as *water* and *mud*, respectively. [The common surface realization of the two distinct expressions, **water** and **tot water**, perhaps explains why Quine (1960, pp. 97–100) was led to treat mass terms as ambiguous, a course followed also by Cresswell (1973, p. 139f)].[14]

In the sentence:

(45)   **Much water ebbs.**

much looks as though it is a determiner like **the** or **a** and, indeed, can be so treated if we are prepared to give it a semantics that divorces it from its other uses (cf. (Wheeler, 1972, pp. 326–329)). What seems more plausible is that we have here a case analogous to the positive in adjectives. **pos** has a null surface realization but means something like "more than average." Here we need a symbol (again with null realization) with a somewhat analogous meaning, something like "a high degree of." We shall use the symbol **deg** in category $\langle 0, \langle 0, 1, 1 \rangle, \langle 0, 1 \rangle \rangle$:

(3.3) $V(\textbf{deg})$ is the function ζ such that for $\omega \in \textbf{D}_{\langle 0, 1, 1 \rangle}$ and $\omega' \in \textbf{D}_{\langle 0, 1 \rangle}$ and $w \in \textbf{W}$, $w \in \zeta(\omega, \omega')$ as follows: Suppose that there is a unique a such that; $w \in \omega'(a)$ and there is some b such that $w \in \omega(a, b)$, and $b = \langle u, > \rangle$, and for any c and d such that $w \in \omega'(c)$ and $w \in \omega(c, d)$, where $d = \langle v, > \rangle$, $u > v$. In such a case $w \in \zeta(\omega, \omega')$ iff u is considerably toward the top of $\mathscr{F}(>)$ when restricted to $\{u : (\exists c)(\exists d)(w \in \omega'(c)$ and $w \in \omega(c, d)$ and $d = \langle u, > \rangle)\}$.

---

[14] In addition, mass nouns have been discussed by Moravcsik (1973), Parsons (1970), Pelletier (1974), and by other authors. The only fact about them that I want to insist on is that they are subject to "more" and "less" and that their underlying semantics involves the notion of a degree. The following few points will, I hope, make clear my attitudes toward some things these and other authors have said.

1. The same surface word can have both a mass and a count sense. It seems to me that what we have here are distinct symbols, though with a very close semantics.
2. The mass/count distinction has no connection with the abstract/concrete distinction. Thus we can have *more water, more virtue, a man, a mistake*.
3. I do not take a logicogrammatical analysis of the syntax and semantics of mass terms to require an analysis of, e.g., what it is to be a volume of water. (Obviously I do not think such an analysis philosophically unimportant, only unnecessary for my present task.) In particular, I have made no statement on whether there can be a volume of water that is not an individual something or collection of individual somethings.

What all this means is that the sentence:

(46) $\langle$**deg, water, ebbs**$\rangle$

will be true iff the total volume of ebbing water is considerably toward the top end of the greater than scale when this scale is restricted to volumes of water in w. Although **deg** has a null realization, the surface degree marker *much* frequently masquerades, as in (45), as the realization of **deg**. [*Much* does not appear in front of adjectives, vide (Bresnan, 1973, p. 278)]. We can, however, say simply:

(47)   **Water ebbs.**

There is in English a species of construction that forms a (complex) count noun out of a mass noun. This construction can be illustrated by the phrase:

(48)   **drop of water**[15]

Drop will be a count noun (and so is in category $\langle 0, 1 \rangle$):

(3.4) $V($**drop**$)$ is the function ω such that for any $a \in \mathbf{D}_1$ and $w \in \mathbf{W}$, $w \in \omega(a)$ iff a is in the form of a drop in w.

Prepositions are difficult words for a λ-categorial language. Perhaps they should not be in the λ-deep structure at all. If they are, we seem to need many different ones with an identical surface realization. This particular **of** will be in category $\langle\langle 0, 1 \rangle, \langle 0, 1 \rangle, \langle 0, 1, 1 \rangle\rangle$:

(3.5) $V($**of**$)$ is the function ζ such that where $\omega \in \mathbf{D}_{\langle 0, 1 \rangle}$ and $\omega' \in \mathbf{D}_{\langle 0, 1, 1 \rangle}$ and $a \in \mathbf{D}_1$ and $w \in \mathbf{W}$, $w \in \zeta(\omega, \omega')(a)$ iff there is some b such that $w \in \omega'(a, b)$ and $w \in \omega(a)$.

This means that $\langle$**drop, of, water**$\rangle$ has the following semantics: $w \in V^+(\langle$**drop, of, water**$\rangle)(a)$ iff $w \in \zeta(\omega, \omega')(a)$, where $V($**of**$) = \zeta$, $V($**drop**$) = \omega$ and $V($**water**$) = \omega'$. By (3.1), (3.4), and (3.5), this will be so iff a is in the form of a drop in w and there is some degree b such that $b = \langle u, > \rangle$ and u is a volume and a is water in w with volume u.

We now want to show that pluralization has a semantic effect that makes plurals behave like mass nouns. In particular, the semantic effect of pluralization is to turn a common count noun like **man** into a two-place predicate that means something like:

(49) x **is a** y**-membered set of men**

---

[15] This point was brought to my attention by G. D. Kennedy, who tells me that John Robert Ross called something like these "measure phrases" in a lecture at UCLA.

This predicate involves a comparison scale that consists of the positive integers under their standard ordering. The collectivizing use of the plural enables us to unify a large number of apparently semantically disparate phenomena in a way that accords neatly with their syntactically similar behavior.[16] Consider:

(50)   **Arabella is more beautiful than Tom is clever.**

(51)   **More water ebbs than mud flows.**

(52)   **More men walk than birds fly.**

It is my belief that in all these sentences **more** has a single meaning, and that the clue to understanding how it works in (52) lies in the following semantics for pluralization of count nouns:

pl is in category $\langle\langle 0, 1, 1\rangle, \langle 0, 1\rangle\rangle$ and has the following semantics:

(3.6) $V(\mathbf{pl})$ is the function ζ such that, for $\omega \in \mathbf{D}_{\langle 0, 1\rangle}$, $a, b \in \mathbf{D}_1$, and $w \in \mathbf{W}$: $w \in \zeta(\omega)(a, b)$ iff $a = \{c : w \in \omega(c)\}$ (i.e., a is the set of all c such that $w \in \omega(c)$), and $b = \langle u, >\rangle$, where $>$ is the standard greater than ordering of the natural numbers and u is the number of members of a.

This means that $\langle \mathbf{pl}, \mathbf{man}\rangle$ indeed means something like (49).[17]

---

[16] Much of what follows replaces the analysis offered by Cresswell (1973, pp. 161–165). It obviously has links with the observations in J. McCawley (1968, pp. 140–155, 161–169), though I have nothing to say here on the "respectively" phenomenon. There are also many similarities with the analysis of plurals offered in Bartsch (1973).

[17] Notice that the analysis of **a drop of water** given earlier will carry over to **a group of men**. Since we have to account anyway for sentences like:

(i)   **The team walked to Cleveland.**

we must suppose that verbs can predicate walking of sets. The plural ending in verbs seems to be sensitive only to **pl**; thus mass nouns and singular count nouns appear on the surface to be more similar than mass nouns and plurals. Probably the verb is sensitive to **pl** because it signals a set whose members can be counted. Where the subject term denotes a set but is not made up using the **pl** morpheme, English seems to be unable to make up its mind, and there is a wide variety of dialectal variation. Thus we can get both:

(ii)   **the team walk**

and

(iii)   **the team walks**

[Some discussion of this occurs in (Perlmutter (1972).]

Certain mass nouns such as *furniture* also seem to denote sets. *Furniture* takes the singular because **pl** is not involved in its underlying representation. But its semantic equivalent *pieces of furniture* takes the plural because **pl** is involved in *pieces*.

The plural can appear on the surface without a determiner. It is not that, as suggested in Cresswell, (1973, p. 191), **pl** is itself a determiner; it is, rather, that the surface sentence *Men run* has as its λ-deep structure:

(53) $\langle$**deg**, $\langle$**pl**, **man**$\rangle$, **run**$\rangle$

Example (53) will (by the semantics for **deg**) be true in w iff the total number of running men in w is considerably toward the top end of the "numerically greater than" scale when restricted to the class of men in w. Where **much** is allowed to appear, it will be realized, in the presence of **pl**, as *many*.

Numerical comparisons work in the following way. Example (52) is:

(54) $\langle\langle$**tot**, $\langle$**pl**, **man**$\rangle$, **walk**$\rangle$, **er than**, $\langle$**tot**, $\langle$**pl**, **bird**$\rangle$, **fly**$\rangle\rangle$

Literally:

(55)   **The degree of the totality of walking men is greater than the degree of the totality of flying birds.**

The collectivizing function of tne plural can explain the difference between:

(56)   **All men walk.**

and:

(57)   **Every man walks.**

and between:

(58)   **Some men walk.**

and:

(59)   **A man walks.**

It has usually been supposed that the plural is without semantic effect in sentences like this. In fact I have taken this view myself (Cresswell, 1973, p. 191). Some of the syntactic differences have been noticed by J. McCawley (1968) and others, but they have not been given a possible-worlds analysis.

The structure that underlies (56) would be something like:

(60) $\langle$**all**, $\langle$**pl**, **man**$\rangle$, **walk**$\rangle$

All would be in category $\langle 0, \langle 0, 1, 1\rangle, \langle 0, 1\rangle\rangle$ and would have the following semantics:

(3.7) $V($**all**$)$ is the function ζ such that if $\omega \in \mathbf{D}_{\langle 0, 1, 1\rangle}$ and $\omega' \in \mathbf{D}_{\langle 0, 1\rangle}$, then for any $w \in \mathbf{W}$: $w \in \zeta(\omega, \omega')$ iff there is an a and a b such that $w \in \omega(a, b)$, and for any such a, $w \in \omega'(a)$.

This semantics makes no reference to pluralization, and **all**, as so defined, will work equally well for mass nouns; thus we can form:

(61)   ⟨**all, water, ebbs**⟩

This is why **all** is different from **every**. **Every** in Cresswell (1973, p. 136) is in category $\langle 0, \langle 0, 1 \rangle, \langle 0, 1 \rangle \rangle$ with the following semantics:

(3.8) V(**every**) is the function ζ such that for ω and $\omega' \in \mathbf{D}_{\langle 0, 1 \rangle}$: $w \in \zeta(\omega, \omega')$ iff for every a such that $w \in \omega(a)$, $w \in \omega'(a)$.

This shows why (56) and (57) are synonymous, though their meanings are obtained differently. A similar distinction obtains between (58) and (59).[18]

4. THE METAPHYSICAL REALITY OF DEGREES OF COMPARISON

The key semantic notion of our logicolinguistic analysis is the concept of a degree of comparison, in terms of a pair $\langle u, > \rangle$, where $>$ is a relation and $u \in \mathcal{F}(>)$. The kinds of degrees that have cropped up in our examples have been things like spatial distances, volumes, etc. In other words, we have chosen relatively unproblematic ones. But what if we say:

(62)   **Arabella is more beautiful than Clarissa.**

(63)   **Bill is more manly than Tom.**

[18] This explains the deviance of:

(i)   *****Some man runs.**

except in logician's English. In Cresswell (1973, p. 191) it was assumed that **some** with the plural meant "at least two." That now seems to me to be wrong. As far as I can see, **some men run** simply means "at least one man runs." The beauty of the semantics presented in this study is that it allows one to see how this can be so. This semantics ought also to be able to deal naturally with sentences like:

(ii)   **The apostles are twelve.**

and the notorious example (Russell's, I believe) of an invalid inference:

(iii)   **Men are numerous.**
Socrates is a man.
Socrates is numerous.

It may, however, be that (3.7) as it stands needs amending to take care of the "collective" flavor of **all**.

Must we postulate the kalon as a degree of beauty or the andron as a degree of manliness? Degrees of beauty may be all right for the purposes of illustration but may seem objectionable in hard-core metaphysics. The first task of this section is to show that the possible-worlds-cum-set-theoretical framework on which our whole semantics is based is rich enough to support all the entities we need for degrees of comparison.

We take as basic data that we can and do make comparisons, i.e., that comparative sentences can be true or false; further, that we have the ability to make counterfactual comparisons. That is to say, our competence in this area is not limited to judgments involving how things actually are but can encompass judgments about how things might be. This means that we can make other-world and even trans-world comparisons.

It is not, in my opinion, the business of logic or linguistics (at least syntax) to explain how it is that we make the comparisons we do make or what the principles are by which we make them. But it is the business of linguistics, and of logic when used in the service of linguistics, to tell us how we put the comparisons we make into the linguistic forms into which we put them.

Consider adjectival comparisons. These can be reduced to sentences of the form:

(64)   x **is more** F **than** y **is** G

This schema generates a relation ϕ between two things. In possible-worlds semantics the things that are compared are in particular possible worlds. E.g., x may be more beautiful than y in w but not in w'; or x in w may be more beautiful than y in w'. So, strictly, the terms of the relation should be pairs consisting of a thing and a world. Let a, b, c, etc. denote such pairs, and let ϕ denote the relation that corresponds to some particular comparison. ϕ determines the following equivalence relation:

(4.1) $a \approx b$ iff for all c, $\phi(a, c)$ iff $\phi(b, c)$ and $\phi(c, a)$ iff $\phi(c, b)$.

Here $\approx$ is obviously an equivalence relation. We can now define the relation $>_\phi$ between degrees based on ϕ. $\mathscr{F}(>_\phi)$ is the set of all the ϕ-equivalence classes. I.e., $u \in \mathscr{F}(>_\phi)$ iff, for some $a \in \mathscr{F}(\phi)$, $u = \{b : b \approx a\}$. In this case we can refer to u as $\bar{a}$.

(4.2) $\bar{a} >_\phi \bar{b}$ iff $\phi(a, b)$

Definition (4.2) is a consistent definition. For suppose that $a \approx c$ and $b \approx c$ and $b \approx d$. Since $\bar{a} = \bar{c}$ and $\bar{b} = \bar{d}$, we must show that $\phi(a, b)$ iff $\phi(c, d)$:

Suppose that $\phi(a, b)$. Then since $a \approx c$, $\phi(c, b)$, and since $b \approx d$, $\phi(c, d)$. Thus if $\phi(a, b)$, then $\phi(c, d)$. The converse is proved analogously.

What all this shows is that to the extent to which we do make comparisons, i.e., to the extent to which there is a body of data to be accounted for, then to that extent the formal theory can be accounted for in the manner of this study.

We have already noted how the method will also account correctly for the semantic deviance of many grammatically well-formed comparative sentences, e.g.:

(65)   ***Bill is taller than Arabella is beautiful.**

On the account given in the present paper this sentence is anomalous because Bill's tallness will be represented on a different scale from Arabella's beauty. We may, if we choose, classify comparison scales using feature theory, as Hale (1970) does, but we must be clear that this is not, strictly, involved in the syntax of comparative sentences.

We do occasionally make comparisons of a prima facie anomalous sort. We sometimes say things like:

(66)   **I am older than you are wise.**

What I would like to suggest here is that in the particular context of this sentence the speaker is using these words AS IF their meanings produced a scale common to age and wisdom. Exactly how this should be represented I do not know, but I am sure that its difficulties arise because the words are not being used literally, and that the difficulties are not solely ones that are tied to the idea of comparison. In some cases what is involved seems to be a sort of order-preserving mapping from one scale to another. This mapping represents the "as if."

A different case arises when the same word alludes to different scales when it modifies different nouns (Hale, 1970, p. 38). Thus although one can say:

(67)   **The meeting was long.**

and:

(68)   **The road is long.**

One cannot say:

(69)   ***The meeting was longer than the road.**

And the reason is that we have in the one case a time scale and in the other a spatial scale. The rule for **long** would be:

(4.3) $V(\textbf{long})$ is the function ζ such that where $\omega \in \textbf{D}_{\langle 0,\, 1\rangle}$, a, $b \in \textbf{D}_1$, and $w \in \textbf{W}$: $w \in \zeta(\omega)(a, b)$ iff $w \in \omega(a)$ and there is some $\langle u, > \rangle$ such that $b = \langle u, > \rangle$ and either (a) a is a physical object and $>$ is the greater than relation of spatial distances and $u \in \mathscr{F}(>)$ and u is the distance between a's extremities, or (b) a is an event and $>$ is the "greater than" of temporal distances and $u \in \mathscr{F}(>)$ and u is the temporal distance between the beginning and end of a.

This explains the semantic anomaly of (69).

Something now on measurability. It seems clear that we can make comparisons without having units of measurement. I hope it is equally clear that nothing in the analysis so far presented has implied that degrees of comparison necessitate units of measurement. A careful look at the metaphysical analysis given at the beginning of this section should be enough to show this. Nevertheless our examples have been taken mainly from cases (the spatial and temporal distances) in which there ARE units of measurement. Or, rather, they have been taken from relations on which units of measurement can be imposed, whether or not the language has chosen to do so. Where a relation $>$ has a natural metric,[19] say d, we can define a new relation $>_d \subseteq \mathscr{F}(>) \times \mathscr{F}(>)$ such that $\langle u_1, u_2 \rangle >_d \langle v_1, v_2 \rangle$ iff $d(u_1, u_2)$ is greater than $d(v_1, v_2)$ by the standard ordering of the real numbers. It is not at all clear how to specify precisely when a relation has a natural metric and just what the metric is, but in many cases we can do so. We can say, e.g., that x is twice as tall as y or twice as large, though when it comes to "twice as beautiful" things are less clear.

The analysis of comparatives and quantities presented in this study has been set in a framework based on possible worlds. This framework has been adopted by Montague, Lewis, Stalnaker, Thomason, myself, and others for the purposes of formal semantics, for what we believe to be adequate reasons. Many problems in formal semantics, however, can be solved independently of the need for possible worlds, and this applies to most, perhaps all, of the analysis so far in this work. Analyses of comparatives have been given by Wallace (1972) and Wheeler (1972). Much of what they have written has affinities with what has been said here, although they have not attempted to tackle the range of linguistic phenomena I have discussed.

One of the strongest reasons for using a possible-worlds approach is so that combinations that involve modality can be accommodated. A typical

---

[19] A METRIC on a set X (Mansfield, 1973, p. 82) is a function from $X \times X$ into the real numbers satisfying certain conditions that ensure that $d(x, y)$ for x and $y \in X$ can be interpreted as the distance between x and y. We need also to ensure that d "respects" $<$; e.g., where $u_1 < u_2$ and $u_2 < u_3$, $d(u_1, u_2)$ is not greater than $d(u_1, u_3)$.

example is a sentence like:

(70)   **If Bill had been a smoker he would be shorter than he is.**

For simplicity I shall adopt the Stalnaker analysis of this conditional[20] and assume that $\alpha \,\Box\!\!\rightarrow \beta$ is to be true in a world w iff in the nearest world to w in which α is true β is true also. Accepting this, we can represent (70) as:

(71) $\langle\langle\lambda, x, \langle\langle\textbf{Bill, smokes}\rangle, \Box\!\!\rightarrow, \langle\textbf{Bill}, \langle\textbf{short, man}\rangle, x\rangle\rangle\rangle$,   **er than**, $\langle\lambda, x, \langle\textbf{Bill}, \langle\textbf{short, man}\rangle, x\rangle\rangle\rangle$[21]

By principles that should by now be clear:

(72) $V^+(\langle\lambda, x, \langle\textbf{Bill}, \langle\textbf{short, man}\rangle, x\rangle\rangle)$

is the function $\omega \in \mathbf{D}_{\langle 0, 1\rangle}$ such that for $a \in \mathbf{D}_1$ and $w \in \mathbf{W}$, $w \in \omega(a)$ iff Bill is a man in w and $a = \langle u, <\rangle$, where $<$ is the "less than" relation for spatial distances and u is Bill's height in w.

The left term is a little more complex and brings out how other worlds come into the picture:

(73) $V^+(\langle\lambda, x, \langle\langle\textbf{Bill, smokes}\rangle, \Box\!\!\rightarrow,\ \langle\textbf{Bill}, \langle\textbf{short, man}\rangle, x\rangle\rangle\rangle)$

is the function $\omega' \in \mathbf{D}_{\langle 0, 1\rangle}$ such that for any $b \in \mathbf{D}_1$ and $w \in \mathbf{W}$: $w \in \omega'(b)$ if in the nearest world w' to w such that $w' \in V^+(\langle\textbf{Bill, smokes}\rangle)$ (and this of course means the nearest world to w in which Bill smokes), $w' \in \omega(a)$ (where ω is as in (72)), and this means that in w' Bill is a man and $b = \langle v, <\rangle$ and v is Bill's height in w'.

When we combine these by (2.3), we find that $w \in V^+(71)$ iff, where $a = \langle u, <\rangle$ and $b = \langle v, <\rangle$, $v < u$.

But u is Bill's height in w, while v is Bill's height in the nearest world to w in which he smokes. So (71) will be true in w iff in the nearest world to w in

---

[20] This conditional appears in various guises in work by Åqvist (1973) and Lewis (1973) as well as Stalnaker (1968) and Stalnaker and Thomason (1970). For illustrative purposes Stalnaker's version, which is the simplest, will suffice. The symbol $\Box\!\!\rightarrow$ is actually due to Lewis (1973). Stalnaker uses $>$, which would obviously lead to confusion in this work.

[21] If one wants an English sentence that gets close to this formula, the following might do:

(i)   **If Bill were to smoke then Bill would be a short man more than Bill is a short man.**

(This sentence is slightly uncouth, but not really bad, I think.) Notice that the **er than** is outside the scope of $\Box\!\!\rightarrow$. I have deliberately avoided an example involving propositional attitudes, such as:

(ii)   **Bill thinks that he is taller than he is** (Ross, 1970, p. 127).

for the reasons mentioned in footnote 2.

which Bill smokes his height is less than his height in *w*—which is precisely what (70) says (assuming that □→ does capture the conditional properly).

5. THE SYNTAX OF COMPARATIVES

So far the analysis has been entirely semantic, and indeed semantics is the burden of my song; but a little needs to be said about how the λ-deep structures are related to the ordinary surface sentences. There are two ways one can go here, and I shall say a little about each. One is to attach the λ-deep structures to the bottom end of a syntactic study, and as an example of this I shall look at how the formulas I have presented might hook onto the underlying representations in Bresnan (1973). The other approach is to proceed, as did Cresswell (1973), directly to the surface with a formula that becomes a sentence of English when certain parts are knocked out. The first approach has the advantage of showing how possible-worlds semantics can fit in with transformational grammar; the second has the advantage of indicating the likelihood that some principles can be found that generate the acceptable structures, without any commitment to the form these principles might take.

The kind of underlying structure Bresnan proposes can be exhibited by the following tree (it is actually made up by using (245) and (251) of Bresnan (1973, p. 318f)):

5.1

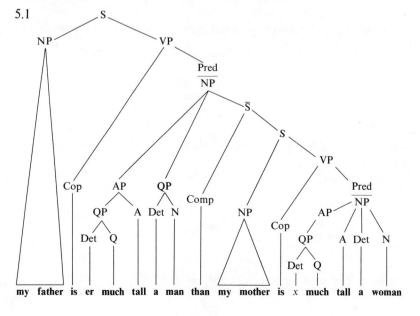

my father is er much tall a man than my mother is *x* much tall a woman

My λ-deep structure when represented as a tree would have to be something like:

5.2

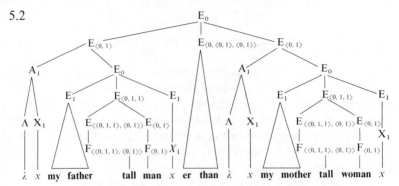

(I trust that the connection between (5.2) and (1.1)–(1.3) is reasonably clear.)

I shall not attempt a detailed formulation of a set of transformations that get us from (5.2) to (5.1) but shall simply say enough to make their possibility plausible. We need principles of two kinds. One set of principles associates the labels of nodes in (5.2) with those in (5.1). Some are obvious, e.g., E_0 corresponds to S. The other principles move elements and insert elements. If we look at the "shapes" of (5.1) and (5.2), and forget about the labels, we see that certain things have to happen.

1. **much** should be inserted immediately after each x with something like the rule:

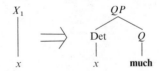

(Suitable restrictions must of course be placed on the environment within which this rule applies.)

2. The subtrees:

must be deleted and the tree "pruned" as a result.

3. In the subtrees in (5.2) ending in [**my father tall man** x] and [**my mother tall woman** x], the phrases [**my father**] and [**my mother**] must be raised to become the subjects of their respective clauses.[22]

4. In some manner the predicates [**tall man** x **much**] and [**tall woman** x **much**] must be turned into [**is** x **much tall a man**] and [**is** x **much tall a woman**]. I shall not make any suggestions about this, since it raises the whole question of the logical priority of the attributive or predicative use of adjectives.[23]

5. **er** must move to replace the x in the leftmost x **much**.

6. The phrase **my father** must be raised so that it becomes the subject of the whole sentence.

As far as I am aware, all these operations are legitimate kinds of transformations, though I have no detailed syntactic arguments for them. If one desired to maintain Bresnan's underlying structures as the deep syntactical level, one would have to postulate a global derivational constraint (see Lakoff, 1971, p. 234) to say that all derivations of comparatives must pass through that level.

The other way of arguing for the validity of a semantic analysis is this: If we can give apparently plausible possible-world semantics for symbols of a λ-categorial language and can then show that a large range of English sentences can be represented as what remains when λ's and variables are deleted and when certain combinations (e.g., **er much**) are realized as single words (e.g., *more*),[24] and if this can be done in such a way that the truth conditions of the λ-categorial sentence correspond with the truth conditions of the original surface sentence, then this is evidence for the correctness of our analysis. It is hard to compare an argument of this kind with the arguments one usually finds in linguistics, because even linguists who advocate a semantic base in formal logic seem to have little to offer on the nature of the entities they are postulating. Notice that a base language that uses possible-worlds semantics can be quite close to the surface because the

---

[22] In (5.2) **my father** is treated as a name, in category 1. It should probably be analyzed as a nominal. And in any case indefinite phrases like **someone** or **many lovers of wisdom** will have to be nominals. In such a case "quantifier lowering" rules of the kind discussed by Lakoff (1971, p. 238f) may have to be brought into play.

[23] Since I adopt an analysis of adjectives that takes their attributive use as prior to their predicative use, the way I would derive the former phrases from the latter would be a little different from the way they would be derived by someone who thinks the predicative use is prior (as I suspect Bresnan does). It might be that the structure that underlies (5.1) is not (5.2) but something more like (74) or (75). Such a structure would be equivalent to (5.2) by λ-conversion, given appropriate rules for **is** and **a** (Cresswell, 1973, pp. 136, 182).

[24] In Cresswell (1973, p. 210) this is done by what is called an "amalgamation function."

detailed semantic analysis can be expressed in a metalinguistic statement
of the meaning of the symbol.

What I shall do is turn (16), (41), and (52) into formulas that become
English sentences when certain changes are made. This section is intended
primarily for readers of Cresswell (1973), and the examples all make use
of λ-conversion. As noted briefly there (p. 224), principles of λ-conversion
look very like principles that underlie many transformations.[25]

In these sentences we shall split **er than** up into its two parts and suppose
that **than** is the operator that carries the semantic weight. **than** is to be in
category $\langle 0, \langle 0, 1 \rangle, \langle 0, 1 \rangle \rangle$, whose semantics satisfies (2.3), while **er** is a
symbol whose function is simply to mark one of the terms of the comparative.
We shall also have **much** sometimes occurring in the same role.

(74) $\langle \langle \lambda, x_1, \langle \textbf{Bill, is, } x_1 \rangle \rangle, \langle \lambda, x_{\langle 0, 1 \rangle}, \langle \langle \lambda, y_1, \langle \lambda, z_1, \langle \textbf{a}, \langle \lambda, y_1,$
        $\langle \langle \langle \textbf{tall, er} \rangle, \textbf{man} \rangle, y_1, z_1 \rangle \rangle, x_{\langle 0, 1 \rangle} \rangle \rangle \rangle, \langle \lambda, x_{\langle \langle 0, 1 \rangle, 1 \rangle}, \langle \langle x_{\langle \langle 0, 1 \rangle, 1 \rangle},$
        $x_1 \rangle, \textbf{than}, \langle x_{\langle \langle 0, 1 \rangle, 1 \rangle}, \textbf{Tom} \rangle \rangle \rangle \rangle \rangle \rangle$

In this example **er** is of category $\langle \langle 0, 1, 1 \rangle, \langle 0, 1, 1 \rangle \rangle$. It is in fact an identity
operator in that category, in that its value is a function ζ such that $\zeta(\omega) = \omega$. (We have to say "an" identity operator, since it will be a partial function
and there could be different ones simply because they had different domains.)
Principles of λ-conversion make this equivalent to:

(75) $\langle \langle \lambda, y_1, \langle \textbf{a}, \langle \lambda, x_1, \langle \langle \langle \textbf{tall, er} \rangle, \textbf{man} \rangle, x_1, y_1 \rangle \rangle, \langle \lambda, x_1, \langle \textbf{Bill},$
        $\textbf{is, } x_1 \rangle \rangle \rangle \rangle, \textbf{than}$ $\langle \lambda, y_1 \langle \langle \langle \textbf{tall, er} \rangle, \textbf{man} \rangle, \textbf{Tom}, y_1 \rangle \rangle \rangle$

Our second example involves mass nouns (**er** is, as before, in category
$\langle \langle 0, 1, 1 \rangle, \langle 0, 1, 1 \rangle \rangle$, and so is **much**; **much** is also an identity function):

(76) $\langle \langle \textbf{tot}, \langle \textbf{much}, \langle \textbf{er, water} \rangle \rangle, \textbf{ebbs} \rangle, \textbf{than}, \langle \textbf{tot, mud, flows} \rangle \rangle$

tot has a null realization, and **much er** is realized as 'more'.

Our third and final example concerns pluralization:

(77) $\langle \langle \textbf{tot}, \langle \textbf{much}, \langle \textbf{er}, \langle \textbf{pl, man} \rangle \rangle \rangle, \textbf{walk} \rangle, \textbf{than}, \langle \textbf{tot}, \langle \textbf{pl, bird} \rangle,$
        $\textbf{fly} \rangle \rangle$

Since **tot** has a null realization, with **much er** *as more* and **pl man** as *men*
and **pl bird** as 'birds' we get the right result.

The task of obtaining these forms for other cases will be tedious but
possible. The examples will, I hope, illustrate both those claims.

---

[25] The principles of λ-conversion allow us to identify (i.e., delete repetitions of) symbols and
permute (i.e., change the order of) symbols. Indeed they look very like the operations licensed by
the elementary transformations. (See Kimball, 1973, pp. 41–43.)

6. ODDS AND ENDS

This section makes a few relatively unsystematic remarks on some of the topics that we have not adequately dealt with.

The first topic is adverbs. Since I regard the attributive use of adjectives as primary, it ought to be clear that most of what has been said will carry over to adverbs. The reason I have not tackled them explicitly is that I am uncertain about their precise semantic analysis. This uncertainty is reflected in the analysis of adverbs that I have presented in Cresswell (1974) (see also Thomason and Stalnaker, 1968), but it is independent of the analysis of degree and quantity adopted in this paper. One use of adverbs is, however, important, and that is adverbs used to modify adjectives, e.g., those called INTENSIFIERS.[26]

Take **considerably**. The semantics of **considerably** should entail that a phrase like ⟨⟨**considerably, tall**⟩, **man**⟩ means a man whose degree of tallness is considerably toward the top end of the degrees-of-tallness scale when this scale is restricted to tallnesses of men. This semantics can be formalized without too great difficulty. The slight problem arises when we intensify comparatives.

For we can say:

(78)   **Bill is considerably taller than Arabella.**

On the semantics given for **er than**, it is not possible to have degrees of "taller-than-ness." In this particular case, given the relation $>$ of *taller than*, there is a very natural metric d that goes with it. Given this metric, we can define a new relation $>$ among degrees of "taller-than-ness" in the way described in Section 4. But it is not clear to me what to do when there is no natural metric. I do not know whether to be worried by this because I am not sure whether we can compare comparatives in the absence of a natural metric.[27]

Where we can compare comparatives we can frequently also put definite measurements on, as with:

(79)   **Bill is a foot taller than Arabella.**

The second topic concerns cases where verb phrases look as though they

---

[26] Wheeler (1972, pp. 325–330) has some interesting things to say about modifiers of adjectives. For example, he takes **very tall man** to mean "tall by comparison with the set of tall men" (**tall man** of course means "tall by comparison with the set of men", so that " 'very' is an instruction to iterate the attributive which follows it [p. 325]."

[27] There is certainly no syntactic objection to the iteration of modifiers of this kind. Bresnan (1973, pp. 289–299) has quite a long section on it.

are subject to comparative constructions, as in:

(80)   **Bill runs more than Arabella swims.**

My inclination with these cases is to say that **more** here really means something like "more often" and is therefore a case of adverbial comparison. However, cases like **weighs more** (Moravcsik, 1973, p. 264) are not so easy, and I recognize that I have not treated these cases in detail.

Finally a slight reservation about the view that *much* is a word without semantic effect at the λ-deep level whose sole function is to be a surface indication of the presence of a degree of comparison. It may be that this is overly simple. Consider, e.g., the difference between:

(81)   **Drink this water.**

and:

(82)   **Drink this much water.**

One possibility is to say that mass nouns are, after all, of category $\langle 0, 1 \rangle$ and do not have a degree of comparison built into them. Thus **water** would mean simply:

(83)   *x* **is an amount of water**

The function of the word **much** would then be to produce the complex expression:

(84) $\langle$**much, water**$\rangle$

and it would be THIS expression that would mean:

(85)   *x* **is an amount of water of degree** *y*

This would explain why *much* is required before mass nouns but not before adjectives. For adjectives, on my account, already have a degree of comparison as part of their meaning. It might also explain why we can say things like:

(86)   **Bill is this much of a man.**[28]

(see Bresnan, 1973, p. 282; Doherty and Schwartz, 1967, p. 924).

My main reason for hesitation at this point is that I find it difficult to give a clear semantics for **much**. What **much** has to do is to discover the appropriate degree of comparison for a predicate, given merely that we know

---

[28] I think the **of** in **much of a man** is a different **of** from the **of** in **a drop of water**, but I am not sure what kind of semantics should be given for it.

what, in each world, satisfies that predicate. For this reason I feel able to do no more than indicate it as a line for further study in the semantics of mass nouns.

Victoria University of Wellington

REFERENCES

Åqvist, L. E. G. son. Modal logic with subjunctive conditionals and dispositional predicates. *Journal of Philosophical Logic*, 1973, **2**, 1–76.
Bar Hillel, Y. Out of the pragmatic wastebasket. *Linguistic Inquiry*, 1971, **2**, 401–406.
Bartsch, Renate, The semantics and syntax of number and numbers. In J. P. Kimball (Ed.), *Syntax and Semantics* Vol. 2, New York: Seminar Press, 1973. Pp. 51–93.
Borowski, E. J. On the extent of John's height. *Foundations of Language*, 1973, **10**, 419–422.
Bresnan, J. W. Syntax of the comparative clause construction in English. *Linguistic Inquiry*, 1973, **4**, 275–343.
Cresswell, M. J. *Logics and Languages*. London: Methuen, 1973.
Cresswell, M. J. Adverbs and events. *Synthese*, 1974, **28**, 455–481.
Cresswell, M. J. Hyperintensional logic. (forthcoming in *Studia Logica*).
Doherty, P. C. and Schwartz, A. The syntax of the compared adjective in English. *Language* 1967, **43**, 903–936.
Green, G. M. More X than not X. *Linguistic Inquiry*, 1970, **1**, 126–127.
Hale, A. Conditions on English comparative clause pairings. ed. R. A. Jacobs and P. S. Rosenbaum (Eds.), *Readings in English Transformational Grammar* Waltham, Massachusetts: Ginn, 1970. Pp. 30–55.
Householder, F. W. On arguments from asterisks. *Foundations of Language*, 1973, **10**, 365–376.
Jennings, R. E. Punctuation and Truth Functionality Unpublished manuscript. (Mimeo)
Kimball, J. P. *The Formal Theory of Grammar*. Englewood Cliffs, New Jersey: Prentice-Hall, 1973.
Lakoff, G. On generative semantics. In D. D. Steinberg and L. A. Jakobovits (Eds.), *Semantics, An Interdisciplinary Reader in Philosophy, Linguistics and Psychology*. Cambridge: Cambridge Univ. Press, 1971. Pp. 232–296.
Lees, R. B. Grammatical analysis of the English comparative construction. *Word*, 1961, **17**, 171–185.
Lewis, D. K. General semantics. In D. Davidson and G. H. Harman (Eds.), *Semantics of Natural Language*. Dordrecht: Reidel, 1972. Pp. 169–218.
Lewis, D. K. *Counterfactuals*. Oxford: Basil Blackwell, 1973.
McCawley, J. D. The role of semantics in a grammar. In E. Bach and R. T. Harms (Eds.), *Universals in Linguistic Theory*, New York: Holt, 1968. Pp. 125–169.
Mansfield, M. J. *Introduction to Topology*. Princeton, New Jersey: Van Nostrand–Reinhold, 1963.
Montague, R. On the nature of certain philosophical entities. *The Monist*, 1969, **35**, 159–194.
Montague, R. Universal grammar. *Theoria*, 1970, **36**, 373–398.
Montague, R. The proper treatment of quantification in ordinary English. In K. J. J. Hintikka, J. M. E. Moravcsik, and P. Suppes (Eds.), *Approaches to Natural Language*, Dordrecht: Reidel, 1973. Pp. 221–242.
Moravcsik, J. M. E. Mass terms in English. In K. J. J. Hintikka, J. M. E. Moravcsik, and

P. Suppes (Eds.), *Approaches to Natural Language*, Dordrecht: Reidel, 1973. Pp. 263–285.

Parsons T. An analysis of mass and amount terms. *Foundations of Language*, 1970, **6**, 362–388.

Partee, B. H. The semantics of belief sentences. In K. J. J. Hintikka, J. M. E. Moravcsik and P. Suppes (Eds.), *Approaches to Natural Language*, Dordrecht: Reidel, 1973. Pp. 309–336.

Pelletier, F. J. Some proposals for the semantics of mass nouns. *Journal of Philosophical Logic*, 1974, **3**, 87–108.

Perlmutter, D. M. A note on syntactic and semantic number in English. *Linguistic Inquiry*, 1972, **3**, 243–246.

Prior, A. N. *Formal Logic*. Oxford: Oxford Univ. Press, 1955.

Prior, A. N. *Time and Modality*. Oxford: Oxford Univ. Press, 1957.

Quine, W. V. *Word and Object*. Cambridge, Massachusetts, M.I.T. Press, 1960.

Rennie, M. K. *Some Uses of Type Theory in the Analysis of Language*. Canberra: Department of Philosophy A.N.U. Monograph series No. 1, 1974.

Ross, J. R. and D. M. Perlmutter, A non-source for comparatives. *Linguistic Inquiry*, 1970, **1**, 127–128.

Seuren, P. A. M. The comparative. Kiefer and Ruwat (Eds.), *Generative Grammar in Europe*, Dordrecht: Reidel, 1973.

Smith, Carlotta S. A class of complex modifiers in English. *Language*, 1961, **37**, 342–365.

Stalnaker, R. C. A theory of conditionals. N. Rescher (Ed.), *Studies in Logical Theory*, Oxford: Blackwell, 1968. Pp. 98–112.

Stalnaker, R. C. Pragmatics. D. Davidson and G. H. Harman (Eds.), *Semantics of Natural Language*. Dordrecht: Reidel, 1972. Pp. 380–397.

Stalnaker, R. C. and Thomason, R. H. A semantic analysis of conditional logic. *Theoria*, 1970, **36**, 23–42.

Thomason, R. H. and Stalnaker, R. C. A semantic theory of adverbs. *Linguistic Inquiry*, 1973, **4**, 195–220.

Vennemann, T. Explanation in syntax. In J. P. Kimball (Ed.), *Syntax and Semantics*, Vol. 2. Seminar Press, New York, 1973. Pp. 1–50.

Wallace, J. Positive, comparative, superlative. *The Journal of Philosophy*, 1972, **69**, 773–782.

Weydt, H. On G. Lakoff, 'Instrumental adverbs and the concept of deep structure'. *Foundations of Language*, 1973, **10**, 569–578.

Wheeler, S. C. Attributives and their modifiers. *Noûs*, 1972, **6**, 310–334.

CAPTURING THE RUSSIAN ADJECTIVE

In Russian there are two forms of qualitative adjective—the long form and the short form.[1] The short form is used in predicate position only, while the long form may be used in predicate position or prenominally as an attributive adjective. The morphological process that relates the two forms is so transparently productive that nearly every qualitative adjective may be said to have both forms, although one or the other may rarely or never be used owing to semantic considerations. To form a short adjective from a long one, one drops the regular long adjectival endings—**yj** (masculine), **aja** (feminine), **oe** (neuter), and **ye** (plural)—and adds, instead, no ending for the masculine (but sometimes an epenthetic stem vowel), **a** for the feminine, **o** for the neuter, and **y** for the plural:

(1)	LONG FORM (LF)	SHORT FORM (SF)		
	Masc.	Masc.	Fem.	
	novyj	**nov**	**nova**	'new'
	umnyj	**umen**	**umna**	'intelligent'
	trudoljubivyj	**trudoljubiv**	**trudoljubiva**	'industrious'

Passive participles, which have the same morphological shape as long-form adjectives, also have short forms, which must always be used when the participle is in predicate position:

(2)   a. **Dver' byla zakrytaja* (LF).
       b. **Dver' byla zakryta** (SF).
         'The door was closed.'

Like the short-form adjectives, short-form passive participles may never be used attributively:

(3)   a. **Nel'zja perexodit' cherez zakrytuju** (LF) **dver'**.
       b. **Nel'zja perexodit' cherez zakryta* (SF) **dver'**.
         'One must not go through a closed door.'

Regular adjectives behave differently from the participles in that long-form adjectives may appear in predicate position. In this study I shall explore

---

[1] There is a class of adjectives in Russian called relational adjectives that have no short forms (for instance, *byvshij* 'former'). I will not discuss them here, although I think that the analysis accounts for them in that it predicts that they will have no short forms, since they have no absolute reading in the sense given in this study.

the conditions under which short- and long-form adjectives are appropriate (Sections 1 and 2) and present an analysis that treats adjectives as members of two distinct underlying categories. First (in Section 3), I shall outline my solution within a framework based on the fragment of English in Montague (1972); then (in Section 4), within an analogous transformational framework like that in Chomsky (1965). Finally (in Section 5), I will discuss briefly some problems encountered in systems in which Russian adjectives form a single underlying category and the long and short forms are transformationally related either to each other or to the underlying category. Section 6 is a summary.

1. THE LONG/SHORT DISTINCTION IN RUSSIAN ADJECTIVES

In this section I present facts that I have found about the long–short distinction in predicate adjectives. First, the long forms, like nouns, inflect fully for case and can appear after many different verbs. The short forms, however, are like verbs in that they do not inflect for case at all and may occur only in the predicates of superficially verbless sentences, as in (6), and after the verb **byt′** 'be' in the past, future, and imperative forms (**byt′** has no overt present tense forms, and short forms may not generally appear after infinitive **byt′**):

(4)   a. **Ulicy kazalis′ ej ochen′ shirokimi** (LF).
        b. *__Ulicy kazalis′ ej ochen′ shiroki__ (SF).
            'The streets seemed to her very wide.'

(5)   a. **Almazov vernulsja domoj radostnyj** (LF).
        b. *__Almazov vernulsja domoj rad__ (SF).
            'Almazov returned home joyful.'

(6)   a. **Nasha molodezh′ talantlivaja** (LF) **i trudoljubivaja** (LF).
        b. **Nasha molodezh′ talantliva** (SF) **i trudoljubiva** (SF).
            'Our youth (is) talented and industrious.'

(7)   a. **Zimnie nochi budut dolgimi** (LF).
        b. **Zimnie nochi budut dolgi** (SF).
            'The winter nights will be long.'

Besides failing to inflect for case, short-form adjectives exhibit one more morphological peculiarity. Russian uses the second-person plural pronoun **vy** for second person singular in nonintimate speech. Long-form adjectives and predicate nouns agree in number with the referent of this pronoun.

If the referent is singular, the adjective will be singular, despite the plural form of the pronoun:

(8) a. **Ivan, vy molodoj** (LF). (singular)
  b. ***Ivan, vy molodye** (LF). (plural)
   'Ivan, you (are) young.'

(9) a. **Ivan, vy artist** (noun). (singular)
  b. ***Ivan, vy artisty** (noun). (plural)
   'Ivan, you (are an) artist.'

In contrast, short-form adjectives, like verbs, agree with the grammatical number of **vy** and so are always plural:

(10) a. ***Ivan, vy molod** (SF). (singular)
   b. **Ivan, vy molody** (SF). (plural)
   .'Ivan, you (are) young.'

(11) a. ***Ivan, vy govoril** (verb) (singular)
   b. **Ivan, vy govorili** (verb) (plural)
   'Ivan, you were speaking.'

While it is important to note that the long forms in (6a), (7a), and (8) are not quite synonymous with the short forms in (6b), (7b), and (10), one can say that, in general, wherever a short-form adjective is possible, that is, after **byt′** or a zero copula, there is also a grammatical counterpart with a long form. Elsewhere only the long form can be used. There are two kinds of exception to this generalization. The first kind is rare: it has to do with short forms that can appear after verbs other than **byt′**. This happens only with adjectives whose short forms have taken on an unpredictably different meaning, separate from that of the long form. Some such words are listed in (12):

(12) **zanjatoj** (LF) 'generally busy'
   zanjat (SF)   'occupied at the moment'

   bol′noj (LF) 'sickly; having poor health'
   bolen (SF)   'ill at the moment'

   pravij (LF)   'right (not left)'
   prav (SF)   'right (not wrong)'

Some of these meanings are special enough to force the use of the short form in otherwise prohibited environments:

(13) **Ded okazalsja prav** (SF).
   'Grandpa turned out to be right.'

The other kind of exception has to do with three constructions that permit no long forms at all. First, only short forms can occur with infinitive complements, as in (14):

(14)   Ja $\begin{cases} \textbf{rada (SF)} \\ \textbf{dolzhna (SF)} \\ \textbf{gotova (SF)} \\ \textbf{soglasna (SF)} \end{cases}$ **pomogat′ vam.**

'I (am) $\begin{cases} \text{glad} \\ \text{obligated} \\ \text{ready} \\ \text{agreed} \end{cases}$ to help you.'

Not only long-form adjectives but nouns as well are barred from taking such complements. Verbs, on the other hand, participate in many similar constructions:

(15)   **Masha** $\begin{cases} \textbf{mogla} \\ \textbf{xotela} \\ \textbf{obeshchala} \end{cases}$ **pomogat′ vam.**

'Masha $\begin{cases} \text{was able} \\ \text{wanted} \\ \text{promised} \end{cases}$ to help you.'

The second construction that allows only short-form adjectives is imperatives with **byt′**, except for those with a hortatory meaning:[2]

(16)   a.   **Priezzhaj zdorovym (LF)**!
        b.   ****Priezzhaj zdorov (SF)**!
               'Go in good health!'

(17)   a.   ****Bud′te zdorovymi (LF)**!
        b.   **Bud′te zdorovy (SF)**!
               'Be well!'

(18)   a.   ****Bud′ ostorozhnym (LF)**!
        b.   **Bud′ ostorozhen (SF)**!
               'Be careful!'

---

[2] Examples of hortatory imperatives, as opposed to those that are commands or warnings are (i) and (ii):

(i)   **Bud′te smelym, soldat!**
        'Be brave, soldier!'
(ii)   **Bud′xoroshim, moj syn!**
        'Be good, my son.'

The last place where only short forms may be used seems to be defined by semantic considerations. Scientific laws and similar statements invariably contain short-form adjectives or verbs, and not long-form adjectives, in predicate position. Sentences with infinitives or certain quantifier phrases as subjects also disallow long forms in the predicate:

(19) a. *Prostrantsvo beskonechnoe (LF).
   b. Prostrantsvo beskonechno (SF).
    'Space is infinite.'

(20) a. *Vse jasnoe (LF).
   b. Vse jasno (SF).
    'Everything is clear.'

(21) a. *Prixodit' domoj ochen' prijatnoe (LF).
   b. Prixodit' domoj ochen' prijatno (SF).
    'To come home is very pleasant.'

Many of the syntactic peculiarities of short forms have been presented as similarities to verbs. But what features of these adjectives could explain their semantic characteristics? I mentioned earlier that the long forms in (6a), (7a), and (8) were not quite synonymous with the corresponding short forms in (6b), (7b), and (10). To see the semantic distinction, let us consider some simpler examples, (22) and (23):

(22) Studentka umna (SF).
   '(The) student (is) intelligent.'

(23) Studentka umnaja (LF).
   '(The) student (is) intelligent.'

Sentence (22) means that the student is intelligent in general, absolute terms. Sentence (23) means that she is intelligent compared with other students; that is, "The student is an intelligent one."

One might wonder how a Russian sentence with the long-form adjective will be understood if the subject is not something like "student," of whom it makes sense to say that someone is an intelligent one. I asked an informant about sentences (24) and (25):

(24) Oleg umen (SF).
   'Oleg (is) intelligent.'

(25) Oleg umnyj (LF).
   'Oleg (is) intelligent.'

Sentence (24), he said, is much like (22). Oleg is just plain generally intelligent ("you can tell by looking at him"). But in (25) Oleg must have somehow actively shown himself to be an intelligent SOMETHING ("maybe he is painting pictures while reciting the pledge of allegiance backwards in Coptic"). This something that the adjective is relative to is unspecified in the syntax but understood uniquely in any given utterance.

The absolute–relative distinction between short- and long-form adjectives helps explain the fact that predicate adjectives in scientific laws and in sentences with certain kinds of abstract subjects must be in their short forms. Examples (19)–(21) are repeated here:

(19)   **Prostrantsvo beskonechno** (SF).
         'Space is infinite.'

(20)   **Vse jasno** (SF).
         'Everything (is) clear.'

(21)   **Prixodit′ domoj ochen′ prijatno** (SF).
         'To come home (is) very pleasant.'

In (19) we can see that the relative reading, "Space is infinite, as spaces go," is impossible; in scientific laws the subject exhausts the class to which it belongs. "Everything" in (20) and "to come home" in (21) similarly fail to admit of a superset to which they belong.

This absolute–relative distinction in Russian seems to be the same one Bolinger (1967) makes in English between adjectives that modify the referent of the noun (26a) and (26b) and those that modify its reference (26c) and (26d):

(26)   a.   *This policeman is honest.*
         b.   **This policeman is rural.*
         c.   *He is an honest policeman.*
         d.   *He is a rural policeman.*

In (26a) and (26b), as in Russian sentences with short-form adjectives, the adjectives *honest* and *rural* are simple properties of the individual that *policeman* refers to. The policeman in question is honest in an absolute sense, honest at his job, in business dealings, and at play. Sentence (26b) is strange because *rural* is not a property of individual people in this way. Sentences (26c) and (26d) are analogous to Russian sentences with long-form adjectives, the ones with the relative meanings. The adjectives here help determine the referents. In (26d), for instance, the whole expression *rural policeman* is a property that picks out referents that are the rural kind of policeman. In (26c), the subject is the honest kind of policeman. He may well cheat at poker, but he is honest as a policeman.

2. SUMMARY OF THE DIFFERENCES BETWEEN LONG-
AND SHORT-FORM ADJECTIVES IN RUSSIAN

Long Forms	*Short Forms*
1. occur in predicate and prenominal position	occur in predicate position only
2. occur in predicates with many different verbs	occur only with **byt′** and zero copula
3. inflect for case	do not inflect for case
4. agree with referent of **vy** in number	agree with grammatical plurality of **vy**
5. take no infinitive complements	may take infinitive complements
6. may not appear in normal imperatives with **byt′**	may appear in most imperatives with **byt′**
7. have a relative meaning; are reference modifying	have an absolute meaning; are referent modifying

3. MONTAGUE ANALYSIS

In this section I propose an analysis of Russian adjectives that captures the generalizations summarized in Section 2. As mentioned earlier, the syntactic distinctions between short- and long-form adjectives can, with the exception of the imperative facts, to which I return later, be seen as similarities between short adjectives and verbs. The semantic distinction of absolute versus relative predication also allies the short adjectives with verbs. After all, in *The woman is walking, is walking* is a property of the individual referred to. The sentence must mean that the woman is walking in an absolute sense, and not relative to other women.

A grammar like Montague's predicts that the syntactic and semantic facts will coincide in this sort of way. The syntax and semantics work side by side in such a way that any two expressions that are the same syntactically will be the same semantically, though not necessarily vice versa. Identical complex semantic types that differ syntactically are distinguished by varying the number of slashes between the components of their syntactic categories. The syntactic categories of IV/IV and IV//IV, for instance, are the same semantically but differ syntactically.

The syntax with which Montague grammar works has a categorial part that has two primitives:

e for entities
t for sentences

Complex categories are built up from these. t/e, for instance, is something that combines with an entity to produce a sentence. Some important complex categories are:[3]

t/e	or	IV	intransitive verbs and verb phrases like **walk, run**
$t//e$	or	CN	common nouns like **woman, unicorn**
$t/$ IV	or	T	terms or noun phrases like **John, she**
IV/T	or	TV	transitive verbs like **find, eat**
IV/IV	or	IAV	verb-phrase-modifying adverbs like **rapidly**
IV//IV			infinitive-taking verbs like **try to**

If we want short-form adjectives to be treated like verbs both syntactically and semantically, they will have to be of the same categories as verbs, IV, TV, and IV//IV.[4] The syntactic rule for combining verbs with their subjects is the following (where P_A is the set of phrases of the category A):

(27)   If $\alpha \in P_T$ and $\beta \in P_{IV}$, then $F_1(\alpha, \beta) \in P_t$, where $F_1(\alpha, \beta)$ is $\alpha\ \beta$.

So we can draw syntactic trees like (28):

(28)

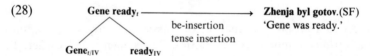

The problem that immediately arises in treating short-form adjectives like verbs is that tense usually jumps right onto verbs, but as we can see in (28), **byt′** is inserted to support it before short-form adjectives.[5] (That **byt′** is a tense support when it appears before short-form adjectives is also suggested by the fact, noted earlier, that short forms do not occur after infinitive **byt′**.) The tense is not too much of a problem, though, as actual verbs before conjugation all end in j or i, and affix hopping could be blocked for the consonantal stems of short adjectives and passive participles with rules

---

[3] In the following chart, in diagrams of sentences, and elsewhere, I use English lexical items as basic expressions of the fragment only for the convenience of the reader. Since the grammar is a fragment of Russian, Russian lexical items should actually appear.

[4] There is ample precedent for treating at least some adjectives as predicates. Bach (1968) and Quine (1960) are two examples.

[5] A similar transformationally inserted "be" has been suggested both for English passives and for English predicate adjectives (Lee, 1974).

like (29):

(29)   If $\alpha \in P_T$ and $\beta \in P_{IV}$, then $F_2(\alpha, \beta) \in P_t$, where $F_2(\alpha, \beta) = \alpha\,\beta'$, where for β ending in a consonant, β' is the past form of **byt′** followed by β, and for β ending in a nonconsonant, β' is the past form of β.

The semantic rule corresponding to (27) is (30):

(30)   If $\alpha \in P_{t/IV}$, $\beta \in P_{IV}$, and α, β translate into α', β', respectively, then $F_1(\alpha, \beta)$ translates into $\alpha'(^\wedge\beta')$.

Since this is the same as the semantic rule we use for verbs, it is not subject to any meaning postulates that might alter its absolute meaning that α is among things that β.

The translation of sentence (28) into intensional logic by means of semantic rules will be (31a); (31b) is the ultimate output of the semantics, achieved through simplifications, definitions, and conventions:

(31)   a. $\overset{\smallfrown}{P}(P\{^\wedge.g\})(^\wedge$**ready′**$)$
        b. **ready′**$_*(g)$

In (31b) readiness is predicated of the individual that **Gene** refers to in absolute terms, just as walking is, in (32), a translation of *Gene is walking*:

(32)   **walk′**$_*(g)$

But what about our long-form adjectives, the modifiers of reference that must yield a relative reading? What category are they in, and how does the semantics work out? In treatments of English (Montague, 1970, for instance), the usual way of handling attributive adjectives is to assign them to category CN/CN. They are things that combine with a common noun to make a new common noun by means of the following syntactic rule:

(33)   If $\alpha \in P_{CN/CN}$ and $\beta \in P_{CN}$, then $F_3(\alpha, \beta) \in P_{CN}$, where $F_3(\alpha, \beta) = \alpha\,\beta$.

The corresponding semantic rule is (34):

(34)   If $\alpha \in P_{CN/CN}$, $\beta \in P_{CN}$, and α, β translate into α', β', respectively, then $F_3(\alpha, \beta)$ translates into $\alpha'(^\wedge\beta')$.

The semantic peculiarities of CN/CN adjectives can now be given by meaning postulates, whose function is to restrict attention to those interpretations of intensional logic that are reasonable candidates for interpretations of natural language. Meaning postulate (35), for instance, applies to the qualitative adjectives discussed here:

(35) $\Box[[\alpha(^\wedge\beta)_*](u) \rightarrow \beta_*(u)]$, where $\alpha \in P_{CN/CN}$, $\beta \in P_{CN}$, and u is a variable of type e.

This is to say that if an individual u is, for instance, an intelligent (α) dog (β), then she is necessarily a dog, but not necessarily intelligent in the absolute sense, as she may be stupid for a pig or for a person. There can be different meaning postulates for different classes of CN/CN adjectives. An "alleged ogre" is not necessarily an ogre or even alleged in an absolute sense, since "alleged" seems to have no absolute sense:

(36)   *They were alleged.

Attributive adjectives in Russian are also CN/CN, although the distinction between common nouns and terms is not quite so obvious in Russian as it is in English, since there are no articles in Russian. In English **woman** and **tall woman** are clearly CNs; they cannot alone combine with a verb to yield a sentence as terms must. We must construct a full term like **the (tall) woman** before we can get a good sentence like **The (tall) woman is walking**. In Russian, though, (37) is a good sentence, having the translations that appear below it:

(37)   **(Vysokaja) zhenshchina guljaet po ulice.**
         'The/a/some (tall) woman is walking along the street.'

However, this does not mean that **zhenshchina** alone is a term, and that attributive adjectives in Russian combine with T's to form new T's. First, syntactically, in Russian as in English, prenominal adjectives may not modify pronouns or proper nouns, which must be terms since they can combine with IVs to make sentences. In addition, limiting long-form adjectives to combining with CNs, and not terms, makes good semantic sense. On the one hand, since CNs are of the same semantic type as IVs, it will ensure that long forms modify reference, and not the referent. The long forms will be combining with properties to form new, modified properties. On the other hand, it will prevent long forms from being interpreted as verblike absolute predicates that apply to individuals, as only terms can combine with such predicates. Therefore we will assume that words like **zhenshchina** are CNs, with which prenominal adjectives can combine to make new CNs by means of the rules given in (33) and (34). There will have to be one or several morphologically empty articles, but they need not concern us here.

Of course the problem of predicate long-form adjectives will now arise. They combine, not with CNs to make new CNs, but with a verb or a zero copula to make an IV phrase:

(38)   **Studentka umnaja (LF).**
         '(The) student (is) intelligent.'

Yet predicate long-form adjectives must not be of a different category from the prenominal ones, as they have the same relative interpretation. Also, we certainly do not want to have to repeat the meaning postulates for a new category of adjective.

A solution to this problem appears if we think of what we have said that (38) actually means. If the adjective had been short, "intelligent" would have been predicated of the individual who is a student absolutely. But (38) has a relative meaning. It says that the student is intelligent as a student. "Intelligent student" is what is predicated of her. What we need to do is to derive all such reference-modifying adjectives attributively, but in the predicate. That is, underlying (38) will be (39):

(39)   **Studentka umnaja (LF) Δ.**
         '(The) student (is an) intelligent Δ.'

Δ is a free variable that ranges over CNs. In (39) Δ is interpreted as "student." As with free variables of category T (deictic pronouns may be an example) in any given sentence, the Δ will have to be interpreted as some particular CN or the sentence will not form an acceptable surface structure. Pragmatic considerations, though, determine the interpretation of Δ. When appropriate, as in (38), it will be interpreted as cointensional with the subject; otherwise it will be interpreted semantically as any other property suggested by the subject or the situation at hand [see (25)]. Syntactically, though, it is always empty and must be deleted from the surface structure. (See the end of this section for motivation for the syntactic rule of dummy CN deletion.)

With this analysis of attributive adjectives, we can have the following kind of tree:

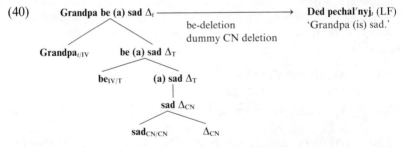

(40)   **Grandpa be (a) sad Δ_t** ⟶ **Ded pechal'nyj$_t$ (LF)**
                                    be-deletion   'Grandpa (is) sad.'
                                    dummy CN deletion

The semantic rules operating on the untransformed t phrase will, with some simplification, give us (41), which eventually reduces to (42):

(41) $\hat{P}(P\{^\wedge g\})(\hat{z}\hat{P} \vee x(\mathbf{sad}'(^\wedge\Delta') \wedge P\{x\}))(\hat{y}(^\vee z = {}^\vee y))$
(42) $\mathbf{sad}'(^\wedge\Delta')_*(g)$

Meaning postulate (35) ensures that in (42) the property of individuals represented by Δ'_* but not $\mathbf{sad}'_*$ is predicated of the individual represented by *g*. So **sad′** pertains only to ^Δ′, which is a function that picks out things that are Δ's. In other words, **sad′** modifies the reference of Δ, just as a long form should.

Notice that in order to have the categories work out right, long predicate adjective phrases must always have some verb in the deep structure, although if the verb is *byt′*, it will be deleted in the present tense, as in (40). It may seem strange to have one form of "be" specially inserted in sentences like (43), while "be" in (44) has been deleted from the verb position:

(43)   **Ljuba byla vesela** (SF).
        'Ljuba was happy.'

(44)   **Ljuba veselaja** (LF).
        'Ljuba (is) happy.'

However, the two types of "be" are semantically quite different.[6] Moreover, this strange outcome helps explain the fact that short forms, but not long forms, can appear after **byt′** in the usual kind of imperative. Although there are no imperatives in the Montague fragments, it is reasonable to suppose that the lexical "be" of the kind that must appear with long-form adjectives is barred from imperatives, except for exhortations to ACT in a certain way, as it is in English, because it is a stative verb. The transformationally inserted "be" is semantically neutral and is probably best viewed as being inserted to support the imperative mood marker as it does tense.

Let us return now to the device of dummy CN deletion, needed to get (38) from (39). Happily Russian not only requires such a rule for an account of long-form adjectives but also supplies some independent motivation for it. It seems that a long-form adjective in Russian "may be used without a noun but the noun to be understood is usually clear from the context [Lunt, 1968, p. 151]":

(45)   **Ax, ty bednaja** (LF)!
        'Oh, you poor (thing)!'

(46)   **Vy prochitali vce ego knigi**? Net, **novaja** (LF) **slishkom dlinnaja** (LF).
        '(Have) you read all his books? No, (the) new (one) (is) too long.'

(47)   **Vy kupili knigu**? Net, **ne bylo novyx** (LF).
        '(Did) you buy (a) book? No, (there) were no new (ones).'

(48)   **Ty gotov k poslednemu** (LF)?
        '(Are) you ready for (the) last (one)?'

---

[6] Lee (1974) gives translations for the "be" of identity and the copula "be" on pages 22 and 24, respectively.

With this final motivation of dummy CN deletion, the sketch of a principled description of short- and long-form adjectives is completed. It will be summarized in Section 6.

4. A TRANSFORMATIONAL ANALYSIS

It is worth pointing out now that, armed with the insight that adjectives do not form a unified underlying category in Russian, we should be able to construct a more standard transformational analysis of the data (see Cooper and Parsons, in this volume). Let us say that only long-form adjectives are members of the category ADJ, while short forms belong to V, for verbs. The following phrase structure rules would then serve to generate long forms only prenominally and short forms only in predicates:

(49)   a.   S → NP AUX VP
       b.   VP → V (COMP)
       c.   NP → DET (ADJ) N

To obtain the surface long adjectives in predicate position, we need a dummy noun deletion rule, as before:

(50)   [X ADJ Δ]$_{NP}$ → [X ADJ $\varnothing$]$_{NP}$

Rules (49a–c) ensure that only long-form adjectives will be generated after regular verbs, including lexical **byt′**, but the tense support **byt′** will have to be transformationally inserted before short-form adjectives in many sentences. As in (29), the be-insertion rule will have to be sensitive to the phonological makeup of the verb or short-form adjective involved, as it applies only when the form ends in a consonant:

(51) $\begin{Bmatrix} \text{past} \\ \text{future} \\ \text{imperative} \end{Bmatrix}$ [... C$_1$]$_V$ → $\begin{Bmatrix} \text{past} \\ \text{future} \\ \text{imperative} \end{Bmatrix}$ **byt′**[... C$_1$]$_V$

The preceding rules will produce the following derivation trees, very much like (28) and (40):

(52)

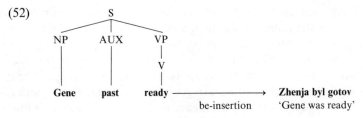

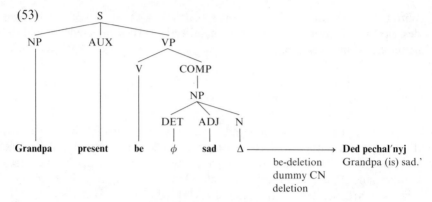

The semantics would presumably work on the untransformed strings in (52) and (53), just as it did in Section 3, only defined in terms of the category names given here.

5. ALTERNATIVE ANALYSES

Other transformational analyses might seem to be possible, but in fact each alternative runs into difficulties. Suppose, for instance, that we tried to list only one form of the adjective and to derive the other transformationally in the right places. Although I think it will make little difference which way we do it, I will start with the long form and derive the short. My reasons for doing it in this direction are two: First, since the long forms appear both prenominally and in the predicate while the short forms appear only as predicates, transforming long-to-short has only one environment, while short-to-long has two. Second, there are classes of long adjectival forms, active participles and the relational adjectives of footnote 1, that have no corresponding short forms, but no such class of short forms that has no corresponding long forms.

A first approximation of a transformation to derive short forms from long forms correctly would be (54):

(54)   NP   (tense **byt′**)   ADJ → NP   (tense **byt′**)   ADJ$_{short}$

Unfortunately there are many things hopelessly wrong with this rule. First of all, in view of the semantic distinction between long forms and short, it must change the meaning of a sentence; the semantics can no longer work on the untransformed string. But even if we are willing to accept such a transformation, the conditions for its application are very strange. The rule must ordinarily be optional, so we can get both (22) and (23) and both (24) and (25), but it is obligatory if the sentence is imperative or has an infinitive complement. Finally, the morphological rules will have to be written to treat verbs and short adjectives similarly with respect to most inflection and agreement phenomena, while long adjectives behave like parts of NPs. The grammar will suggest no explanation of these facts.

Let us try, then, deriving both forms of the adjective—long and short—from a single underlying verbal category as in Babby (1971). This is quite plausible if one assumes that all long forms come from reduced relative clauses. The underlying difference between (55) and (56) would then be the difference between deep structures like (57) and (58):

(55) **Ona umnaja** (LF).
'She (is) intelligent.'

(56) **Ona umna** (SF).
'She (is) intelligent.'

(57) **She is a Δ who is intelligent.**

(58) **She is intelligent.**

However, there are adjectives that can appear in relative clauses but appear not at all or with a different meaning prenominally, and vice versa.[7] In fact long-form predicate adjectives are not even grammatical in unreduced relative clauses on the surface. Most important, though, the deep structures in (57) and (58) cannot accurately reflect the semantic differences between long and short forms. Relative clauses in Russian, as in English, express an absolute, referent-modifying property. Sentences (59) and (60) are equally surprising, because they seem to be claiming that a mouse is big in absolute terms. Sentence (61), however, is an unnoteworthy comment on the relative size of mice:

(59)   *This mouse is big.*

(60)   *This is a mouse that is big.*

(61)   *This is a big mouse.*

So the semantics working on a deep structure like (57) will have to give us something like **She is a Δ and she is intelligent**, where both Δ and **intelligent** are referent modifiers. But long forms are supposed to be relative. Sentence (55) actually means "She is intelligent as a Δ."

---

[7] Compare, for instance, (i) and (ii):

(i)   **Eto plat′e, kotoroe gotovo.**
       'This (is) (a) dress which is ready.'

(ii)   **Eto gotovoe plat′e.**
       'This (is) (a) ready-made dress.'

There are other possible analyses to try, but it seems that under the assumptions about the interrelationship of syntax and semantics common to Montague grammar and transformational grammar we have no choice but to treat Russian adjectives as belonging to two separate syntactic–semantic categories. The resulting complication of the lexicon is of a kind independently needed to account for other kinds of words. Verbs that can have different kinds of complements, for instance, must behave semantically in a manner appropriate to each permissible syntactic construction. In other words, under the assumption that the semantics works up the syntactic tree, many verbs, too, must belong to more than one syntactic–semantic class. It can then be taken as support for such assumptions that the double-adjective analysis of Russian that they have forced us into actually explains part of the language. With either of the systems suggested in this study, the facts recorded in Section 2 can be captured, as outlined in Section 6.

6. SUMMARY

1. Long forms appear in both predicate and prenominal position; short forms, only in the predicate. We can now say that long forms actually are generated only prenominally and short forms only in predicate position. Long forms appear sometimes to be predicative because of the effects of the independently motivated rule of dummy CN deletion.

2. Long forms can occur with many verbs; short forms, only with **byt′**. This is because short forms, being of the same category as verbs themselves, leave no room for any verb other than the transformationally inserted kind of **byt′**.

3–5. Long forms are like nouns in inflection, agreement, and in not taking infinitive complements. Short forms are like verbs in inflection, agreement, and in their ability to take infinitive complements. Long-form adjectives are of category CN/CN, so they are always part of a noun phrase and behave accordingly. Short forms are of the same category as verbs and so follow verb rules.

6. Long forms cannot appear in most imperatives with **byt′**; short forms can. This is because the kind of **byt′** that can appear with long-form adjectives is a stative lexical verb that does not normally occur in imperatives, while the kind of **byt′** that appears with short forms is a transformationally inserted dummy support for tense and mood.

7. Long-form adjectives are reference modifying; short forms are referent modifying. This difference is captured by assigning each type of adjective to a different syntactic category and, hence, to a different semantic type. The CN/CN version (long form) combines with a property to make a new property. The IV version (short form) is itself a predicate that applies to individuals.

University of Massachusetts, Amherst

ACKNOWLEDGMENTS

I am grateful to Alex Shishin for his lively services as an informant, to Maurice Levin for reading some of the examples, and to David Dowty. And, for their help and encouragement, I would like to thank Emmon Bach and especially Barbara Partee.

REFERENCES

Babby, L. H. A Transformational Analysis of Russian Adjectives. Unpublished doctoral dissertation. Harvard University, Cambridge, Massachusetts, 1971.

Babby, L. H. The deep structure of adjectives and participles in Russian. *Language*, 1973, **49**, 349–360.

Bach, E. Nouns and noun phrases. E. Bach and R. T. Harms (Eds.), *Universals in Linguistic Theory*. New York: Holt, 1968. Pp. 90–122.

Bolinger, D. Adjectives in English: Attribution and predication. *Lingua*, 1967, **18**, 1–34.

Chomsky, N. *Aspects of the Theory of Syntax*. Cambridge, Massachusetts: M. I. T. Press, 1965.

Danilenko, L. P. *Russkij Jazyk dlja Inostrancev*. Number 20. Leningrad: Leningrad Univ. Press, 1968.

Lee, K. The Treatment of Some English Constructions in Montague Grammar. Unpublished doctoral dissertation, University of Texas at Austin, Austin, Texas, 1974.

Lunt, H. H. *Fundamentals of Russian*. New York: Norton, 1968.

Montague, R. The proper treatment of quantification in ordinary English. In J. Hintikka, J. Moravcsik, and P. Suppes (Eds.), *Approaches to Natural language: Proceedings of the 1970 Stanford Workshop on Grammar and Semantics*. Dordrecht: Reidel, 1973. Pp. 221–242. [Reprinted in R. Thomason (Ed.), *Formal Philosophy: Selected Papers of Richard Montague*. New Haven: Yale Univ. Press, 1974.]

Montague, R. English as a formal language. In B. Visenti *et al.*, *Linguaggi nella Societa e nella Tecnica*. Milan: Edizioni di Communità, 1970. [Reprinted in R. Thomason (Ed.), *Formal Philosophy: Selected Papers of Richard Montague*. New Haven: Yale Univ. Press, 1974.]

Quine W. V. O. *Word and Object*. Cambridge, Massachusetts: M.I.T. Press, 1960.

Stilman, G., and Harkins, W. E. *Introductory Russian Grammar*. Waltham, Massachusetts: Blaisdell, 1964.

Stilman. L. *Russian Verbs of Motion*. New York: Columbia Univ. Press, 1951.

ROBIN COOPER AND TERENCE PARSONS

MONTAGUE GRAMMAR, GENERATIVE SEMANTICS, AND INTERPRETIVE SEMANTICS

INTRODUCTION

In "Universal Grammar" (in Montague, 1974; hereafter UG) Montague complains that work in transformational grammar is not yet rigorous enough to merit serious consideration. As an alternative he gives a system of grammar (= syntax plus semantics) that generates a fragment of English syntax and assigns meanings to the sentences so generated. The grammar generates only a portion of English, but it does so by means of a theory that meets the high standards of mathematical rigor and precision he advocates.

Linguists complain, in turn, that for all their rigor, Montague's techniques are unfamiliar, and do not fit into the framework of phrase structure and transformational rules that they have found so fruitful in analyzing (at least the syntax of) natural language.

The conflict is, at least in part, ill-founded. To show this we will describe a transformational grammar that is exactly equivalent to Montague's system in "The Proper Treatment of Quantification in Ordinary English" (in Montague, 1974; hereafter PTQ). That is, it generates exactly the same English sentences as Montague's system, and it assigns the same meanings to them. At the same time, it is possible to preserve Montague's theory of translation and interpretation.

This system (which we call "Cooper grammar") bears some resemblance to certain systems of generative semantics[1] insofar as it contains higher quantified NPs and variables in its deep structures together with "lowering" rules that operate on them. However, this gives no edge to generative semantics; for there is a third system ("interpretive grammar"), equivalent to the first two,[2] that resembles systems of interpretive semantics[3] in that quantifier scope ambiguities are not represented syntactically but are accounted for by interpretive rules.

Our paper follows this outline: Section 1 contains expositions of Montague syntax and Cooper syntax. Section 2 shows how to convert Montague's

---

[1] As proposed, for example, in Lakoff (1972) or McCawley (1972).

[2] With certain qualifications—cf. Sections 5.3, 5.4.

[3] As proposed, for example, by Jackendoff (1972).

analysis trees (similar to deep structures) into deep structures of Cooper syntax. We state theorems about this conversion process that entail the equivalence of the two syntactic theories. Section 3 contains expositions of Montague's theory of translation and semantic interpretation, and shows how Cooper syntax can be interpreted in accordance with it. Section 4 contains theorems that entail the semantic equivalence of the two systems. Section 5 contains an exposition of a system of interpretive semantics, which is equivalent to the earlier systems, and shows that it, too, can be viewed as a system that is in accordance with Montague's theory of translation and interpretation.

1. MONTAGUE SYNTAX AND COOPER SYNTAX

1.1. *Montague Syntax*

Montague generates phrases of English by a many-claused recursive definition. Familiarity with this technique is presupposed here; for an exposition (directed specifically at the system of Montague's rules in PTQ), see Partee (1975).

Hereafter we will refer to the system of PTQ as M GRAMMAR; M SYNTAX, and M SEMANTICS will designate its syntactic and semantic parts, respectively. We begin with a formulation of M syntax like that in PTQ, except that we replace Montague's terminology with terminology more familiar to linguists. For example, instead of Montague's P_{CN} (common noun phrase) we use Nom (nominal); instead of his P_t we use S (sentence).

M syntax consists of 17 rules, S1–S17. Rule S1 resembles a lexicon; the rest are used to build up complex phrases from simpler ones. The "building up" is done by means of syntactic operations F_0-F_{15} defined in S2–S17.

S1: *The words on the right are basic members of the indicated categories:*

VP	(verb phrase):	**run, walk, talk, rise, change**
NP	(noun phrase):	**John, Mary, Bill, ninety, he$_0$, he$_1$, he$_2$, . . .**
V_t	(transitive verb):	**find, lose, eat, love, date, be, seek, conceive**
Adv$_{VP}$	(verb phrase adverb):	**rapidly, slowly, voluntarily, allegedly**
Nom	(nominal):	**man, woman, park, fish, pen, unicorn, price, temperature**
Adv$_S$	(sentence adverb):	**necessarily**
P	(preposition):	**in, about**
V_S	(sentential verb):	**believe-that, assert-that**
V_{VP}	(verb phrase verb):	**try-to, wish-to**

S2: If ζ is a Nom, then $F_0(\zeta)$, $F_1(\zeta)$ and $F_2(\zeta)$ are all NPs, where $F_0(\zeta) =$ **every** ζ, $F_1(\zeta) =$ **the** ζ, and $F_2(\zeta) =$ **a** ζ or **an** ζ, according as the first word in ζ takes **a** or **an**.

S3: If ζ is a Nom and if ϕ is an S (sentence), then $F_{3,n}(\zeta, \phi)$ is a Nom, where $F_{3,n}(\zeta, \phi) = \zeta$ **such that** ϕ' and ϕ' comes from ϕ by replacing each occurrence of **he**$_n$ or **him**$_n$ by

$$\begin{Bmatrix} \text{he} \\ \text{she} \\ \text{it} \end{Bmatrix} \quad \text{or} \quad \begin{Bmatrix} \text{him} \\ \text{her} \\ \text{it} \end{Bmatrix},$$

respectively, according as the first basic Nom in ζ is of

$$\begin{Bmatrix} \text{masc} \\ \text{fem} \\ \text{neuter} \end{Bmatrix}$$

gender.

S4: If α is an NP and δ is a VP, then $F_4(\alpha, \delta)$ is an S, where $F_4(\alpha, \delta) = \alpha \delta'$ and δ' is the result of replacing the first verb in δ by its third-person singular present (where a VERB is any basic VP, V_t, V_S, or V_{VP}).

S5: If δ is a V_t and β is an NP, then $F_5(\delta, \beta)$ is a VP, where $F_5(\delta, \beta) = \delta \beta$ if β does not have the form **he**$_n$ and $F_5(\delta, \beta) = \delta$ **him**$_n$ if β has the form **he**$_n$.

S6: If δ is a P and β is an NP, then $F_5(\delta, \beta)$ is an Adv$_{VP}$.

S7: If δ is a V_S and β is an S, then $F_6(\delta, \beta)$ is a VP, where $F_6(\delta, \beta) = \delta \beta$.

S8: If δ is a V_{VP} and β is a VP, then $F_6(\delta, \beta)$ is a VP.

S9: If δ is an Adv$_S$ and β is an S, then $F_6(\delta, \beta)$ is an S.

S10: If δ is an Adv$_{VP}$ and β is a VP, then $F_7(\delta, \beta)$ is a VP, where $F_7(\delta, \beta) = \beta \delta$.

S11: If ϕ and ψ are S's, then so are $F_8(\phi, \psi)$ and $F_9(\phi, \psi)$, where $F_8(\phi, \psi) = \phi$ **and** ψ, and $F_9(\phi, \psi) = \phi$ **or** ψ.

S12: If γ and δ are VPs, then so are $F_8(\phi, \psi)$ and $F_9(\phi, \psi)$.

S13: If α and β are NPs, then so is $F_9(\alpha, \beta)$.

S14: If α is an NP and ϕ an S, then $F_{10,n}(\alpha, \phi)$ is an S, where either
  (a) α does not have the form **he**$_k$ and $F_{10,n}(\alpha, \phi)$ comes from ϕ by replacing the first occurrence of **he**$_n$ or **him**$_n$ by α and all other occur-

rences of $\mathbf{he}_n$ or $\mathbf{him}_n$ by

$$\left\{\begin{array}{c}\mathbf{he}\\\mathbf{she}\\\mathbf{it}\end{array}\right\} \quad\text{or}\quad \left\{\begin{array}{c}\mathbf{him}\\\mathbf{her}\\\mathbf{it}\end{array}\right\},$$

respectively, according as the gender of the first basic Nom or NP in α is

$$\left\{\begin{array}{c}\text{masc}\\\text{fem}\\\text{neuter}\end{array}\right\},$$

or

(b) $\alpha = \mathbf{he}_k$ and $F_{10,n}(\alpha, \phi)$ comes from ϕ by replacing all occurrences of $\mathbf{he}_n$ or $\mathbf{him}_n$ by $\mathbf{he}_k$ or $\mathbf{him}_k$, respectively.

S15: If α is an NP and ζ is a Nom, then $F_{10,n}(\alpha, \zeta)$ is a Nom.

S16: If α is an NP and δ is a VP, then $F_{10,n}(\alpha, \delta)$ is a VP.

S17: If α is an NP and δ is a VP, then $F_{11}(\alpha, \delta)$, $F_{12}(\alpha, \delta)$, $F_{13}(\alpha, \delta)$, $F_{14}(\alpha, \delta)$, and $F_{15}(\alpha, \delta)$ are all S's, where $F_{11}(\alpha, \delta) = \alpha\,\delta'$ and δ' is the result of replacing the first verb in δ by its negative third-person singular present; $F_{12}(\alpha, \delta) = \alpha\,\delta''$ and δ'' is the result of replacing the first verb in δ by its third-person singular future; $F_{13}(\alpha, \delta) = \alpha\,\delta'''$ and δ''' is the result of replacing the first verb in δ by its negative third-person singular future; $F_{14}(\alpha, \delta) = \delta''''$ and δ'''' is the result of replacing the first verb in δ by its third-person singular present perfect; $F_{15}(\alpha, \delta) = \alpha\,\delta'''''$ and δ''''' is the result of replacing the first verb in δ by its negative third-person singular present perfect.

If a phrase of some particular category is constructed by these rules, we can record the history of that construction in an ANALYSIS TREE. Such a tree contains as nodes all phrases constructed along the way. A numeral following each node tells which syntactic operation was used to reach the node; the nodes immediately dominated by a given node contain the inputs to the operation used. For example, the following is an analysis tree for a construction of the Nom **woman such that Mary loves her**:

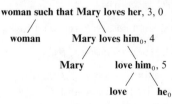

Analysis trees will be particularly important in what follows; here are three samples of analysis trees for sentences (taken from **PTQ**):

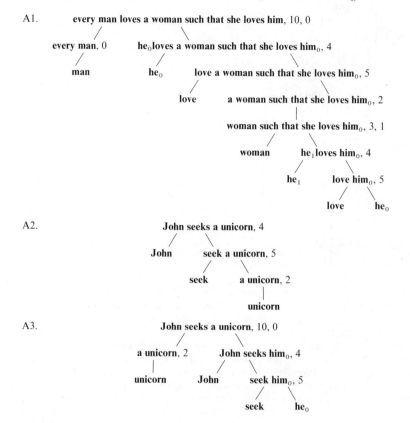

A1.   every man loves a woman such that she loves him, 10, 0

A2.   John seeks a unicorn, 4

A3.   John seeks a unicorn, 10, 0

Although category markings are missing from the trees, they are easily recoverable from the structures of the trees. For example, A1 classifies **love him$_0$** as a VP, **he$_1$ loves him$_0$** as an S, etc., eventually classifying its top node as an S. Trees A2 and A3 both yield the same sentence at the top node; the two trees correspond to the de dicto and de re readings of this sentence, respectively.

1.2. *Cooper Syntax (C-Syntax)*

This syntax has two parts. There is a set of phrase structure or rewrite rules, which generate phrase structure trees, or deep structures.[4] Then there is an ordered set of transformational rules that convert these trees into other trees and ultimately into surface structures.

PHRASE STRUCTURE RULES:

$$1.\ S \rightarrow \begin{cases} S \begin{Bmatrix} \textbf{and} \\ \textbf{or} \end{Bmatrix} S \\ NP \quad Vbl \quad S \\ Adv_S \quad S \\ \begin{Bmatrix} Neg \\ \varnothing \end{Bmatrix}^5 \quad NP \quad Aux \quad VP \end{cases} \quad \begin{matrix} a \\ b \\ c \\ d \\ e \\ f \end{matrix}$$

$$2.\ VP \rightarrow \begin{cases} VP \begin{Bmatrix} \textbf{and} \\ \textbf{or} \end{Bmatrix} VP \\ NP \quad Vbl \quad VP \\ VP \quad Adv_{VP} \\ V_i \\ V_t \quad NP \\ V_{VP} \quad VP \\ V_S \quad S \end{cases} \quad \begin{matrix} a \\ b \\ c \\ d \\ e \\ f \\ g \\ h \end{matrix}$$

$$3.\ Aux \rightarrow Pres \begin{Bmatrix} \varnothing \\ M \\ Perf \end{Bmatrix} \quad \begin{matrix} a \\ b \\ c \end{matrix}$$

---

[4] Readers acquainted with the present state of transformational syntax will notice some peculiarities here. These have been introduced either to generate just Montague's original fragment (although more general rules generating a larger fragment of English are well established in the linguistic literature) or to comply with Montague's theory of translation. An example of the former type of peculiarity is seen in the rule expanding Aux. Examples of the latter type are seen in the absence of a lexicon and the expansion of VP into V_S S, representing a verb and sentential object (though Emonds (1970) has argued for this). It has been necessary to do this in order to preserve that part of Montague's theory of translation which requires that each category in the syntax represent one and only one type (or category) in the logic. For example, if a lexicon with strict subcategorization were included, the node V would be allowed to dominate transitive verbs, intransitive verbs, and verbs taking a sentential object. All of these represent different types in the logic, and thus the category V would not map into just one type in the logic. Similarly, if verbs with sentential objects occurred in the following more traditional structure:

```
        VP
       /  \
      V    NP
           |
           S
```

it would be required that S and NP represent the same logical type, which they do not in our fragment.

[5] We use

$$\begin{Bmatrix} A \\ \varnothing \end{Bmatrix}$$

as a notational variant for more normal (A), indicating optionality of the element A, in order to facilitate numbering of each unabbreviated phrase structure rule.

4. $Adv_{VP} \rightarrow P \quad NP$

5. $NP \rightarrow \begin{cases} NP \quad \textbf{or} \quad NP \\ Det \quad Nom \\ N_{prop} \end{cases}$

   a
   b
   c

6. $Nom \rightarrow \begin{cases} NP \quad Vbl \quad Nom \\ Nom \quad Vbl \quad \textbf{such-that} \quad S \\ N_{com} \end{cases}$

   a
   b
   c

7. $V_i \rightarrow$ **run, walk, talk, rise, change**

8. $N_{prop} \rightarrow$ **John** [+masc], **Mary** [+fem], **Bill** [+masc], **ninety** [+neuter], **he$_0$, he$_1$, he$_2$,** . . .

9. $V_t \rightarrow$ **find, lose, eat, love, date, be, seek, conceive**

10. $Adv_{VP} \rightarrow$ **rapidly, slowly, voluntarily, allegedly**

11. $N_{com} \rightarrow$ **man** [+masc], **woman** [+fem], **park** [+neuter], **fish** [+neuter], **pen** [+neuter], **unicorn** [+neuter], **price** [+neuter], **temperature** [+neuter]

12. $Adv_S \rightarrow$ **necessarily**

13. $P \rightarrow$ **in, about**

14. $V_S \rightarrow$ **believe-that, assert-that**

15. $V_{VP} \rightarrow$ **try-to, wish-to**

16. $Det \rightarrow$ **every, the, a**

17. $M \rightarrow$ **will**

18. $Perf \rightarrow$ **have en**

19. $Neg \rightarrow$ **n't**

20. $Vbl \rightarrow x_0, x_1, x_2,$ . . .

TRANSFORMATIONAL RULES:

There are eight of these rules. They are obligatory, and they cycle on S nodes, VP nodes, and Nom nodes.[6]

There is the following PRUNING CONVENTION: (*a*) Any node that exhaustively dominates a single element is itself deleted if that element is

[6] See Appendix A for an explanation of the cycling mechanism.

deleted; (b) any node that immediately and exhaustively dominates a similar node is removed. The rules are as follows.[7]

21. NP LOWERING:[8]

$$\text{NP}[x_i]_\text{Vbl}[X[\text{he}_i]_\text{NP}(Y\ \text{he}_i)^*\ Z]\ \begin{Bmatrix} \text{S} \\ \text{VP} \\ \text{Nom} \end{Bmatrix}$$

$$
\begin{array}{ccccccc}
1 & 2 & 3 & & 4 & 5 & 6 & 7 \\
\end{array}
$$

$$\Rightarrow\quad \varnothing\ \ \varnothing\ \ 3\ \ \ \ 1\ \ 5 \begin{Bmatrix} \text{a.} & \textbf{he} \\ \text{b.} & \textbf{she} \\ \text{c.} & \textbf{it} \\ \text{d.} & \textbf{he}_j \end{Bmatrix} 7$$

where i, j are any natural numbers and X, Y, Z do not contain $\textbf{he}_i$.

The choice of pronoun is (a) iff the leftmost N_prop or N_com dominated by 1 has the feature [+masc]; (b) iff the leftmost N_prop or N_com dominated by 1 has the feature [+fem]; (c) iff the leftmost N_prop or N_com dominated by 1 has the feature [+neut]; (d) iff the leftmost N_prop dominated by 1 is $\textbf{he}_j$.

22. VACUOUS QUANTIFICATION DELETION:[9]

$$
\text{NP}\quad \text{Vbl}\quad \begin{Bmatrix} \text{S} \\ \text{VP} \\ \text{Nom} \end{Bmatrix}
$$

$$
\begin{array}{ccc}
1 & 2 & 3 \\
\Rightarrow\quad \varnothing & \varnothing & 3
\end{array}
$$

---

[7] The rules are stated here in an unnecessarily redundant fashion in order to increase perspicuity of the proofs of Theorems 2–4. We believe that an equivalent statement of the same rules would be that given in Appendix B.

[8] Some explanation of this notation is in order. See Appendix C.

[9] This rule requires some explanation. It is necessitated by the fact that the phrase structure rules will generate quantified NPs that cannot be lowered because they do not have the same index as any variable in the sentence, as in (i):

(i)

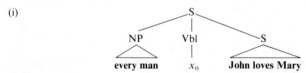

Rule 22 deletes the higher NP and Vbl, so the surface form of (i) would be simply **John loves Mary**. But the semantics of our system (see Section 3) incorporates the meaning of the higher NP into the meaning of (i). I.e., it assigns to (i) the meaning of **every man is such that John loves Mary**. This is NOT equivalent to simply **John loves Mary**, and thus structures like (i) should not appear in an adequate grammar of English. We have retained such structures because our task here is to produce a system exactly equivalent to Montague's, which is also defective in this respect. (The defect is easily correctable by filtering out structures of the form of (i) when $\textbf{he}_0$ does not occur in the lower S.)

23. RELATIVE CLAUSE FORMATION:

Nom $[x_i]_{Vbl}$ **such-that** $[(X \textbf{ he}_i)^*\ Y]_S$

1   2   3   4   5   6

$\Rightarrow$ 1 $\emptyset$ 3 $4 \begin{Bmatrix} \textbf{he} \\ \textbf{she} \\ \textbf{it} \end{Bmatrix} 6$

where i is any natural number, **he**$_i$ is not in X or Y, and the pronoun is
he if the leftmost common noun in 1 has the feature [+masc], **she**
if the leftmost common noun in 1 has the feature [+fem], and **it** if the
leftmost common noun in 1 has the feature [+neuter].

24. NEG PLACEMENT:[10]

n't NP Pres$\left(\begin{Bmatrix} \textbf{will} \\ \textbf{have} \end{Bmatrix} \right)$ Y

1   2   3   4

$\Rightarrow$ $\emptyset$ 2 3 + 1 4

25. DO SUPPLETION:

X   Pres   **n't** Y

1   2   3   4

$\Rightarrow$ 1 2 + **do** 3 4

26. AFFIX HOPPING:[11]

X   Pres   Y   (**en** Z)   W

1   2   3   4 5   6

$\Rightarrow$ 1 $\emptyset$ 3 + 2 $\emptyset$ 5 + 4 6

where Y, Z represent trees consisting of single morphemes rooted by
themselves.

27. CASE MARKING:

X $\begin{bmatrix} \begin{Bmatrix} V_t \\ P \end{Bmatrix} \textbf{he}_i \end{bmatrix}_{\begin{Bmatrix} VP \\ Adv_{VP} \end{Bmatrix}}$ Y

1   2 3   4

$\Rightarrow$ 1 2 3   4

[+acc.]

In addition to Rules 1–27, we suppose the existence of certain morphophonemic spelling rules, which we will not state here. For example, from

---

[10] The notation 3 + 1 in this transformation indicates that the subtree referred to by term 1
in the structural description is to be sister-adjoined to the right of the subtree referred to by term 3
(i.e., it is to be attached to the node immediately dominating the root of that subtree).

[11] We assume the principle of strict cyclicity, which requires that a transformation not apply
on a given cycle if its structural description is met by a subtree already cycled on and the only
elements affected by the application of the transformation are within that subtree. This principle
entails that each affix may be hopped only once. See Chomsky (1973) for a detailed discussion
of this principle.

love + **en** they would produce **loved**; from **love** + Pres they would produce
loves; from **he** they would produce **him**, etc.
[+acc]

Let us illustrate C syntax by mimicking the Montague analysis tree given
earlier for **woman such that Mary loves her**. Rules 1–20 yield the following
deep structure:

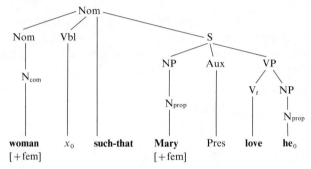

In cycling on the VP node, Rule 27 changes **he**_0 to **he**_0 ; no other rules apply
[+acc]
here. In cycling on the S node, Rule 26 "hops" Pres, and we get:

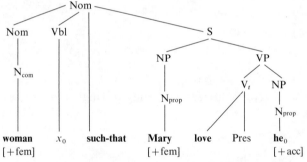

In cycling on the leftmost Nom node, no rules apply. In cycling on the top
Nom node, Rule 23 deletes the variable and changes **he**_0 to **she**, yielding:
[+acc]   [+acc]

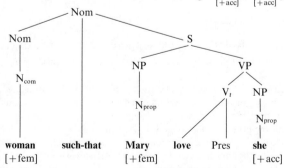

The conversion of **she** [+acc] to **her** and of **love** + Pres into **loves** (by the morphophonemic rules) and the omission of the remaining features yields a bottom string identical to the top node of the Montague analysis tree given earlier.

Corresponding to the Montague analysis trees A1–A3 are the following Cooper deep structure trees. (The notion "corresponding to" will be defined explicitly later.) The reader can ascertain that in each case the transformational rules convert these trees into trees whose terminal (= "bottom") elements constitute the English sentences that form the top nodes of the corresponding Montague trees.

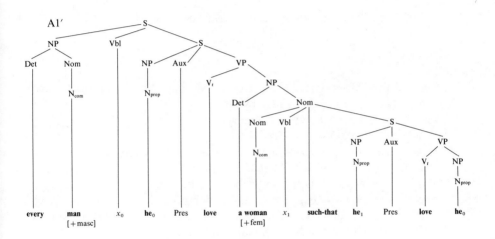

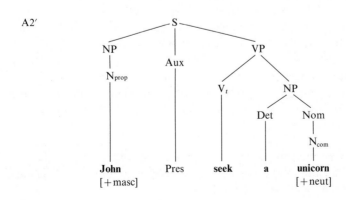

A3′

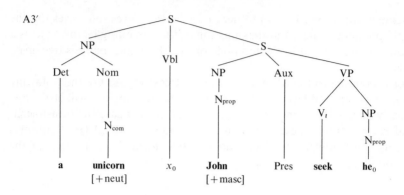

2. COMPARISON OF M SYNTAX AND C SYNTAX

2.1. *Metamorphosis*

Let us call a Montague analysis tree an M TREE. And let us use C TREE for any deep structure generated by the C syntax phrase structure rules from ONE OF THE FOLLOWING category symbols: S, NP, VP, Nom, V_t, Adv_{VP}, Adv_S, P, V_S, V_{VP}.

In this section we describe a process that converts any M tree into a C tree. We call the resulting C tree the METAMORPHOSIS of the M tree. Each M tree is equivalent to its metamorphosis in the sense that they both give rise to the same English expression, and they both assign the same meaning to it (by semantic rules to be discussed). Thus metamorphosis is the key to the general equivalence of M grammar and C grammar.

Let us use t to stand for any arbitrary M tree, and $m(t)$ for its metamorphosis. We will use $[\alpha]$ to stand for any arbitrary M tree whose top node is α, n or α, k, n. The metamorphosis of an M tree is produced in three stages; i.e., $m(t)$ is the result of successively performing three operations on t: STRUCTURE DEVELOPMENT, STRUCTURE LABELING, and EMERGENCE.

STAGE 1: STRUCTURE DEVELOPMENT
At each node of the M tree, make one of the following changes; which change you make depends on which of Montague's Rules S1–S17 generated the node in that tree.

S1: A node generated by S1 is a bottom element of an M tree. Do not change these nodes at all, EXCEPT add features to nouns. E.g., change **John** to **John** [+masc].

S2: Replace **every** α, 0   by   **every** α, 0

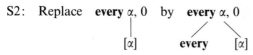

Likewise for **the** and **a**.

S3: Replace α **such that** β', 3, n by α **such that** β', 3, n

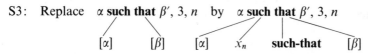

S4: Replace $\alpha\delta'$, 4   by $\alpha\delta'$, 4

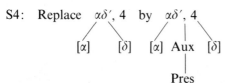

S5–S9: No changes.

S10: Replace $\beta\delta$, 7   by $\beta\delta$, 7

     $[\delta]$ $[\beta]$ $[\beta]$ $[\delta]$

S11: Replace α **and** β, 8   by α **and** β, 8

     $[\alpha]$ $[\beta]$ $[\alpha]$ **and** $[\beta]$

Likewise for **or**.

S12, S13: Like S11.

S14: Replace $F_{10,n}(\alpha, \beta)$, 10, n by $F_{10,n}(\alpha, \beta)$, 10, n

     $[\alpha]$ $[\beta]$ $[\alpha]$ x_n $[\beta]$

S15, S16: Like S14.

S17: This has five clauses.

   Replace $\alpha\delta'$, 11   by $\alpha\delta'$, 11

     $[\alpha]$ $[\delta]$ **n´t** $[\alpha]$ Aux $[\delta]$

                      Pres

   Replace $\alpha\delta''$, 12   by $\alpha\delta''$, 12

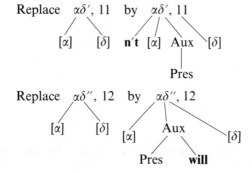

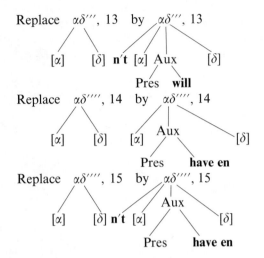

Replace $\alpha\delta'''$, 13 by $\alpha\delta'''$, 13

[α] [δ] **n't** [α] Aux [δ]

Pres **will**

Replace $\alpha\delta''''$, 14 by $\alpha\delta''''$, 14

[α] [δ] [α] Aux [δ]

Pres **have en**

Replace $\alpha\delta''''$, 15 by $\alpha\delta''''$, 15

[α] [δ] **n't** [α] Aux [δ]

Pres **have en**

STAGE 2: STRUCTURE LABELING

At this stage we put category symbols at the nodes. First we change (some of) the nodes that are not bottom nodes; then we change (some of) the bottom nodes.

1. At each node other than Aux that is not a bottom node, replace its string by the category assigned to it by the original M tree; but rewrite that string to the right in curly brackets. E.g.,

replace α **such that** β', 3, n by Nom $\{\alpha$ **such that** β', 3, $n\}$

[α] x_n **such-that** [β] [α] x_n **such-that** [β]

2. For bottom nodes α other than Pres, **and, or,**

replace α by β
         |
         α

if β is the category symbol assigned to α by any of C Rules 9, 10, 12–20, and

replace α by NP or by Nom or by VP
         | | |
         N_{prop} N_{com} V_i
         | | |
         α α α

according as α occurs in C Rule 8, 11, or 7, respectively.

STAGE 3: EMERGENCE

Now erase the curly brackets and their contents. This ends the description of metamorphosis. We will illustrate the metamorphosis process by giving the results of applying stage 1 and stage 2 to the M trees A1–A3. In each case stage 3 is left as an exercise for the reader. Also, the reader can easily check that in each case the final result of the metamorphosis is a C tree; in fact the metamorphoses of A1, A2, A3 are A1′, A2′, and A3′, respectively.

A1. STAGE 1

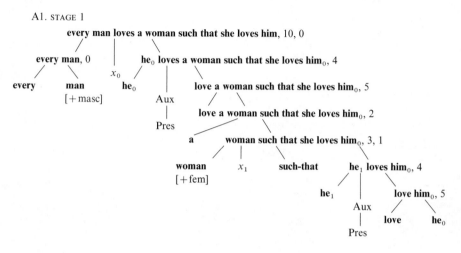

STAGE 2

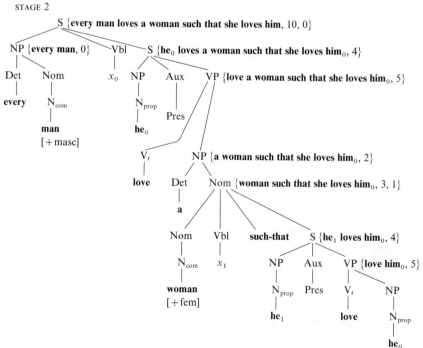

A2. STAGE 1

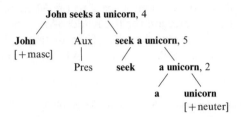

STAGE 2

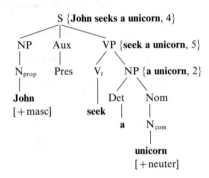

A3. STAGE 1

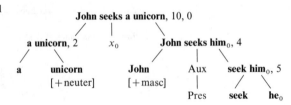

STAGE 2

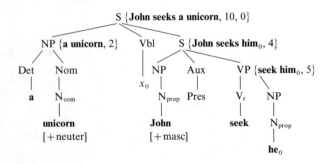

2.2 *The Equivalence of M Syntax and C Syntax*

Stage 1 of the metamorphosis process alters the structure of an M tree, but the alteration is minimal. Indeed slight alterations in M syntax and C syntax would eliminate all such difference in structure.

If we ignore this minor structural difference, we can characterize a Montague analysis tree as follows: It is simply a deep structure tree of C syntax, except that its nonterminal nodes do not consist of category symbols; instead, each such node consists of the string of terminal symbols that that node WILL dominate after all transformations have been applied to the deep structure. (The missing category symbols are recoverable by reading up the tree.) The results of stage 2 in the metamorphoses of A1–A3 illustrate this point. The proof of this point is in Theorem 3.

The following theorems show the syntactic equivalence of M grammar and C grammar.[12]

THEOREM 1: *If t is an M tree, then m(t) is a C tree.*

This has been illustrated in the case of A1–A3. The full proof of the theorem is by induction on the structure of M trees. It is easily shown that unit M trees (trees that consist simply of a single output of rule S1) metamorphize into small C trees. That is, the BOTTOM nodes of M trees all metamorphize into C trees. Then it can be shown that for any NONBOTTOM node of an M tree, if its branches metamorphize into C trees, then so does the tree dominated by that node. This is shown case by case, depending on which of Rules S2–S17 generated the node.

We will say that a C tree t GENERATES a string α if after applying all possible transformations to t you get a tree t' such that α is the string of terminal items of t' read from left to right.

THEOREM 2: *If t is a C tree, t generates exactly one string.*

This is true because all transformations of C syntax are obligatory, and you never have a choice of which order to apply them in (except for occasional choices of which subtree to work on first). The proof of this theorem is by induction on the structure of C trees.

If t is a C tree, we will use gen(t) to stand for "the unique string generated by t." As before, we use [α] to stand for any arbitrary M tree whose top node is α, k or α, k, n.

---

[12] More detailed outlines of the proofs of these theorems are available from T. Parsons, Department of Philosophy, University of Massachusetts, Amherst, Massachusetts 01002.

THEOREM 3: *If* [α] *is an M tree, then* α = *gen(m([α]))*.[13]

That is, the top node of an M tree = the unique string generated by the metamorphosis of that tree. The proof is by induction on the structure of M trees. (The property holds for unit M trees, and it also holds for any M tree if it holds for its branches).

COROLLARY: *C syntax yields all of the sentences that M syntax yields.*

THEOREM 4: *The function m is one-to-one from the set of M trees onto the set of C trees.*

So the metamorphosis process can be reversed and applied to any C tree. (Show this in part by showing that each STAGE of *m* is one–one.) Now we can conclude:

COROLLARY: *C syntax yields exactly the same sentences as M syntax.*

This corollary shows that M syntax and C syntax have the same weak generative capacity. But the interesting fact is the close resemblance in the syntactic structures underlying the sentences in the two theories; this resemblance is articulated in the metamorphosis function. The theories generate the same sentences in metamorphically similar ways. One natural consequence of this fact is that a sentence is *n* ways (syntactically) ambiguous in M syntax if and only if it is *n* ways (syntactically) ambiguous in C syntax.

---

[13] This theorem has one minor exception—M trees whose top nodes are prepositional phrases containing pronouns. For example, the M tree:

metamorphizes into:

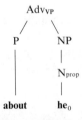

which generates **about he$_0$** instead of **about him$_0$**; the pronoun does not change case until the Adv$_{VP}$ is combined with a VP. This exception could easily be eliminated by allowing transformations to cycle on Adv$_{VP}$ nodes.

3. MONTAGUE SEMANTICS AND COOPER SEMANTICS

In Section 3.1, we give an informal discussion of Montague's theory of translation and semantic interpretation.[14] A formal exposition of this theory is found in UG (there is also a detailed description in Thomason, 1974). In Section 3.2, we define a translation relation between C trees and sentences of intensional logic. And in Section 3.3, we show how this translation relation fits into Montague's theory.

3.1. *Montague's Theory of Translation and Semantic Interpretation*

According to Montague, an interpretation of a language L is a triple consisting of (*a*) a set of meanings corresponding to each of the meaningful

---

[14] It is important to distinguish the meaning of the terms SEMANTICS and INTERPRETATION in the logical sense employed by Montague from the meaning commonly ascribed to them in the linguistic literature. The aim of a logical semantics is to define precisely under what conditions a given sentence would be true. Thus given the sentence of the predicate calculus (i), the semantics would tell us that it would be true just in case there were at least one man who loved Mary:

(i) $\exists x[\mathbf{man}(x) \wedge \mathbf{love}(x, \mathbf{Mary})]$

Without an explicitly defined semantics (i) would be just a meaningless collection of shapes. To illustrate this point we construct an artificial language that consists of the elements A, B, and C. The syntax of this language specifies correct sentences as those consisting of a simple concatenation of all three symbols, with the condition that B is in the middle. Thus there are two possible sentences in this language, given in (ii):

(ii)   a. ABC
          b. CBA

The syntax tells us nothing about the meaning of the sentences in (ii). This language becomes meaningful only when we define a semantics for it. We do this by rules of interpretation that map the symbols of the language into either objects or relations that might be found in the real world. We represent the mapping as a function f such that $f(A) =$ **The White House**, $f(C) =$ **Washington**, and $f(B) =$ a relation such that the object denoted by the symbol to the left of B is IN the object denoted by the symbol to the right of B. Now (iia) and (iib) become meaningful sentences. We can determine that in the actual world (iia) is true and (iib) false. Note that this language is not ambiguous. Ascertaining whether the sentences were true or not would be considerably more complicated if we allowed A to denote either **The White House** or **Buckingham Palace**. We would have to disambiguate the sentence in some way before we could give it a truth value. We might make a statement such as "the sentence is true in the real world if A denotes The White House and false if it denotes Buckingham Palace." It is because natural language is ambiguous that logicians constructed unambiguous artificial languages in order to make semantics more perspicuous. Much of what is called semantics in linguistic literature has to do with disambiguating natural language. Generative semantics disambiguates natural language by creating an underlying level of logical form from which ambiguous surface structures can be derived. Interpretive semantic theories disambiguate language by means of interpretive rules, which are not to be confused with the rules of semantic interpretation in a logical system.

expressions of L; (*b*) a set of operations defined on the set of meanings (these operations correspond to the syntactic operations of L that are de-fined on the set of meaningful expressions); (*c*) a function that maps the basic meaningful expressions (or lexical items) of L into meanings. Let us take as an example a language L, which is a very small fragment of English. It has the following three basic meaningful expressions (lexical items): **John**, **loves**, **Mary**. Syntactic operations on this set define more nonbasic meaning-ful expressions. These state that (*a*) **loves Mary** is a meaningful expression of the category VP and (*b*) **John loves Mary** is a meaningful expression of the category S (sentence). Thus our fragment contains one sentence, **John loves Mary**, whose structure might be represented as:

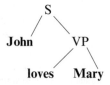

Now let us assign an interpretation to L. We will consider first item (*c*) of the interpretation referred to earlier. This is the function that maps lexical items onto meanings. Call this function f. Then the value of $f(\textbf{John})$, or the meaning of **John**, will itself be that function from possible worlds and con-texts of use which maps each such world and context to the individual John. (It happens that Montague's theory of proper names requires that the meaning of **John** pick out the same individual no matter which world or context of use is chosen.) Similarly, the value of $f(\textbf{Mary})$, the meaning of **Mary**, picks out the individual Mary in each world and context. $f(\textbf{loves})$, the meaning of **loves**, picks out from each world and context a relation that can exist between two people. Two people are included in this relation only if the first one loves the second. These functions from possible worlds and contexts of use to John, Mary, and the relation of loving are all elements in the set of meanings that make up item (*a*) of the interpretation. This set also contains meanings for the remaining meaningful expressions of L, i.e., the VP **loves Mary** and the S **John loves Mary**. The VP is formed syntactically by a function applied to **loves** and **Mary**. Item (*b*) of the interpretation con-tains a corresponding semantic function that operates on the meanings of **loves** and **Mary** and produces from them the meaning of the VP **loves Mary**. The result is a function from possible worlds and contexts of use to sets of entities that love Mary. Similarly, there is a syntactic function that applies to **John** and a VP to form an S, and a corresponding semantic function that takes the meaning of **John** and the meaning of the VP and produces from them the meaning of S, a function from possible worlds and contexts of use to either true or false, depending on whether John is included in the set of people who love Mary or not (in the given world and context).

Montague (UG) states that one of the basic aims of semantics is to characterize the notion of a true sentence under a given interpretation. Why, then, do we have to assign meanings to all syntactic expressions of English whether sentences or not? The arguments for assigning meanings to members of each syntactic category run parallel to the arguments for having sub-sentence syntactic categories in syntax when really one of the basic aims of syntax is to characterize the well-formed sentences of the language under consideration. If we assigned meanings only to the category S we would have to assign a meaning to each atomic sentence of the language in an arbitrary fashion. Given two sentences of English, for example, **John loves Mary** and **Bill loves Mary**, we would have to assign truth or falsity to these sentences quite independently and miss such generalizations as that each of them is true just in case their subject belongs to the set of people who love Mary. The semantics would be analogous to a syntax that admitted only the category S and listed all the atomic sentences of the language. Semantic interpretations of this nature derive from a considerable philosophical tradition in the study of formal languages. Montague was attempting to show that it is also possible to define such a semantics for English. In PTQ he did this not by interpreting English directly but by first translating it into a formal language that was more perspicuously related to the semantics. However, in order to show that it is possible to define such a semantics on English itself it was necessary for the disambiguated version of English and the formal language to be homomorphic (in a specific sense that he defines) so that the interpretation induced by translation assigned meanings to all the syntactic expressions of English (and not just a subset of those expressions such as the category S sentence). In order to achieve this he restricted the relation between the logic and English approximately as follows:

1. There is one and only one category in the logic corresponding to each category in the syntax of English.

2. Each basic expression (lexical item) has only one translation into a member of some category in the logic (which may be a complex member of a category in the logic; e.g., the basic expression **John** translates into $\hat{P}P\{^{\wedge}j\}$, the set of properties belonging to the intension of the individual John. This logical expression is a member of a category but is not a basic expression).

3. For each complex expression in the disambiguated version of English, there is one and only one corresponding expression in the logic, whose constituents correspond to the translation of the constituents of the English expression. In addition, there is just one syntactic operation in the logic which corresponds to the syntactic operation in English that combines the constituent expressions. A complex syntactic operation in the logic may correspond to a simple syntactic operation in English. For example, there

is a simple syntactic operation in English that combines a proper name such as **John** with an intransitive verb such as **run** and produces the sentence **John runs**. The translations of the constituents are $\hat{P}P\{^\wedge j\}$ and **run**′, respectively. The syntactic operation of the logic that corresponds to that of English consists of two separate operations—one that takes **run**′ into $^\wedge$**run**′ and another that combines this with $\hat{P}P\{^\wedge j\}$ to form the expression $\hat{P}P\{^\wedge j\}$ ($^\wedge$**run**′).

4. Sentences of English correspond only to sentences in the logic.[15]

3.2. *Translating Deep Structures into Intensional Logic*

Like Montague, we shall not interpret the C syntax directly but, rather, translate it into the intensional logic Montague defines in PTQ, while preserving the translation relation. As the logic and the semantics defined on it have been discussed in detail in PTQ, Partee (1975), and Thomason (1974), we shall assume some familiarity with it here. The translation rules presented here are similar in an important way to projection rules as they have been defined, for example, in Katz and Fodor (1964). They may be viewed as first processing the terminal nodes of the deep structure and then assigning readings to each higher node[16] progressively until the root of the tree is reached. The reading assigned to any given node will be the result of a specific operation applied to the readings assigned to the nodes it immediately dominates. The translation procedure differs from the Katz–Fodor system insofar as it assigns meaningful expressions of intensional logic to each node rather than sets of semantic features.

We define first a notion of lexical item in the present system. A LEXICAL ITEM is any terminal node that is exhaustively dominated by some node A in any tree generated by the grammar. The set of lexical items thus defined includes all the terminal nodes except **and**, **or**, Pres, and **such-that**. Except for Pres, which does not exist in the M grammar, these items are introduced syncategoramatically (i.e., they do not belong to any basic lexical category) in both C syntax and M syntax. In both systems such items are translated only as part of the configuration in which they appear and, thus, are not assigned any meanings of their own.

---

[15] These four principles of translation are meant to be an approximate informal prose version of the definition of a translation base given in Montague (UG, Section 5). Item 1 corresponds to (1) of Montague's definition; 2 corresponds to (2) and (3); 3 corresponds approximately to (4) and (5); 4 corresponds to (6).

[16] More precisely, one should say that a reading is assigned to the tree dominated by each higher node, thus obtaining a reading for the whole tree when the root is reached.

We now define a function j that maps lexical items of the deep structure syntax into expressions of the intensional logic:

$j(x_0) = x_0$
$j(x_1) = x_1$
   etc.
$j(\mathbf{n't}) = \sim$
$j(\mathbf{have\ en}) = H$
$j(\mathbf{will}) = W$
$j(\mathbf{every}) = \lambda Q \hat{P} \forall x[Q\{x\} \supset P\{x\}]$
$j(\mathbf{the}) = \lambda Q \hat{P} \exists y[\forall x[Q\{x\} \equiv x = y] \wedge P\{y\}]$
$j(\mathbf{a}) = \lambda Q \hat{P} \exists x[Q\{x\} \wedge P\{x\}]$
$j(\mathbf{necessarily}) = \hat{p}[\Box \hat{p}]$
$j(\mathbf{be}) = \lambda \mathscr{P} \lambda x \mathscr{P}\{\hat{y}[^{\vee}x = {}^{\vee}y]\}$
$j(\mathbf{John}) = j^*$
$j(\mathbf{Mary}) = m^*$
$j(\mathbf{Bill}) = b^*$
$j(\mathbf{ninety}) = n^*$
$j(\mathbf{he}_i) = \hat{P}P\{x_i\}$
$j(X) = X'$,

where X is any lexical item not in the preceding list.

We now define translation rules for each of the structural configurations generated by the phrase structure rules. A rule of the form:

is to be read as follows:

If [A], [B] are trees rooted by the nodes A, B and are immediately dominated by a node C, then the tree [C] translates as ϕ. A tree whose topmost node exhaustively dominates the node immediately below it (i.e., is of the

form $\begin{array}{c} A \\ | \\ [B] \end{array}$) has as its translation the result of applying the identity function

to the translation of the tree without the topmost node. Thus the translation

of any tree $\begin{array}{c} A \\ | \\ [B] \end{array}$ is the same as the translation of [B]. This immediately pro-

vides us with translation rules corresponding to 19–20c, 7–18, 6c, 5c, 3a, and 2f. We now specify the other translation rules in detail, where A′ is to be read as "the translation of the tree [A]."

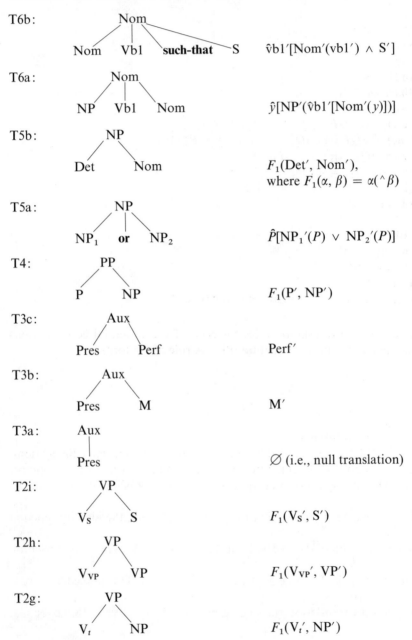

T6b:

Nom
/ | \
Nom   Vbl   **such-that**   S

$\hat{v}bl'[\text{Nom}'(vbl') \wedge S']$

T6a:

Nom
/ | \
NP   Vbl   Nom

$\hat{y}[\text{NP}'(\hat{v}bl'[\text{Nom}'(y)])]$

T5b:

NP
/ \
Det   Nom

$F_1(\text{Det}', \text{Nom}')$,
where $F_1(\alpha, \beta) = \alpha(^\wedge\beta)$

T5a:

NP
/ | \
NP$_1$ **or**   NP$_2$

$\hat{P}[\text{NP}_1'(P) \vee \text{NP}_2'(P)]$

T4:

PP
/ \
P   NP

$F_1(\text{P}', \text{NP}')$

T3c:

Aux
/ \
Pres   Perf

Perf′

T3b:

Aux
/ \
Pres   M

M′

T3a:

Aux
|
Pres

$\emptyset$ (i.e., null translation)

T2i:

VP
/ \
V$_S$ S

$F_1(\text{V}_S', \text{S}')$

T2h:

VP
/ \
V$_{VP}$ VP

$F_1(\text{V}_{VP}', \text{VP}')$

T2g:

VP
/ \
V$_t$ NP

$F_1(\text{V}_t', \text{NP}')$

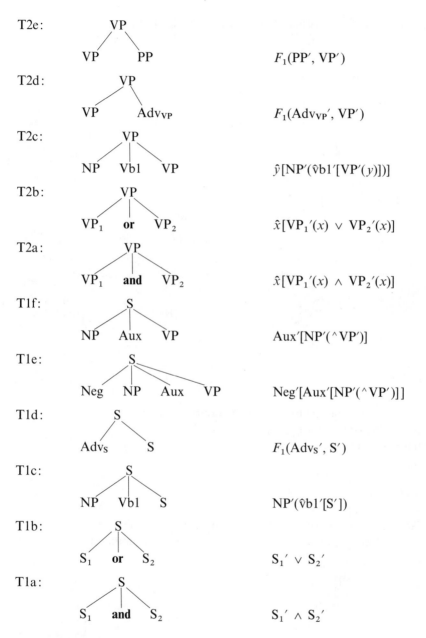

T2e: $F_1(PP', VP')$

T2d: $F_1(Adv_{VP}', VP')$

T2c: $\hat{y}[NP'(\hat{v}b1'[VP'(y)])]$

T2b: $\hat{x}[VP_1'(x) \vee VP_2'(x)]$

T2a: $\hat{x}[VP_1'(x) \wedge VP_2'(x)]$

T1f: $Aux'[NP'(^\wedge VP')]$

T1e: $Neg'[Aux'[NP'(^\wedge VP')]]$

T1d: $F_1(Adv_S', S')$

T1c: $NP'(\hat{v}b1'[S'])$

T1b: $S_1' \vee S_2'$

T1a: $S_1' \wedge S_2'$

By way of illustration we show a detailed translation of the deep structure corresponding to the de re reading of **John seeks a unicorn**, repeated here for convenience. It will be noted that for each application of a phrase structure rule the corresponding translation rule applies:

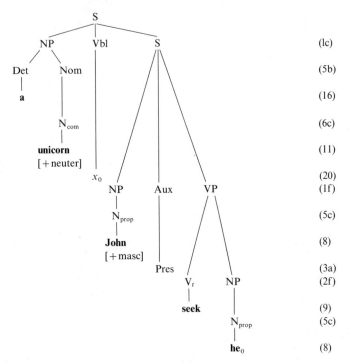

	(1c)
	(5b)
	(16)
	(6c)
	(11)
	(20)
	(1f)
	(5c)
	(8)
	(3a)
	(2f)
	(9)
	(5c)
	(8)

TRANSLATION OF LEXICAL ITEMS ACCORDING TO j:

a—$\lambda Q \hat{P}[\exists x[Q\{x\} \wedge P\{x\}]]$

unicorn—**unicorn**′

x_0—x_0

John—j^*

seek—**seek**′

he$_0$—$\hat{P}P\{x_0\}$

According to the rule for translation of nonbranching nodes, these will also be the translations of the nonbranching nodes dominating these items, e.g.:

$$
\begin{array}{c}
\text{NP} \\
| \\
\text{N}_{\text{prop}} \\
| \\
\textbf{John}\,[+\text{masc}]
\end{array}
$$

translates as j^*. By applying T5b to the leftmost NP, we obtain $\lambda Q \hat{P} \exists x[Q\{x\} \wedge P\{x\}]$ (^**unicorn**′). Now, turning to the embedded S, we already know the translation of the subject NP. The translation of Aux according to T3a is null. The translation of the VP according to T2g is **seek**$'(\hat{P}P\{x_0\})$ (recall that for Montague $\hat{P}P\{x_0\}$ is an abbreviation for $^\wedge\hat{P}P\{x_0\}$). The whole embedded sentence is, then, according to Tlf, $j^*(^\wedge\textbf{seek}'(\hat{P}P\{x_0\}))$. Finally, Tlc yields

$$\lambda Q\hat{P}\exists x[Q\{x\} \;\wedge\; P\{x\}](^\wedge\textbf{unicorn}')(\hat{x}_0[j^*(^\wedge\textbf{seek}'(\hat{P}P\{x_0\}))],$$

which reduces to $\exists x[\textbf{unicorn}'(x) \;\wedge\; \textbf{seek}'(\hat{P}P\{x\})(^\wedge j)]$.

3.3. *Deep Structure Translation and the Translation Relation*

Montague characterizes the translation relation as a particular relation between disambiguated languages (for which he gives a precise definition (UG) that we shall refer to later). In order to demonstrate that this relation holds between C syntax and the logic, we must show (*a*) that the language of the deep structure trees is a disambiguated language in his sense and (*b*) that there is a translation relation of the type he specifies between the deep structure syntax and the intensional logic.

In the following demonstration we shall make use of a redefinition of phrase structure grammar that is equivalent to more usual definitions such as those given in Chomsky and Miller (1963). We shall consider phrase structure rules to be of the form $f([A], [B]) = [C]$, where [A], [B], and [C] are subtrees rooted by the nodes A, B, and C, respectively, and where [C] is obtained from [A] and [B] by f by sister-adjoining [A] and [B] under a node C so that [A] is to the left of [B]. For example, a rule of the form $f([NP], [Aux], [VP]) = [S]$ will sister-adjoin a tree rooted by NP, followed by a tree rooted by Aux, followed by a tree rooted by VP under a node S to produce a new tree rooted by S. Terminal nodes are considered specific types of subtrees that are rooted by themselves. In addition, it is required that each syntactic operation apply only to terminated trees (i.e., trees whose leaves may root only themselves according to the grammar). It is easy to see that this is a redefinition of phrase structure grammars, since for any grammar of this type there will be an isomorphic phrase structure grammar defined in the traditional way, where there is a one-to-one mapping between rules (any rule of the new type can be formed from the old type by making the right-hand side the arguments of the function and the left-hand side the result of the function, and changing the reference from node labels to subtrees) and a one-to-one mapping between terminated trees generated such that each corresponding tree is generated by similar applications of corresponding rules.

Viewing a phrase structure grammar in this way allows us to show that it fits Montague's definition of a disambiguated language. Montague (UG) defines a disambiguated language as a system $\langle A, F_\gamma, X_\delta, S, \delta_0 \rangle_{\gamma \in \Gamma, \delta \in \Delta}$, where:

1. $\langle A, F_\gamma \rangle_{\gamma \in \Gamma}$ is an algebra
2. for all $\delta \in \Delta$, X_δ is a subset of A
3. Γ is the smallest set including as subsets all the sets X_δ (for $\delta \in \Delta$) and closed under all the operations F_γ (for $\gamma \in \Gamma$)
4. X_δ and the range of F_γ are disjoint whenever $\delta \in \Delta$ and $\gamma \in \Gamma$
5. for all $\gamma, \gamma' \in \Gamma$, all sequences a in the domain of F_γ, and all sequences a' in the domain of $F_{\gamma'}$, if $F_\gamma(a) = F_{\gamma'}(a')$, then $\gamma = \gamma'$ and $a = a'$
6. S is a set of sequences of the form $\langle F_\gamma, \langle \delta_\xi \rangle_{\xi < \beta}, \varepsilon \rangle$, where $\gamma \in \Gamma$, β is the number of places of the operation F_γ, $\delta_\xi \in \Delta$ for all $\xi < \beta$, and $\varepsilon \in \Delta$
7. $\delta_0 \in \Delta$

We interpret this system in the following way into deep structure syntax:

A is the set of terminated (sub) trees.
F_γ is the function f mentioned in the redefinition of phrase structure rules for all $\gamma \in \Gamma$.
X_δ is a category of lexical items for all $\delta \in \Delta$. All lexical items that are immediately and exhaustively dominated by the node δ in any tree generated by the grammar are members of the set X_δ. $\bigcup_{\delta \in \Delta} X_\delta$ is the set of lexical items.
S is the set of phrase structure rules.
δ_0 is the node S.
Γ is the set of indices on syntactic operations F.
Δ is the set of nonterminal nodes or category indices that represent sets of trees.

It can be shown that each of the seven parts of the definition of disambiguated language hold true under this interpretation. We shall now define a translation relation of the type specified in Montague (UG) between the present deep structure syntax and the intensional logic in Montague (PTQ). We represent the logic as a disambiguated language $\langle A', F_\gamma', X_\delta', S', \delta_0' \rangle_{\gamma \in \Gamma', \delta \in \Delta'}$. This has the following interpretation:

A' is the set of meaningful expressions.
F_γ' is a syntactic operation for all $\gamma \in \Gamma'$.
X_δ' is a subset of basic meaningful expressions for all $\delta \in \Delta'$.
S' is the set of syntactic rules.
δ_0' is the category index t.
Γ' is the set of indices on syntactic operations.
Δ' is the set of category indices.

The translation base given by Montague (UG) that determines the translation relation is a system $\langle g, H_\gamma, j \rangle_{\gamma \in \Gamma}$ such that:

1. g is a function from Δ into Δ'
2. j is a function with domain $\bigcup_{\delta \in \Delta} X_\delta$
3. whenever $\delta \in \Delta$ and $\xi \in X_\delta$, $j(\xi) \in C'_{g(\delta)}$, where C' is the family of syntactic categories generated by the logic
4. for all $\gamma \in \Gamma$, H_γ is a polynomial operation of the same number of places as F_γ over the algebra $\langle A', F_\gamma' \rangle_{\gamma \in \Gamma'}$
5. whenever $F_\gamma, \langle \delta_\xi \rangle_{\xi < \beta}, \varepsilon \rangle \in S, \langle H_\gamma, \langle g(\delta_\xi) \rangle_{\xi < \beta}, g(\varepsilon)$ is a derived syntactic rule of the logic
6. $g(\delta_0) = \delta_0'$

We shall now define the translation relation, showing as we go how each of these clauses is met.

CLAUSE 1: g is a function from the set of nonterminal nodes or category indices of the deep structure syntax into the indices of the logical types. The values of this function are expressed in the following list, where the indices of the logical types are represented as sequences of s, e, and t:[17]

$g(\text{Vbl}) = \langle s, e \rangle$

$g(\text{Neg}) = \langle t, t \rangle$

$g(\text{Perf}) = \langle t, t \rangle$

$g(\text{M}) = \langle t, t \rangle$

$g(\text{Det}) = \langle\langle s, \langle\langle s, e \rangle, t \rangle\rangle, \langle\langle s, \langle\langle s, e \rangle, t \rangle\rangle, t \rangle\rangle$
$\quad = \langle\langle s, g(\text{N}_{\text{com}}) \rangle, g(\text{NP}) \rangle$

$g(\text{V}_{\text{VP}}) = \langle\langle s, \langle\langle s, e \rangle, t \rangle, \langle\langle s, e \rangle, t \rangle\rangle = \langle\langle s, g(\text{VP}) \rangle, g(\text{VP}) \rangle$

$g(\text{V}_{\text{S}}) = \langle\langle s, t \rangle, \langle\langle s, e \rangle, t \rangle\rangle$

$g(\text{P}) = \langle\langle\langle s, \langle\langle s, e \rangle, t \rangle\rangle, t \rangle, \langle\langle s, \langle\langle s, e \rangle, t \rangle, \langle\langle s, e \rangle, t \rangle\rangle\rangle$
$\quad = \langle\langle s, g(\text{NP}) \rangle, g(\text{Adv}_{\text{VP}}) \rangle$

$g(\text{Adv}_{\text{S}}) = \langle\langle s, t \rangle, t \rangle$

$g(\text{N}_{\text{com}}) = \langle\langle s, e \rangle, t \rangle$

$g(\text{Adv}_{\text{VP}}) = g(\text{V}_{\text{VP}})$

$g(\text{V}_t) = \langle\langle s, \langle\langle s, \langle\langle s, e \rangle, t \rangle\rangle, t \rangle\rangle, \langle\langle s, e \rangle, t \rangle\rangle$

$g(\text{N}_{\text{prop}}) = \langle\langle s, \langle\langle s, e \rangle, t \rangle\rangle, t \rangle$

$g(\text{V}_i) = g(\text{N}_{\text{com}})$

$g(\text{Nom}) = g(\text{N}_{\text{com}})$

$g(\text{NP}) = g(\text{N}_{\text{prop}})$

---

[17] See Montague (PTQ) for an explanation. Appendix C of Partee (1975) has been invaluable in writing the details of this function.

$$g(\text{Aux}) = g(\text{Neg})$$
$$g(\text{VP}) = g(\text{V}_i)$$
$$g(\text{S}) = \langle t \rangle$$

CLAUSES 2 AND 3: j is a function with its domain as the set of lexical items in the deep structure syntax. The result of j for some lexical item that is a member of the category δ is a meaningful expression (not necessarily basic) of the logical type $g(\delta)$. The values of this function are given in Section 3.2.

CLAUSES 4 AND 5: For every syntactic operation in the deep structure syntax, there is a corresponding (complex of) operation(s) in the logic. Furthermore, for each phrase structure rule there is a corresponding (complex of) rule(s) in the logic consisting of a corresponding (complex of) operation(s) and corresponding category indices (according to g).

The translation rules defined in Section 3.2 meet these conditions when viewed as defined on syntactic rules of the type mentioned in our redefinition of phrase structure grammars.

CLAUSE 6 requires that the syntactic category S corresponds to the type of t phrases in the logic according to g. This also holds true.

4. THE SEMANTIC EQUIVALENCE OF M GRAMMAR
AND C GRAMMAR

Both M grammar and C grammar yield semantic accounts of sentences by means of translating structures underlying the sentences into a semantically interpreted intensional logic. They do so in equivalent ways. In particular, we can prove the following:

THEOREM 5: *The translation into intensional logic of any M tree in Montague grammar is logically equivalent to the translation into intensional logic of its metamorphosis in Cooper grammar.*

COROLLARY: *M grammar and C grammar assign exactly the same meanings to exactly the same sentences.*

(In this corollary we think of meanings as being "the same" if they are expressible by logically equivalent sentences.) Theorem 5 is proved by a straightforward induction on the structure of M trees: Unit M trees metamorphize into C trees that have equivalent translations, and a complex M tree does this if its branches do.

Theorem 5 refers to logically equivalent translations rather than identical ones because M trees do not always have the SAME translations as their metamorphoses. For example:

every boy, 0
|
boy

translates into (*a*) $\hat{P}\forall x[\textbf{boy}'(x) \supset P\{x\}]$, whereas its metamorphosis:

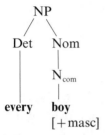

translates into (*b*) $\lambda Q\hat{P}\forall x[Q\{x\} \supset P\{x\}](^\wedge\textbf{boy}')$. The translations in (*a*) and (*b*) are logically equivalent; (*b*) can be turned into (*a*) by elimination of the abstract and amalgamation of $^\wedge{}^\vee\textbf{boy}'$ to $\textbf{boy}'$ [recall that $Q\{x\}$ is Montague's abbreviation of $^\vee Q(x)$]. It would be a fairly straightforward task to alter C grammar so that M trees always had EXACTLY the same translations as their metamorphoses. This could be done in two ways. First, we could alter the translation relation. For example, the case discussed here could be handled by altering the translation rule (in C grammar) for:

NP
/ \
Det   Nom

from $F_1(\text{Det}', \text{Nom}')$ to the result of eliminating the initial abstraction from $F_1(\text{Det}', \text{Nom}')$ and then erasing the resulting $^\vee{}^\wedge$. This was not done above because it would violate Montague's methodological principle that the logical syntactic operation involved in a translation should be a polynomial operation over the algebra of the logic.

Alternatively, C syntax could be made to look more like M syntax, e.g., by introducing Det's syncategorematically in the same manner as **and**, **or**, and **such-that**. This would be achieved by introducing phrase structure rules of the following form in place of Rule 5b in the C syntax:

$$\text{NP} \rightarrow \left\{ \begin{array}{l} \textbf{every} \\ \textbf{a} \\ \textbf{the} \end{array} \right\} \text{Nom}$$

The quantifiers now would not be lexical items according to the definition in Section 3.2 and, therefore, would not receive a translation except when combined with a nominal in exactly the same fashion as in M syntax.

5. INTERPRETIVE GRAMMAR

C grammar resembles a system of generative semantics in that it contains variables in its deep structures that are eliminated by NP-lowering rules. In this section we present a system that more closely resembles that of interpretive semantics. The basic idea is to keep the syntactic component of the theory as simple as possible while doing all the work in the semantic translation. We will call the system INTERPRETIVE GRAMMAR (or I GRAMMAR), and its components I SYNTAX and I SEMANTICS.

5.1. *I Syntax*

I syntax is essentially a purification of C syntax. We eliminate or modify the rules of C syntax that introduce variables and that lower NPs, and we add one new rule to generate pronouns. Specifically, we ELIMINATE from C syntax the following:

1c:	$S \rightarrow NP$ Vbl S
2c:	$VP \rightarrow NP$ Vbl VP
6a:	Nom $\rightarrow NP$ Vbl Nom
20:	Vbl $\rightarrow x_0, x_1, x_2, \ldots$

We CHANGE Rule 6b from Nom $\rightarrow$ Nom Vbl **such-that** S to

6b′:   Nom $\rightarrow$ Nom **such-that** S.

We eliminate the transformations dealing with variables, i.e.:

21:	NP Lowering
22:	Vacuous Quantification
23:	Relative Clause Formation

Since these were the only rules that required cycling on Nom and VP nodes, we may now simplify the grammar to cycle only on S. Finally, we ADD three clauses to Rule 8 to freely generate anaphoric pronouns:

8′:   NP $\rightarrow$ **he** [+masc], **she** [+fem], **it** [+neuter]

(We then expand Transformations 27 and 28 so as to change the cases of THESE pronouns, as well as of **he**$_i$.)

Notice that I syntax will still contain the subscripted pronouns **he**$_i$, **she**$_i$, **it**$_i$. This is in keeping with both M syntax and C syntax, which generate quasi-English sentences containing these items. The translation schemes of both such systems translate these items into free variables, which seem to resemble DEMONSTRATIVE pronouns of English. We will persist in viewing

subscripted pronouns as demonstrative pronouns and the others as anaphoric pronouns—items that behave like bound variables. In M grammar
and C grammar, such behavior is guaranteed by the form of the syntax.
In I grammar, anaphoric pronouns are freely generated; the trick is to get
them to behave like bound variables in the semantics.

As an illustration of the rules of I syntax, we generate trees A1″–A3″
which correspond to trees A1′–A3′ discussed earlier:

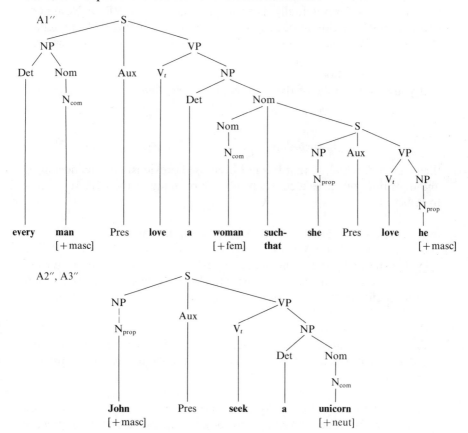

Notice that A2″ and A3″ are identical. In this fragment, unlike the earlier
ones, the ambiguous sentence **John seeks a unicorn** comes from only one
deep structure. So here deep structures themselves will be ambiguous.

5.2. *I Semantics*

The first step in I semantics is to INDEX deep structure trees. Our method
will resemble indexing proposals in the literature, except that in addition

to putting indices on pronouns and their NP antecedents, we also index nodes to indicate scope.[18]

An INDEXING is the result of a finite number of applications of the following two processes to a phrase structure tree of I syntax. They are applied to cyclic nodes in the following manner. We find an S, VP, or Nom node that does not itself dominate any such node; we first apply Abstraction Marking once, if possible; then we apply Quantification Marking as many times as we like (or not at all). Then we go to any new S, VP, or Nom node that does not itself dominate any untreated S, VP, or Nom node, and repeat the process. We continue until we have treated the top node of the tree.

ABSTRACTION MARKING
If you are at a node of the form Nom in a configuration of this sort:

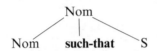

then pick a numeral, n, that has not been used previously in the indexing[19] and does not appear as a subscript on any pronoun in the tree. Write prefixes as follows:

1. ABSTRACTION SCOPE: Write An preceding the upper Nom.
2. VARIABLE: Write Vn preceding no, some, or each NP node that is dominated by the S above and (a) exhaustively dominates an unsubscripted pronoun that agrees with the lower Nom in gender and (b) has no prefix before it already.

QUANTIFICATION MARKING
Pick a numeral, n, that has not been used previously in the indexing and that does not appear as a subscript on any pronoun in the tree. Write prefixes as follows:

1. QUANTIFICATION SCOPE: Write Sn preceding the node on which you are cycling, and preceding any other prefixes that already precede that node.
2. QUANTIFIER: Write Qn preceding some NP node that (a) is dominated by the cycling node, (b) does not exhaustively dominate a pronoun,

[18] Note that nothing hinges on the fact that we mark the indexing on the trees. It would be possible, though less perspicuous, to represent the indexing as a separate object, not unlike Jackendoff's (1972) tables of coreference, and then define the translation procedure on a tree and its indexing in a way strictly analogous to the present proposal.

[19] This is for simplicity only; see discussion at the beginning of section 5.3.

(*c*) has no prefix before it yet, and (*d*) does not dominate any node
with a V*k* or Q*k* prefix, unless it also dominates a node with the corresponding S*k* or A*k* prefix.[20]

3. VARIABLE: Write V*n* before no, some, or each NP node that (*a*) ex-
    haustively dominates an unsubscripted pronoun that agrees with the
    NP node of 2 in gender, (*b*) has no prefix before it already, (*c*) is dom-
    inated by the cycling node, and (*d*) is to the right of the NP node of 2.

We will say that an unsubscripted pronoun is BOUND in an indexed tree
if its NP node is preceded by V*n*, for some numeral, *n*. And we define a
VIABLE INDEXING as an indexing of a tree in which every unsubscripted
pronoun is bound.

Viable indexings are important for two reasons. First, it will turn out
that I syntax is NOT equivalent to M syntax and C syntax, because I syntax
generates some English sentences that are not generated by the others.
However, if we were to remove from I syntax all deep structures for which
no viable indexings exist, then we would have a system that IS syntactically
equivalent (i.e., generates the same set of sentences) to M syntax and C
syntax (see Section 5.3). Second, viable indexings provide the foundation
for the semantic interpretation of I syntax deep structures. Specifically, we
will provide a translation procedure that maps viably indexed I syntax deep
structures into sentences of intensional logic. The procedure works only for
viably indexed trees.

Before giving the semantics we illustrate viable indexings by giving three
viably indexed trees, A1‴–A3‴; these are produced from A1″–A3″, and
they will correspond in their semantic interpretation to trees A1–A3 of
M syntax and A1′–A3′ of C syntax:

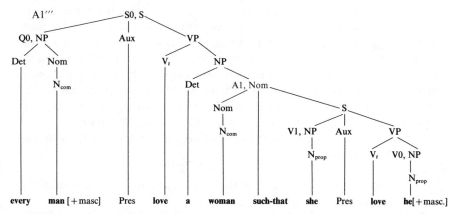

<hr />

[20] Condition (*d*) is important in proving Theorem 9. One of its effects is to deny indexings to
Bach–Peters sentences; see d scussion preceding Theorem 9 in Section 5.3.

A2‴

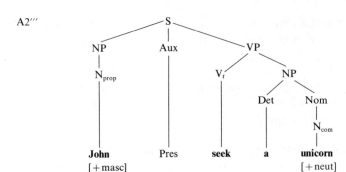

Note that A2‴ = A2″; i.e., by the definition of viable indexing A2″ is ALREADY viably indexed. Still, that does not prevent us from giving it OTHER indexings, e.g.:

A3‴

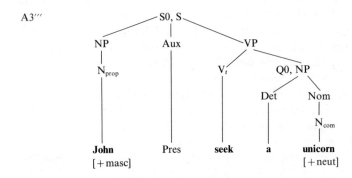

We are now in a position to state the rules that translate I syntax deep structures into sentences of intensional logic. The first step is to viably index the tree. If no viable indexing is possible, then stop here; no translation is given to the tree (see Section 5.3 for comments on this). Otherwise, the next step is to go up the tree in a manner like that described in Section 3.2 for Cooper grammar. There are two differences: First, we have to deal with prefixes on nodes. The idea here is first to translate the node ignoring its prefixes, then translate it together with its innermost (= rightmost) prefix, etc., finally getting a translation of the entire node, including all of its prefixes. Second, there are a few differences in detail. Here are the rules:

For lexical items, we employ the function j (see Section 3.2), with the following alterations:

1. j is no longer defined for variables as arguments, since variables do not appear in the syntax of I grammar.
2. $j(\textbf{he}) = \hat{P}P\{x_n\}$, where Vn is the prefix to the NP node that exhaustively dominates **he**. Similarly for $j(\textbf{she})$, $j(\textbf{it})$.

For nodes, the translation rules are as in Cooper grammar, except that we replace T1c, T2c, T6a, T6b by T1c′, T2c′, T6a′, and T6b′, and we add Rule Q:

RULE Q:

translates as $\hat{P}P\{x_n\}$.
(Note that

translates as something rather complex by Rule T5b, which we inherit from Cooper grammar. In giving Rule Q we do not alter this fact; we simply "store" it for later use in T2c′, T6a′, or T1c′.)

T2c′:   Sn, α

translates as $\hat{y}[\beta(\hat{x}_n[\alpha'(y)])]$, where α is either VP or VP together with some prefixes, and where β is the translation of the subtree of the form

whose top node has Qn as a prefix.

T6a′: Just like T2c′, except replace VP by Nom.

T1c′:   Sn, α

translates as $\beta(\hat{x}_n[\alpha'])$, where α is either S or S preceded by some prefixes, and where β is the translation of the subtree of the form

whose top node has Qn as a prefix.

T6b′:

translates as $\hat{x}_n[\beta'(x_n) \wedge \gamma']$, where α is either Nom or Nom plus some prefixes.

Let us illustrate these rules in application to A2''' and A3'''. The tree A2''' is translated exactly as in C grammar, so there is nothing new there. The tree A3''' is translated as follows:

$$j(\textbf{John}) = j^*$$
$$j(\textbf{seek}) = \textbf{seek}'$$
$$j(a) = \lambda Q \hat{P} \exists x[Q\{x\} \wedge P\{x\}]$$
$$j(\textbf{unicorn}) = \textbf{unicorn}'$$

By Rule T5b:

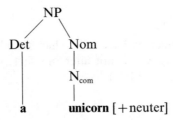

translates as $\lambda Q \hat{P} \exists x[Q\{x\} \wedge P\{x\}](^\wedge \textbf{unicorn}')$.

By Rule Q:

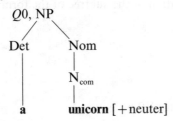

translates as $\hat{P}P\{x_0\}$.

By Rule T2g:

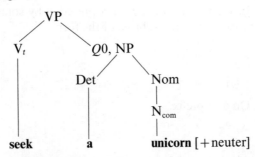

translates as $\textbf{seek}'(\hat{P}P\{x_0\})$.

Then by Rule T1F:

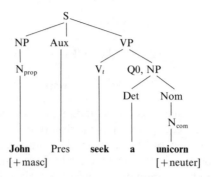

translates as $j*(^\wedge\mathbf{seek}'(\hat{P}P\{x_0\}))$.

Finally, Rule T1c' translates the entire tree A3''' as

$$\lambda Q\hat{P}\exists x[Q\{x\} \wedge P\{x\}](^\wedge\mathbf{unicorn}')(\hat{x}_0[j*(^\wedge\mathbf{seek}'(\hat{P}P\{x_0\}))])),$$

which is the same as the translation of A3'' in C grammar (see Section 3.2).

5.3. Comparison of I Grammar with M Grammar and C Grammar

The system of I grammar described earlier was not designed to be an analog of M grammar and C grammar but, rather, to be an analog of certain variants of these systems. The variants stem from two idiosyncrasies of M grammar. First, M grammar allows for vacuous quantification. E.g., an analysis tree for **John walks** might look like this:

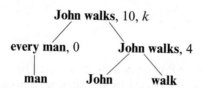

Here the extra **every man** is syntactically superfluous; it does not carry over in any way into the top string. Semantically it is objectionable, since it gives an incorrect meaning to the English sentence (cf. footnote 9).

The other idiosyncrasy has to do with "quantification" by a pronoun. You can produce **he$_i$ walks** directly by:

$$\begin{array}{c} \mathbf{he}_i\ \mathbf{walks},\ 4 \\ \diagup\quad\diagdown \\ \mathbf{he}_i\qquad\mathbf{walk} \end{array}$$

Or you can generate it by "quantifying" something else with he_i, or as in:

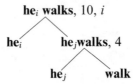

Here the original presence of he_j is redundant; the second tree has the same meaning (up to logical equivalence) as the first tree.

From the point of view of M grammar, these idiosyncrasies are tolerated because they are special cases of a general rule, S14, which would have to be specially constrained to eliminate the idiosyncrasies. But for purposes of comparison with I grammar they turn out to be complications. Thus we will compare I grammar NOT with M grammar but with M′ grammar, which is M grammar minus these idiosyncrasies. Specifically, we suppose that S14 is constrained so that clause (*a*) applies only when ϕ actually contains he_n, and by omitting clause (*b*).

We wish to emphasize that this move is for simplicity only; the points we wish to make would merely be more complicated without these changes.

We also suppose C grammar to be constrained in a similar way. That is, we filter out deep structures of the form:

$$
\left\{ \begin{array}{c} S \\ VP \\ Nom \end{array} \right\}
$$

$$
NP \qquad \begin{array}{c} Vbl \\ | \\ x_n \end{array} \qquad \left\{ \begin{array}{c} S \\ VP \\ Nom \end{array} \right\}
$$

(*a*) when the leftmost NP exhaustively dominates he_j, or (*b*) when x_n does not occur somewhere dominated by the rightmost node. We also filter out C trees in which Vbl is rewritten as the SAME variable in more than one place.[21] We will call the result C′ grammar. Note that M′ grammar and C′ grammar are equivalent to M grammar and C grammar in the sentences they generate and in the meanings they assign to them (up to logical equivalence), except for those meanings produced via the objectionable vacuous quantifications discussed in footnote 9.

---

[21] This does not weaken the system in any significant way. The same sentences are still generable, and they have the same meanings up to interchange of bound variables.

Now we can define a new metamorphosis function that converts C′ trees into syntactically and semantically equivalent viably indexed I trees. The idea behind the new metamorphosis function is that we can view a viably indexed I tree as the result of applying Transformational Rules 21 (NP Lowering) and 23 (Relative Clause Formation) to a C′ tree, where the indexing encodes the structure of the original C′ tree. In fact we define the METAMORPHOSIS OF A C TREE as the result of applying Rules 21 and 23 to the tree, cycling as before on S, VP, and Nom nodes, with the addition of prefixes as follows:

Rule 21: (a) Add Si as a prefix to the resulting top node.

(b) Add Qi as a prefix to the lowered NP node.

(c) Add Vi as a prefix to each NP node that originally exhaustively dominated **he**$_i$.

Rule 23: (a) Add Ai as a prefix to the top node.

(b) Add Vi as a prefix to each NP node that originally exhaustively dominated **he**$_i$.

We illustrate this metamorphosis process by applying it to A3′:

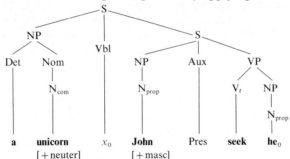

Neither rule applies until the topmost S node, where our revised Rule 21 yields:

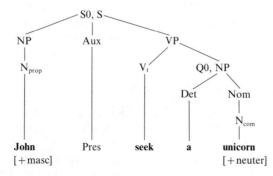

which is A3‴. The reader can easily check that the metamorphoses of A1′ and A2′ are A1‴ and A2‴ respectively.

We can now state the following theorems:

THEOREM 6: *If t is a C' tree, m(t) is a viably indexed I tree.*

Again this is proved by induction; unit C' trees metamorphize into viably indexed I trees, and complex ones do if their branches do.

THEOREM 7: *If t is a C' tree, then gen(t) = gen(m(t)), where gen(m(t)) is the terminal string of the tree generated from m(t) by first erasing all the prefixes and then applying the transformational component of I syntax.*

COROLLARY: *I syntax generates every sentence that C' syntax generates.*

THEOREM 8: *If t is a C' tree, then t' = m(t)'.*

That is, if *t* is a C' tree, then its translation into intensional logic by the rules of C grammar is identical with the translation into intensional logic of its metamorphosis by the rules of I grammar. In short, C' grammar and I grammar agree about sentence meaning.

We do NOT have the result that every sentence generable by I syntax is also generable by C' syntax. An example of a sentence of I syntax that is not generable by C' syntax is **The man such that he deserves it will get the prize such that he wants it**. The reason is that I syntax is more flexible regarding the production of "anaphoric" (unsubscripted) pronouns than C' syntax or M' syntax.[22] However, a certain FRAGMENT of I syntax IS equivalent to C' syntax—namely, the fragment that you get by filtering out all I trees for which no viable indexings exist.

THEOREM 9: *The metamorphosis function is a one-to-one function from the set of C' trees onto the set of viably indexed I trees.*

So if we have a viably indexable I tree, we can reverse the metamorphosis process and get an equivalent C' tree—i.e., a C' tree that generates the same sentence as the I tree and assigns it the same meaning (relative to the chosen indexing).

5.4. *I Grammar and Montague's General Theory*

I grammar as defined in Sections 5.1–2 is not in accordance with Montague's theory of language, since the syntax generates an ambiguous language that is subsequently disambiguated by the indexing procedure. Thus there can be no one-to-one correspondence between the syntactic rules

[22] For a discussion of the inability of C' syntax (actually M syntax) to generate such sentences, see Partee (1973 Section 8).

and the semantic rules, and the translation relation that ensures this in M grammar and C grammar cannot be defined for this system.

However, it can be shown that I grammar can be defined in a different way that is in accordance with Montague's general theory. In UG Montague defines a language as consisting of a pair [$\mathfrak{A}$, R], where $\mathfrak{A}$ is a disambiguated language (in the specific sense we have discussed in Section 3.3) and R is a function that maps expressions of $\mathfrak{A}$ into expressions of an ambiguous language. For example, if we take the analysis trees of PTQ as the disambiguated language, the range of R would be obtained by erasing all but the meaningful expression at the topmost node of any tree. To redefine I grammar in accordance with this, we can generate the viably indexed trees directly by syntactic rules and show that they are meaningful expressions of a disambiguated language that stands in the appropriate translation relation to the intensional logic. We then define the relation R that maps this disambiguated language into the ambiguous deep structure language of I syntax by deleting the indexing. Thus we show that I syntax is a reversed definition of a system that meets Montague's theory. Whereas Montague would require that the disambiguated language be generated directly by the syntax and then mapped by R into the ambiguous language, I grammar generates the ambiguous language with the syntax and maps it into the disambiguated language by the process of viable indexing that is the converse of R. (In doing this we are of course ignoring those trees which are generated by the phrase structure rules of I syntax and which do not receive a viable indexing.)

The syntax of the disambiguated language whose meaningful expressions are viably indexed trees consists of the following rules from the original C syntax (suitably reformulated as backwards phrase structure rules in the manner suggested in Section 3.3: 1a, b, d–f; 2a, b, d–h; 3a–c; 4; 5a–c; 6c; 7–19. In addition, we add the following rules of RELATIVE CLAUSE FORMATION and QUANTIFICATION.

RELATIVE CLAUSE FORMATION:

If [Nom] is a tree rooted by $\langle \zeta \rangle$, Nom and [S] is a tree rooted by $\langle \xi \rangle$, S (where $\langle \zeta \rangle$, $\langle \xi \rangle$ are possibly null sequences of prefixes assigned by the Relative Clause Formation or Quantification rules), which has at least one occurrence of he_n in its terminal string (n is not an index in [Nom], [S]), then $F_{100,n}([Nom], [S])^{23}$ is a tree of the form:

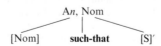

An, Nom

[Nom]   such-that   [S]′

----

[23] Where 100 is an index not used in the explicit reformulation of the phrase structure rules mentioned earlier. Similar remarks hold for the quantification rules given later.

where [S]′ is obtained from [S] by performing the following operations in order: (a) Write Vn before each NP exhaustively dominating an occurrence he_n; (b) replace each occurrence of he_n by he[+masc], she[+fem], or it[+neut], according as the leftmost N_{com} in [Nom] immediately dominates a lexical item of the form α[+masc], α[+fem], α[+neut] for any α.

QUANTIFICATION:

1. If [NP] is a tree rooted by a node NP not exhaustively dominating he_i for any i, and [S] is a tree rooted by $\langle \xi \rangle$, S (with $\langle \xi \rangle$ as before), which has at least one occurrence of he_n in its terminal string (n is not an index in [S], [NP]), then $F_{101,n}$([NP], [S]) is a tree of the form [S]′ obtained from [S] by performing the following operations in order: (a) Write Sn before the topmost node of [S]; (b) write Qn before the topmost node of [NP]; (c) replace the tree containing the leftmost occurrence of he_n and rooted by a node NP exhaustively dominating he_n by the tree obtained from (b); (d) write Vn before each remaining NP node exhaustively dominating an occurrence of he_n. (e) replace each remaining occurrence of he_n by he[+masc], she[+fem], or it[+neut], according as the leftmost N_{com} in [NP] immediately dominates a lexical item of the form α[+masc], α[+fem], α[+neut] for any α.

Rules 2 and 3 are analogous rules for VP and Nom quantification.

It can be shown that:

1. The syntax characterized here generates the language of viably indexed trees of I grammar.
2. This language is a disambiguated language according to the specific definition repeated in Section 3.3.[24]
3. This language stands in an appropriate translation relation to Montague's intensional logic, which is characterized in a similar manner as the original C syntax, with a few obvious changes, and the

---

[24] Actually by excluding vacuous quantification and quantification by pronouns we are violating Montague's definition of the family of categories of a disambiguated language (see UG, p. 226), which requires that an operation defined over a sequence of categories should apply to all members of those categories. This minor nonequivalence of the two systems is actually to be regarded as an advantage of the present system, since requiring vacuous quantification creates the problem noted in footnote 9. As pointed out in Section 5.3, we think it is probably also possible to construct an interpretive system that does allow for vacuous quantification in the same way as the original M grammar, but it would be much increased in complexity.

   interpretation induced by this procedure corresponds in an obvious way to the interpretation of viably indexed trees as characterized by I grammar.

4. It is possible to obtain the deep structure language of I syntax by means of an ambiguating function R, which erases the prefixes from all nodes of any given tree.

Thus I grammar is a redefinition of a system that complies with Montague's general theory of language (except for the restriction mentioned in footnote 24). An objection might be that it lacks the original elegance of Montague's system, where semantic interpretation and English syntax are directly related and are not mediated by a disambiguating process such as indexing. This inelegance is offset, however, by the possibility of constructing an autonomous theory of English syntax. All the rules of I grammar are syntactically motivated,[25] since the rules that were eliminated were just those needed for semantic disambiguation. Also, the transformations of I syntax meet the Boolean conditions of analyzability (and also recoverability of deletion, since there are no deletion transformations) proposed by Chomsky (1965) and, thus, are consistent with a more constrained theory of natural language syntax. We regard as a promising result the fact that it is possible to construct such a syntactic theory while preserving the spirit of Montague's semantic theory.

6. REMAINING QUESTIONS

We have shown that quite different systems of grammar are roughly equivalent with regard to a certain fragment of English. This leaves several open questions, to which we have proposed no answers.

In spite of the rough equivalence, might one system be preferable to others? The interpretive system employs a syntax that is motivated and articulated independently of semantic considerations, whereas the two earlier systems utilize syntactic components that are designed with the semantics in mind. Interpretive grammarians have taken this contrast as an advantage of the interpretive approach, whereas others have cited the same contrast as an advantage of the other systems. Our results suggest that, for the present fragment of English, considerations other than generative adequacy (both syntactic and semantic) must be what is at issue in this dispute.

---

[25] With the exception of those rules that generate subscripted pronouns. These rules could also be eliminated in a fairly simple way by allowing unbound pronouns to be produced by the indexing procedure.

Perhaps a more crucial question is the extent to which this sort of equivalence will carry over to extensions of the fragment of English treated in PTQ. One obvious issue is the treatment of anaphoric pronouns. Our interpretive system generates them freely but fails to assign meanings to some sentences containing them; M grammar and C grammar simply fail to generate those sentences at all. Perhaps the approaches will diverge in their treatments of the problem cases.

Other extensions of M grammar are discussed in this volume; an obvious question is whether these can be carried over into extensions of C grammar and I grammar in a neat way.

Finally, it is known that both Montague's general approach and transformational grammar (in some forms, anyway) are capable of generating all recursively enumerable languages. Thus all approaches will be potentially equivalent with respect to (syntactic) weak generative capacity. What additional constraints are appropriate to grammatical systems, and will the approaches discussed here diverge with respect to their abilities to meet those constraints? We have discussed the extent to which M grammar, C grammar, and I grammar meet constraints on the relation between syntax and semantics proposed in Montague (1974), but this barely scratches the surface of the general issue.

University of Texas, Austin
University of Massachusetts, Amherst

ACKNOWLEDGMENTS

The ideas in this study can be apportioned between the coauthors ROUGHLY as follows: Cooper, Sections 1, 3, 4, 5.4; Parsons, Sections 2, 4, 5.1–5.3. We wish to thank Frank Heny and Barbara Partee for helpful discussion, and Barbara Partee especially for specific suggestions too numerous to detail here. Research for this paper was partially supported by NSF grant GS 39752.

APPENDIX A. CYCLIC RULE APPLICATION

The transformational rules of C syntax (Section 1.2) are applied as follows: We start with any phrase structure tree. We pick any S, VP, or Nom node that does not itself dominate any such node, and we apply Rule 21 (if possible) to the (maximal) subtree dominated by that node. Then we apply Rule 22 to the resulting subtree, etc. Our original tree has now been converted into a new tree (or maybe left unaltered). We take this new tree, look for any S, VP, or Nom node that does not dominate any S, VP, or Nom node AT WHICH THE TRANSFORMATIONS HAVE NOT YET BEEN APPLIED, and go through the rules again. We repeat until the rules have applied once at every S, VP, or Nom node. Then we stop. We now have a surface structure tree.

It is necessary to cycle on all three of these nodes because the phrase structure rules generate deep structures of the types represented by (i)–(iv):

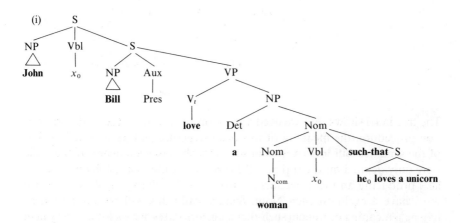

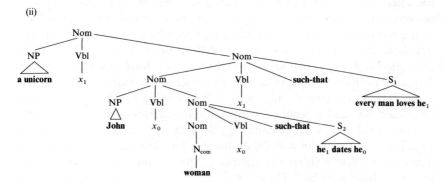

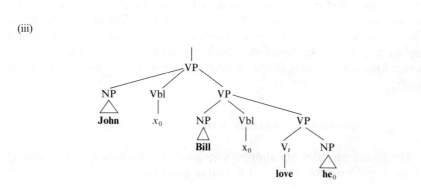

(iv)

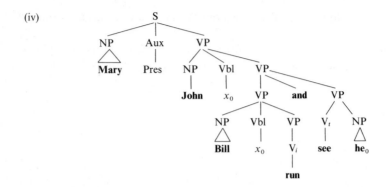

The tree in (i) shows that we need a cycle on each S. In virtue of the translation procedure, the meaning of this deep structure will be specified as that
of the sentence **Bill loves a woman such-that she loves a unicorn**. If the cycle
were only defined on the top S, NP Lowering would insert **John** in place of
he_0, producing an incorrect surface structure. Similarly, (ii) shows that we
must have a cycle on each Nom. Semantically this will be interpreted as
having a meaning of **woman such-that a unicorn dates her such-that every man
loves her**; i.e., **woman** will be associated with he_0 in S_2 and he_1 in S_1; **a
unicorn** will be associated with he_1 in S_2. Again incorrect surface structures
would result if the cycle was not defined on each Nom. The trees in (iii) and
(iv) show that the cycle must also be defined on VPs. In (iii) **Bill** will be
associated with he_0 semantically, and the fact that **John** appears in a higher
quantifier position will not make any difference to the truth value. However,
if the cycle were defined only on S, NP Lowering could apply to either
quantified NP, and Vacuous Quantification Deletion would delete whichever remained. This would mean that a possible surface structure of English
would contain **love John** with the meaning of **love Bill**. The tree in (iv) shows
a similar problem involving conjunction. The semantics this time will only
associate **John** with he_0. However, if the cycle were defined only on S,
either **John** or **Bill** could be lowered into the place held by he_0. With cycling
on VP nodes the lower quantified NP containing **Bill** must be deleted,
since it cannot be lowered on the relevant VP cycle. Thus only **John** can
replace he_0. It will be noted that the cyclic nodes are just those nodes to
which Montague's rules of Quantification and Relative Clause Formation
apply.

APPENDIX B: SIMPLIFIED FORMS OF TRANSFORMATIONS

The following rules are simpler statements (as promised in footnote 7)
of the transformational rules of C syntax given in Section 2.1.

NP LOWERING:

$$\begin{array}{ccccccc} \text{NP} & x_i & \text{X} & [\text{he}_i]_{\text{NP}} & (\text{Y} & \text{he}_i)^* & \text{Z} \\ 1 & 2 & 3 & 4 & 5 & 6 & 7 \end{array}$$

$$\Rightarrow \quad \varnothing \quad \varnothing \quad 3 \qquad 1 \qquad 5 \left\{\begin{array}{l} \text{a. } \textbf{he} \\ \text{b. } \textbf{she} \\ \text{c. } \textbf{it} \\ \text{d. } \textbf{he}_j \end{array}\right\} 7$$

where i, j are any integers and X, Y, Z do not contain **he**$_i$ and there is no element to the right of Z.

The choice of pronoun is (a) iff the leftmost N_{prop} or N_{com} dominated by 1 has the feature [+masc], (b) iff the leftmost N_{prop} or N_{com} dominated by 1 has the feature [+fem], (c) iff the leftmost N_{prop} or N_{com} dominated by 1 has the feature [+neut], and (d) iff the leftmost N_{prop} dominated by 1 is **he**$_j$,

VACUOUS QUANTIFICATION DELETION:

$$\begin{array}{cc} \text{NP} & \text{Vbl} \\ 1 & 2 \end{array}$$

$$\Rightarrow \quad \varnothing \quad \varnothing$$

RELATIVE CLAUSE FORMATION:

$$\begin{array}{cccccc} \text{Nom} & x_i & \textbf{such-that} & (\text{X} & \textbf{he}_i)^* & \text{Y} \\ 1 & 2 & 3 & 4 & 5 & 6 \end{array}$$

$$\Rightarrow \quad 1 \quad \varnothing \quad 3 \qquad 4 \left\{\begin{array}{l} \text{a. } \textbf{he} \\ \text{b. } \textbf{she} \\ \text{c. } \textbf{it} \end{array}\right\} 6$$

where i is any natural number and X, Y do not contain **he**$_i$ and there is no element to the right of Y.

The SC contains (a) iff the leftmost N_{com} dominated by 1 has [+masc], (b) iff the leftmost N_{com} dominated by 1 has [+fem], and (c) iff the leftmost N_{com} dominated by 1 has [+neut].

NEG PLACEMENT:

$$\begin{array}{cccc} \textbf{n't} & \text{NP} & \text{Pres} & \left(\left\{\begin{array}{l}\textbf{will} \\ \textbf{have}\end{array}\right\}\right) \\ 1 & 2 & 3 & \end{array}$$

$$\Rightarrow \quad \varnothing \quad 2 \qquad 3 + 1$$

DO SUPPLETION:

$$\begin{array}{cc} \text{Pres} & \textbf{n't} \\ 1 & 2 \end{array}$$

$$\Rightarrow \quad 1 + \textbf{do} \ 2$$

AFFIX HOPPING:

$$\begin{array}{ccccc} \text{Pres} & \text{X} & (\textbf{en} & \text{Y}) \\ 1 & 2 & 3 & 4 \\ \Rightarrow & \varnothing & 2+1 \varnothing & 4+3 \end{array}$$

X, Y represent trees consisting of single morphemes rooted by themselves.

CASE MARKING:

$$\begin{array}{cc} \left\{ \begin{matrix} V_t \\ P \end{matrix} \right\} & \textbf{he}_i \\ 1 & 2 \\ \Rightarrow \quad 1 & 2 \\ & [+\text{acc}] \end{array}$$

Of these transformations, NP Lowering and Relative Clause Formation do not meet the Boolean conditions on analyzability required by Chomsky (1965). Also, Vacuous Quantification Deletion does not meet the recoverability-of-deletion condition as it is normally viewed.

APPENDIX C: TRANSFORMATIONAL NOTATION

The transformational rules of C syntax (Section 2.1) tell how to convert one (sub)tree into another. The symbols above the numbers represent a structural description of the complete subtree dominated by the relevant cyclic node. A tree meets this description if it can be factored into a sequence of subtrees such that the first tree is rooted by the constant directly over 1, the second by that over 2, etc. The variables X, Y, and Z represent arbitrary, possibly null sequences of trees. The complete factorization must exhaust the terminal symbols of the subtree cycled on. When a string of symbols is enclosed in square brackets, the sequence of trees represented by that string must be exhaustively dominated by the symbol occurring as a subscript on the right bracket. If the numeral is directly below the subscript (as is the case with term 4 of this transformation), then the tree referred to is rooted by the subscript, which must, in addition, exhaustively dominate the contents of the brackets. The material in parentheses followed by an asterisk stands for zero, one, or many sequences of trees of the indicated form, where the subsequent Y may be different in each repetition.

The second pattern of numerals, the structural change, tells how to rearrange and modify the original tree so as to yield the derived tree. Placing a different numeral or new material below a term indicates that the subtree in the structural change is to be substituted for that in the structural description. $\varnothing$ ("zero") indicates the null tree and, thus, represents a deletion when substituted for a particular subtree.

For illustration suppose that we apply NP Lowering on an S cycle. The rule tells us to convert a tree of this form (where the portions enclosed by dotted lines are those referred to by the numbered terms of the structural description of the transformation):

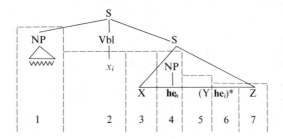

into a tree of the form:

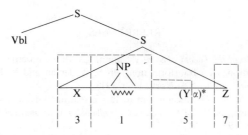

In this tree, α is a pronoun chosen in accordance with the stated restrictions. The pruning convention, which may be regarded as a rule applying after each transformation (and as many times as possible), removes Vbl by its first part and the topmost S by its second part.

In particular, Rule 21 changes the following tree (where 5 and 6 are empty):

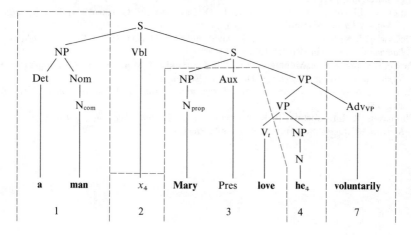

362

into (after pruning):

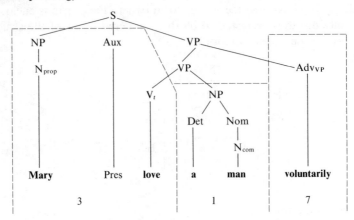

REFERENCES

Chomsky, N. *Aspects of the Theory of Syntax*. Cambridge, Massachusetts: M. I. T. Press, 1965.

Chomsky, N. Conditions on transformations. In S. Anderson and P. Kiparsky (Eds.), *A Festschrift for Morris Halle*. New York: Holt, 1973.

Chomsky, N., and Miller, G. Introduction to the formal analysis of natural languages. In R. D. Luce, R. Bush, and E. Galanter (Eds.), *Handbook of Mathematical Psychology*, Vol. II. New York: Wiley, 1963.

Emonds, J. Root and Structure Preserving Transformations. Unpublished manuscript, 1970. [Available through the Indiana University Linguistics Club, Bloomington, Indiana.]

Jackendoff, R. *Semantics in Generative Grammar*. Cambridge, Massachusetts; M. I. T. Press, 1972.

Katz, J., and Fodor, J. The structure of a semantic theory. In J. Fodor and J. Katz (Eds.), *The Structure of Language: Readings in the Philosophy of Language*. Englewood Cliffs, New Jersey: Prentice-Hall, 1964.

Lakoff, G. Linguistics and natural logic. In D. Davidson and G. Harman (Eds.), *Semantics of Natural Language*. Dordrecht: Reidel, 1972.

McCawley, J. A program for logic. In D. Davidson and G. Harman (Eds.), *Semantics of Natural Language*. Dordrecht: Reidel, 1972.

Partee, B. Comments on Montague's paper. In J. Hintikka, J. Moravcsik, and P. Suppes (Eds.), *Approaches to Natural Language*. Dordrecht: Reidel, 1973.

Partee, B. Montague grammar and transformational grammar. *Linguistic Inquiry*, 1975, **6**, 203–300.

Thomason, R. Introduction. In R. Thomason (Ed.), *Formal Philosophy: Selected Papers of Richard Montague*. New Haven: Yale Univ. Press, 1974.

INDEX